Psychopharmacology

R. H. Ettinger
Eastern Oregon University

PEARSON
Prentice
Hall

Pearson Education International

Boston   Columbus   Indianapolis   New York   San Francisco   Upper Saddle River
Amsterdam   Cape Town   Dubai   London   Madrid   Milan   Munich   Paris   Montreal   Toronto
Delhi   Mexico City   São Paulo   Sydney   Hong Kong   Seoul   Singapore   Taipei   Tokyo

If you purchased this book within the United States or Canada you should be aware that it has been imported without the approval of the Publisher or the Author.

Executive Acquisitions Editor: Susan Hartman
Editorial Assistant: Laura Barry
Director of Marketing: Brandy Dawson
Executive Marketing Manager: Jeanette Koskinas
Marketing Manager: Nicole Kunzmann
Senior Production Project Manager: Roberta Sherma
Editorial Production Service: Chitra Ganesan/Pr
Manufacturing Buyer: Debbie Rossi
Cover Administrator: Bernadette Travis
Editorial Production and Composition Service: PreMe
Photo Researcher: Meghan Lessard/PreMediaGlobal

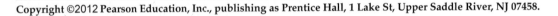

10 9 8 7 6 5 4 3 2 1

Prentice Hall
is an imprint of

ISBN 13: 978-0-13-278764-2
ISBN 10: 0-13-278764-4

CONTENTS

PREFACE

With the increase in the prevalence of psychiatric and behavioral disorders and rapid advances in the development of new drug therapies, there is an ever-increasing need to present the science behind these developments to undergraduate and preprofessional students. Students and educators are often confronted with conflicting and potentially exaggerated claims about the effectiveness of drugs and how they work. As recently as ten years ago, the mechanisms of action of many medications prescribed for common psychological disorders were not well understood, even by the scientists developing them. Now drug treatment has advanced to a stage where drugs are designed for their effects on specific receptors, membrane proteins, or secondary messengers in particular cells in the brain. Unfortunately, because students do not always receive a sufficient introduction to neural and physiological sciences, they often lack the appropriate preparation for courses in psychopharmacology. This text introduces a sufficient background in neuroanatomy and physiology so that students can comprehend the necessary details of drug action.

This text also presents psychopharmacology in the context of the behavioral disorders they are designed to treat, not necessarily by traditional drug classification. Students are often familiar with the major diagnostic categories (for example, affective disorders, psychoses, and attention disorders); so presenting psychopharmacology as it pertains to these familiar disorders strengthens students' understanding of the physiology and neurochemistry underlying the disorders as well as the approaches to their treatment. Each disorder is discussed from a historical context along with diagnostic criteria and descriptions of typical cases. In addition, what is presently known about the underlying pathology of each disorder is carefully described.

A critical examination of drug claims is sorely missing from most psychopharmacology texts, but it is offered here. For instance, antidepressants do not simply make patients "happier." In fact, many patients recognize that the drug has had an effect only when they recall how they felt weeks before commencing treatment. That is, the antidepressant effects are quite subtle and in many cases are less noticeable than a drug's side effects. From a critical perspective, students will read about the most current research available. When alternatives to traditional drug therapies are supported by research, these studies are presented as well. A discussion of how drug effectiveness is measured in both human and animal studies is included throughout the text.

Over the past 75 years, psychopharmacology has contributed significantly to the treatment of severe psychological disorders as well as to an understanding of the brain and human behavior. Drug discovery and development depends heavily on neural and behavioral studies. Likewise, understanding the complex neural mechanisms underlying human behavior has benefited from pharmacological studies. This symbiotic relationship between psychopharmacology and the neural and behavioral sciences will continue long into the future. You are invited to approach one of the most fascinating and challenging sciences of our time.

I would like to thank the numerous reviewers of this text. Because of their thoughtful comments, this text was greatly improved. Michael R. Davey, Western Illinois University; Joshua Dearborn, University of Missouri-St. Louis; Kevin Doyle, University of Virginia; Chris Jones, Palo Verde College; Brian M. Kelley, Bridgewater College; Kimberly Kennard, Modesto Junior College; Roland Lamarine, California State University, Chico; Gloria J. Lawrence, Wayne State College; Steven E. Meier, University of Idaho; Kanoa Meriwether, University of Hawaii–West Oahu; Lawrence J. Nolan, Wagner College; Richard L. Port, Slippery Rock University; George T. Taylor, University of Missouri- St. Louis; Linda Walsh, University of Northern Iowa; Christopher Wilson, Sam Houston State University; Irene Young, St. Phillips College. I also would like to thank those of you who have chosen to read this text and hope that you too will feel free to make suggestions for future changes. It is only through these thoughtful exchanges that textbooks can continue to evolve, rather than merely undergo revision to incorporate the newest developments.

SUPPLEMENTS

For Instructors

Test Bank (0-13-601310-4) Skillfully prepared by R. H. Ettinger, the test bank is a wonderful tool for classroom preparation and management. The test bank contains a set of questions for each chapter, including over 400 multiple choice and 100 essay questions.

Computerized Test Bank (0-205-09362-0) The test bank is also available in the MyTest (X) computerized format, which lets instructors prepare tests for printing as well for network and online testing.

Standard Lecture and Art-Only PowerPoint Presentation (0-13-601312-0) The PowerPoint Presentation is an exciting interactive tool for use in the classroom. Brian Kelley created a PowerPoint package with detailed outlines of key points for each chapter, supported by charts, graphs, diagrams, and other visual aids from the textbook to reinforce student learning. The PowerPoint Presentation is also available as art only slides.

For Students

MyPsychKit (0-205-63793-0) MyPsychKit is a new online tool designed to accompany this text and aid students with interactive media and other study resources. MyPsychKit provides a wealth of study tools for students looking to clarify and deepen their understanding of Psychopharmacology concepts.

CHAPTER 1

Organization and Function of the Nervous System

People's behaviors, including their thoughts, sensations, emotions, memory, and even states of consciousness, are a result of complex interactions between neurons distributed throughout the brain. These neurons form elaborate systems that communicate their activity by releasing small amounts of transmitter substances that act on neurons receiving the message as well as on neurons sending the message. To understand how drugs act to treat certain psychological conditions, you must understand the intricate and sometimes subtle ways in which neurons function to regulate behavior. You also must appreciate the complex systems of neurons in the brain that specialize in different functions, including movement, emotions, learning and memory, and motivational states.

The average human brain weighs approximately 1400 grams (or roughly 3 pounds) and contains nearly 200 billion neurons. In turn, each of these neurons may communicate with just a few neurons or with as many as tens of thousands of neurons. How the structure and organization of neurons and their surrounding environment allows for such communication is the topic of the first part of this chapter. The chapter then describes the structures and functions of systems in the brain that allow humans and other organisms to function in and adapt to their continuously changing environments. This background is necessary if you are to understand how psychological disorders arise and how drugs may help to alleviate them.

THE STRUCTURE AND FUNCTION OF NEURONS

As mentioned previously, the brain contains approximately 200 billion individual nerve cells or neurons. These neurons are the basic units of the brain as well as the rest of the nervous system. Neurons vary in shape, size, and other characteristics according to their location and specific function.

There are three major classes of neurons: sensory neurons, motor neurons, and interneurons. Sensory, or afferent, neurons carry ascending messages to the central nervous system (CNS) from receptors in the skin, ears, nose, and eyes as well as from some organs, muscles, and joints. The brain and sometimes the spinal cord interpret these messages and send appropriate responses through descending motor, or efferent, neurons. These neurons lead to sensory organs, muscles, glands, and other peripheral tissues to control movement and the functioning of glands, sensory organs, and other tissues. **Interneurons** reside only in the CNS and function to bridge communication between sensory and motor neurons. Without these connecting neurons, sensory messages would not result in appropriate bodily responses. Interneurons also communicate with each other throughout the nervous system. Although neurons vary in size, shape, and function, they share four common structures: the cell body, dendrites, axon, and terminal buttons (see Figure 1.1.).

Cell Body, or Soma

The cell body, or soma, is the largest part of the neuron. It contains structures that control the cell's metabolic functions (cell respiration and metabolism). It also contains the nucleus, which contains the cell's genetic information encoded in DNA. The membrane of the cell body may have receptors, in which case it can receive messages from other neurons, although the cell body is not typically the cell's primary receiving target.

Dendrite

Neurons typically receive messages from other cells at a collection of extensions from the cell body called dendrites, which branch out from the cell body like roots of a tree. (The word *dendrite* comes from the Greek word for tree.) Dendrites may

Structure of a Typical Neuron

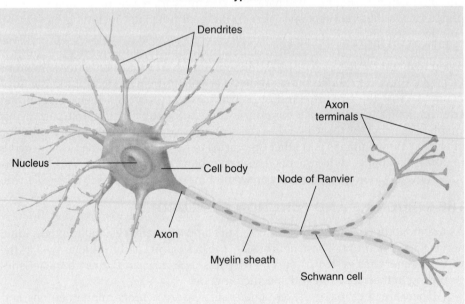

FIGURE 1.1 Neuron structure.   © Carlson, *Physiology of Behavior*, Fig. "The Principle Parts of a Multipolar Neuron." Copyright 2007. Reproduced by permission of Pearson Education, Inc.

receive information from a few to thousands of surrounding neurons. The more extensive the neuron's network of dendrites, the more connections can be made with other neurons. Interneurons in the brain typically contain far more dendritic branches than neurons in the spinal cord or the peripheral nervous system (PNS). Signals received by dendrites are passed on to the membrane of the cell body, where excitatory and inhibitory signals are integrated and a decision is made whether to transmit the signal along its axon.

Axon

The axon is typically an extended branch of the cell that functions to transmit the electrical signal from the surface of the cell body toward receiving cells. The point on the cell body where both the axon and the electrical signal originate is called the **axon hillock.** The electrical signal is transmitted along the entire length of the axon, which ranges from several feet in length in spinal cord and PNS neurons to fractions of millimeters in neurons within the brain. The axon may divide into two or more major branches called collaterals, thereby increasing its capacity to communicate with other neurons. Axons may be myelinated or unmyelinated. Myelin is a type of glial cell that wraps around the axon, providing it with insulation. Most peripheral axons are myelinated, and most (but not all) of the axons in the brain are unmyelinated. Myelin serves to insulate the axon, much like insulation on a wire, and to increase the speed of conduction along the axon. It is myelin that gives brain tissue, which is normally grayish brown, a white color (white versus gray matter).

Terminal Button

The transmitting end of the axon consists of small bulblike structures known as terminal buttons (see Figure 1.2.). The terminal buttons store and release neurotransmitters, which excite or inhibit adjacent neurons. Terminal buttons also are where neurotransmitter substances are taken back into the cell after their release. The structure that allows for neurotransmitter reuptake is a protein called a reuptake transporter. The text will give these transporter proteins considerable attention because they are the site where many psychotropic drugs are designed to work.

Once the recycled neurotransmitters (or their precursor chemicals) have been taken back into the terminal button, they are transported further back into synaptic vesicles, where they are stored for subsequent release. The amount of neurotransmitter available in synaptic vesicles for release depends on the availability of its metabolic precursors and on the frequency of cell firing.

Neural Transmission

For a message to travel from neuron to neuron, it must move from the terminal button at the end of one neuron's axon to the dendrites or cell body of an adjacent neuron. The process by which impulses are transmitted in the CNS is called neural transmission, and it involves both electrical and chemical processes.

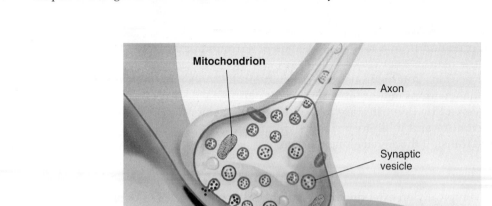

FIGURE 1.2   Terminal button of axon.   © Carlson, *Physiology of Behavior*, Fig. "Details of Synapse." Copyright 2007. Reproduced by permission of Pearson Education, Inc.

In the PNS, messages are transmitted along the extended axonal fibers of both motor and sensory neurons that are contained in bundles of neural fibers called nerves. The multitude of neural circuits or pathways in the CNS are made up of hundreds of thousands of individual neurons. These fibers extend as continuous structures from sensory receptors or muscles to the CNS. For example, a sensory message from a pain receptor in the skin of the finger is transmitted along a single axonal fiber that extends the length of the arm to a point at which it enters the spinal cord and transfers its message to an interneuron.

Neuron Electrical Activity

All cells, including neurons, are enclosed in a lipid membrane composed of two layers of lipid molecules called a lipid bilayer (see Figure 1.3.). This membrane acts as a skin that permits the cell to maintain an internal environment that is different from the fluid outside the membrane. The membrane communicates with its external environment through specialized integrated proteins that are distributed throughout the lipid structure. These proteins carry glucose to internal cell structures and carry metabolic waste back out. They also serve to carry chemical ions back and forth across the membrane. These ions carry a positive or a negative electric charge, which changes the membrane's electrical potential. Ions that are particularly important in neural transmission are negatively charged organic ions (An$^-$),

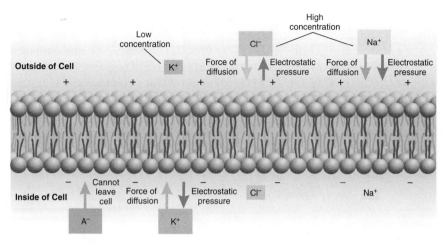

FIGURE 1.3 Electrostatic and diffusion pressures act on charged ions. At rest, the membrane is impermeable to Na^+; so it is not at equilibrium. The concentration of Na^+ is greater on the outside and is attracted toward the negative inside charge. Although K^+ is relatively free to pass through the membrane, the positive electric charge outside keeps it from escaping. K^+ ions are at equilibrium as these forces are balanced at rest. © Carlson, *Physiology of Behavior*, Fig. "The Relative Concentration of some important ions inside and outside the Neuron and the Forces acting on Them." Copyright 2007. Reproduced by permission of Pearson Education, Inc.

chlorine ions (Cl^-), positively charged sodium ions (Na^+), and potassium ions (K^+). If the cell membrane did not act as a barrier, these ions would be equally distributed inside and outside the neuron. However, the negative organic ions do not pass through the cell membrane to the surrounding fluid and the membrane is only semipermeable to other ions. For instance, sodium and chlorine ions pass through only when gates are open for them. These gates, called **ion channels,** are proteins embedded in the cell membrane. They become activated by changes in the membrane potential or by the presence of specific chemicals on their surface.

Resting Potentials

Essentially two forces act on these charged ions. The first force is diffusion, which is the pressure on ions to distribute themselves equally in a medium (that is, to move from high to lower concentrations). For example, perfume diffuses from an open bottle throughout a room. The second force is electrostatic. Similarly charged ions repel each other, as do similarly charged sides of a magnet. This electrostatic force acts to move ions toward the opposite charge and away from a similar charge. When these two forces are at equilibrium, the neuron is said to be in its resting state. The distribution of negatively and positively charged ions on either side of the membrane determines the cell's electrical potential during this resting state. Therefore, this **resting potential** is determined in large part by the concentrations of charged ions in the fluids on both sides of the cell membrane. The ion transport proteins that are embedded in the cell membrane also can contribute to the resting potential to some extent because they too carry an electric charge.

The negative and positive charges are unequal on either side of the membrane when the two forces are at equilibrium, so its interior has a negative electrical potential with respect to its exterior. This phenomenon is due primarily to the negatively charged organic ions inside the membrane and a high concentration of positively charged sodium ions outside the membrane. Most neurons at rest (that is, when their membrane potential is not changing) have a net negative charge of about −70 millivolts (70/1,000 of a volt) relative to their outside environment. The membrane is said to be in a polarized state when the neuron is at rest (see Figure 1.4.).

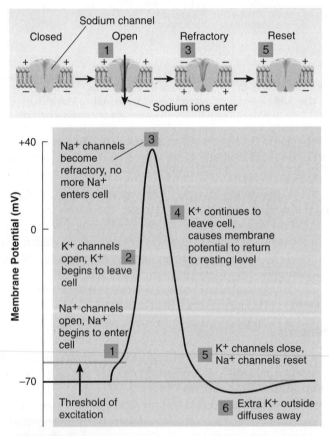

FIGURE 1.4   The action potential. Once the membrane reaches its threshold voltage of about −55mV, Na$^+$ channels open and begin to depolarize the membrane further. Because K$^+$ is no longer at equilibrium, after Na$^+$ influx, it begins to leave the cell. Na$^+$ channels close, and the membrane returns to its resting potential. Na$^+$/K$^+$ transporters reinstate the resting concentrations of these charged ions.   © Carlson, *Physiology of Behavior*, Fig "Action Potential . . ." Copyright 2007. Reproduced by permission of Pearson Education, Inc.

This differential charge gives the resting neuron a state of potential energy known as the resting potential. In other words, it is in a state of readiness to be activated by an impulse from an adjacent neuron. Maintaining this resting potential allows the neuron to store the energy it utilizes when it transmits an impulse. The resting potential is maintained because the membrane is relatively impermeable to the positively charged sodium (Na^+) ions concentrated outside the neuron and to the negatively charged organic ions inside the neuron. Potassium ions can move relatively freely until the two forces operating on the neuron are at equilibrium. That is, the diffusion force trying to expel the ions from the neuron is counteracted by the higher positive charge outside the neuron. Chlorine also is essentially at equilibrium and cannot enter the more negatively charged inside the cell.

Graded Potentials

The resting potential is disturbed when the neuron receives an impulse from another neuron. This disturbance is referred to as a **graded potential,** and its strength varies with the intensity and frequency of stimulation. If you were to measure the charge on the axon during a graded potential, you would observe a change from approximately −70 to −60 millivolts depending on the amount of excitatory stimulation the cell receives (see Figure 1.5.). A graded potential by itself is of little consequence. However, when several graded potentials occur simultaneously or in rapid succession, together they may be sufficient enough to depolarize the neuron to a threshold value (the minimum voltage change sufficient to allow Na^+ ions to enter the cell) of about −55 millivolts.

The determination of whether a graded potential is sufficient to bring the axon to its threshold level is made at the axon hillock, a specialized region of the cell body near the base of the axon. The axon hillock integrates all of the graded potentials that reach it. If the sum of these graded potentials reaches a sufficient magnitude or threshold, a sudden depolarization begins at the axon hillock. This depolarization is referred to as an action potential.

Action Potentials

An **action potential** is initiated when the axon is depolarized to its threshold level (approximately −55 millivolts). When the membrane reaches this threshold level, a sudden complete depolarization results. That is, the axon goes from approximately −55 to +30 millivolts (see Figure 1.4.). This rapid depolarization is the result of the membrane changing its permeability to sodium (Na^+) ions. When the membrane is no longer impermeable to Na^+, it enters the cell, bringing the charge on the inside of the membrane to a positive value (about +30 millivolts). Some potassium ions begin to leave the axon at this time because the electrostatic gradient inside the axon becomes weakened as sodium ions enter. However, the number of potassium ions that leave the inside of the axon is far outweighed by the number of sodium ions that enter.

The change in permeability to Na^+ is extremely brief, and the resting potential is quickly restored by the closing of the Na^+ gates and the rapid expulsion of

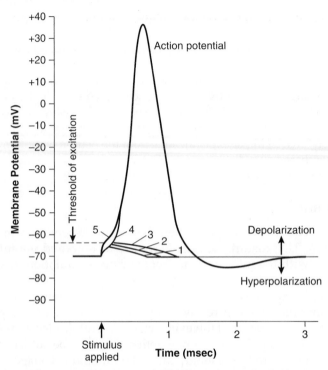

FIGURE 1.5   Graded potentials (1 and 2) are not sufficient to open Na$^+$ channels and initiate an action potential. At position 3, the graded potential reaches threshold. At positions 4 and 5 an action potential is initiated by either summation of graded potentials (4) or by sufficient depolarization by the initial stimulus (5).   © Carlson, *Physiology of Behavior*, Fig "An Action Potential." Copyright 2007. Reproduced by permission of Pearson Education, Inc.

K$^+$ from within the axon. Potassium ions are repelled because of the positive charge now inside the membrane. As potassium ions leave, the charge across the membrane returns to its resting state. In fact, an excess of potassium outflow briefly hyperpolarizes the membrane. This complete process for an action potential takes about 1 millisecond (1/1,000 of a second). Some drugs disrupt this process and prevent the propagation of action potentials by blocking Na$^+$ channels. Local anesthetics such as lidocaine block pain messages this way.

Once an action potential occurs at the axon hillock, sufficient depolarization occurs further down the axon to reach threshold and initiate another one. This process is repeated rapidly as the action potential flows (or propagates) along the entire surface of the axon to the terminal button. Once the action potential reaches the terminal button, it initiates processes that lead to the release of neurotransmitter substances that carry the message to adjacent neurons. You will learn about this process in more detail later.

Unlike the graded potential, the strength of an action potential does not vary according to the degree of stimulation. Once an action potential is triggered, it is transmitted the entire length of the axon with no loss of intensity. Partial action potentials or nerve impulses do not occur; thus, an axon is said to conduct without decrement. Because of this, the action potential is said to follow the all-or-none law: If the sum of the graded potentials reaches a threshold, an action potential will occur; if the threshold is not reached, no action potential will occur.

According to the all-or-none law, a neuron fires at only one level of intensity. Even though a single neuron's impulse level is always the same, two important variables still may change: the number of neurons affected by stimulation and the frequency with which neurons fire. Very weak stimuli may trigger graded potentials in only a few neurons, whereas very strong stimuli may cause thousands of neurons to fire. The frequency in which neurons fire also can vary greatly—from fewer than 100 times per second for weak stimuli to as often as 1,000 times per second for strong stimuli. Thus, the combination of how many neurons fire and how often they fire allows you to distinguish different intensities of stimuli.

The speed with which an impulse travels through a neuron varies with the properties of the axon, ranging from less than 1 meter per second to as fast as 100 meters per second (roughly 224 miles per hour). At least two important factors affect speed. One is the resistance to current along the axon—an inverse relationship exists between resistance and conduction speed, meaning that speed is reduced as resistance increases. Resistance is decreased most effectively by an increase in axon size, which helps explain why large axons, such as those in PNS neurons, tend to conduct impulses at a faster rate than do small axons.

However, if the nervous system had to depend only on axon size to transmit impulses quickly, there would not be enough room in the human body for all of the large axons that would be needed. Fortunately, a second property helps to increase the speed of transmission of nerve impulses. Specialized cells, called glial cells, wrap around some axons, forming an insulating cover called a myelin sheath. (One type of glia cell, the oligodendrocyte, forms the myelin in the CNS. In the PNS, the insulating sheaths are built from another type of glia cell known as the Schwann cell.) Between each glia cell, the axon membrane is exposed by a small gap called a **node of Ranvier.** It is at these small gaps in the myelin where Na^+ influx occurs. So compared to an unmyelinated axon, an action potential at one node of Ranvier can sufficiently depolarize the neuron further down the axon (see Figure 1.6.).

In these myelinated neurons, nerve impulses do not propagate down the axon smoothly. Instead, they jump from node to node in a process called *saltatory conduction* (from the Latin *saltare*, meaning "to leap"). Saltatory conduction is so efficient that a small myelinated axon can conduct a nerve impulse just as quickly as an unmyelinated axon 30 times larger. Because myelin plays such a critical role in the nervous system, the effects of diseases that involve progressive breakdown in these insulating sheaths, such as multiple sclerosis (MS), can be devastating. In MS, the loss of myelination may short-circuit or delay the transmission of signals from the brain to the muscles of the arms and legs. As a consequence, a person

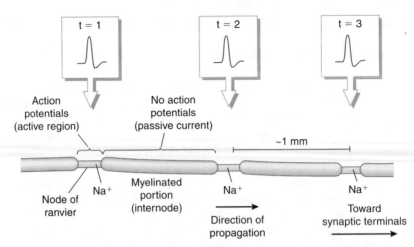

FIGURE 1.6   Myelinated axon. The passive current beneath the myelin remains above threshold, so sodium channels at times $t = 1 - 3$ open almost simultaneously and depolarize the membrane quickly. A myelinated axon can transmit signals about 200 times faster than an unmyelinated neuron.
© Morris, Charles G.; Maisto, Albert A.; *Psychology: An Introduction*, 12th Edition. © 2005, p. 49, fig 2.1. Adapted by permission of Pearson Education, Inc., Upper Saddle River, NJ. (Originally appeared in the text Fundamentals of Human Neuropsychology by B. Kolb/Q. Whishaw (c) 1996 W.H. Freeman.)

with MS experiences a weakness or loss of control over the limbs. As the disease progresses, more neurons become disrupted by demyelination.

Glial cells appear to play numerous other significant roles in the development and function of the nervous system. For instance, astrocytes (named after their starlike structure) form long processes that guide developing neurons to their final destinations. Once these neurons develop and form connections, the glial processes disappear. Other astrocytes are involved in the formation of synaptic connections between neurons. They essentially form the "glue" that holds synapses together. These astrocytes do not assist merely in the formation and structure of synapses; they may be involved in other essential neuronal functions, such as the synthesis of neurotransmitter substances and neurotransmitter removal after it has been released. In addition, astrocytes are involved in subtitle neuronal communication in what are termed **tripartite synapses** that may function to regulate neuronal activity. Tripartite synapses are mentioned here because drugs of the future may target glial functioning and some forms of depression appear to be associated with glial cell loss (Allen et al., 2009).

The transmission of an electrical impulse from one neuron to another (or to other types of cells) involves a series of events beginning with the arrival of the action potential at the terminal button. Neurons communicate primarily through the release of neurotransmitters. Far less common is the electrical synapse, in which an electrical potential is conducted from one neuron to the next because of a tight junction between them. These rare electrical synapses will not be discussed here.

Because several steps are involved in synaptic transmission and pharmacologists can take advantage of each of them in designing drugs, the remainder of this chapter will discuss these processes in some detail.

SYNAPTIC TRANSMISSION

Neurotransmitter Release

When the axon fires, the action potential travels along the axon to the terminal button. When it arrives at the terminal button, the membrane there changes its permeability to another ion, calcium (Ca^{++}). Calcium then enters the terminal button and allows the synaptic vesicles to migrate to the presynaptic membrane, where they fuse with the membrane and release their contents into the synapse. (Refer to Figure 1.7 for an illustration of the fusing of synaptic vesicles to the post synaptic membrane.) The total amount of neurotransmitter released depends on how much Ca^{++} enters the terminal button. More intense stimulation produces a greater frequency of action potentials, which in turn allows more Ca^{++} to enter, thus increasing the amount of neurotransmitter released. The Ca^{++} channel proteins control how much calcium enters the terminal button, but these proteins can be regulated by other proteins that can be activated by endogenous substances as well as by specific drugs that target them. For example, THC in marijuana attaches to a specific cannabinoid receptor (CB2) that controls Ca^{++} channel protein activity.

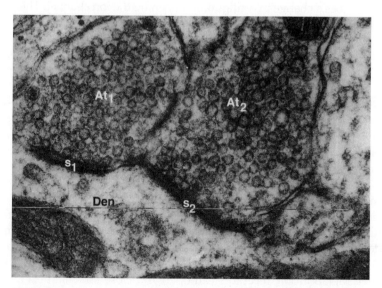

FIGURE 1.7   Electron micrograph of an active synapse. At_1 and At_2 refer to axon terminals with synaptic vesicles; s_1 and s_2 are active synapses on a cell dendrite (Den).   © Image courtesy of Dr. John Heuser, M.D., Washington University School of Medicine.

Receptors

Once a neurotransmitter is released into the synaptic gap, it diffuses toward the post-synaptic membrane of a receiving cell. The postsynaptic membrane contains sites on specific proteins or chains of amino acids called receptors. These receptors are composed of highly specific molecular structures on the end of an amino acid string exposed in the synaptic gap. The specific molecular configuration of the receptor determines which substances can bind with it temporarily. When a neurotransmitter binds with the receptor complex, the postsynaptic membrane's permeability to ions changes briefly, allowing them to flow in or out depending on the synapse. Drugs also may be designed to bind with receptors, and their effects can be to mimic the neurotransmitter or to block or prevent the neurotransmitter from binding. These drug effects will be discussed throughout the remaining chapters of this text.

Synapses not only vary in which ions flow in or out of the cell, but also vary in how their receptors are configured and how they ultimately control an ion channel. When a receptor controls an ion channel directly, often because it is part of the same protein, the receptor is called an **ionotropic receptor.** When the receptor is not part of the ion channel and other proteins are involved in controlling an ion channel, the receptor is classified as a **metabotropic receptor.**

IONOTROPIC RECEPTORS   Ionotropic receptors contain a binding site for their specific neurotransmitter, and they control an ion channel that opens when the neurotransmitter is bound to it. Upon binding with the neurotransmitter, the receptor protein undergoes a change in configuration opening the ion channel. The passage of ions in or out of the cell membrane results in a graded membrane potential. Ionotropic receptors operate quickly to depolarize the postsynaptic membrane. The ion channels they control remain open for only a few milliseconds as the neurotransmitter is released quickly from the binding site and is degraded by a breakdown enzyme.

METABOTROPIC RECEPTORS   Unlike ionotropic receptors that are relatively simple and quite fast, metabotropic receptors do not directly control ion channels. Rather, when the neurotransmitter is bound to the receptor site, a series of events requiring cellular energy are initiated—thus, the term *metabotropic*. Metabotropic receptors are located in close proximity to another membrane protein called a G protein, short for guanine nucleotide binding protein. When the receptor is activated by neurotransmitter, the G protein undergoes a change in conformation and a subunit of the protein dissociates, or breaks away. The detached subunit of the G protein is called an α subunit. The α subunit then activates an enzyme that facilitates the formation of cyclic adenosine monophosphate (AMP) (cAMP) from adenosine triphosphatase (ATP). cAMP acts as a **second messenger** by activating a third protein that controls an ion channel. Metabotropic receptors can open and close ion channels for all three polarizing ions (Cl^-, K^+, and Na^+). Because these receptors require several steps involving enzyme action, the formation of a second messenger, and the activation of an ion channel protein, they are relatively slow when compared to ionotropic receptors. In addition, the ion channels controlled by metabotropic receptors remain

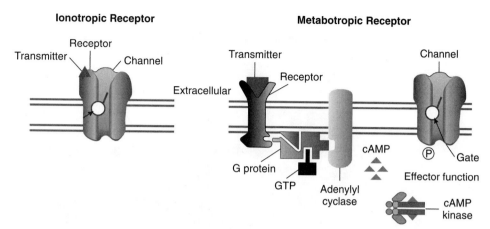

FIGURE 1.8 Comparison of ionotropic and metabotropic receptors. Ionotropic receptors control an ion channel allowing the rapid influx of Na^+ [excitatory or Cl^- (inhibitory)] or the outflow of K^+ (also inhibitory). Metabotropic receptors activate G proteins. When the receptor is activated by neurotransmitter, the G protein undergoes a change in conformation and a subunit of the protein dissociates. The dissociated units then activate an enzyme that facilitates the formation of cAMP from ATP. cAMP acts as a second messenger by activating a third protein that controls an ion channel. Metabotropic receptors can be excitatory or inhibitory depending on the ion channel they control. © Carlson, *Physiology of Behavior*, Figs "Ionotropic Receptors" and "Metabotropic Receptors." Copyright 2007. Reproduced by permission of Pearson Education, Inc.

in their open or closed state for much longer. In fact, they may remain in their altered state for as long as several minutes. Finally, metabolic receptors may be located on the neuron releasing the neurotransmitter and thereby control the amount of neurotransmitter released. Later chapters will have more to say about these receptors. Many of the drugs discussed in later chapters alter the functioning of metabolic receptors. Because there are numerous steps and these receptors control the functioning of several cell processes, they provide pharmacologists with more options for altering receptor functioning using drugs (see Figure 1.8.).

Neurotransmitter Reuptake

Some neurotransmitters are broken down by enzyme action once they have accomplished their function. The enzymes that function to break down neurotransmitter substances are manufactured and released by the same neuron releasing the neurotransmitter. One such enzyme, acetylcholinesterase, breaks down the neurotransmitter acetylcholine (ACh) into acetate and choline molecules. These breakdown products then reenter the terminal buttons to be recycled for further use. In some cases, the neurotransmitter substance reenters the terminal button intact without enzyme degradation. The **neurotransmitter reuptake** processes is controlled by specialized membrane proteins called transporters. The

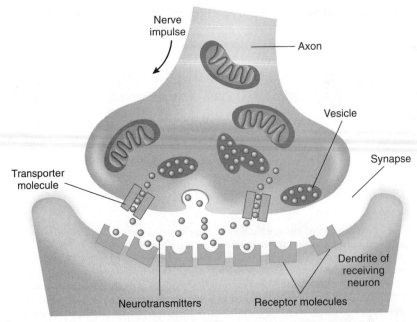

FIGURE 1.9   Reuptake transporter. Reuptake transporters transport a neurotransmitter in the synaptic cleft back into the terminal button. Once the neurotransmitter is in the terminal button, it is transported into the synaptic vesicles by vesicular transport.   © Carlson, *Physiology of Behavior*, Fig ". . . reuptake of Choline." Copyright 2007. Reproduced by permission of Pearson Education, Inc.

density and availability of these transporter proteins determine how quickly a neurotransmitter is cleared from the synapse (see Figure 1.9.).

These breakdown and reuptake processes, which are essential for normal neuronal functioning, can be influenced by a number of drugs. For example, drugs such as amphetamine and cocaine inhibit the reuptake of several neurotransmitters, resulting in heightened alertness and activity. Other drugs block the breakdown process, resulting in prolonged neurotransmitter action. Some of the antidepressants discussed later work in this manner.

Excitatory and Inhibitory Synapses

The postsynaptic membrane of the receiving neuron contains specialized receptor sites that respond to a variety of neurotransmitters. Neurotransmitters act on these receptor sites to produce a change in the permeability of the postsynaptic membrane. Depending on the receptor site and the type of neurotransmitter, this change in permeability can excite or inhibit action potentials in the receiving neuron.

As stated earlier, neurotransmitters exert their effects by opening ion channels in the postsynaptic membrane, letting positively or negatively charged ions pass through. If positively charged sodium ions enter, the membrane is excited, or depolarized. Neurotransmitters that cause these changes are called excitatory neurotransmitters, and their effects are referred to as **excitatory postsynaptic potentials (EPSPs).** Conversely, if positively charged potassium ions pass to the outside of the postsynaptic membrane or if negatively charged chloride ions enter, the membrane is inhibited and the graded potential results in making the membrane more negative—a process called hyperpolarization. Neurotransmitters that act in this way are called inhibitory neurotransmitters, and their effects are called **inhibitory postsynaptic potentials (IPSPs)** (see Figure 1.10.).

Because hundreds, even thousands, of axon terminals may form synapses with any one neuron, EPSPs and IPSPs may be present at the same time. The combination of all of these excitatory and inhibitory signals determines whether the receiving neuron will fire. For an action potential to occur, EPSPs must predominate and do so to the extent of reaching the neuron's threshold. To prevent this from happening, a sufficient number of IPSPs must be present to prevent the summation of EPSPs and IPSPs from reaching the threshold of depolarization.

Some neurotransmitters seem to be exclusively excitatory or inhibitory; others seem capable of producing either effect depending on which ion channel it opens in a specific pathway or neural structure. When transmitters have both excitatory and inhibitory capabilities, the postsynaptic receptor protein determines the effect. Thus, these neurotransmitters may have an inhibitory effect at one synapse and an excitatory effect at another synapse.

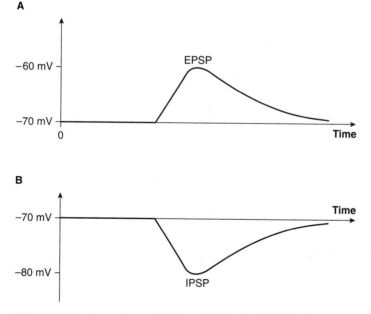

FIGURE 1.10 Comparison of EPSPs and IPSPs. An EPSP depolarizes the membrane, while an IPSP hyperpolarizes it, moving it further from its threshold.

Neurotransmitters interact with receptors on the postsynaptic cell membrane to change its electrical potential. If the change is sufficient to depolarize the cell membrane, a graded potential is initiated, thus beginning the cycle outlined earlier.

Autoreceptors

As mentioned previously, some receptors for neurotransmitters are located on the sending cell. These receptors, called **autoreceptors,** regulate the activity of the sending neuron (see Figure 1.11.). Autoreceptors can excite or inhibit the neuron's activity and thus the amount of neurotransmitter it produces and releases, but it does not do this by controlling ion channels. Instead, autoreceptors regulate the internal process of the cell through the activity of second messenger systems. Most often autoreceptors are proteins of a distinct subset of metabotropic receptors for a specific neurotransmitter. That is, for each known neurotransmitter, there are several subtypes of receptor proteins with which it binds. These receptor subtypes have unique functions and are located on different regions of the cell or on

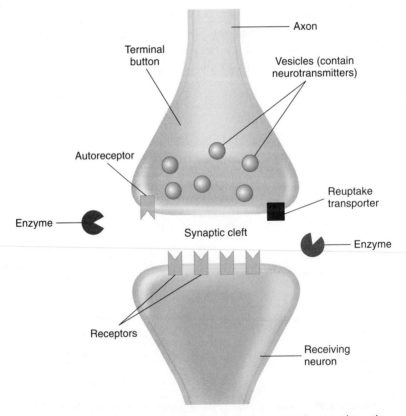

FIGURE 1.11 Neurotransmitter binds to an autoreceptor that regulates the amount of neurotransmitter synthesized and released.

different neural pathways or structures. Interestingly, drugs designed to alter the function of a particular neurotransmitter system may be targeting only a specific subtype of receptor. This approach often results in drugs that alter behavior appropriately without producing undesirable side effects.

Heteroreceptors

Heteroreceptors function nearly the same as autoreceptors except that heteroreceptors receive a neurotransmitter released by another neuron. These receptors may excite or inhibit internal processes that control the synthesis and release of a neurotransmitter. As with autoreceptors, heteroreceptors are metabotropic and it is the activity of a second messenger, not the control of ion channels, that determine their effects.

PRESYNAPTIC EFFECTS   So far the discussion has focused on synapses between terminal buttons and receptor sites located on dendrites or cell bodies of receiving neurons. Synapses between axon terminal buttons and the axons of receiving neurons (axoaxonal synapses) also are common. These synapses differ in one significant way, however. Recall from the discussion of neural transmission that a receiving cell integrates the excitatory and inhibitory influences it is receiving at any given moment. If the neuron is receiving sufficient excitatory input to reach threshold, an action potential will occur. With axoaxonic synapses, there is no contribution to neural integration, but an effect that contributes to the amount of neurotransmitter released. When the axoaxonal synapse is facilitatory, it is called **presynaptic facilitation;** when the axoaxonal synapse is inhibitory, it is called presynaptic inhibition. Some analgesics reduce pain by presynaptic inhibition of pain-signaling neurotransmitters. The pain-signaling neuron is still producing action potentials, but the amount of neurotransmitter released is significantly reduced.

NEUROTRANSMITTER SUBSTANCES

Since the discovery of the first neurotransmitter by Otto Loewi in the 1920s, about 50 additional substances have been identified as neurotransmitters. A large number of other neuroactive substances called **neuromodulators** have been described that modulate the effects of neurotransmitters but meet all of the identifying criteria themselves. For a substance to be considered a neurotransmitter it must (1) be synthesized and stored in the presynaptic neuron, (2) be released into the synapse when the neuron fires, (3) cause a postsynaptic effect after it interacts with a receptor, and (4) have some mechanism for degradation or reuptake. Table 1.1 presents a list of several important substances known to be neurotransmitters, as well as the functions they are thought to perform.

Although the list of substances identified as neurotransmitters is quite large, later chapters will discuss a few that are well understood and that play important roles in psychological disorders.

TABLE 1.1 Chemicals Known to Be Major Neurotransmitters or Neuromodulators

Neurotransmitter-Neuromodulator Effects	Location	Functions
ACh Excitatory	Cortex, spinal cord, target organs activated by the PNS	Excitation in brain. Excitation or inhibition in target organs of PNS. Involved in learning, movement, and memory.
Norepinephrine (NE) Excitatory, Inhibitory	Spinal cord, limbic system, cortex, target organs of the sympathetic nervous system	Arousal of reticular system. Involved in eating, emotional behavior, learning, and memory.
Dopamine (DA) Inhibitory	Limbic system, basal ganglia, cerebellum	Involved in movement, emotional behavior, attention, learning, memory, and reward.
Serotonin (SE) Inhibitory	Brainstem, most of brain	Involved in emotional behavior, arousal, and sleep.
Gamma-aminobutyric acid (GABA) Inhibitory	Most of brain and spinal cord	Involved in regulating arousal and anxiety. The major inhibitory neurotransmitter in the brain.
Endorphins Inhibitory	Spinal cord, most of brain	Function as natural analgesics for pain reduction. Also involved in emotional behavior, eating, and learning.
Glutamate Excitatory	Brain and spinal cord	Major excitatory neurotransmitter in brain. Most neurons in the brain receive excitatory input from glutamate.
Glycine Inhibitory	Brain and spinal cord	Colocated on glutamate receptors. Widespread inhibitory effects throughout the brain.
Substance P Excitatory	Spinal cord	Released by pain-transmitting neurons in the dorsal horn of the spinal cord.
Anandamide Inhibitory	Brain, spinal cord, and PNS	Neuromodulator that acts on heteroreceptors to regulate neurotransmitter release.
Adenosine Inhibitory	Brain and PNS	Neuromodulator released by neurons and glia. Plays significant roles in sleep and wakefulness and controls vasodilatation.

Acetylcholine (ACh)

ACh was the first neurotransmitter discovered. Its discovery by Otto Loewi in 1921 was a bit serendipitous and through its many retellings may only slightly resemble the real occasion. However, prior to Loewi's discovery, it was not known whether neuron signaling was electrical or chemical. There was considerable speculation about possible chemical agents that might be neurotransmitters, but no one had discovered them. Loewi apparently awoke from a dream about an experiment that would demonstrate chemical signaling. He quickly scribbled it down and went back to sleep. The next morning he found, to his dismay, that he could not read his scribbles, although he could recall that he had dreamt something important. The next night the dream returned, and Loewi rushed to his laboratory to complete it. His experiment involved removing the heart from two frogs. One heart was dissected with the vagus nerve intact. (The vagus nerve controls heart rate.) The other heart was removed without the vagus nerve. Next, Loewi placed the hearts in separate dishes filled with saline solution and stimulated the vagus nerve of the first frog. After demonstrating a reduction in heart rate, he removed some of the saline solution and applied it to the heart of the second frog. Heart rate decreased in this frog as well, demonstrating that a chemical released from the vagus nerve controls heart rate. For this work, Loewi was the corecipient of the Nobel Prize in Physiology or Medicine in 1936.

In addition to controlling heart rate, ACh plays an important role in motor movement, as it is the neurotransmitter released from motor neurons onto muscle fibers to make them contract. Several toxins such as botulism, nerve gas, and black widow spider venom interfere with ACh transmission and produce paralysis in their victims. This form of paralysis is a consequence of sustained muscle contraction, which also can disrupt respiratory muscles and result in suffocation. A common disorder that involves ACh is Alzheimer's disease, which involves a degeneration of ACh neurons in the basal forebrain. Although the causes of Alzheimer's disease are not well understood and no treatment is available at present, drugs that increase the availability of ACh are being used to treat the symptoms of this debilitating disease (Tabet, 2006).

There are two subtypes of ACh receptors, named after substances that are known to bind to them. Muscarinic receptors are metabotropic receptors named after an alkaloid found in the mushroom *Amanita muscaria*. These receptors are distributed throughout the brain but particularly in the cortex, thalamus, hippocampus, mesolimbic system, and basal ganglia. They play important roles in cognitive and motor functions as well as in opiate reward. Muscarinic receptors in the ventral tegmental area regulate the release of DA in the nucleus accumbens. This effect may contribute to opiate addiction.

The other receptor subtype is called nicotinic, named after the alkaloid nicotine found in tobacco plants. All nicotinic receptors are ionotropic, and they are found on all muscle cells at neuromuscular junctions. When bound with Ach, these receptors control sodium channels, which leads to muscle contraction. On other nonmuscular synapses, nicotinic receptors are associated with EPSPs. Often nicotinic receptors are located on axon terminals (axoaxonal synapses), and they contribute to neurotransmitter release by presynaptic facilitation. Nicotinic receptors also contribute to increased DA activity in the ventral tegmental area.

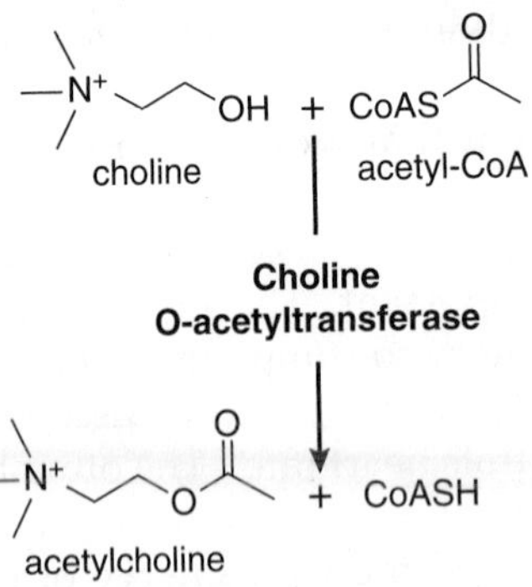

FIGURE 1.12 Synthesis of ACh from choline and acetyl-CoA.
© Carlson, *Physiology of Behavior*, "The Biosynthesis of Acetylcholine." Copyright 2007. Reproduced by permission of Pearson Education, Inc.

ACETYLCHOLINE (ACH) SYNTHESIS AND BREAKDOWN   ACh is synthesized in cholinergic neurons from two precursor compounds: choline and acetyl coenzyme A (acetyl-CoA) (see Figure 1.12.). Choline is made available from dietary fat, and acetyl-CoA results from glucose metabolism in most cells. ACh neurons produce choline acetyltransferase (CoASH), the enzyme required to synthesize ACh from these precursors. How much ACh is produced depends on whether its precursors are available (not typically a problem) and how active these neurons are. Adjusting diet to increase ACh production or ingesting choline has little or no effect.

Once ACh has been released into the synapse, it is quickly broken down by the enzyme acetylcholinterase (AChE). AChE not only breaks down ACh that is free in the synapse, but also breaks down ACh that is in the terminal buttons and not in synaptic vesicles and ACh that is attached to postsynaptic receptors. The breakdown of ACh into choline and acetic acid helps regulate the amount of ACh available in the neuron and helps terminate its effects on receiving neurons quickly. Choline is taken back into the neuron by activating the choline transporter protein located on the terminal button. Later chapters will have more to say about the synthesis and breakdown of ACh in the discussion about drugs that alter these processes. The distribution of acetylcholinergic neurons throughout the brain is illustrated in Figure 1.13.

Norepinephrine (NE)

NE is distributed throughout the CNS and PNS. The noradrenergic neurons originate in the pons of the brainstem in a region called the locus coeruleus. They form an excitatory pathway to the cortex known as the reticular activating system (RAS). This system is primarily responsible for maintaining cortical arousal. Structures that are innervated along the way include the thalamus, the hypothalamus, and all other limbic structures where the RAS is involved in controlling

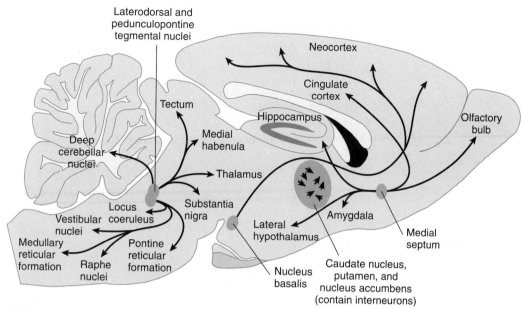

FIGURE 1.13 Major acetylcholinergic pathways originate in several brainstem regions and in the *muscarinic receptors*. They project throughout the brainstem, limbic system, basal ganglia, and cortex. © Carlson, *Physiology of Behavior*, Fig. 4.9, "Major Acetylcholingeric Pathways . . . " Copyright 2010. Reproduced by permission of Pearson Education, Inc.

attention, emotion, and eating. Noradrenergic neurons also play important roles in the PNS-regulating organs such as the heart. Deficiencies in NE activity are linked to depression and attention deficit disorders (Biederman, 2005).

NE binds to several different receptors subtypes that control widely different functions. NE α and β subtypes are separated into two further subtypes 1 and 2 (α_1, α_2, β_1, and β_2). All four of these receptor types are found in the brain and the PNS, where they control various organs. The α_2 receptor also is an autoreceptor that regulates the synthesis and release of NE from sending neurons. All noradrenergic receptors are metabotropic, and they activate second messenger systems in these neurons. Noradrenergic receptors can produce both excitatory and inhibitory effects depending on the specific receptor. The α_1 and both β_1 and β_2 receptors are excitatory, while the α_2 receptors are inhibitory.

NOREPINEPHRINE (NE) SYNTHESIS AND BREAKDOWN NE belongs to a family of neurotransmitters and hormones called catecholamines, a name that describes their primary molecular structure. All catecholamines are synthesized from the same precursor compound, tyrosine, which is made available from dietary proteins. The synthesis of NE from tyrosine involves several enzymes produced by noradrenergic neurons (see Figure 1.14.). The first phase of the synthesis involves the conversion of tyrosine into DOPA by the enzyme tyrosine hydroxylase. As you might expect by its name, this enzyme facilitates the reaction that adds two hydroxyl groups to

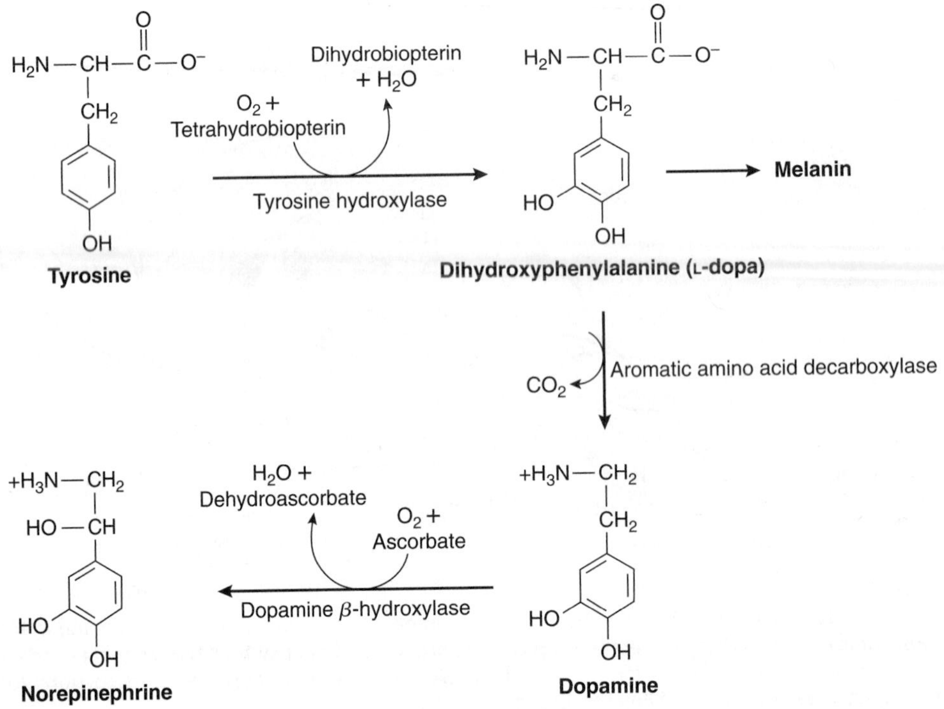

FIGURE 1.14   NE and DA are synthesized from dietary tyrosine. Synthesis is terminated at DA in dopaminergic neurons.   © Carlson, *Physiology of Behavior*, Fig "Biosynthesis of the Catecholmines." Copyright 2007. Reproduced by permission of Pearson Education, Inc.

tyrosine. The second phase of synthesis from DOPA to DA involves the enzyme aromatic amino acid decarboxylase, which cleaves a carbon and several oxygen molecules from DOPA. Finally, DA is converted into NE with the aid of a third enzyme, dopamine β-hydroxylase, which adds another hydroxyl group to the molecule. The rate of synthesis depends on the availability of tyrosine and tyrosine hydroxylase, which is termed a rate limiting enzyme. When NE levels are high in the terminal, button tyrosine hydroxylase is inhibited, thus decreasing synthesis. When noradrenergic neurons are firing at a high rate, this enzyme is facilitated. As long as a person has a sufficient source of tyrosine in his or her diet, there is no way to alter NE levels without drugs. And because the pathways to NE synthesis are complex, there are numerous opportunities to alter its synthesis pharmacologically.

NE is quickly removed from the synapse by two processes: reuptake and breakdown by the enzyme monoamine oxidase (MAO). Much of the available NE in the synapse is transported back into the terminal button intact through the NE transporter protein. The remaining transmitter is broken down by MAO. Later chapters about depression will discuss drugs that block the NE transporter and the activity of MAO. The major pathways of noradrenergic neurons are illustrated in Figure 1.15.

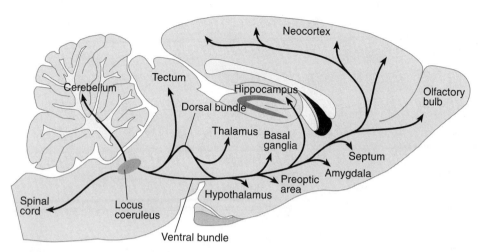

FIGURE 1.15 Major noradrenergic pathways originate in the locus coeruleus of the brainstem and project throughout the limbic system and cortex. Adapted from Cotman, C.W. and McGaugh, J.L. *Behavioral Neuroscience: An Introduction*. New York: Academic Press, 1980.

Dopamine (DA)

DA is located in three distinct pathways that all begin in the brainstem. First, the **nigrostriatal pathway** begins in the brainstem area called the substantia nigra, meaning "dark substance," as its color appears somewhat darker than surrounding neural tissues. Axons extending from the cell bodies of DA neurons in this region terminate in all regions of the basal ganglia. The primary function of these structures involves voluntary movement, particularly the initiation of movement. Deficiencies in DA in the nigrostriatal pathway result in Parkinson's disease, which is a severe motor disorder resulting from progressive degeneration of these DA neurons. Presently, Parkinson's disease is most effectively treated with a drug (L-dopa) that is converted into DA in the brain (Hurley & Jenner, 2006).

The second major DA pathway originates in the ventral tegmental area adjacent to the pons. Axons projecting from the cell bodies of these DA neurons form the **mesolimbic system** and project to the nucleus accumbens, septum, amygdala, and hippocampus. Other axons from the ventral tegmental area form the third pathway and project to the frontal cortex. This system is sometimes referred to as the **mesocortical system,** or the reward system (see Figure 1.16.). As the name implies, these neurons and their targets have been implicated in reinforcement, and they are activated by all addictive drugs. Discussions of drug abuse in later chapters will have more to say about this pathway. The DA pathways also are implicated in the psychotic disorder schizophrenia.

The receptors for DA fall into five groups: D_1–D_5. D_1 and D_2 receptors, which are most common, are distributed throughout the basal ganglia and the mesolimbic system as described earlier in this chapter. Both of these receptors are metabotropic and regulate the activity of **second messenger systems,** but they

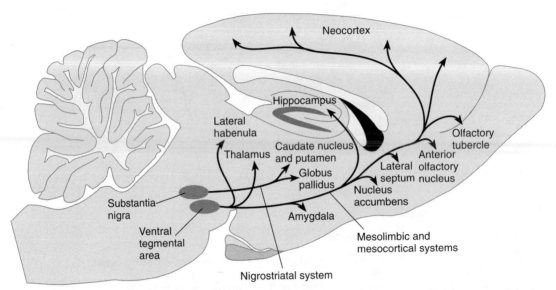

FIGURE 1.16 Major DA pathways originate in the brainstem and midbrain. The mesolimbic system originates in the ventral tegmental area of the midbrain. The nigrostriatal system originates in the substantia nigra. © Carlson, *Physiology of Behavior*, Fig 4.13 "Major Dopamine Pathways . . ." Copyright 2010. Reproduced by permission of Pearson Education, Inc.

have opposite effects. D_1 receptors activate the formation of the second messenger adenylyl cyclase, while D_2 receptors inhibit it. D_2 receptors are primarily inhibitory, resulting in hyperpolarization of the receiving neuron. Because DA receptors differ widely in function and distribution, they control a large number of important functions. Modern pharmacology attempts to target specific receptor subtypes to produce the desired effects while minimizing unwanted side effects that also may be mediated by DA receptors.

DOPAMINE (DA) SYNTHESIS AND BREAKDOWN   DA, a catecholamine related to NE, also is synthesized from dietary tyrosine. The major difference between DA and NE synthesis is that DA neurons do not produce the enzyme dopamine β-hydroxylase, which converts DA into NE. Like NE, the rate limiting enzyme for DA production is tyrosine hydroxylase. DA is quickly removed from the synaptic gap by both reuptake and breakdown. The dopamine transporter protein (DAT), located on the presynaptic membrane, transports DA back into the terminal button intact, where it can be integrated back into synaptic vesicles and released again. Other DA is metabolized by the enzyme MAO. There are two subtypes of MOA: MAO-A and MAO-B. Which one plays the major role in breakdown depends on brain location and the neurotransmitter involved. MAO-A has greater specificity for NE and SE, while both MAO-A and MOA-B metabolize DA. Drugs that block the activity of MAO are referred to as monoamine oxidase inhibitors (MAOIs), and they have been widely used to treat depression.

FIGURE GALLERY

Structure of a Typical Neuron

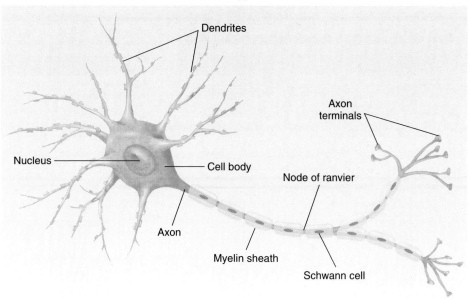

▲ **FIGURE 1.1** Neuron structure (see page 2 for text discussion).

FIGURE 1.2 Terminal button of axon (see page 4 for text discussion). ▶

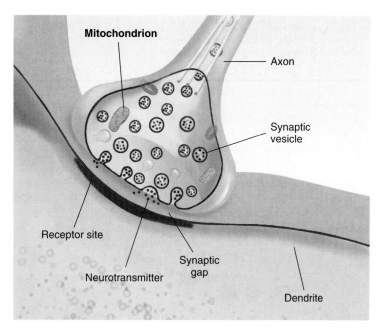

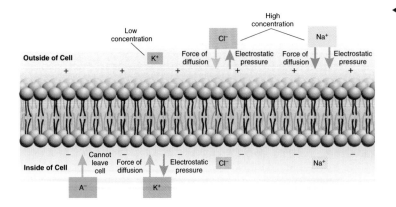

◀ FIGURE 1.3 Electrostatic and diffusion pressures act on charged ions. At rest, the membrane is impermeable to Na$^+$; so it is not at equilibrium. The concentration of Na$^+$ is greater on the outside and is attracted toward the negative inside charge. Although K$^+$ is relatively free to pass through the membrane, the positive electric charge outside keeps it from escaping. K$^+$ ions are at equilibrium as these forces are balanced at rest (see page 5 for text discussion).

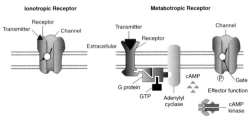

▲ FIGURE 1.8 Comparison of ionotropic and metabotropic receptors. Ionotropic receptors control an ion channel allowing the rapid influx of Na$^+$ [excitatory or Cl$^-$ (inhibitory)] or the outflow of K$^+$ (also inhibitory). Metabotropic receptors activate G proteins. When the receptor is activated by neurotransmitter, the G protein undergoes a change in conformation and a subunit of the protein dissociates. The dissociated units then activate an enzyme that facilitates the formation of cAMP from ATP. cAMP acts as a second messenger by activating a third protein that controls an ion channel. Metabotropic receptors can be excitatory or inhibitory depending on the ion channel they control (see page 13 for text discussion).

FIGURE 1.21 Central and peripheral nervous systems (see page 32 for text discussion). ▶

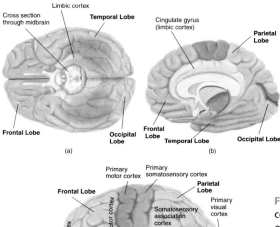

Limbic cortex

Cross section through midbrain

Temporal Lobe

Cingulate gyrus (limbic cortex)

Parietal Lobe

Frontal Lobe

Occipital Lobe

Frontal Lobe

Temporal Lobe

Occipital Lobe

(a)

(b)

Primary motor cortex

Primary somatosensory cortex

Parietal Lobe

Frontal Lobe

Primary visual cortex

Prefrontal cortex

Premotor cortex

Somatosensory association cortex

Auditory association cortex

Visual association cortex

Visual association cortex

Primary auditory cortex (mostly hidden from view)

Temporal Lobe

Occipital Lobe

(c)

Rostral ← → *Caudal*

▲ **FIGURE 1.22** Cortex with major fissures and gyri and lobes identified (see page 34 for text discussion).

FIGURE 1.23 Brainstem with pons, medulla, and cerebellum. The reticular formation is a complex array of neurons that ascend through the midline of the brainstem and project to the thalamus. These neurons are essential for vital functions such as respiration, heart rate, and blood pressure, as well as for cortical arousal (see page 35 for text discussion). ▼

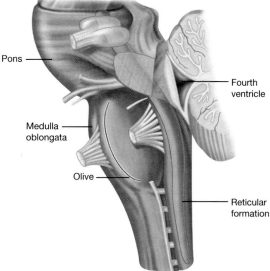

Pons

Fourth ventricle

Medulla oblongata

Olive

Reticular formation

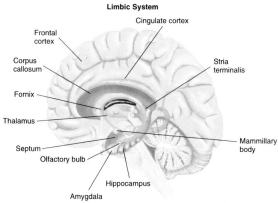

Limbic System

Cingulate cortex

Frontal cortex

Corpus callosum

Stria terminalis

Fornix

Thalamus

Septum

Mammillary body

Olfactory bulb

Hippocampus

Amygdala

◀ **FIGURE 1.25** Limbic structures revealed from a sagittal section of the brain (see page 38 for text discussion).

FIGURE 1.27 The structures of the basal ▶ ganglia include the caudate nucleus, putamen, and globus pallidus (see page 41 for text discussion).

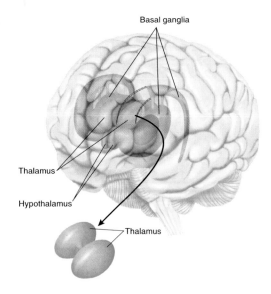

Basal ganglia

Thalamus

Hypothalamus

Thalamus

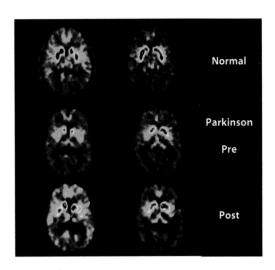

Normal

Parkinson

Pre

Post

◀ **FIGURE 1.28** PET scans revealing the activity of neurons in the caudate nucleus in normal subjects as well as in a patient with Parkinson's disease before (pre) and after (post) L-dopa treatment. Red and yellow colors indicate more neural activity than do green and blue colors (see page 42 for text discussion).

FIGURE 2.2 Cell membrane. The ▶ arrangement of phospholipid molecules into a bilayer with negatively charged hydrophobic heads. This arrangement keeps fluids from passing through the cell membrane. Molecules may pass through the cell membrane if they are carried through by proteins imbedded in the cell membrane or if they are fat-soluble and enter by diffusion (see page 49 for text discussion).

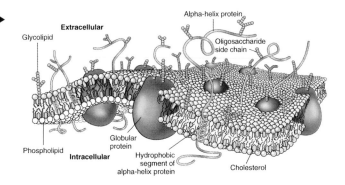

Alpha-helix protein

Extracellular

Glycolipid

Oligosaccharide side chain

Phospholipid

Intracellular

Globular protein

Hydrophobic segment of alpha-helix protein

Cholesterol

FIGURE 2.3 Blood-brain barrier. Tight junctions between astrocytic (glial cell) end feet and capillary endothelial cells (A). Electron micrograph showing tight junctions between capillary endothelial cells and astrocytic feet (B) (see page 50 for text discussion).

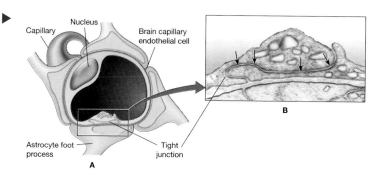

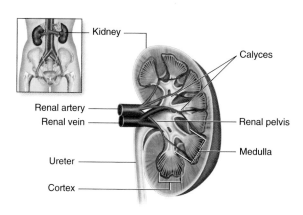

◀ **FIGURE 2.4** Each kidney filters about 1 liter of blood each minute. Drug metabolites are excreted through the kidneys (see page 52 for text discussion).

FIGURE 2.10 The distinctive context for morphine administration (see page 58 for text discussion). ▼

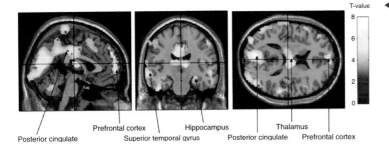

Posterior cingulate | Prefrontal cortex | Hippocampus | Thalamus | Posterior cingulate | Prefrontal cortex
Superior temporal gyrus

T-value

◀ FIGURE 4.4 Areas with decreased GABA$_A$ receptor binding in PTSD patients are indicated in yellow (see page 106 for text discussion).

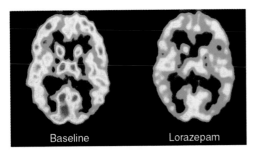

Baseline   Lorazepam

▲ FIGURE 4.11 PET image showing decreased neural activity throughout the brain after benzodiazepine treatment. Red and orange indicate more neural activity than the yellow, green, and blue colors (see page 118 for text discussion).

FIGURE 4.12 Valeriana officinalis (see page 121 for text discussion). ▼

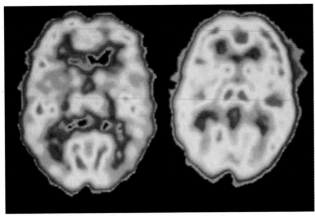

Schizophrenic   Normal

FIGURE 5.2 PET images of schizophrenic brain (left) and normal brain (right). The frontal lobes are at the top of each image. These images reveal decreases in frontal lobe activity in schizophrenics (top of each image) as well as enlarged ventricles (blue areas in the center) (see page 137 for text ◀ discussion).

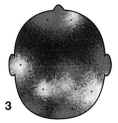

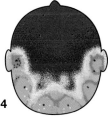

1 Normal 14-year-old female
low theta wave activity.

3 ADD 14-year-old female
high theta wave activity.

2 Normal 9-year-old male
low alpha wave activity.

4 ADD 9-year-old male
high alpha wave activity.

◀ **FIGURE 6.1** Quantitative EEG (Q-EEG) patterns from normal children and children affected by ADHD. Excessive slow wave activity (alpha and theta activity) is characteristic of ADHD (see page 153 for text discussion).

FIGURE 6.5 Amphetamines (including methamphetamine) increase the availability of DA in several distinct ways: (1) by binding to the presynaptic membrane of dopaminergic and noradrenergic neurons, thereby increasing the release of NE and DA from synaptic vesicles; (2) by causing the transporters for DA to act in reverse, transporting vesicular DA back into the terminal and transporting this "free" DA into the synaptic cleft; and (3) by blocking the reuptake transporter for NE (see page 158 for text discussion). ▶

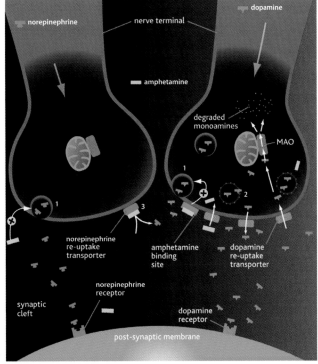

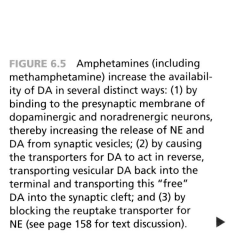

A Autism group

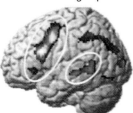

B Control group

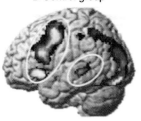

Sentence Comprehension

◀ FIGURE 6.9 Brain activity measured by fMRI in autistic and normal control subjects during a sentence comprehension task. Autistic subjects (top) showed less activity in the left inferior frontal gyrus but more activation in the left superior temporal gyrus (circled areas) than control subjects (bottom) (see page 168 for text discussion).

▲ FIGURE 7.1 Pink flowers of the opium poppy *Papaver somniferum*, which is grown mainly in Afghanistan, India, and Mexico. The milky latex sap (opium) extracted from immature seed pods contains morphine and codeine, which can be easily transformed into heroin (see page 173 for text discussion).

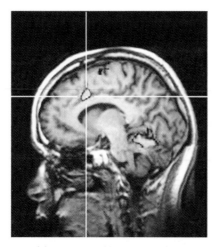
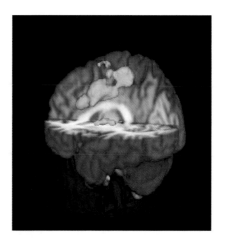

▲ FIGURE 7.6 (a) Pain caused by extreme heat is perceived in the anterior cingulate gyrus as well as the somatosensory cortex. (b) Pain-induced activation of the thalamus, the somatosensory cortex, and the anterior cingulate cortex (see page 177 for text discussion).

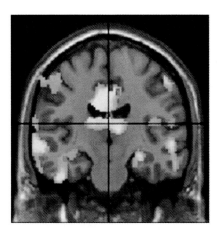

FIGURE 8.4 Functional MRI scan showing activity in the nucleus accumbens. Activation of the ◀ nucleus accumbens is correlated with positive subjective feelings (see page 194 for text discussion).

FIGURE 8.13 EEG recordings from the ▶ midline of brains in casual versus excessive video game players. The green trace shows the pattern of electrical potentials evoked by video game visual cues. The black trace was evoked by neutral cues; the blue, by alcohol-related cues. These EEG records were recorded from electrodes placed along the midline of the head (see page 204 for text discussion).

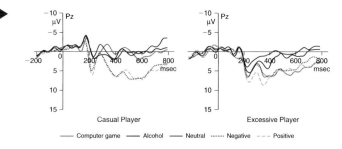

◀ FIGURE 9.3 Coca shrubs grow readily in mountainous regions throughout South America. The coca leaves from these shrubs can be harvested several times a year (see page 211 for text discussion).

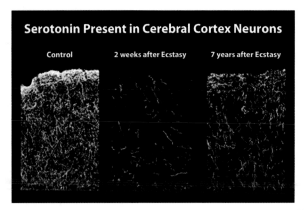

Serotonin Present in Cerebral Cortex Neurons

Control   2 weeks after Ecstasy   7 years after Ecstasy

▲ FIGURE 9.19   Cortical serotonergic axons in a squirrel monkey after saline (control) or 5 mg/kg MDMA twice daily for four days. Animals were sacrificed and examined after two weeks or after seven years. Some cortical regeneration can be seen after seven years (see page 227 for text discussion).

FIGURE 9.21   A popular way to deliver and administer LSD is on small stamps that contain 50–100 micrograms of LSD. These stamps are placed on the tongue, where the drug is rapidly absorbed (see page 229 for text discussion). ▼

FIGURE 9.22   Psilocybin mushroom (*Psilocybe semilanceata*). A common species of psilocybin mushroom found in the Pacific Northwest and in the northeastern United States (see page 230 for text discussion).

▲ FIGURE 9.24   Marijuana plant (left) and dried mature flower (right) (see page 233 for text discussion).

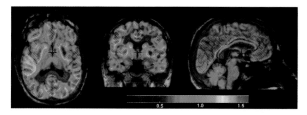

▲ FIGURE 9.26 Positron emission tomography (PET) images of a brain following the injection of a radioactive CB_1 receptor ligand. High densities of cannabinoid receptors are expressed in the cerebral cortex, cerebellum, caudate nucleus, putamen, globus pallidus, substantia nigra, and hippocampus (see page 236 for text discussion).

FIGURE 10.8 A field of tobacco plants (*Nicotiana tabacum*) growing in North America (see page 257 for text discussion). ▼

FIGURE 10.15 (A) MRI images showing eight brain regions. (1) PFC = prefrontal cortex; (2) Acg = anterior cingulate gyrus; (3) NAcc = nucleus accumbens; (4) VP = ventral pallidum; (5) HP = hippocampus; (6) VTA = ventral tegmental area; (7) VC = visual cortex; (8) SEP = septum. (B) Activation in many brain structures in response to a single dose of nicotine. (C) Increased activation in response to the fifth dose of nicotine shows upregulation and sensitization (see page 264 for text discussion). ▼

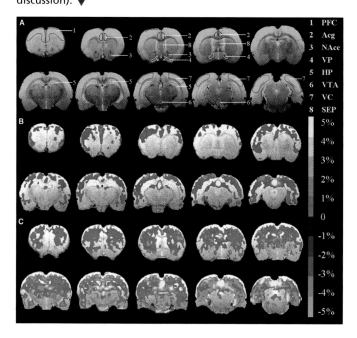

FIGURE 10.17 Coffee (*Coffea*) is a genus of small trees and shrubs native to Africa and Southern Asia. Of the more than 90 species of *Coffea, Coffea arabica* is considered most suitable for making fine coffee. The fruits or beans of the *Coffea* plant are dried and roasted for brewing (see page 268 for text discussion).

FIGURE 10.18 Tea plants are evergreens of the *Camellia* family native to China, Tibet, and northern India. The two main varieties of the tea plant are *Camellia sinensis,* which is grown in the mountainous regions of central China and Japan, and *Camellia assamica,* which grows in tropical climates of Northeast India and the Szechuan and Yunnan provinces of China (see page 268 for text discussion).

Serotonin (SE)

SE, or 5-hydroxytryptamine (5-HT), belongs to a class of compounds known as monoamines because of its single amine molecular structure. It is distributed throughout the brain and spinal cord and is involved in the control of the sleep-wake cycle, mood, aggressive behavior, and appetite. In fact, since its discovery in the 1970s, it has been implicated in numerous behavioral problems, including sleep disorders, aggression, obesity, anorexia, and depression. A common myth is that simply increasing or decreasing the levels of this neurotransmitter may be the cure to any of these problems. The treatment of behavioral disorders is never that simple.

SE neurons also originate in the brainstem in a region of cell bodies called the raphe nuclei. (The term *nucleus* refers to brain regions that are predominantly cell bodies of a specific neuron type.) Two of the regions of greatest interest are the dorsal raphe nucleus and the median raphe nucleus. Axons from these cells travel throughout the cortex and other main brain structures, including the basal ganglia, thalamus, hypothalamus, and mesolimbic system. Receptors for SE include ionotropic and, more predominantly, metabotropic types. They are classified into several subgroups, including the 5-HT$_1$, 5-HT$_2$, 5-HT$_3$ . . . 5-HT$_7$. These are further divided into 5-HT$_{1A}$ and 5-HT$_{1B}$ for this subgroup. Each of these receptor types seems to have specific functions, and they are distributed in different regions of the brain. This text will discuss a few of these, as they have been main targets for pharmacological research. The 5-HT$_{1A}$ subtype functions as autoreceptors on SE cell bodies, regulating the synthesis and release of SE, and are located mainly in the hippocampus and amygdala. 5-HT$_{1B}$ receptors as well as autoreceptors are found predominantly on serotonin axon terminals, and 5-HT$_{2A}$ receptors are located throughout the cortex, basal ganglia, and mesolimbic system. The 5-HT$_{2A}$ receptors are metabotropic receptors that activate a second messenger system in the receiving cell.

SEROTONIN (SE) SYNTHESIS AND BREAKDOWN SE is synthesized from tryptophan, an amino acid found in a variety of foods, including dairy products, meats, fish, and poultry. Tryptophan is converted into 5-hydroxytryptophan by the enzyme tryptophan hydroxylase, which is produced by sertotonergic neurons (see Figure 1.17.). This intermediate is converted into 5-HT by amino acid decarboxylase. The amount of SE produced depends on the availability of tryptophan and the rate limiting enzyme tryptophan hydroxylase. However, eating foods rich in tryptophan

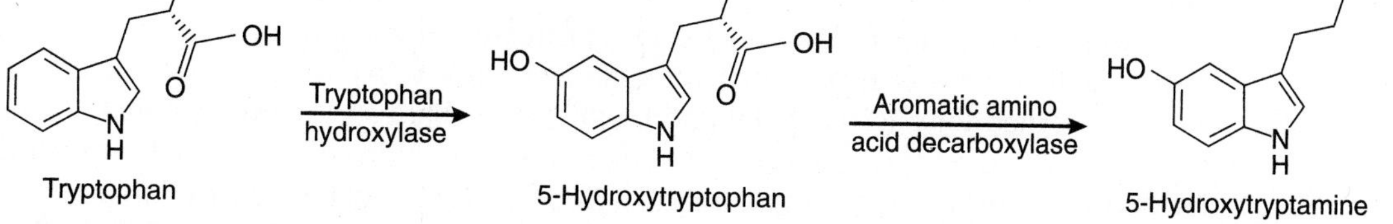

FIGURE 1.17 5-HT is synthesized from dietary tryptophan. © Carlson, *Physiology of Behavior*, Fig. "Serotonin is synthesized from Dietary Tryptophan." Copyright 2007. Reproduced by permission of Pearson Education, Inc.

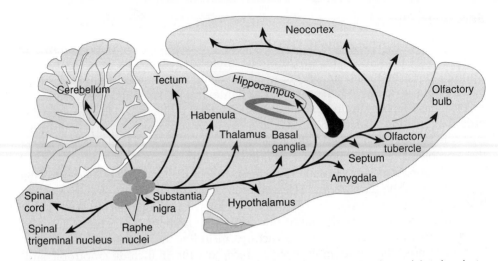

FIGURE 1.18   Major serotonergic pathways in the brain originate in the raphe nuclei and project throughout the limbic system and cortex.   © Carlson, *Physiology of Behavior*, Fig. 4.18. "Major Serotonergic Pathways . . ." Copyright 2010. Reproduced permission of Pearson Education, Inc.

or taking the supplement may increase SE levels only slightly. It is interesting that SE levels may increase to a greater extent by eating carbohydrate-rich food. Apparently, the amount of tryptophan that can cross from the blood into serotonergic neurons depends on the ratio of carbohydrate-rich to tryptophan-rich protein. This may be why some people are soothed by chocolate.

SE, as with NE and DA, is removed from activity by reuptake and by enzymatic breakdown. Reuptake is accomplished through the SE transporter protein imbedded in the presynaptic membrane. Once inside the terminal button, SE can be transported further into the synaptic vesicles for later release. The remaining SE is rapidly degraded by MOA, which breaks SE into its metabolite 5-hydroxyindolacetic acid. The amount of this metabolite is an index of SE activity and can be easily measured. Both of these processes are targets for drug development, and some of the most popular antidepressants used today are designed to block the reuptake process. These drugs are called serotonin specific reuptake inhibitors (SSRIs). The major serotonergic pathways are illustrated in Figure 1.18.

Glutamate

Glutamate or glutamic acid is an amino acid derived from glutamine. It is used by cells for protein synthesis and other cellular functions and is one of the most important excitatory neurotransmitters in the brain. It is known to play an important role in a process called long-term potentiation, which is a change in neuronal functioning that mediates some forms of learning and memory (Robbins et al., 2006). Because of its ubiquitous presence throughout the brain, you should not be surprised that its activity will play a role in several of the disorders discussed in later chapters. Unlike the neurotransmitters ACh, NE, DA, and SE, glutamate neurons do not originate in the brainstem and do not form pathways through the limbic and cortical areas of the brain. Rather, glutamate neurons are found in most brain regions with large projections throughout the cerebral cortex, hippocampus, and cerebellum.

Glutamate receptors can be ionotropic or metabotropic. Ionotropic receptors have been classified as **AMPA** (α-amino 3-hydroxy 5-methyl 4-isoxazole proprionic acid), **kainate** (after kainic acid, which binds to it), or **NMDA** (N-methyl D-aspartate). All of these ionotropic receptors control sodium influx, which produces fast depolarization of postsynaptic membranes. In addition to controlling sodium influx, the NMDA receptor controls calcium (Ca^{2+}) influx, which contributes to fast depolarization and it initiates a slower and prolonged acting second messenger system. In this sense, the NMDA receptor has both ionotropic and metabotropic properties. Of these three receptor types, the NMDA receptor has received the most attention because of its role in mediating the cellular changes that underlie learning and memory. The NMDA receptor has several unique properties, including functioning as both an ionotropic and a metabotropic receptor. In its resting polarized state, the glutamate receptor channel is occupied by a magnesium ion (Mg^{2+}) that prevents the influx of Ca^{2+}. In order for the membrane to become permeable to Ca^{2+}, it must be sufficiently depolarized to eject Mg^{2+}. Additionally, the NMDA receptor requires the presence of a second neurotransmitter, glycine (an inhibitory neurotransmitter), before the ion channel for Ca^{2+} is opened and complete depolarization can occur. In summary, the NMDA receptor controls both Na^+ and Ca^{2+} channels and it is both voltage- and neurotransmitter-dependent. The Ca^{2+} channel is opened only when glutamate and glycine are bound to it and the postsynaptic membrane is sufficiently depolarized to eject Mg^{2+} that is blocking the Ca^{2+} channel. Once Ca^{2+} enters, it initiates a second messenger system that leads to cellular changes that underlie learning and memory (see Figure 1.19.). This cellular change is called **long-term potentiation,** referring to the fact that the postsynaptic membrane can now more readily depolarize when stimulated. Long-term potentiation is believed to be one of several important long-term synaptic changes that mediate learning. Drugs that disrupt NMDA receptors can interfere with learning and memory.

At least eight metabotropic glutamate receptors have been identified. These metabotropic receptors mediate second messenger systems that lead to synaptic and cellular changes that contribute to a host of physiological functions, including learning, motor control, and pain.

GLUTAMATE SYNTHESIS AND BREAKDOWN Glutamate is synthesized from glutamine, an abundant nonessential amino acid in all cells that is readily available from proteins in meats, fish, eggs, and dairy products. The synthesis of glutamate from glutamine is facilitated by the enzyme glutaminase. Because all cells can synthesize glutamate, cells that store it in synaptic vesicles and release it when the cell is activated are called glutaminergic neurons. Glutamate also can be ingested directly. The food preservative monosodium glutamate (MSG) contains glutamate. Eating foods containing large amounts of glutamate, including MSG, may produce symptoms of dizziness and numbness. In large amounts, glutamate is known to be neurotoxic and can lead to cell death. Excessive exposure of

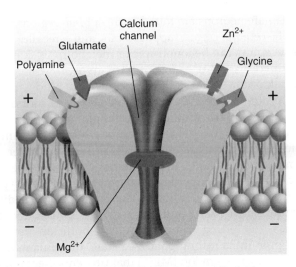

FIGURE 1.19   Glutamate receptor. Normally the ion channel is blocked by Mg^{2+}. Activation of the receptor displaces Mg^{2+} and allows Na^+ or Ca^{2+} to enter. The glutamate receptor requires the presence of glycine (an inhibitory neurotransmitter) before the ion channel for Ca^{2+} is opened.   © Carlson, *Physiology of Behavior*, Fig. "A Schematic Illustration of an NMDA Receptor, with it's Binding Sites." Copyright 2007. Reproduced by permission of Pearson Education, Inc.

postsynaptic neurons to glutamate is referred to as **excitotoxicity,** which, as you will see later, may contribute to symptoms of schizophrenia.

Glutamate is removed from the synapse by several reuptake mechanisms. All of these are mediated by a glutamate transporter found on the presynaptic terminal button or on surrounding glial cells. If glutamate is taken up by glial cells, it is converted back to glutamine before its transport back to a glutaminergic neuron. Once inside the terminal button, glutamine is converted into glutamate and transported into synaptic vesicles for storage and later release.

Gamma-aminobutyric Acid (GABA)

GABA is the major inhibitory neurotransmitter in the brain and spinal cord. Like neural excitation, neural inhibition is critical for the regulation and control of all physiological and behavior functions. Alterations in GABA functioning result from a variety of drugs, including alcohol, and they all have profound effects on behavior and mood. GABAergic neurons are distributed throughout the cortex, hippocampus, limbic structures, basal ganglia, and brainstem and cerebellum. Often GABA neurons are interneurons, but GABAergic neurons also may project along pathways between brain structures. The receptors for GABA can be ionotropic or metabotropic. The ionotropic receptor is classified as GABA$_A$; the metabotropic receptor, as

GABA$_B$. GABA produces neural inhibition by opening Cl$^-$ channels so that chlorine can move from the outside to the inside of the membrane. This movement of negatively charged ions to the inside hyperpolarizes the membrane from about -70 mV to an even greater negative charge, making it more difficult for an action potential to occur. The GABA$_A$ receptor is composed of a membrane-spanning protein that contains at least five different binding sites. The primary site is for GABA, but there are additional sites for barbiturates, benzodiazapines, steroids, picrotoxin, and perhaps alcohol. These binding sites are named after compounds or classes of drugs that bind specifically to them. For example, all of the benzodiazepine drugs appear to bind specifically to the benzodiazepine site. Each of the other compounds or classes of drugs can cause the Cl$^-$ channel to open on is own, and they can facilitate and prolong GABA binding (see Figure 1.20.).

The GABA$_B$ receptor is a metabotropic receptor that facilitates the opening of K$^+$ channels, also hyperpolarizing the postsynaptic membrane. The GABA$_B$ receptor is less widely distributed than the GABA$_A$ receptor, and it functions as a postsynaptic receptor and as an autoreceptor that regulates the synthesis and release of GABA. Most of the GABA drugs discussed in this text affect primarily the GABA$_A$ receptor.

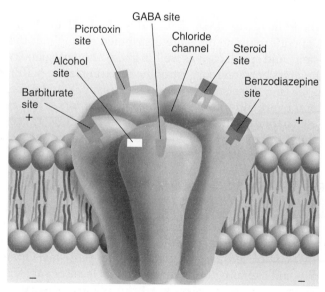

FIGURE 1.20   GABA$_A$ receptor complex. Contains binding sites for GABA, barbiturate, benzodiazepine, and alcohol.
© Carlson, *Physiology of Behavior*, Fig. "A Schematic Illustration of a GABA Receptor, with its Binding Sites." Copyright 2007. Reproduced by permission of Pearson Education, Inc.

GABA SYNTHESIS AND BREAKDOWN   Ironically, GABA is synthesized from the excitatory neurotransmitter glutamate discussed previously by neurons that produce the enzyme glutamic acid decarboxylase. The amount synthesized is regulated by this enzyme, not necessarily the amount of glutamate present in the cell. Drugs that block the synthesis of GABA can produce excessive neural excitation and even seizures.

GABA is removed from the synapse in a manner similar to that of glutamate. That is, GABA is transported intact back into the terminal button or it is taken up by glial cells and converted into glutamate, then into glutamine. Glutamine is transported into the terminals of GABA cells for resynthesis and reintegration into synaptic vesicles for storage and release. Excess GABA in the terminal button is degraded by the enzyme GABA aminotransferase, which breaks GABA into its precursor glutamate. Drugs that block the activity of this enzyme may be useful for the treatment of seizures because they result in increased amounts of GABA available for release. Drugs that increase the activity of GABA are used to treat anxiety, insomnia, and seizures associated with epilepsy and some forms of depression.

Endorphins

Endorphins are a family of peptide neurotransmitters chemically similar to opiates such as morphine. Their name is derived from *endo* (for endogenous) and *orphin* (from morphine). They are widely distributed throughout most of the brain and spinal cord. Extensive research has linked endorphins to an array of behavioral and physiological processes, including inducing analgesia, inducing a sense of euphoria, counteracting the influence of stress, and modulating food and liquid intake. High concentrations of endorphin neurons are distributed throughout the cortex, thalamus, limbic system, and spinal cord as well as in the pituitary gland, which controls the release of the stress hormone corticotrophin releasing factor (CRF). Receptors for the endorphins fall into three subtypes; μ (mu), κ (kappa), and δ (delta). All of the endorphin receptors are inhibitory metabotropic receptors. They control mechanisms in the postsynaptic cell that regulate K^+ or Ca^{++} influx or second messenger systems that inhibit cell excitability. Later you will learn about several drugs that bind selectively to these opiate receptors, including the opiate morphine.

Substance P

Substance P belongs to the peptide class of neurotransmitters, thus its name. Its primary function appears to be signaling messages from pain receptors called **nocioceptors** to the dorsal horn of the spinal cord. Substance P activates ascending pain neurons that comprise the spinothalamic pain pathway. Opiates and other drugs can inhibit pain signaling by decreasing the release of substance P.

The preceding discussion is only a brief review of several of the most important neurotransmitters and neuromodulators, which will be discussed further in later chapters. New neurotransmitters and other neuroactive substances are still being discovered and investigated. Such discoveries have been central to the development of psychopharmacology. At present, the number of substances identified and believed to be neurotransmitters or neuromodulators exceeds 150.

THE ORGANIZATION AND STRUCTURE OF THE NERVOUS SYSTEM AND BRAIN

The nervous system is separated into two distinct components: the **central nervous system (CNS),** which consists of the brain and spinal cord, and the **peripheral nervous system (PNS),** which transmits and receives information to and from muscles, glands, and internal organs to the skin (see Figure 1.21.). Both of these systems must work in synchrony for normal adaptive behavior. For instance, information from the stomach (PNS) communicates its state of fullness to the CNS. Although peripheral signals from the stomach are only part of the complex regulation of hunger and eating, they are critical for normal eating behavior. Communication also can originate in the CNS without an eliciting stimulus. A decision to stop reading this text and go outside might originate in the CNS and direct motivational and motor systems to initiate the movement. Drugs used to treat psychological disorders may have both central and peripheral effects. While the CNS effects are often critical for therapy, a drug's peripheral effects (side effects) may be even more salient. Some drugs used to treat schizophrenia, for example, can produce sexual dysfunction, dry mouth, blurred vision, and high heart rate. The following sections will review the major components of the CNS and examine the structure and function of the cells of which the CNS is composed.

Central Nervous System (CNS)

As stated at the beginning of the chapter, the average human brain weighs approximately 1400 grams (or roughly 3 pounds) and contains nearly 200 billion neurons. The brain is organized into numerous structures that interact to regulate eating and drinking; to produce movement, emotion, learning, and memory; and to allow a person to experience the world through his or her senses. This section will examine some of these structures and their functions.

If a person's skull were removed so that you could look at the surface of the brain, you would see the surface of the cerebral cortex. In its natural state, the human cortex looks much like a soft, wrinkled walnut, its outer surface filled with crevices and folds. The left and right sides appear to be separated by a long, deep fissure (called the longitudinal sulcus). The cortex is divided into two sides, or cerebral hemispheres, that, while not identical, are almost mirror images of each other. Under the cortex are many other structures. Starting from the spinal cord and working roughly upward through the base of the brain, these include the medulla; pons; cerebellum; hypothalamus and other structures of the limbic system; thalamus; and structures of the basal ganglia including the substantia nigra, the caudate nucleus, and the putamen.

Cerebral Cortex

The cerebral cortex consists of the thin outer layer of the brain. Its average thickness is about 3 mm, and its surface area is estimated to be about 2400 cm². The Latin *cortex* means "bark," and the cortex covers the brain in much the same way

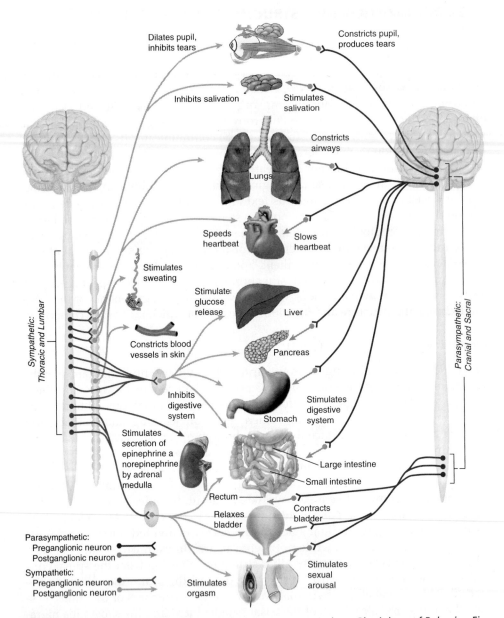

Dilates pupil, inhibits tears

Constricts pupil, produces tears

Inhibits salivation

Stimulates salivation

Constricts airways

Lungs

Speeds heartbeat

Slows heartbeat

Stimulates sweating

Stimulates glucose release

Liver

Constricts blood vessels in skin

Pancreas

Inhibits digestive system

Stimulates digestive system

Stomach

Stimulates secretion of epinephrine a norepinephrine by adrenal medulla

Large intestine

Small intestine

Rectum

Relaxes bladder

Contracts bladder

Sympathetic: Thoracic and Lumbar

Parasympathetic: Cranial and Sacral

Parasympathetic:
Preganglionic neuron
Postganglionic neuron

Sympathetic:
Preganglionic neuron
Postganglionic neuron

Stimulates orgasm

Stimulates sexual arousal

FIGURE 1.21 Central and peripheral nervous systems. © Carlson, *Physiology of Behavior*, Fig "the Autonomic Nervous System and the Target Organs . . ." Copyright 2010. Reproduced by permission of Pearson Education, Inc.

bark covers a tree trunk. This portion of the brain also is called the **neocortex,** or new cortex, because it was the last part of the brain to develop during evolution. A deep grove in the cortex is referred to as a fissure or sulcus, and a protuberance is called a gyrus. Names for specific regions of the cortex include these terms as identifiers to distinguish and locate them. The wrinkled and convoluted appearance of the cortex is nature's solution to the problem of cramming the huge neocortical area into a relatively small space in the skull. The size of the skull is essentially fixed because increases in skull size would require commensurate increases in the size of female pelvic structures to allow for full-term child birth. As this example illustrates, evolutionary changes to one structure often require changes to others.

The cortex is divided into four lobes named after the bones of the skull that cover them. The frontal lobes include everything in front of (rostral to) the central sulcus, the temporal lobes on either hemisphere are located below the lateral fissure, the parietal lobes are behind (caudal to) the central sulcus, and the occipital lobes are at the caudal tip of each hemisphere. These lobes are further separated into functional areas. Three of these areas receive and process sensory information: the primary auditory cortex, the primary visual cortex, and the primary somatosensory cortex. Adjacent to each of these sensory areas is an association cortex where sensory processing, perception, and memories occur. In addition to sensory processing, the cortex includes large areas for motor control and movement. The primary motor cortex is located in the frontal lobes in the gyrus immediately rostral to the central sulcus. Areas for processing emotion are located in both prefrontal regions of the frontal lobes and in the cingulate cortex, which lies deep in the longitudinal sulcus that separates the two hemispheres. In addition to processing emotion, the prefrontal areas, along with the sensory association cortices, are involved in the processing of short-term memories (see Figure 1.22.).

Later chapters will discuss many of these cortical areas because they are implicated in several psychological disorders and are sites of action for a number of psychotropic drugs.

Spinal Cord

Because the brain occupies the commanding position in the CNS, the spinal cord is often overlooked in discussions of the biological bases of behavior. However, the spinal cord fills the very important function of conveying messages to and from the brain. In addition, the spinal cord controls reflexes, which are simple circuits of sensory and motor neurons that initiate responses to specific stimuli.

All complex behaviors require integration and coordination at the level of the brain. However, certain basic reflexive behaviors (such as a leg jerk in response to a tap on the kneecap or the quick withdrawal of a hand from a hot stove) do not require brain processing. Different parts of the spinal cord control different reflexes. For example, hand withdrawal is controlled by the upper spinal cord, whereas the knee jerk response is controlled by an area in the lower cord. The brain is not directly involved in controlling these simple reflexive responses, but it

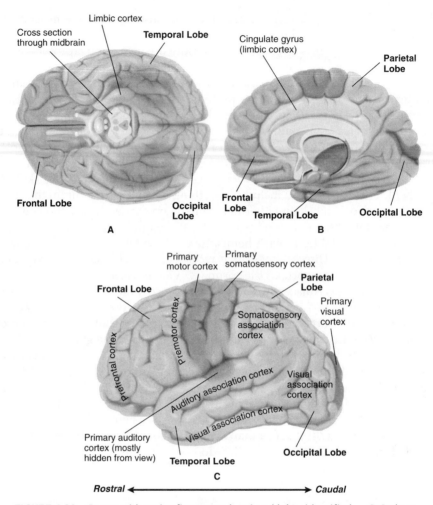

FIGURE 1.22 Cortex with major fissures and gyri and lobes identified. © Carlson, *Physiology of Behavior*, Fig "Cortex with Major Fissures and Gyri and Lobes Identified." Copyright 2010. Reproduced by permission of Pearson Education, Inc.

is clearly aware of what action has transpired. The top of the spinal cord and the brainstem are illustrated in Figure 1.23.

Before beginning discussion of the CNS and its various structures and systems, you need to review the terms that describe how the brain is dissected and the locations of structures relative to these dissections. Anatomists typically describe the brain from one of several transections through it. Sections along the axis from front to back are referred to as sagittal sections. The most common of these sections is a midsagittal section through the midline of the brain. Another way of observing structures in the brain that do not fall along the midline is to take a series of sections horizontally through the brain. These horizontal sections reveal the relative positions

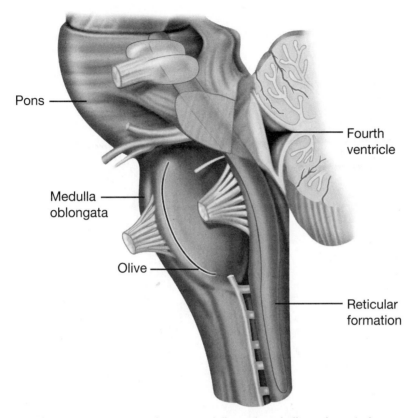

Pons

Fourth ventricle

Medulla oblongata

Olive

Reticular formation

FIGURE 1.23   Brainstem with pons, medulla, and cerebellum. The reticular formation is a complex array of neurons that ascend through the midline of the brainstem and project to the thalamus. These neurons are essential for vital functions such as respiration, heart rate, and blood pressure, as well as for cortical arousal.   © Medical Look. Reprinted by permission.

of structures that do not lie along the midsagittal plane. Finally, sections may be taken vertically through the brain. These views of the internal structures of the brain are referred to as coronal sections (see Figure 1.24.). These anatomical terms will be used throughout this chapter to describe various structures and systems of the brain.

Medulla

The medulla is the lowest part of the brain, located just above (superior to) the spinal cord. This structure is in a well-protected location, deep and low within the brain. It contains centers that control many vital life-support functions such as breathing, heart rate, and blood pressure and plays an important role in con- sciousness and in the regulation of other reflexive functions such as sneezing, coughing, and vomiting. The medulla also forms the base of the RAS, which is discussed later in the chapter (see Figure 1.23.).

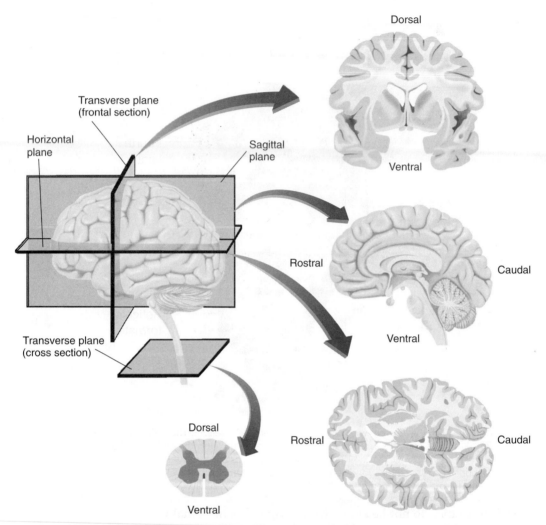

FIGURE 1.24   Sections of the human brain from different anatomical perspectives. Each of these views reveals the relative positions of various structures in the brain.   © Carlson, *Foundations of Physiological Physiology*, Fig "Planes of Section as they pertain to the Huan Nervous System." Copyright 2008. Reproduced by permission of Pearson Education, Inc.

Pons

The pons is a large bulge in the lower brain core, dorsal to the medulla. The pons plays an important role in fine-tuning motor messages as they travel from the mo-tor area of the cerebral cortex down to the cerebellum. Species-typical behaviors (such as fear and feeding behaviors) and facial expressions are mediated by the pons, which appears to program the patterns of muscle movement required for the expressions.

The pons also plays a role in processing some sensory information, particularly visual information. In addition, the pons contains specialized nuclei that help control respiration and that mediate pain and analgesia.

Cerebellum

The cerebellum, a distinctive structure about the size of a fist, is tucked beneath the posterior part of the cerebral hemispheres. It consists of two wrinkled hemispheres covered by an outer cortex. The cerebellum's primary function is to coordinate and regulate motor movements that are broadly controlled by higher brain centers, including the cortex and structures of the basal ganglia, to be discussed later in the chapter. The cerebellum fine-tunes and smoothes out movements, particularly those required for rapid changes in direction. For example, when you reach out to catch a moving ball, your cerebellum is involved in the timing of your movements. This kind of timed movement clearly involves learning. Experiments with animals have shown that the activity of specific cells in the cerebellum changes during the course of learning and that blocking projections from cells in the cerebellum disrupt learned responses (Wikgren et al., 2006).

Damage to the cerebellum results in awkward, jerky, uncoordinated movements and may even affect speech. Professional boxers are especially susceptible to slight damage to the cerebellum, which results in a condition called punch-drunk syndrome. Motor impairment following alcohol intoxication also may be related to alcohol's effects on cells in the cerebellum.

Reticular Formation

The reticular formation consists of a set of neural structures that extend from the medulla up to the thalamus. Research has demonstrated that the reticular formation plays a critical role in consciousness and in controlling arousal and alertness. For this reason, it has become common to refer to this collection of structures as the **reticular activating system (RAS)** (see Figure 1.23.). Attention-deficit hyperactivity disorder (ADHD) may result from insufficient, rather than excessive, arousal produced by the reticular system, explaining why treatment with psychostimulants is often successful. The chapter on attention disorders will discuss this topic in more detail.

Some of the neural circuits that carry sensory messages from the lower regions of the brain to the higher brain areas have ancillary or detouring fibers that connect with the reticular system. Impulses from these fibers prompt the reticular formation to send signals upward, making a person more responsive and alert to his or her environment. Experiments have shown that mild electrical stimulation of certain areas in this network causes sleeping animals to awaken slowly, whereas stronger stimulation causes animals to awaken rapidly, with greater alertness.

The reticular formation also seems to be linked to sleep cycles. When you fall asleep, your reticular systems cease to send alerting messages to your brain. While sleeping, you may screen out extraneous stimuli, with the possible exception of critical messages such as the sound of a squeaking floor or a baby's cry. Although the role of the reticular formation in sleep is still not fully understood, scientists do know that reticular neurons inhibit sleep-active neurons during wakefulness (Osaka, 1994) and that serious damage to this structure may cause a person to be extremely lethargic or to enter into a prolonged coma. Recent evidence also suggests that patients in a severe coma may be aroused by electrical stimulation of the reticular system (Cooper et al., 1999).

LIMBIC SYSTEM

The **limbic system** is the portion of the brain most closely associated with emotional expression and motivation; it also plays a significant role in learning and memory. The limbic system is a collection of structures located around the central core of the brain, along the innermost edge of the cerebral hemispheres. The key structures of the limbic system include the amygdala, the hippocampus, the nucleus accumbens, parts of the hypothalamus, and the bundles of axons that connect these structures. The limbic system also includes the cingulate gurus, which is located above the corpus callosum in the fissure that separates the two cerebral hemispheres. Damage to or stimulation of sites in this system may profoundly affect emotional expression by causing excessive reactions to situations or by greatly reducing emotional responses. Limbic structures also are implicated in major depression, and drugs that are discussed later will act on some of these structures. Structures of the limbic system are illustrated in Figure 1.25.

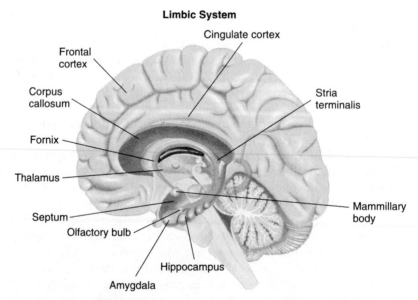

FIGURE 1.25 Limbic structures revealed from a sagittal section of the brain. © Carlson, *Physiology of Behavior*, Fig "The Major Components of the Limbic System." Copyright 2010. Reproduced by permission of Pearson Education, Inc.

Amygdala

The amygdala, a small structure located in the inferior temporal lobe, plays an important role in expressing anger, rage, and aggressive and in learning fear-motivated behavior. Electrical stimulation or surgical damage to areas in the amygdala may cause an animal to go into a blind rage, whereas in other parts of the amygdala, the same procedures may produce extreme passivity. The amygdala also plays significant roles in social cognition and decision making. Amygdala damage in humans results in the inability of memories to trigger emotional states. These emotional states are essential to normal social functioning and decision making. For example, when you make a decision to invest a large sum of money, an emotional state induced by the thought of making more money or losing it all guides your decision to invest. People with amygdala damage lose these functions, making normal decisions difficult (Bechara et al., 2002, 2003; Adolphs et al., 1995).

Nucleus Accumbens

The nucleus accumbens, located near the amygdala, is part of a group of structures that form the pathway for DA neurons originating in the upper pons and terminating in the frontal cortex. This pathway, referred to as the **mesolimbic-cortical system,** begins in the ventral tegmental area of the pons and passes through the nucleus accumbens, where it is routed to the frontal cortex. The nucleus accumbens is associated with the reinforcing properties of a category of highly valued stimuli, including addictive drugs. The DA-containing neurons of the mesolimbic system have an excitatory effect on the frontal cortex.

Hippocampus

The hippocampus also is located in the inferior temporal lobe. This structure plays significant roles in the formation of new memories. Individuals who experience damage to this structure have difficulty storing new information in memory. Recent evidence suggests that the hippocampus also may undergo significant alterations as a result of stress and its size may be smaller in patients who have experienced prolonged periods of stress, have post-traumatic stress disorder, or who may have schizophrenia. The stress hormone cortisol, a glucocorticoid, can cause neuronal atrophy in the hippocampus as well as inhibit the growth of new neurons in adults. Both of these consequences result in a decline in memory.

Hypothalamus

The hypothalamus is a grape-sized structure that lies inferior to the thalamus and above the optic chiasm. Although it is relatively small, it is essential for many physiological functions and for the motivation of behavior. The hypothalamus integrates information from a number neurotransmitters and hormones that indicate changes in body states. The maintenance of a relatively constant internal environment, including fluid and nutrient levels, requires the integration of information about the status of these systems as well as the initiation of motivational systems to ensure that they remain relatively stable. For example, neurons in the lateral hypothalamus secrete the peptide neurotransmitter **orexin** in response to signals indicating depletion in energy stores. Orexin, in turn, stimulates appetite and a reduction in metabolic rate to conserve remaining energy.

A person shivering when cold and perspiring when hot are homeostatic processes that act to restore normal body temperature and are controlled by neurons in the anterior hypothalamus. The hypothalamus also is critical to sexual motivation, and it contains distinct nuclei for males and females that are critical for normal sexual motivation. The medial preoptic nucleus of the hypothalamus contains a greater number of cells in males than in females. The growth of these neurons depends on androgens during development, and they are responsible for normal male sexual behavior. In females, the ventromedial hypothalamus controls sexual motivation, and this region contains large numbers of estrogen receptors (see Figure 1.26.).

The hypothalamus also is the center of the neuroendocrine system, which controls the activity of the pituitary gland and various other hormone-secreting endocrine glands. The hypothalamus contains specialized secretory cells that produce and release hormones that stimulate the **pituitary gland.** The pituitary gland produces and secretes a variety of essential hormones, including male and female sex hormones, growth hormone, adrenocorticotropic hormone, antidiuretic hormone, and oxytocin. Figure 1.26 illustrates the hypothalamus and many of its nuclei.

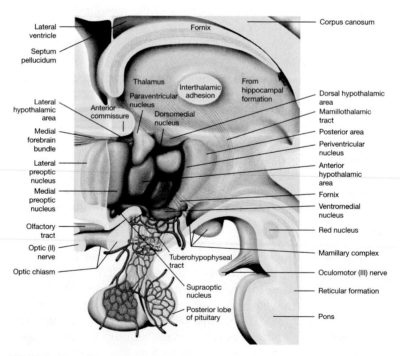

FIGURE 1.26 Hypothalamus and thalamus revealed from an animated sagittal section.   © Newscom.

Thalamus

The thalamus is located above the hypothalamus in the center of the cerebral hemispheres. It is composed of two oval-shaped lobes that lie side by side, one in each hemisphere. Sensory input to the cortex is routed through specific regions in the thalamus with the sole exception of the sense of smell. These distinct regions are specialized for certain kinds of sensory information. Auditory messages from the inner ear travel to the medial geniculate nucleus of the thalamus before being routed to the primary auditory cortex and visual messages transmitted from a person's eyes pass through the lateral geniculate nucleus in route to the primary visual cortex. In addition to this function, the thalamus also appears to work in conjunction with the reticular formation to help regulate sleep cycles and to control the excitability of all regions of the cortex. The chapter on attention disorders will provide more information about the thalamus and its control over the excitability of the cortex.

BASAL GANGLIA

The basal ganglia consist of several subcortical brain structures, including the caudate nucleus, putamen, and substantia nigra (see Figure 1.27.). These structures

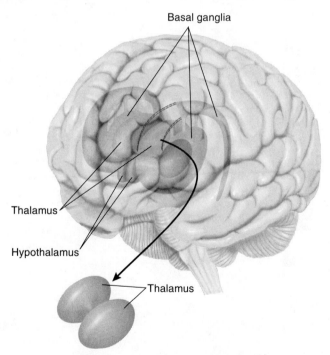

FIGURE 1.27   The structures of the basal ganglia include the caudate nucleus, putamen, and globus pallidus.   *Source:* © Carlson, *Physiology of Behavior*, Fig, 3.18 "The Location of the Basal Ganglia and Diencephalon, ghosted in to a Semitransparent Brain," Copyright 2007. Reproduced by permission of Pearson Education, Inc.

receive messages from the cortex and the thalamus. The primary function of the basal ganglia is in the control and initiation of motor movement. One of the most common disorders of the basal ganglia is Parkinson's disease. Parkinson's disease results from the progressive destruction of the DA-containing neurons of the substantia nigra. This destruction leads to decreased activity of other structures in the basal ganglia, including the caudate nucleus and putamen. This disease occurs most often in the elderly; however, it may occur in individuals in their late forties or fifties (for example, Michael J. Fox). Parkinson's disease is characterized by difficulty in initiating movement, rigidity, and tremors in the hands. Parkinson's disease is commonly treated with drugs such as L-dopa that increase DA neural transmission, but embryonic and stem cell transplants into the substantia nigra may be the most promising treatments for the future (Correia et al., 2006).

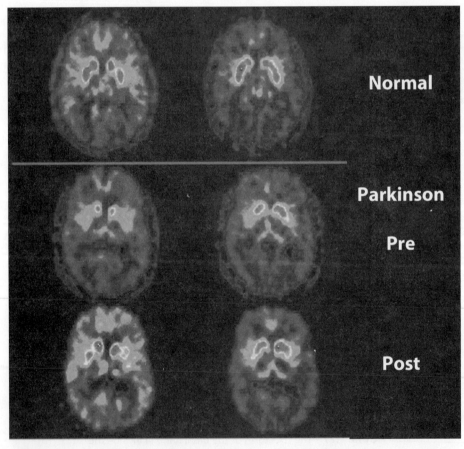

FIGURE 1.28 PET scans revealing the activity of neurons in the caudate nucleus in normal subjects as well as in a patient with Parkinson's disease before (pre) and after (post) L-dopa treatment. Lighter shading indicates more neural activity than grey regions after treatment.

A related movement disorder, **tardive dyskinesia,** may result from long-term use of antipsychotic medication. These drugs block a subset of DA receptors referred to as D_2 receptors. As a result, these DA receptors may become sensitized, causing the excessive movement associated with this disease. In a sense, Parkinson's and tardive dyskinesia are opposite diseases—Parkinson's occurring when DA pathways begin to degenerate in the basal ganglia; tardive dyskinesia, when DA receptors in the same region become too sensitive (see Figure 1.28.). The chapter on antipsychotic medication will provide more information about tardive dyskinesia.

2

Psychopharmacology
Pharmacokinetics and Pharmacodynamics

Have you ever wondered whether getting that morning coffee might work just a little bit better if you could hook yourself up to an IV? While being tied to a drip bag with a long thin tube might get caffeine into your bloodstream more quickly, missing out on the sensory aspects of this morning ritual would make your experience much less pleasant. As you will see in this chapter, the action of a drug can and often does depend not only on its pharmacological properties, but also on how rapidly it enters the brain, the context in which it is administered, and your expectations of its effects. The chapter begins by examining how routes of administration and drug dose affect how much and how long drugs are available at target sites. It also explores how repeated exposure to a drug alters its effectiveness. These are all topics of **pharmacokinetics,** the science of how drugs are absorbed, distributed to body tissues, and eliminated from the body after being metabolized.

DRUG NAMES

Before beginning a discussion of pharmacokinetics, however, a brief introduction to the drug naming convention is in order. Students often are confused over drug names, as most drugs have several. For example, drugs can be named after their chemical structure, which may be useful to a chemist, but these names are far too awkward to use in any other context. The **chemical name** for the popular antidepressant Prozac is N-methyl-3-phenyl-3-[4-(trifluoromethyl)phenoxy]-propan-1-amine. A drug's chemical name reveals its chemical composition and molecular structure. Pharmaceutical companies also may patent **brand names,** or trade names, for their product. These brand names reveal little if anything about the

TABLE 2.1	Examples of several common drug names. Note that the drug brand name is always capitalized; the generic name is not		
Chemical Name		**Brand (trade) Name**	**Generic Name**
N-methyl-3-phenyl-3-[4-(trifluoromethyl)phenoxy]-propan-1-amine		Prozac	fluoxetine
methyl alpha-phenyl-2-piperidineacetate		Ritalin	methylphenidate
N,N,6-trimethyl-2-(4-methylphenyl)-imidazo(1,2-a)pyridine-3-acetamide		Ambien	zolpidem
7-chloro-1-methyl-5-phenyl-1,3-dihydro-2H-1,4-benzodiazepin-2-one		Valium	diazepam
4,5-epoxy-14-hydroxy-3-methoxy-17-methylmorphinan-6-one		Percoset, Percodan	oxycodone

drug's makeup or structure. You are probably familiar with drug brand names because they are the names used in advertising. When drugs are marketed in different countries, they may have several brand names. The name Prozac is a brand, or trade, name. Pharmaceutical companies typically receive exclusive rights to manufacture and distribute brand name drugs they have developed. Once this exclusivity has expired (typically after five to seven years), a drug can be manufactured and distributed by other drug manufacturers as a **generic drug.** The generic drug name can be used by any number of companies that market and distribute the same generic drug. The generic name for Prozac is fluoxetine. Generic drugs must contain the same active ingredients as the original brand name drug, and they must be pharmacologically equivalent. Because several manufacturers may compete to produce and market generic drugs, the cost is often considerably less than their equivalent brand name drug. Table 2.1 presents several common drugs and their respective brand and generic names.

PHARMACOKINETICS: DRUG ABSORPTION, METABOLISM, AND TOLERANCE

Drug Absorption

Drug absorption refers to the mechanisms by which drugs get into the bloodstream and are distributed throughout the body. Because the focus of this text is on psychopharmacology, a topic of particular interest is how drugs get into the brain. How quickly and how much of a drug reaches the brain depends on several factors, including how it is administered and how readily molecules of the drug pass from the bloodstream into neural tissues. The chapter examines routes of administration first, then discusses factors that influence a drug's passage from blood to the brain.

ORAL ADMINISTRATION (PO)   Perhaps the most common route of drug administration is the ingestion of a pill or tablet, but drug administration also includes the oral ingestion of liquids. To be taken orally, a drug must be soluble in gastric fluids and not be destroyed or broken down by them so it can cross from the lining of the stomach and upper intestine into the bloodstream. To pass through the tissues lining of the gastric tract, a drug must be fat-soluble to some extent. The greater its solubility in fat, the more rapidly it can permeate the mucosal lining into the blood. Fat solubility also is a factor in determining how rapidly a drug can pass from the bloodstream into neural tissues in the brain. The reason fat solubility is important is that the tissues lining the stomach, upper intestine, blood vessels, and neurons are composed primarily of fats, or lipids. Fat-soluble compounds literally dissolve in these tissues and pass through by diffusion. Oral ingestion of drugs is often the most preferred method of administration, but absorption may take between one-half and three hours depending on how fat soluble a drug is and where it is absorbed. For instance, some drugs are designed to dissolve quickly in the mouth and are absorbed through the mucosal lining in the mouth and throat. Other drugs are more slowly absorbed in the lining of the upper intestine. You may be familiar with how long it takes an oral analgesic to relieve the pain associated with an extracted tooth. When a drug may not be stable in stomach acids and enzymes or when it needs to reach the brain more quickly, other methods are sometimes preferred.

INHALATION   A number of illicit and legal drugs are typically administered by inhalation, including nicotine and marijuana. This method is preferred for drugs of abuse because they are absorbed quickly through the lungs into the bloodstream. Because the lungs have a large surface area and blood volume, absorption takes only a few seconds. Drugs used to administer anesthesia (e.g., halothane) are often administered by inhalation. The level of anesthesia is carefully monitored and regulated throughout its duration. For drugs used to treat psychological disorders, inhalation is not preferred because therapeutic doses of these drugs require a stable blood level unlike the rapid spike in levels preferred by drug users. You may be familiar with the variety of bronchial and nasal inhalers used to treat asthma and congestion. Other drugs such as methamphetamine, cocaine, and heroin vaporize when heated, and these vapors are inhaled. This is often preferable to oral or nasal administration because it produces an intense state of euphoria and is often less risky than intravenous administration, when needle sharing may spread diseases such as AIDS.

INTRAVENOUS (IV)   An IV injection is a rapid and precise way to administer a drug. Drug absorption is rapid because the drug is delivered directly into venous blood, where it is quickly distributed throughout the circulatory system. The drug does not pass through membranes of the gastric system or the lungs.

IV administration is more precise because the entire amount of the drug gets into the bloodstream. Following oral administration, unpredictable amounts of the drug temporarily get trapped in fat tissue, making the amount reaching the blood difficult to determine. Because drugs administered intravenously have such rapid onset, they are more dangerous. Overdose by intravenous administration can cause death by respiratory or heart failure and can cause severe allergic reactions. The intravenous use of recreational drugs is of particular concern because they are often administered in unsanitary conditions, increasing the risk of infections and diseases spread by shared needles. In addition, drugs mixed and prepared outside specialized laboratories often contain contaminants. The soluble contaminants may be toxic, and those that are insoluble may lodge in the lungs and blood vessels, causing damage to them and to other organs.

INTRAMUSCULAR (IM)   Drugs also can be delivered into skeletal muscle, where they are absorbed more slowly. Depending on the injection site and the amount of blood flow to the muscle tissue, absorption typically occurs within one hour. Often drugs administered intramuscularly are mixed in an oil base to further slow their absorption. Several hormones are commonly administered intramuscularly, including Depo-Provera (medroxyprogesterone) as a female contraceptive and testosterone for hormone replacement in men.

TRANSDERMAL   Nicotine patches, motion sickness patches, testosterone replacement gel, and some forms of female contraceptives are examples of transdermal drug administration. Because the skin is relatively impermeable to water-soluble substances, these drugs must be fat-soluble to pass through the skin. Absorption is slow and can be sustained over several days or weeks.

SUBCUTANEOUS (SC)   SC administration may consist of a subdermal injection or implantation of a drug in pellet form. Several hormones are available in pellet form, including the newly approved female contraceptive Implanon. For each implant, Implanon delivers contraceptive hormones for up to three years.

INTRAPERITONEAL (IP)   The delivery of a drug directly into the abdominal cavity beneath the peritoneum is a common route of administration in small laboratory animals. This method of drug administration is not used for humans because of the risks of contaminating the abdominal cavity and damaging internal organs. This procedure is used to administer drugs to small animals when rapid absorption is required. You might wonder why researchers do not prefer intravenous injections in these cases because accurate dosing can be achieved. However, as you might imagine, delivering drugs intravenously to small laboratory rats and mice can be difficult.

The time course of plasma concentrations of cocaine following different routes of administration are presented in Figure 2.1. Table 2.2 describes advantages and disadvantages of each administration method.

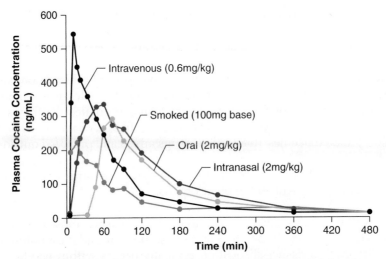

FIGURE 2.1 Comparison of absorption times for different administration routes.   Based on Carlson, N. R. (2010). *Physiology of Behavior*, 10th Ed, Boston: Allyn and Bacon.

TABLE 2.2   Routes of drug administration

Route of Administration	Main Advantages	Main Disadvantages
Oral (PO)	Patient administration, relatively safe	Delayed and variable absorption
Inhalation	Rapid availability, patient administration, reliable absorption, accurate blood levels	Irritation of nasal passages or the throat and lungs, possibility of overdose
Intravenous (IV)	Rapid availability, reliable absorption, accurate blood levels	Patient administration difficult, possibility of contamination and infection from needles, possibility of overdose
Intramuscular (IM)	Prolonged and reliable absorption, easy to administer	Patient administration difficult, possibility of contamination and infection from needles
Transdermal	Prolonged and reliable absorption, easy to self-administer	Local irritation, variable absorption, more difficult to regulate blood levels
Subcutaneous (SC)	Prolonged and reliable absorption, easy to administer	Patient administration difficult, possibility of contamination and infection from needles
Intraperitoneal (IP)	Primarily for administering drugs to smaller laboratory animals when intravenous administration is not feasible	Possibility of damage to internal organs, local irritation at injection site, delayed absorption compared to intravenous injection

Cell Membrane Permeability

Once a drug is administered, it must pass through several membranes before it reaches the brain. The first membranes that drugs encounter are the cell membranes that make up the linings of the gastric system, skin cells, muscle and fat cells, and mucosal lining of the lungs. All of these tissues are composed of a phospholipid bilayer made up of complex lipid (fat) molecules arranged in two rows. These phospholipid molecules are composed of a head region that is negatively charged and an uncharged tail region that is split into two segments. These molecules are arranged such that their heads form both the inner and outer surfaces of the membrane and their tails remain between these charged segments. The negatively charged heads of these molecules are hydrophilic (attracted to water) and are exposed to both the intra and extra cellular fluids. The uncharged tails are hydrophobic (repel water) and therefore prevent fluid and water-soluble substances from easily passing through the membrane. Imbedded in this arrangement of phospholipid molecules are protein molecules that serve a variety of transport functions. For substances to pass through the cell membrane, they must be carried through by one of the specialized transporter molecules or they must be fat-soluble and essentially dissolve in the membrane and pass through by diffusion. Figure 2.2 shows how the plasma membrane is constructed and how it incorporates various proteins.

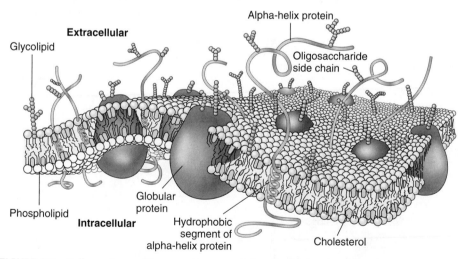

FIGURE 2.2 Cell membrane. The arrangement of phospholipid molecules into a bilayer with negatively charged hydrophobic heads. This arrangement keeps fluids from passing through the cell membrane. Molecules may pass through the cell membrane if they are carried through by proteins imbedded in the cell membrane or if they are fat-soluble and enter by diffusion.
© 1995–2009 by Michael W. Davidson and The Florida State University. All Rights Reserved.

Substances also must pass through small blood vessels, called capillaries, to enter and leave the bloodstream. Capillary membranes are constructed of tightly packed single layers of cells that have small gaps between them. Substances that fit through these gaps can enter and leave the bloodstream by diffusion. That is, diffusion pressure forces a substance through the membrane and down its concentration gradient until the concentration is essentially equal on both sides of the capillary wall. Most drugs easily pass through capillary membranes this way and become distributed throughout the body's tissues. The greater the blood flow to tissue, the greater the concentration of drug. Because the brain has relatively high blood flow, higher concentrations of drug would be expected there. However, drugs must cross an additional membrane before they can enter the brain.

BLOOD-BRAIN BARRIER The capillaries that circulate blood throughout most of the brain are constructed differently than capillaries in other tissues. Because the brain requires a stable and protected environment to function effectively, substances cannot easily pass between small gaps in the capillary membrane. These capillaries are constructed of cells with tight junctions that allow only very small molecules to pass. In addition, the capillary walls are surrounded by a type of glial cell called an astrocyte. These astrocytic feet provide an additional barrier by tightly adhering to the capillary endothelial membrane. This impermeable construction is referred to as the **blood-brain barrier (or BBB)** (see Figure 2.3). Some essential substances such as glucose and some amino acids are carried through by specialized transporters in the capillary membrane. Fat-soluble substances, including all psychoactive drugs, can dissolve in the membrane and

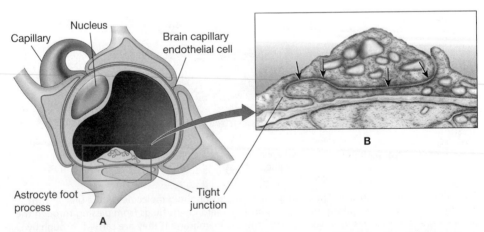

FIGURE 2.3 Blood-brain barrier. Tight junctions between astrocytic (glial cell) end feet and capillary endothelial cells (A). Electron micrograph showing tight junctions between capillary endothelial cells and astrocytic feet (B). © Based on Goldstein, Goldstein, and Betz (1986).

pass through by diffusion. The blood-brain barrier provides an effective means to protect the brain from perturbations in the chemical environment of the blood-stream. In addition, the blood-brain barrier protects the brain from potentially toxic substances, including most viruses and bacteria.

In a few areas of the brain, the blood-brain barrier is relatively weak, allow-ing some substances to be detected by specialized neurons. For example, neu-rons in the area postrema of the medulla detect some toxic substances; it triggers vomiting to rid the body of potentially toxic substances still in the stomach. Others areas, including the subfornical organ located on the underside of the fornix between the lateral ventricles, has a weak blood-brain barrier and detects the presence of hormones involved in the regulation of fluid balance. The blood-brain barrier poses a significant obstacle to drug development. For drugs to reach their target receptors in the brain, they must pass through the blood-brain barrier.

PLACENTAL BARRIER   Pregnant females have an additional barrier that separates the blood system of the mother from that of the fetus. However, this barrier must allow essential substances, including nutrients and oxygen in the mother's blood, to enter the fetal blood supply. In addition, it must allow metabolic waste produced by the fetus to be eliminated through the mother's circulatory system. Because the placenta is an ineffective barrier to drugs ingested by the mother, the fetus can have drug levels that are equally high. This explains why it is so important for women to avoid potentially harmful drugs, such as alcohol, during pregnancy. Fetuses exposed to addictive drugs such as heroin, metham-phetamine, and cocaine show symptoms of withdrawal during maternal abstinence. However, most drugs used to treat psychological disorders are not harmful to a developing fetus.

Drug Metabolism

Once a drug enters the bloodstream and begins to circulate throughout the body, much of it is attaching to inactive proteins or is being dissolved in fat tissue and some of the drug begins to undergo metabolism and excretion. The drug bound to inactive sites is referred to as **depot binding.** As the blood concentration of the drug begins to drop, some drug bound to depot sites reenters the bloodstream (down its concentration gradient), thereby prolonging its activity. The drug remaining in circulation begins to be excreted.

Drugs and their metabolites leave the body in several ways: through exhala-tion (breathalyzer tests for alcohol rely on this), perspiration through the skin, and excretion through the kidneys. Only small amounts of volatile drugs such as alcohol are exhaled, but significant amounts are excreted through perspiration and the kidneys after they are metabolized. If fat-soluble drugs did not undergo metabo-lism, they would continue to be reabsorbed and released by tissues. The liver's metabolism of foreign material is an essential mechanism that rids the body of potentially toxic substances, which sometimes damage the liver. For this reason, liver function is routinely monitored in individuals taking certain drugs because the drugs or their metabolite may be toxic. And, as you may know, the liver is often severely damaged in alcoholics.

Drug metabolism by enzymes in the liver typically results in inactive water-soluble metabolites that are filtered out by the kidneys. In some cases, however, the metabolite of a drug may be as active or even more active than the parent drug. These active metabolites reenter the blood system and are reabsorbed. Drugs with active metabolites have significantly longer durations of action compared to drugs without active metabolites. The active metabolite is eventually metabolized into inactive water-soluble compounds and filtered out of the blood by the kidneys.

The kidneys are located in the back of the abdomen below the ribs. Their function is to filter and excrete by-products of metabolism and to regulate body fluids. Once a drug is metabolized by liver enzymes, its water-soluble metabolites are captured in the kidneys and excreted in urine. Drug testing for illicit drugs (actually their metabolites) is often conducted on urine samples. Approximately 1 liter of blood plasma is filtered by the kidneys each minute, and more than 99.5 percent of this fluid is returned to circulation. The remaining fluid is excreted as urine. The structure of the kidney is illustrated in Figure 2.4.

DRUG HALF-LIFE   As the body continues to metabolize and excrete a drug that is in circulation, the drug's concentrations in the blood and other tissues begin to decline. The time course of this decline can be accurately measured by assays of blood taken at specific intervals after drug administration. One useful measure

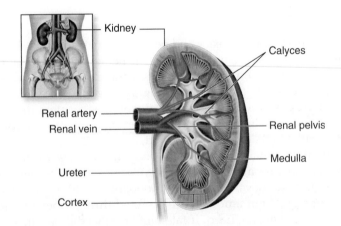

FIGURE 2.4   Each kidney filters about 1 liter of blood each minute. Drug metabolites are excreted through the kidneys.

of the time course of drug elimination is called elimination **half-life.** A drug's half-life is the amount of time it takes for the drug's initial blood level to be decreased 50 percent by metabolism and elimination (i.e., one-half of its peak level). Figure 2.5 shows that the drug reaches a peak blood plasma level of approximately 20 mg/L and is quickly redistributed to tissues over the first hour. After one hour, plasma concentrations fall linearly as plasma and tissue concentrations are at equilibrium. From hour 2 to hour 5, the plasma concentrations fall by one-half (from 8 mg/L to 4 mg/L), indicating a drug half-life of three hours. This three-hour half-life remains constant for this drug. Therefore, in the next three hours, the plasma level will be decreased by another 50 percent, or down to 2 mg/L, and to 1 mg/L after 11 hours or 3 half-lives (see Figure 2.5). Different drugs have different half-lives, ranging from hours to days. For example, cocaine has a half-life of about one hour. The antidepressant Prozac has a half-life of about 48 hours, but it has an active metabolite with a half-life of almost six days. Because of its relatively long half-life, missing a daily dose may not be problematic.

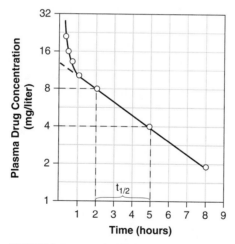

FIGURE 2.5   Drug half-life. Plasma concentrations of a drug following an intravenous injection. Concentrations were measured every 15 minutes following administration for the first hour, then at hour 1, hour 5, and hour 8. During the first hour, plasma concentrations fell rapidly as the drug was redistributed to tissues. After one hour, the plasma concentration was essentially equal to tissue concentrations and levels fell in a linear manner. In this example, the half-life ($t_{1/2}$) is three hours.

The concept of elimination half-life is important for when considering drug dose and frequency of administration. For instance, knowing a drug's half-life allows for predicting its duration of action. And this knowledge of a drug's half-life allows for adjusting dose intervals to achieve a steady blood level of the drug. Drugs used to treat most conditions, including psychological disorders and pain, are most effective when blood levels fall within a narrow range. When blood levels fall below this range, the drug response is too low to be effective. When blood levels are above this range, the drug may be toxic or lethal.

This relationship between a drug dose and it physiological effects is called a **dose response curve.** As shown in Figure 2.6, there is little physiological response until the dose is increased. Then as the dose continues to increase, there is a sharp rise in its effectiveness until a point at which no further increase in effectiveness is produced. Regarding the effectiveness of oxycodone on pain, for instance, doses below 0.01 ug/mL of blood result in little relief from pain. Doses above 0.01 to about 0.10 ug/mL result in a sharp rise in analgesia. Above doses of 0.10 ug/mL, the analgesic response is essentially flat. Most drugs produce several physiological effects, which is true for the opiates (e.g., oxycodone). In addition to analgesia, the effects of drugs can be observed on respiration. At low therapeutic doses, there is little **respiratory depression** (decrease in respiratory rate). At doses approaching 3.0 ug/mL, respiratory depression begins to become a concern. And at blood levels over 4.0 ug/mL, the drug may be lethal, producing complete respiratory depression (see Figure 2.6). This discussion reveals that drugs may have several dose response curves, one for each physiological response. Furthermore, these dose response curves may not overlap. The next section examines how repeated exposure to a drug can actually shift a dose response curve.

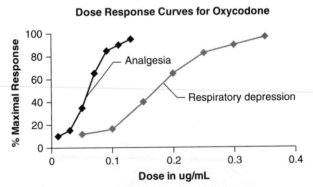

FIGURE 2.6   Dose response curves for oxycodone. The dose response curve for analgesia rises rapidly from about 0.01 through 0.05 ug/mL. After about 0.10 ug/mL, there is little increase in analgesia. However, the dose response curve for respiratory depression rises gradually from doses of about 0.05 ug/mL through 0.25 ug/mL. At doses exceeding 0.30 ug/mL, respiratory depression is almost certain.

Tolerance

As implied above, dose response curves are not static. After repeated administration, the effectiveness of a dose of the analgesic oxycodone, for example, diminishes considerably. The decrease in effectiveness of a dose of drug (a shift to the right in the dose response curve as illustrated in Figure 2.7) following repeated administration is called **tolerance.** Tolerance occurs to all drugs taken over a period of time, but it occurs most rapidly to drugs in the opiate family (e.g., oxycodone and morphine). In fact, when an individual experiences tolerance to oxycodone, he or she is tolerant to other opiates as well, including morphine. This phenomenon is called **cross-tolerance.**

A variety of mechanisms contribute to drug tolerance, and some mechanisms may contribute to tolerance to a greater extent than other mechanisms for different classes of drugs. For this reason, tolerance may develop at different rates for different drugs. In some cases, tolerance can develop over the course of a week; in other cases, it may take many months or even years. Furthermore, some changes in drug responsiveness that contribute to tolerance are easily reversed when the drug is discontinued, while other mechanisms may persist long after use of the drug ends. We know the most about tolerance to drugs in the opiate and stimulant families because these families of drugs have been studied most extensively.

METABOLIC TOLERANCE   As discussed previously, before they can be excreted, psychoactive drugs must undergo metabolism by liver enzymes. The enzymes responsible for the metabolic enzymes that break drugs into water-soluble compounds increase after repeated exposure to a drug. This results in more rapid metabolism as more enzymes are available for degradation. For example, alcohol is metabolized by the liver enzyme alcohol dehydrogenase, which catalyzes the oxidation of alcohol into acetylaldehyde. Acetylaldehyde is further converted into

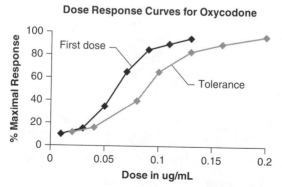

FIGURE 2.7   Tolerance to the analgesic effects of oxycodone is expressed as a shift to the right in the dose response curve for analgesia.

acetic acid by acetaldehyde dehydrogenase. The amount of these liver enzymes increases with exposure to alcohol, contributing to alcohol tolerance.

CELLULAR TOLERANCE   In addition to enzymatic degradation, cellular adaptations to some drugs appear to diminish their effects on target cells. One cellular adaptation that follows drug-induced increases in neurotransmitter availability is **downregulation**. When synaptic activity increases significantly, the number of postsynaptic receptors may actually be reduced, making the post synaptic cell less responsive to chemical transmission (see Figure 2.8). Another mechanism of downregulation is an increase in the sensitivity of autoreceptors on the transmitting neuron. Autoreceptors essentially function to slow down the activity of the firing cell, resulting in less neurotransmitter being synthesized and released. Both mechanisms of downregulation contribute to drug tolerance.

ASSOCIATIVE TOLERANCE   Given what you have learned about tolerance so far, it might be surprising to observe an organism that can display tolerance to a drug in one context but not in another. After all, if tolerance results from downregulation and more efficient enzymatic degradation, why would the context in which a drug was administered make any difference in how someone

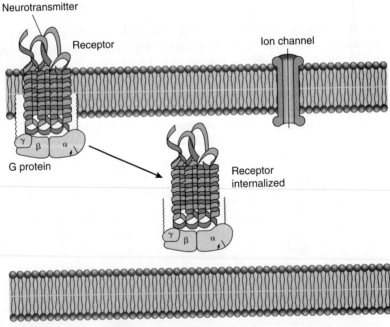

FIGURE 2.8   Downregulation of receptors. Metabotropic receptors may become internalized during the development of tolerance. The expression or the internalization of receptors may occur rapidly and underlie the dynamics of conditioned tolerance.

responds to it? In an experiment conducted by Siegel (1975), rats were administered progressively increasing doses of morphine over a period of several weeks. At the end of this period, all of the animals had developed tolerance and were receiving a dose of morphine that would be lethal to most untreated animals. On the final day of morphine administration, half of the animals received their injections in a novel context, while the remaining half received their injections in the familiar drug environment. Most of the animals that received their drug in the novel context demonstrated signs of overdose, while none of the rats receiving their drug in the familiar context did. This experiment, and many that have followed, reveals that contextual cues associated with drug onset become conditioned stimuli that can elicit tolerance. When animals received a drug injection in a novel context, tolerance was not expressed. In this case, the conditioning is a form of Pavlovian conditioning where contextual cues (conditioned stimuli) associated with drug onset (unconditioned stimulus) come to elicit conditioned tolerance (a conditioned response). In this example, the conditioned response is called a compensatory response to the effects of the drug. Compensatory conditioned responses function to maintain relatively stable internal conditions. Tolerance compensates for the large perturbation caused by opiate administration. This phenomenon is not habituation that could be defined as a decrease in the effectiveness of a stimulus (in this case a drug) to elicit a response. Because habituation is not an associative form of conditioning, it would not be context-specific.

The author's laboratory has further demonstrated that these contextual cues can undergo extinction of tolerance when animals are exposed to the drug context without drug injections. After extinction, tolerance to morphine is not expressed. However, extinction can be reversed when a single morphine dose is administered in the original drug context. This reinstatement of tolerance can occur months after extinction, suggesting that conditioned tolerance to drugs may never be completely reversed. The neural mechanisms underlying associative tolerance are still unknown, but rapid internalization of receptors and downregulation are likely to mediate it. (Results from these experiments are presented in Figures 2.9 and 2.10.)

Reinstatement of conditioned tolerance and other drug responses may contribute to the high recidivism rates for recovering drug addicts. After treatment, reexposure to the context in which drugs were previously used may elicit drug behaviors, including drug craving and withdrawal. Furthermore, rapid reinstatement of tolerance and addiction will appear following drug use after abstinence.

BEHAVIORAL TOLERANCE   The associative tolerance just described involves conditioned associations between a context in which drugs are administered and drug onset. This form of conditioning is referred to as Pavlovian conditioning, and it appears to contribute to a rapid decrease in receptor availability. Operant conditioning also can contribute to drug tolerance. For example, when animals are given intoxicating doses of alcohol before learning a complex motor task, they tend to perform that task better when they are under the influence of alcohol than

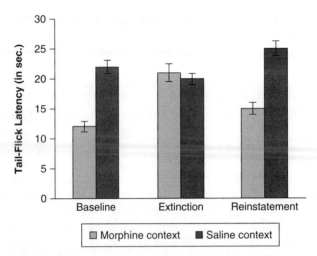

FIGURE 2.9 Conditioned tolerance, extinction, and reinstatement. Animals administered morphine in a distinctive context show tolerance (a decrease in tail-flick latency) in that context but not in a context where saline was administered (longer tail-flick latencies). After several trials in which the animals were exposed to the distinctive morphine context without drug administration, tolerance was extinguished (longer latencies). Tolerance can be reinstated following a single exposure to the morphine context using a morphine injection. (From author's laboratory).

FIGURE 2.10 The distinctive context for morphine administration. (Photo from author's laboratory).

when they are in a sober state. In this example, alcohol becomes a discriminative stimulus that occasions a set of behavioral adaptations to motor behavior (Wenger et al., 1981). Behavioral adaptations such as these are referred to as behavioral tolerance or **state-dependent learning.**

Drug Toxicity and Overdose

As you can see in the dose response curves in Figures 2.6 and 2.7, psychoactive drugs often have several distinct effects, and not all of them are desirable. In addition, some drug effects are caused by the pharmacological actions of the drug; others are not. For example, morphine is well known for its analgesic properties. But it also produces hypothermia; constipation; and, at high doses, respiratory depression. All of these side effects are attributable to its pharmacological actions. It also is possible to have nonpharmacological reactions to drugs, such as an allergic reaction. Although allergic reactions are quite rare with morphine, they can occur with any drug and can be lethal. Other nonpharmacological reactions include damage to the liver or kidneys where drugs are concentrated, as they are responsible for drug metabolism and excretion. Certain drugs also may be harmful to a developing fetus and cause developmental abnormalities or damage to developing organs. All of these drug reactions are examples of drug toxicity, which is a measure of the potentially harmful effects of a drug. Some toxic reactions may be minimized by carefully adjusting drug dosages, but others, such as allergic reactions, can occur with any dose.

At high doses, all drugs can produce toxic reactions and even death. A drug's toxic reactions that are attributable to an excessive dose is called an *overdose* reaction. Overdose reactions can be lethal, and they are most likely attributable to respiratory, kidney, or liver failure. In experimental animals, where drug toxicity is investigated, the dose that is lethal (LD) to 50 percent of the animals receiving it is called the LD_{50} dose. When the dose is lethal to all of the experimental animals, it is the LD_{100} dose. A drug's safety is determined by comparing the drug's therapeutically effective dose (ED) with its lethal dose. The area between these two dose response curves is called the **therapeutic index.** Typically, the wider the range or therapeutic index between a drug's effective and lethal doses, the safer it is.

As cellular and conditioned tolerances to a drug develop, synaptic changes, including downregulation of receptors, occur and the dose response curve shifts to the right. These changes may not occur at the same rate at all sites of drug action. As a result, tolerance to some drug effects may occur at different rates than other drug effects. If tolerance to the therapeutic effect occurs at a faster rate compared to a drug's adverse or toxic affects, the therapeutic index narrows. For example, tolerance appears to occur more quickly to an opiate's analgesic effects (its ED) than to effects on respiratory centers (its LD). This contributes to the high risk of overdose observed in experienced, tolerant drug users. In Figure 2.11, the effective and lethal dose response curves are shown for the analgesic oxycodone.

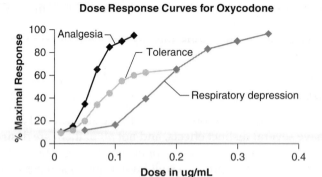

FIGURE 2.11   As tolerance develops to oxycodone's analgesic effects, the effective dose response curve moves to the right, narrowing the therapeutic index.

As tolerance to the analgesic effects begins to develop, the dose response curves for effective and lethal doses merge, increasing the risk of overdose considerably.

Placebo Effects

Not all drug effects are caused by pharmacological properties or even drug interactions with receptors. In fact, recent research on the effectiveness of antidepressant medication has confirmed that about one-half of the improvement in depression symptoms can be attributed to the **placebo** effect. What is the placebo effect, and how can it contribute to the treatment of depression and chronic pain? A placebo is a pharmacologically inert substance administered under the guise of medication. In well-designed clinical studies, neither the patients nor the physician know which patient group receives the placebo or the actual medication. This **double-blind** approach is intended to rule out patient compliance as well as physician biases that can flaw the results. As shown in Figure 2.12, the proportion of patients who respond to treatment for depression has increased steadily over the past 20 years. While it would be tempting to say that this increase reflects improvements in antidepressant drugs over the years, how would it account for the same increase in the effectiveness of placebo treatment that contributes to the same rate of improvement? The figure also reveals that in 2000, about 55 percent of the patients treated with medication responded positively, while about 30 percent of the patients receiving placebos improved. In other words, the placebo effect appears to account for more than 50 percent of the improvement in depression symptoms.

Similar results on the effectiveness of placebos are regularly observed in comparisons of placebos with analgesics for postoperative and chronic pain. And a number of these studies have further revealed that the placebo effect for analgesia is mediated by the endogenous opiate system (e.g., Zubieta et al., 2005). In fact, the drug naloxone, which blocks opiate activity, also blocks the placebo effect,

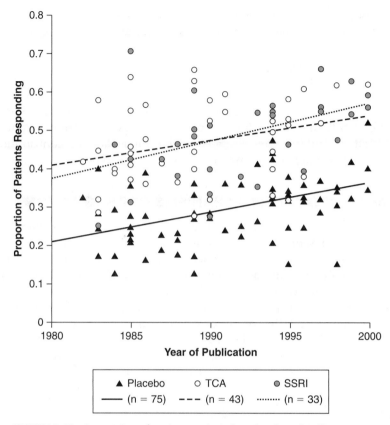

FIGURE 2.12 Proportion of patients assigned to placebo, tricyclic antidepressants (TCAs), and selective serotonin reuptake inhibitors (SSRIs) who showed a 50 percent or greater improvement in Hamilton Rating Scale for depression score by year of publication.   © Walsh, B. T., Seidman, S. N., Ryski, R., Sysko, R., & Gould, M. (2002). Placebo response in studies of major depression. *Journal of the American Medical Association*, 287, 1840–1847.

suggesting that ingesting a placebo can activate the endogenous opiate system and alleviate pain by the very same mechanisms opiate analgesics can (Levine et al., 1978). Because the neural mechanisms for pain and analgesia are well understood, this has been an ideal model used to investigate the neural mechanisms of placebo effects.

Progress also has been made in revealing the mechanisms mediating the antidepressant action of placebos. While investigators have observed neural changes in the cortex of placebo-treated patients, which are similar to the effects observed after antidepressant therapy, the neurochemical mechanisms for the placebo effect in the treatment of depression is still unknown (Benedetti et al., 2005). Thus, the placebo effect accounts for a significant amount of the treatment effect observed following drug therapy and must be taken into account in studies of drug effectiveness. Simply comparing the efficacy of drug treatment to nontreated control subjects may lead to flawed conclusions about the value of drug treatment.

This section examined how the effects of a drug depend on how it is administered, how rapidly and completely it is absorbed, and how repeated exposure and drug administration can alter drug effectiveness by contributing to the development of tolerance. In addition, it examined how to evaluate the safety and effectiveness of a drug by comparing dose response curves for the drug's therapeutic and toxic effects. You also saw that the placebo effect can contribute significantly to a drug's effects and that well-designed studies can isolate this contribution. The next section looks at how drugs interact with receptors to produce their effects.

PHARMACODYNAMICS: MECHANISMS OF DRUG ACTION

Once a drug has passed from the blood supply into the brain, it can begin to exert its effects on neuronal functioning. A basic principle of **pharmacodynamics** is that drug effects are mediated by their influence on target cells. While many of these effects are caused by the interaction between a drug and specific receptors, other effects may be mediated by a drug's effects on neurotransmitter synthesis, storage, release, reuptake, or its metabolism. Ultimately, all psychoactive drugs alter neural function by facilitating or inhibiting neurotransmission. When a drug acts to facilitate neurotransmission, the drug is called an **agonist;** when a drug acts to inhibit or decrease neurotransmission, the drug is referred to as an **antagonist.** A variety of these mechanisms of action are described in Figure 2.13.

Drug Agonists

Because there is a long chain of events leading the synthesis, storage, release, and breakdown of neurotransmitter substances, there are numerous opportunities to alter these processes with drugs. Some of these drug effects are transient, lasting only as long as the drug is present. Other effects are longer-term, affecting receptor expression and protein synthesis. This section will examine some of the most common ways drugs act to facilitate neural communication. Drugs that bind directly to and activate receptor sites are called direct agonists. Drugs that facilitate neurotransmission by increasing neurotransmitter availability or release are called indirect agonists.

NEUROTRANSMITTER SYNTHESIS AND AVAILABILITY   Some drugs function as agonists by increasing the synthesis of a neurotransmitter or by increasing the amount released into the synapse. As you recall, neurotransmitters are synthesized from precursor compounds in the neurons that release them. Increasing the availability of precursor compounds and/or the rate-limiting enzymes necessary for their production can increase neurotransmitter availability. For example, the dopamine agonist L-dopa (3, 4-dihydroxy-L-phenylanine), which is commonly used to treat Parkinson's disease, is the metabolic precursor to dopamine. L-dopa

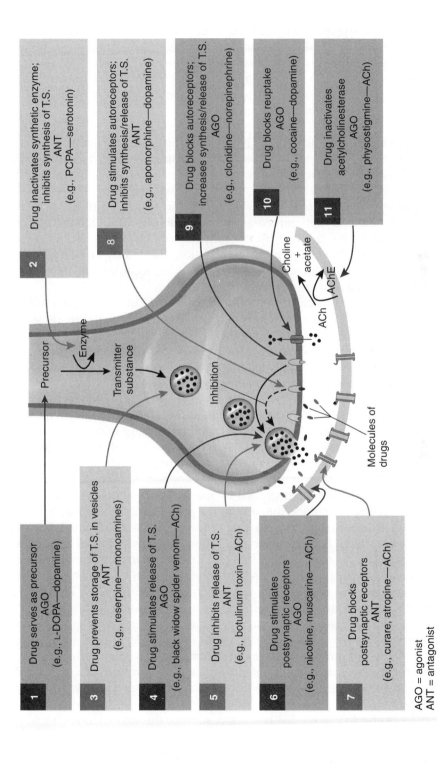

FIGURE 2.13 Mechanisms of drug action. © Carlson, *Physiology of Behavior*, Fig. "Drug Affects of Synaptic Transmission." 2010. Reproduced by permission of Pearson Education, Inc..

AGO = agonist
ANT = antagonist
T.S. = transmitter substance

readily crosses the blood-brain barrier, unlike dopamine, and is quickly converted into dopamine by the enzyme aromatic amino acid decarboxylase. Because this enzyme also is found in peripheral tissues, some of the L-dopa is converted into dopamine before it reaches dopaminergic neurons. To prevent this from occurring, peripheral inhibitors of aromatic amino acid decarboxylase, such as carbidopa, are coadministered with L-dopa.

NEUROTRANSMITTER RELEASE Neurotransmitter is typically released from synaptic vesicles directly into the synaptic gap only after the synaptic vesicles have fused with the presynaptic membrane. However, some drugs may actually enhance the amount of neurotransmitter released by causing it to be released into the presynaptic terminal, where it is then transported into the synaptic gap. Amphetamine and methamphetamine are examples of dopamine agonists that increase dopamine activity by causing dopamine to leak from the synaptic vesicles into the terminal button. In addition, these drugs cause the dopamine transporter to operate in reverse and carry this intracellular dopamine outside the cell, where it can activate dopamine receptors.

Although not a drug, the venom from black widow spiders, as well as some poisonous snakes, acts as an acetylcholine (ACh) agonist by increasing the amount of ACh released into the synapse. This results in overactivity of ACh neurons at neuromuscular synapses, causing muscular contraction. In humans, black widow spider venom is rarely lethal, but the venom from snakes, which is delivered in much larger quantities, can be.

NEUROTRANSMITTER BREAKDOWN AND REUPTAKE The breakdown and reuptake processes that terminate the activity of neurotransmitter released into the synapse are essential for normal neuronal activity. However, these processes may be altered by drug action that results in prolonged neurotransmitter activity. The catecholamine neurotransmitters dopamine and norepinephrine as well as the monoamine serotonin are degraded by the synaptic enzyme monoamine oxidase (MAO). Drugs that block the activity of this enzyme, called MAO inhibitors (MAOIs), enhance neural activity that prevents the metabolic breakdown of these neurotransmitters. Because all three of these neurotransmitters are degraded by MAO, MAOIs are not selective in agonizing any one neurotransmitter. MAOIs such as phenelzine (Nardil) are used as antidepressants and will be discussed later.

Blocking the **reuptake** of intact neurotransmitter is an effective way to enhance neurotransmission selectively or in combination with other neurotransmitters. Blocking reuptake prolongs the action of neurotransmitters on their receptors. This has the immediate effect of increasing neurotransmission and a delayed effect of prompting downregulation of the receptors. The popular antidepressant fluoxetine (Prozac) acts as a **selective serotonin reuptake inhibitor (SSRI)** by blocking the serotonin transporter. Several new generation antidepressants act to inhibit the reuptake of serotonin and norepinephrine. These drugs may be as effective as the SSRIs without some of the adverse side effects.

NEUROTRANSMITTER RECEPTOR ACTIVATION   Some drugs, because of their chemical structure, bind selectively with specific receptors and agonize neurotransmission directly (direct agonist). In these cases, the drug is said to have a high binding affinity for the receptor. Occasionally, a drug has such high affinity that it competes effectively with the natural ligand or neurotransmitter for these receptors. Because there are no reuptake transporters for drugs and they are not degraded quickly by synaptic enzymes, these drugs may have prolonged effects. The hallucinogenic drug lysergic acid diethylamide (LSD) is an example of such a drug. LSD has a high affinity for most serotonin receptors, but its hallucinogenic effects are believed to be mediated by the 5-HT_2 subtype. Other hallucinogenic drugs have similar agonistic actions on serotonin receptors. Table 2.3 presents several common drugs and their mechanisms of action.

Drug Antagonists

If a heroin overdose victim suffering from respiratory and cardiac failure is fortunate enough to make it to an emergency room, he or she will likely receive an intravenous injection of naloxone (Narcan). Within a minute, respiration and heart function will return to normal and the patient will again be responsive to pain and to his or her surroundings. Without the injection of this powerful opiate antagonist, the patient may not have survived. Drug antagonists function to inhibit, or block, neurotransmission. In this example, naloxone competes for the same opiate

TABLE 2.3   Common drugs that act as agonists and antagonists

Drug	Mechanism of Action
cocaine	Dopamine Agonist
L-dopa	Dopamine Agonist
amphetamine	Dopamine/Norepinephrine Agonist
Prozac	Serotonin Agonist
Valium	GABA Agonist
alcohol	GABA Agonist
Thorazine	Dopamine Antagonist
Atropine	ACh Antagonist
marijuana	Cannabinoid Agonist
LSD	Serotonin Agonist
Narcan	Opiate Antagonist

receptors as heroin, but more effectively. The difference is that naloxone does not activate the receptor; it merely blocks it so that neither heroin nor the endogenous ligand (an endorphin) can exert its effects. Within a few hours, naloxone is metabolized and excreted and opiate receptors may return to normal. Not all antagonists work this directly on receptors. As you saw with drug agonists, the neurotransmission process has many steps and drugs can antagonize them all.

NEUROTRANSMITTER SYNTHESIS AND AVAILABILITY   The synthesis of catecholamine neurotransmitters is dependent upon the availability of both dietary tyrosine and the enzyme tyrosine hydroxylase, which converts tyrosine it into DOPA. The drug α-methyl-para-tyrosine (AMPT) acts as an indirect antagonist by blocking the ability of tyrosine hydroxylase to catalyze this conversion, thus depleting both dopamine and norepinephrine. In animal studies, this depletion causes behavioral depression and movement disorders. In humans, AMPT has been used to treat dyskinesia, a movement disorder, and has been shown to induce relapse of major depression and seasonal affective disorder—a type of depression associated with low levels of ambient light.

Neurotransmitter availability also can be disrupted by drug. For example, the antihypertensive drug reserpine binds to the vesicular transporter protein, preventing newly synthesized or recycled catecholamines and serotonin from being transported into synaptic vesicles. As you may recall, neurotransmitter remaining in the terminal button is quickly degraded by MAO. Reserpine nonselectively antagonizes dopamine, norepinephrine, and serotonin by depletion, producing behavioral depression and sedation. Because of these central effects, today reserpine is only rarely used to treat hypertension. Reserpine is used in animal studies that are investigating the roles of catecholamine and serotonin depletion in depression.

NEUROTRANSMITTER RELEASE   The release of catecholamine neurotransmitters is regulated by presynaptic autoreceptors. The receptor subtypes of these autoreceptors are the α_2 receptor for norepinephrine and the D_2 receptor for dopamine. Drugs that stimulate these receptors actually reduce the amount of neurotransmitter released. Because very few drugs have affinities for specific subtypes of receptors, the effects of drugs can be contradictory. That is, a drug such as apomorphine (derived from morphine) stimulates dopamine receptors, but because it agonizes D_2 receptors, it actually decreases dopamine release from neurons containing them. So apomorphine, although a dopamine agonist, has antagonistic effects on some dopamine neurons.

Botulism toxin is another example of a substance that inhibits the release of neurotransmitter. In this case, it antagonizes ACh by preventing synaptic vesicles from fusing with the presynaptic membrane. The effect of poisoning is muscle weakness, and in severe cases, botulism toxin can cause asphyxiation and death. In extremely small doses, botulism toxin (Botox) is used as a cosmetic to eliminate facial wrinkles. It does this by paralyzing small groups of muscle cells that, in their contracted state, cause wrinkles.

NEUROTRANSMITTER RECEPTOR ACTIVATION   In the early 1950s, well before the catecholamine neurotransmitters were identified, the drug chlorpromazine (Thorazine) was introduced as the first drug to treat schizophrenia, which may be the most debilitating of all psychological disorders. While chlorpromazine was rapidly becoming the treatment of choice for severe psychosis, its mechanism of action remained a mystery for nearly a decade. Scientists now know that chlorpromazine acts as a direct antagonist on dopamine receptors. This discovery has led to modern theories describing the molecular basis of schizophrenia as well as to the development of many new drugs for its treatment. By blocking dopamine receptors, chlorpromazine disrupts dopamine neurotransmission in the basal ganglia, the mesolimbic system, and the cortex.

Drugs that directly antagonize receptors vary in their affinity for specific receptor subtypes. Newer drugs being developed for schizophrenia treatment are focused on minimizing the severe motor side effects associated with older medications by targeting specific dopamine receptors. This topic will be discussed in more detail in the chapter on antipsychotic medication.

This section provided examples of how drugs can act to facilitate and disrupt neurotransmission. Because the neurotransmission process has many steps, there are many ways to alter neural activity with drugs. Using drugs to alter neurotransmission has led to a greater understanding of how different neurotransmitter systems contribute to both normal and disordered behavior. It also has led to more effective treatment for behavior disorders while at the same time minimizing troubling side effects.

As you will see in the following chapters, modern drug development is going beyond altering drug-receptor interactions by examining ways to alter the expression of genes in specific populations of neurons. These manipulations can affect receptor expression as well as other properties of cell functioning that may contribute to the treatment of psychological disorders.

CHAPTER

3

Mood Disorders
Major Depression and Bipolar Disorders

Jamie is a 28-year-old woman who was recently divorced after a six-year marriage. She remembers feeling depressed during most of her high school years, especially during her senior year when she sought help following a suicide attempt. Jamie had an unremarkable childhood. Both parents worked, but she was rarely alone during her pre–high school years. She has two younger brothers, both of whom appear without symptoms of depression. She has always had several close friends. After graduating from college with a degree in interior design, Jamie held several jobs and is now employed with an architectural firm. She enjoys her job but believes it is getting more stressful and contributing to her overwhelming fatigue.

After Jamie's suicide attempt, she was prescribed medication, which she took regularly for about a year. The medication helped somewhat, but she still felt depressed and the drug made her drowsy and interfered with her concentration at work. Since her diagnosis, Jamie has gained over 50 pounds and she no longer swims or runs, activities she enjoyed throughout college. She now reports that she does not look forward to spending evenings with friends, traveling, or even visiting her parents or brothers—all things she did when she was married. She spends her time after work watching television and talking with girlfriends on the phone. She gets little pleasure from reading and finds that she is often distracted by extreme loneliness and sadness. Although Jamie has had no other suicide attempts, she has contemplated it frequently since her divorce as the only solution to her pain. During these periods, she finds herself soothed by chocolate, which she blames for her weight problem.

Jamie's case is not untypical. She has done well in her job, has a number of close friends, and is relatively healthy. In fact, most of her coworkers and friends would not consider her to be depressed. She is seeking help again because she wants more from life. She is tired of being alone and would like to begin dating in the hopes of finding a romantic partner. She does not like being with herself and feels no one else would like to be with her either. She also hopes that treatment will help her lose weight since attempts at dieting have failed.

Depression is the most common of the psychological disorders, affecting the lives of nearly everyone. It affects people because they are among the many who live with depression or because they have family members or close friends who suffer from depression. Each year nearly 1 out of every 10 adults is diagnosed with depression, and many more may go undiagnosed. The lifetime prevalence (at least one occurrence during a person's lifetime) is as high as 17 percent, affecting about 24 percent of all women and 12 percent of all men. Depression can occur at any age, but it first appears most frequently in late adolescence and early adulthood. It contributes significantly to suicide risk, which is the third leading cause of death in adolescents and young adults. Depression also is a major contributor to substance use disorders (for instance, alcohol, methamphetamine, cocaine, and opiate abuse) and to eating disorders, including obesity and bulimia. Because depression adversely affects the lives of so many, it isn't surprising that the economic impact of depression on the productivity of the workforce and healthcare system is estimated to exceed $40 billion annually. On the other hand, the sales of prescription drugs to treat depression are escalating and now exceed $20 billion each year.

This chapter discusses several severe mood disorders, emphasizing **major depressive disorder** and **bipolar disorder.** It will examine their diagnostic criteria, their pathology, and the pharmacological approaches to their treatment. Other depressive disorders, including **dysthymic disorder,** are not discussed because their pathology and treatment do not differ significantly from those of major depressive disorder.

MAJOR DEPRESSIVE DISORDER

Defining and Diagnosing Depression

The point at which someone who is experiencing symptoms of depression becomes diagnosed with major depressive disorder is never clear and will vary depending on who is making the clinical judgment. The reason is because the symptoms of depression are subjective and assessing them through patient interviews can be challenging. The diagnostic criteria for depression (and for all other psychiatric disorders) are presented in the *Diagnostic and Statistical Manual of Mental Disorders (DSM).* The DSM, published by the American Psychiatric Association, is widely accepted as the standard guide for defining and diagnosing all recognized behavioral and psychological disorders. Presently the DSM is in its fourth text revision (DSM-IV-TR).

The diagnostic criteria for major depressive disorder (unipolar depression) require that an individual experience at least five of the following symptoms on most days during the two-week period leading to the diagnosis:

- *A depressed mood for most of the day.* This may be characterized by a persistent sadness or irritability, a tendency to cry easily, and a feeling of hopelessness and discouragement. Some patients describe their mood as "gray," meaning it lacks any change in emotion.

- *A diminished interest and pleasure in most activities.* This includes recreational activities that the individual enjoyed previously (e.g., golf, tennis, or skiing) as well as social activities with friends and family. Depression also may contribute to a diminished interest is sexual activity.

- *A significant change in appetite and weight.* Although appetite and weight often increase during depressive episodes, some individuals may experience a diminished appetite and unwanted weight loss. In some cases, carbohydrate cravings occur, which may be associated with serotonin depletion. As mentioned in Chapter 1, carbohydrate diets can contribute to increases in serotonin synthesis and availability.

- *Insomnia or hypersomnia.* A disruption in normal sleeping patterns is common in all types of depression as well as in nondepressed individuals. Because sleeping difficulties can be caused by many things, including diet, alcohol consumption, medication, lack of physical activity, and stress, their prevalence in depression is not surprising. Chronic sleep problems, whether insomnia or hypersomnia, can exacerbate other symptoms of depression, making them even more debilitating.

- *Motor agitation or retardation that is observable by others.* Often patients do not recognize these changes in their behavior, but others may notice increased agitation or lethargy. Pacing, frequent urges to get up and move about, or the inability to complete tasks are examples of behavioral agitation. Not initiating activities, sleeping excessively, or sitting for hours at a time are examples of behavioral retardation.

- *Fatigue or diminished energy.* Very common in depression, these symptoms are often described as a lack of motivation or excessive tiredness and are clearly related to other symptoms listed here. Some patients experience such extreme fatigue that they may spend much of their day inactive or in bed.

- *A diminished ability to think or to concentrate.* Concentration may be frequently disrupted by thoughts of guilt or remorse or the urge to move. Depression makes most activities and work difficult, contributing to a loss of productivity and the enjoyment that most people get from work and leisure activities.

- *Feelings of helplessness, worthlessness, or guilt.* Depressed individuals often describe their lives as being worthless and not having significant meaning. In addition, they believe that their efforts rarely result in gratification. Efforts to do well in school or work begin to diminish, leading to even less gratification and less future effort.

- *Recurrent thoughts of suicide or attempted suicide.* Many people have thought of suicide at some point in their life, but depression is often associated with persistent suicide thoughts and plans. Suicide attempts are a clear sign of depression and must be taken seriously. Over 30,000 people commit suicide each year, making it the third leading cause of death among the youth.

Everyone experiences these symptoms from time to time. They can be associated with the loss of a significant other, the end of a relationship, or the unexpected termination of employment. Depression associated with significant changes in one's life does not typically escalate into a major depressive disorder even though it can be disruptive and make normal daily activities difficult. This **reactive depression** is relatively transient, often disappearing on its own within a few weeks or months without treatment. Moreover, reactive depression tends to be intermixed with periods of normal mood. Major depressive disorder is more persistent and debilitating, and although it can go into remission, during a depressive episode, there is little or no relief from its symptoms.

Major depressive disorder is often accompanied by anxiety. The anxiety may be related to an unrealistic fear of public or open places (**agoraphobia**), for example, or it may be generalized in that there are no particular contexts or occasions that trigger it. Generalized anxiety can be acute and is often associated with greatly elevated sympathetic activity. In these instances, it is difficult to know whether the feelings of anxiety follow the elevated sympathetic response or contribute to it. Anxiety is mentioned here because when depression occurs with significant anxiety, it may be treated differently than when depression is the only or primary feature of the disorder. Anxiety disorders and their treatment will be discussed in a later chapter.

Pathology of Major Depressive Disorder: Monoamine Hypothesis

Most of the evidence available today suggests that abnormalities in the serotonergic and/or noradrenergic systems, including the brain structures they innervate, underlie severe depression. Beginning in the 1960s, researchers began to speculate that these neurotransmitter systems were involved in depression because drugs that were effective in its treatment altered neurotransmitter availability and breakdown. Likewise, drugs that depleted neurotransmitter availability could cause depression-like symptoms. These observations led to the prominent **monoamine hypothesis** of depression. According to this hypothesis, deficiencies in the monoamine (single amine group in their molecular structure) neurotransmitters dopamine, norepinephrine, and/or serotonin would be sufficient to cause depression. Some of the earliest evidence for this hypothesis came from observations of patients being treated for high blood pressure with the drug reserpine. As discussed in Chapter 2, reserpine not only reduces blood pressure, but also blocks the vesicular transport of monoamine neurotransmitters into synaptic vesicles. Left in the terminal button, these monoamines get degraded by monoamine oxidase (MAO), resulting in a depletion of available neurotransmitters. One serious side effect observed in patients being treated with reserpine is depression. This drug-induced depression disappears quickly once reserpine treatment is discontinued. Although reserpine is not used as an antihypertensive today, it is still used in animal studies to examine the effects of amine depletion on behavior.

Consideration of the monoamine neurotransmitters as factors in depression was also reasonable given their distributions throughout the limbic system and frontal cortex—areas known for their roles in behavioral arousal, emotion, and motivation. Because reserpine nonspecifically depletes monoamine neurotransmitters, the earliest versions of the monoamine hypothesis could not distinguish which of the monoamine neurotransmitters were involved in behavioral depression, nor could they suggest how these deficiencies caused it.

Since its inception, the monoamine depletion hypothesis has generated considerable support and is presently the most widely accepted account of the pathology of depression. And although this hypothesis has undergone revision, there is still no consensus about its details. In fact, depression may result from several different alterations in the structure and function of monoamine neurotransmitter systems and in their target neuronal structures. It is becoming increasingly clear, however, that depression is a neurological disease that is reversible or partially reversible by pharmacotherapy in many patients.

Revised Monoamine Hypothesis of Depression

One observation that has plagued the monoamine hypothesis since its beginning has been that even though antidepressant treatment produces rapid changes in neurotransmitter availability, the symptoms of depression do not disappear as quickly. The **lag time** between drug-induced changes in neurotransmitter availability and any corresponding changes in symptoms may be two weeks or longer. If depression were merely the result of monoamine depletion, we would expect more rapid improvement. What kinds of neuronal changes might take longer to be expressed?

The most recent revisions to the monoamine hypothesis propose that depression may be a consequence of neural degeneration in the hippocampus and the frontal cortex caused by monoamine neurons in these areas failing to produce sufficient amounts of tropic or growth factors. One protein that has received considerable attention is **brain-derived neurotropic factor (BDNF).** This is a nerve growth factor essential for normal cell survival, receptor growth, and growth of new neurons. BDNF acts within the cell nucleus to maintain normal cell functioning and to facilitate synaptic growth by signaling the expression of new receptor sites. The synthesis of BDNF is dependent on a series of cellular events, beginning with the influx of Ca^{++} upon activation of monoamine metabotropic receptors. In turn, Ca^{++} activates second messengers that regulate the **transcription** of BDNF from the cell's DNA (see Figure 3.1). The second messenger mediating BDNF transcription appears to be a protein called **CREB,** which stands for cyclic adenosine monophosphate (or **cAMP**) **r**esponse **e**lement **b**inding protein (Tao et al., 1998). In summary, **downregulation** of monoamine neurons may lead to further downregulation of an essential growth factor in neurons in the hippocampus and the frontal cortex. This downregulation disrupts neuronal signaling and plasticity and may lead to cellular degeneration.

Downregulation of monoamine activity also occurs as a result of neuronal inhibition by autoreceptors. As discussed in Chapter 2, autoreceptors on both the soma and terminal buttons regulate neuron excitability and the amount of neurotransmitter synthesized and released from the terminal button. Patients with

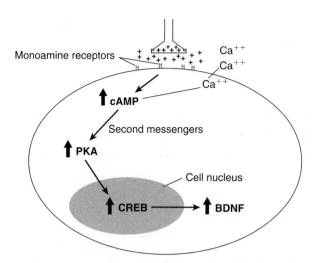

FIGURE 3.1   The neurotropic factor BDNF regulates receptor growth and expression. Activation of monoamine metabotropic receptors allows for the influx of Ca^{++}, which activates second messenger systems and an increase in CREB and BDNF synthesis. BDNF is essential for the expression of new receptors, cell maintenance, and cell survival.

major depression may have increased numbers of these autoreceptors, which may contribute to decreases in serotonin and norepinephrine release. Chronic treatment with antidepressants downregulates these autoreceptors, resulting in increased postsynaptic activity (Levin et al., 2007).

How do depressed patients get downregulated BDNF transcription and the cascade of neuronal consequences resulting from it? There are several possibilities, including genetic predispositions to autoreceptor expression and downregulated BDNF transcription or to the CREB activity that regulates it. Evidence to support this explanation comes primarily from animals that have been genetically altered not to express the BDNF gene (knockout mice). These animals demonstrate depression-like behavior and a resistance to antidepressant treatment. Both of these effects are consistent with the idea that BDNF **downregulation** contributes to depression and that antidepressant treatment can reverse it (Monteggia et al., 2007). In addition, environmental stress has been shown to contribute to BDNF downregulation. Animals exposed to stressors, including maternal separation or forced swimming, show decreased CREB and BDNF activity, suggesting that chronic stress may contribute to behavioral depression by altering BDNF transcription from DNA (Nair et al., 2007). The stress hormone contributing to BDNF downregulation and to cell damage appears to be the glucocorticoid cortisol (Haynes et al., 2004; Schule et al., 2006).

Evidence for decreased or downregulated synthesis of BDNF in depression comes from both animal and human studies. For example, as shown in Figure 3.2, patients with depression have low levels of BDNF in their blood when compared to nondepressed subjects; patients with recurring depression have even lower levels (Lee et al., 2006, 2007; Post, 2007; Yoshida et al., 2007). Antidepressant

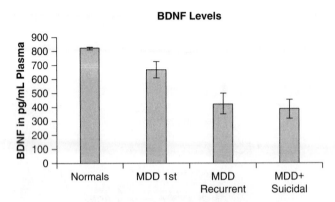

FIGURE 3.2 BDNF levels in depression (mean pg/mL +− SE). Blood plasma levels of BDNF decrease as the severity of depression increases. Lee, B.-H., Kim, H., Park, S-H., Kim, Y.K. (2006). Decreased plasma BDNF level in depressive patients. © Reprinted from the *Journal of Affective Disorders*, 101(1-3), 293–244 with permission from Elsevier.

therapy acts to downregulate presynaptic autoreceptors and to stimulate the formation of BDNF, reinstating normal cell functioning and growth. The lag time between the initiation of antidepressant treatment and the neuronal adaptations resulting from it correspond well with improvements in mood.

Animal studies continue to play an important role in pharmacology research and drug development. Experimental methods and the measurement of behaviors indicative of depression have become more standardized. For example, chronic mild stress, forced swimming, and removal of the olfactory bulbs have been used effectively to induce behavioral symptoms of depression. These symptoms include decreases in forced swim time, decreases in sexual behavior, depressed appetite, and impairments in learning and memory (see Figure 3.3). In addition to inducing behavioral depression, these manipulations have been shown to suppress the synthesis of BDNF in several brain regions. Chronic, but not acute,

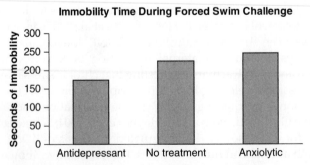

FIGURE 3.3 Antidepressants significantly decrease immobility in a forced swim challenge with laboratory rats. Data from Porsolt et al., 1977.

treatment with antidepressant drugs appears to reverse the downregulation of BDNF synthesis and the symptoms of depression in these experimental animals (Grønli et al., 2006; Khundakar et al., 2006; Rogóz et al., 2005).

It appears that all antidepressants have the ability to downregulate autoreceptor expression and to activate the second messenger systems that lead to BDNF synthesis. These neuronal adaptations may be the critical mechanisms of antidepressant action (Blom et al., 2002; Nibuya et al., 1998; Thome et al., 2000; Thomas et al., 2003; Tiraboschi et al., 2004). Long-term, but not acute, antidepressant treatment may act to upregulate BDNF transcription and synthesis by activating CREB directly or by increasing Ca^{++} influx, which then activates CREB. Increases in BDNF activity promote the growth and expression of postsynaptic serotonin receptors, thereby enhancing serotonergic neurotransmission (Altar, 1999; Koponen et al., 2005).

PHARMACOLOGICAL TREATMENT OF MAJOR DEPRESSIVE DISORDER

The following sections review the history and evolution of drug development and the pharmacological treatment of depression. The first drugs used to treat depression were introduced in the late 1950s, well before their mechanisms of action were understood. As the monoamine neurotransmitters and their pathways were being described in the 1960s, drugs were being used as research tools to investigate the functions of neurotransmitter systems, as well as therapy for a variety of behavioral disorders. This interrelationship between drug development and neuroscience research continues to the present.

Tricyclic Antidepressants

The tricyclic category of antidepressant drugs share a common three-ring molecular structure from which they derive their name and classification (see Figure 3.4). Discovered in the late 1950s, these drugs were first used, unsuccessfully, to treat

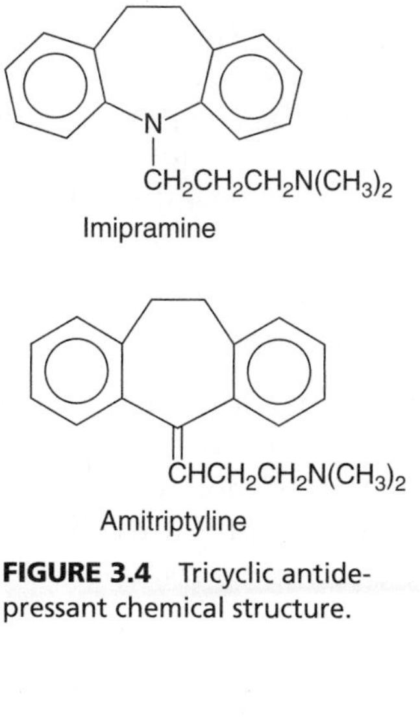

Imipramine

Amitriptyline

FIGURE 3.4 Tricyclic antidepressant chemical structure.

TABLE 3.1	Tricyclic Antidepressants	
Drug Name	**Common Trade Names**	**Half-Life Hours**
Amitriptyline	Elavil	10–28
Desipramine	Norpramin	24
Doxepin	Sinequan	8–24
Imipramine	Tofranil, Imipramin	10–20
Nortriptyline	Pamelor	36
Protriptyline	Triptil, Vivactil	74
Trimipramine	Surmontil	7–23

schizophrenia. Their ability to treat major depression was discovered quite by accident in hospitalized patients. The tricyclic antidepressants include about eight compounds, each marketed under different brand names. Imipramine, the first **tricyclic antidepressant** produced, is currently marketed under several brand names, including Imipramin, Deprinol, and Tofranil. Other tricyclics, their common brand names, and their pharmacokinetics are included in Table 3.1. These drugs differ only slightly in their molecular structure, and their mechanisms of antidepressant action are essentially the same. They differ only in their relative specificities for different monoamine neurotransmitters and in their side effects on acetylcholine and histamine receptors.

MECHANISMS OF TRICYCLIC ANTIDEPRESSANT ACTION   All tricyclic antidepressants bind effectively to the reuptake transporter proteins for both norepinephrine and serotonin. By competitively binding to transporter proteins, they interfere with the normal reuptake of these neurotransmitters, thereby increasing the duration they remain in the synaptic gap. The longer neurotransmitters remain in the synapse, the longer they may exert their effects on pre- and postsynaptic receptors. Because blocking reuptake of neurotransmitters is an immediate effect of antidepressant treatment and their effects on symptoms of depression, if they occur at all, are often delayed by several weeks, their antidepressant effects may result from synaptic adaptations and neuronal growth following the downregulation of presynaptic autoreceptors and the **upregulation** of BNDF synthesis (see Figure 3.5).

SIDE EFFECTS OF TRICYCLIC ANTIDEPRESSANTS   While the antidepressant action of the tricyclic antidepressants appears to be their effects on reuptake mechanisms, they also block histamine and acetylcholine receptors to some extent. Histamine blockade (an antihistamine effect) produces drowsiness and fatigue in most patients. This antihistamine effect can be minimized to some degree by taking it at

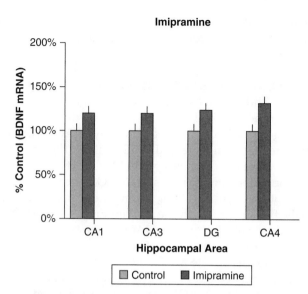

FIGURE 3.5   Imipramine significantly increased BDNF synthesis in all hippocampal areas examined. Data from Russo-Neustadt et al., 1999.

night rather than early in the day. If insomnia and agitation are part of the complex of symptoms, the drowsiness and fatigue may be an attractive side effect. In addition, tricyclic antidepressants block acetylcholine receptors and may cause dry mouth, dizziness, hypotension, constipation, blurred vision, and difficulty with concentration and memory formation. While all of these cholinergic effects are unwanted, patients experience them to varying degrees. Some patients find that the effectiveness and relatively low cost of the drugs outweigh their annoying side effects, while other patients find the drugs (and their accompanying side effects) intolerable. Several common tricyclic antidepressants and their respective half-lives are shown in Table 3.1.

Overdosing with tricyclic antidepressants can and does occur and may lead to seizures, cardiac arrhythmias, severe hypotension, and even death. Unintentional overdose would be quite rare, however, because there is a relatively wide therapeutic index (AD_{50}–LD_{50}) for these drugs. The toxic effects of the tricyclic drugs are typically seen at doses exceeding 10 times their normal dose (i.e., 1000 mg or more).

Monoamine Oxidase Inhibitors (MAOIs)

Monoamine oxidase inhibitors (MAOIs) were developed in the late 1950s and were found, by coincidence, to function as antidepressants. Iproniazid, the first MAOI, was actually developed to treat tuberculosis. Unexpectedly, Iproniazid was observed to have mood-elevating and **psychostimulant** effects and soon after was recruited to treat major depression. Because of often severe and life-threatening side effects and newer alternatives for pharmacotherapy, these drugs have only limited usefulness today.

MECHANISMS OF MAOI ANTIDEPRESSANT ACTION MAO is produced by all monoamine neurons and functions to deaminate (remove the amine group) these neurotransmitters in the terminal button. Therefore, the amount of monoamine available for storage and release is regulated by MAO. MAOIs prevent this oxidative reaction, resulting in increased availability of the neurotransmitters for storage and release. There are two subtypes of MAO that preferentially **deaminate** different monoamines: Monoamine oxidase-$_A$ (MAO-$_A$) deaminates norepinephrine, dopamine, and serotonin, while MAO-$_B$ deaminates dopamine and phenylanine but has less specificity for norepinephrine and serotonin. The early MAOIs inhibited MAO-$_A$ and MAO-$_B$ equally, but newer MAOIs have been developed to be more specific in attempts to reduce their side effects. MAOIs are typically irreversible, meaning that once they deactivate MAO, the enzyme remains unavailable in the terminal button until it has been replaced. The resynthesis of MAO may take as long as several weeks. Reversible MAOIs have been developed, but they are not commercially available in the United States. Presumably, the MAO inhibiting effect could be more carefully regulated by dose with reversible MAOIs (see Table 3.2).

As with the tricyclic antidepressants, the lag time from initial treatment to the observation of therapeutic effects, if observed, is typically about two weeks. That corresponds to the time for synaptic adaptations resulting from downregulated autoreceptor expression to upregulated BDNF synthesis.

SIDE EFFECTS OF MAOI ANTIDEPRESSANTS All MAOIs have significant and sometimes serious side effects, including sedation and fatigue, dizziness, movement disorders including tremors, blurred vision, decreased libido, dry mouth, and weight gain. A more serious side effect may occur if MAOIs are taken with foods containing tyramine (derived from the amino acid tyrosine), an amine formed as a by-product of fermentation. Foods such as cheese, yogurt, aged meats, certain

TABLE 3.2 MAOIs

Drug Name	Common Trade Names	Selectivity
Isocarboxazid	Marplan	MAO-$_A$, MAO-$_B$
Phenelzine	Nardil	MAO-$_A$, MAO-$_B$
Selegiline	Eldepryl	MAO-$_B$
Tranylcypromine	Parnate	MAO-$_A$, MAO-$_B$

Note: Because these MAOIs are irreversible, elimination half-life does not affect their clinical effectiveness.

breads, wine, and some fruits contain tyramine, which is normally deaminated in the liver by MAO. However, MAOIs even deactivate liver MAO, resulting in excess levels of tyramine, which may increase norepinephrine storage and release. Excessive norepinephrine activity can cause severe headaches; sweating; nausea; and a hypertensive crisis, which can cause a stroke.

In 2003, the FDA approved a newer selective MAOI called selegiline for treating Parkinson's disease; in 2006, it approved a selegiline skin patch for treating major depression. Selegiline acts primarily on MAO-$_B$, so it increases dopamine storage and release without interacting with tyramine-containing foods as significantly as do nonselective MAOIs. At higher doses, selegiline also inhibits MAO-$_A$, producing its antidepressant effect. The other side effects associated with nonselective MAOIs, including dry mouth, decreased libido, weight gain, and fatigue, do not appear to be as bothersome with the use of selegiline.

Selective Serotonin Reuptake Inhibitors (SSRIs)

By the late 1970s, researchers were beginning to distinguish between the behavior-stimulating and mood-elevating effects of antidepressants that acted on both the noradrenergic and serotonergic systems. Researchers believed that the behavior-stimulating effects were mediated by blocking norepinephrine reuptake, while the mood-enhancing effect was mediated by serotonin. In attempts to target these systems individually, research focused on developing drugs to specifically enhance serotonin (or 5-HT) neurotransmission while at the same time minimizing effects on histamine and acetylcholine receptors that mediated most of the troublesome side effects. In 1988, after more than ten years of pharmacology research, fluoxetine (Prozac) was approved for the treatment of major depression. Since the development of Prozac, a number of similar compounds have been developed and approved for the treatment of depression as well as other psychological disorders (see Table 3.3). These drugs are known as **second-generation** antidepressants. These drugs differ considerably from the **first-generation** MAOIs and tricyclics in

TABLE 3.3 SSRIs		
Drug Name	**Brand Name**	**Half-Life**
Citalopram	Celexa	23–45 hrs
Escitalopram	Lexapro	27–32 hrs
Fluoxetine	Prozac	24–48 hrs[*]
Fluvoxamine	Luvox	9–28 hrs
Paroxetine	Paxil	24 hrs
Sertraline	Zoloft	22–36 hrs

*Active metabolite

their mechanisms of antidepressant action as well as their effects on histamine and acetylcholine receptors. In addition, second-generation antidepressants were developed specifically for treating depression, unlike the MAOIs and tricyclics that were developed to treat other diseases and only later were identified for their antidepressant effects. With the development of these second-generation compounds came the first significant advance in the 30-year history of treating depression with drugs.

MECHANISMS OF SSRI ANTIDEPRESSANT ACTION   As their name implies, SSRIs were developed specifically to inhibit the reuptake of serotonin by competitively binding with the serotonin transporter protein. This competitive binding effectively blocks the reuptake of a significant amount of extracellular serotonin, leaving it available to engage pre- and postsynaptic receptor sites for longer durations. The SSRIs do not specifically target subtypes of serotonin receptors, so they effectively increase serotonin activity at 5-HT_1, 5-HT_2, and 5-HT_3 receptor types. Recall from Chapter 1 that the 5-HT_1 receptor types function as metabotropic postsynaptic receptors and as inhibitory autoreceptors. It is believed that the antidepressant effects of SSRIs are mediated primarily by the 5-HT_{1A} receptor types while some of their adverse side effects may be mediated by 5-HT_2 receptors. Specifically, the 5-HT_{1A} autoreceptor is believed to be overexpressed in major depression, resulting in excessive inhibition of serotonergic neurons in the raphe nucleus, amygdala, and hippocampus. Chronic treatment with SSRIs leads to downregulation of these inhibitory autoreceptors and a corresponding increase in serotonergic activity. Selectively blocking the effects of SSRIs on 5-HT_2 receptors may enhance the effectiveness of SSRI treatment and decrease some unwanted side effects (Levin et al., 2007; Marek et al., 2005; Parsey et al., 2006).

In summary, SSRIs increase serotonergic activity by blocking the reuptake transporter, leaving serotonin in the synapse for longer durations. Increases in serotonin activity result in neuronal adaptations and downregulation of 5-HT_{1A} autoreceptors (see Figure 3.6). The 5-HT_2 type receptors may mediate many of the troubling side effects associated with SSRI use. Research employing selective 5-HT_2 antagonists in combination with SSRIs further confirms the role of 5-HT_1 receptors in major depression and provides promise for an even more effective therapy with reduced side effects. Drugs with this property will be described in the next section. Several of the most common SSRIs are listed in Table 3.3.

SIDE EFFECTS OF SSRI ANTIDEPRESSANTS   All of the antidepressants discussed thus far have had significant side effects; the SSRIs are no exception. As mentioned previously, most of the side effects, including sexual dysfunction in males, decreased libido, gastrointestinal problems, decreased appetite, insomnia, and agitation, are mediated primarily by the 5-HT_2 receptor types. In addition, a life-threatening condition referred to as **serotonin syndrome,** a toxic reaction caused by excessive serotonin activity, may occur. Symptoms of serotonin

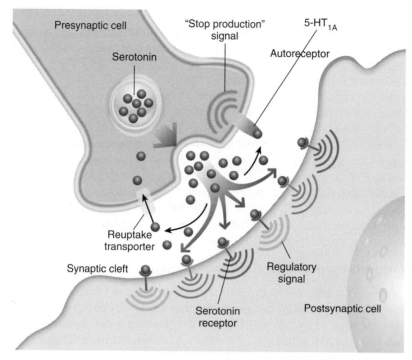

FIGURE 3.6 5-HT$_{1A}$ autoreceptors may be overexpressed in depression, contributing to decrease serotonin activity. SSRIs downregulate inhibitory 5-HT$_{1A}$ autoreceptors in several regions of the brain, including the hippocampus, raphe nucleus, and the amygdala.

syndrome include disorientation, confusion, visual disturbances, severe agitation, mania, hypertension, hyperthermia, cold sweats, and diarrhea. In severe cases, serotonin syndrome can lead to coma and perhaps death. This syndrome is most likely when SSRIs are taken with other medication that can increase serotonin activity, including all non-SSRI antidepressants and St. John's Wort, an herbal remedy for depression (Izzo, 2004). However, serotonin syndrome also can occur as an overdose to any SSRI taken by itself.

Recent years have seen considerable attention surrounding cases of suicide in children and adolescents taking SSRIs. In fact, in early 2004, the Food and Drug Administration (FDA) issued a warning that antidepressant drugs significantly increased the risk of **suicide ideation** and **suicidality** in children and adolescents. In 2007, this warning was revised to included warnings about increased risks of suicide ideation and attempts in young adults aged 18–24. Additional language was added stating that scientific data do not show this increased risk in adults older than 24 and that adults aged 65 and older taking antidepressants actually have a decreased risk of suicidality. The contribution of SSRIs to suicidality is quite small (e.g., Tiihonen et al., 2006), and not all studies have found it (e.g., Nilsson et al., 2004). In a recent analysis of all research published between 1988 and 2006, investigators found no significant difference in suicidality between adolescents with major depression taking antidepressants and those taking placebos. However, antidepressants were found to be more effective than placebos in treating symptoms of depression (Bridge et al., 2007).

Since the regulatory warning regarding SSRI and suicide risk was issued, SSRI prescriptions rates for adolescents have dropped significantly (about 22 percent for 2003–2004). During this same time, as shown in Figure 3.7, researchers report a concerning increase in suicides in this age group. In the United States, suicide rates among youth increased by 14 percent between 2003 and 2004, corresponding to a drop in prescription rates (Gibbons et al., 2007).

Clearly, the debate about whether antidepressants can increase suicide ideation and attempts will continue with mixed results well into the future. Suicidality is a common symptom of major depression in all age groups and must be considered in every treatment program.

Serotonin-Norepinephrine Reuptake Inhibitors (SNRIs)

The most recent additions to the antidepressant arsenal come from attempts to minimize drug side effects, shorten the lag time in therapeutic effectiveness, and increase the range of symptoms treated. Depression often includes depressed mood and depressed behavior. For instance, overwhelming fatigue, excessive sleepiness, and prolonged sleep duration are common in depressed patients. Increasing noradrenergic activity promotes arousal by enhancing activity of the reticular activating system. While drugs that target norepinephrine more

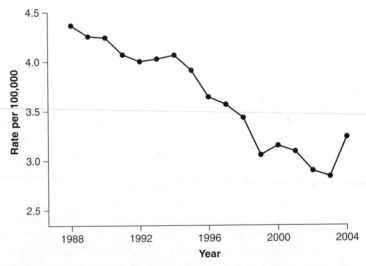

FIGURE 3.7   Suicide rate among youth in the United States (5–19 years of age).   © Reprinted with permission from the *American Journal of Psychiatry*. (Copyright 2007). American Psychiatric Association.

specifically, such as amphetamine, are not affective in treating depression, the SNRIs, which block the reuptake of serotonin and norepinephrine, are. In addition, because the antagonism of acetylcholine and histamine receptors (and increasing activity of the 5-HT$_{2-3}$ receptors) mediate most of the troublesome side effects of antidepressants, new dual-action drugs are being designed to evade these receptor effects.

MECHANISMS OF SNRI ANTIDEPRESSANT ACTION   The SNRIs differ considerably in their effects on serotonin and norepinephrine neurons, and several increase dopamine activity to some extent (see Table 3.4). Duloxetine (Cymbalta) was approved in 2004 for treating depression and neuropathic pain. Its mechanisms of action include blockade of the serotonin and norepinephrine reuptake transporters as well as the reuptake transporter for dopamine. Dopamine activity in the frontal cortex also may be increased indirectly by increasing noradrenergic activity to those neurons.

Because duloxetine does not antagonize 5-HT$_{2\ and\ 3}$ receptors, as do the other SNRIs, sexual dysfunction in men and decreased libido in both sexes still may occur. In addition, duloxetine can cause nausea, intestinal upset, hypertension, and sedation.

Mirtazapine   Mirtazapine (Remeron) is a unique antidepressant that increases noradrenergic and serotonergic activity by blocking both noradrenergic α-2 and 5-HT$_{1A}$ autoreceptors that normally decrease neurotransmitter synthesis and release. Mirtazepine also antagonizes 5-HT$_{2-3}$ postsynaptic receptors, thereby decreasing some of the most troublesome sexual side effects associated with SSRIs.

Nefazodone   Besides blocking the reuptake transporters for serotonin and norepinephrine, Nefazodone (Serzone) also acts as a 5-HT$_{2-3}$ antagonist. By blocking 5-HT$_{2-3}$ receptors, nefazodone minimizes the side effects associated with

TABLE 3.4	**SNRIs**		
Drug Name	**Brand Name**	**Receptor Effects**	**Half-Life**
Duloxetine	Cymbalta	NE, 5-HT, and DA reuptake blockade	12 hours
Mirtazapine	Remeron	Blocks α-2 NE and 5-HT$_1$ autoreceptors and 5-HT$_{2-3}$ antagonism	20–40 hours
Nefazodone	Serzone[+]	NE and 5-HT reuptake blockade and 5-HT$_{2-3}$ antagonism	12 hours*
Venlafaxine	Effexor	NE and SE reuptake blockade, DA reuptake blockade is weak	3–7 hours*

[+]No longer available in the U.S. or Canada

*Active metabolite

SSRI treatment. In particular, the adverse effects on sexual functioning and libido are reduced with nefazodone when compared to SSRI antidepressants (Clayton et al., 2006). Because of a risk of liver toxicity, however, the drug was withdrawn in Canada in late 2003 and was subsequently discontinued in the United States in 2004. It it is still available under other brand names in some countries.

With the major difference between the SSRIs and the SNRIs being their effects on norepinephrine reuptake, these drugs appear to contribute to the same neuronal adaptations as other antidepressants. And although their side effects may not be as bothersome, they are no more effective than any of the other antidepressants already mentioned. Ultimately, all antidepressants contribute to upregulation of BDNF synthesis and the neuronal growth and adaptation it promotes. Several additional dual-action antidepressants are listed in Table 3.4.

Atypical Antidepressants

Not all antidepressants alter the availability or activity of serotonin and norepinephrine, as the antidepressants discussed thus far. Because their mechanisms of action do not follow this traditional approach, these drugs are often referred to as **atypical antidepressants.** Originally, the SNRIs were classified as atypical because of their effects on norepinephrine and serotonin, but now they are classified by their dual mechanisms of action. A few atypical antidepressants are available today. Only one of these, bupropion, will be discussed in any detail. Others are listed in Table 3.5.

BUPROPION   Bupropion has been approved to treat depression (as Wellbutrin) and to diminish cravings associated with smoking cessation (as Zyban). Bupropion is as effective as other antidepressants, but its mechanism of action is quite different. Bupropion acts primarily as a selective dopamine reuptake inhibitor by blocking the dopamine transporter protein. To a lesser extent, it acts

| TABLE 3.5   Atypical Antidepressants | | | |
Drug Name	Brand Name	Receptor Effects	Half-Life
Amoxapine	Asendin	Blocks norepinephrine reuptake	8 hours*
Bupropion	Wellbutrin, Zyban	Blocks dopamine reuptake, partially blocks norepinephrine reuptake, blocks nACh receptors	10–14 hours*
Maprotiline	Ludiomil	Blocks norepinephrine reuptake (NRI)	51 hours
Reboxetine	Norebox, Edronax	Blocks norepinephrine reuptake (NRI)	13 hours
Trazodone	Desyrel	Blocks 5-HT reuptake, blocks 5-HT$_2$ receptors	3–9 hours

*Active metabolite

to inhibit the reuptake of norepinephrine (Stahl et al., 2004). Bupropion also acts as an antagonist on acetylcholine nicotinic receptors. Because bupropion does not act on serotonergic receptors, it has few of the side effects associated with SSRIs and SNRIs. In fact, bupropion may act to enhance sexual functioning and libido and may be used with SSRIs to augment their effectiveness and to diminish their side effects (Clayton et al., 2004). Interestingly, although bupropion does have stimulant properties, it does not possess the reinforcing properties or the abuse potential associated with other dopamine-norepinephrine agonists such as amphetamine and cocaine. This may be due to its relatively slow absorption rate and to its lower occupancy of transporter sites compared to the abused drugs.

Notable side effects caused by buropion include restlessness, agitation, motor tics or tremors, decreased appetite and weight loss, abdominal discomfort, and rare seizures. Because of these effects, bupropion is not used with patients exhibiting anxiety, panic disorder, or manic episodes.

How Effective Are Antidepressants?

There is little doubt that treating major depression with medication is effective, and literally tens of thousands of scientific articles support their use. However, it is well known that not all patients respond to medication. Most available research suggests that as many as 40 percent of patients with major depression will not respond to initial antidepressant therapy, and for others, the effectiveness of medication can diminish over time. This rate of nonresponding is high, but it can be misleading because many patients who were labeled as nonresponders after initial therapy do in fact respond to a different antidepressant (Rosack, 2002; Ruelaz, 2007).

Another complication in interpreting the effectiveness of antidepressants is the observation that many placebo-treated patients improve throughout their initial treatment period. Well-designed studies on the effectiveness of medication must include placebo controls to rule out effects not attributable to the drugs being investigated. According to Kirsch and Sapirstein (1998), placebos accounted for about 75 percent of antidepressant effectiveness in the 19 clinical trials they investigated. They concluded that the remaining 25 percent might be attributable to **active placebo** effects as opposed to antidepressant effects. Active placebo effects include perceptible side effects of a drug that do not contribute to its clinical effectiveness. For example, sedation, dry mouth, and dizziness may lead patients to believe their medication is working because these side effects are common with antidepressants. Consequently, patients might report fewer, less severe symptoms than other patients taking inert placebos that do not cause these effects.

Clearly, not all researchers are as critical of antidepressant effectiveness. More recent research comparing the effectiveness of antidepressants versus placebos in over 7,000 patients found that antidepressants provided a more sustained treatment effect for major depression than did placebos, which tend to lose their effectiveness quickly (Papakostas et al., 2006).

In summary, methodological issues continue to plague research on the efficacy of antidepressants, but the vast majority of research confirms their effectiveness when compared for sustained, not merely short-term, outcomes. Clearly, the debate on whether antidepressants are significantly more effective than placebos will continue into the future. Better objective methods are needed to measure treatment outcomes, as are more standardized double-blind research methodologies incorporating active placebos. At present, outcomes are measured in human studies using a number of subjective depression rating scales, which can reveal inconsistent outcomes.

ST. JOHN'S WORT (*HYPERICUM PERFORATUM*)   Are there effective herbal treatments for major depressive disorder? Perhaps the most extensively studied and most widely used herbal product for the treatment of depression is St. John's Wort, which is the common name for the flowering plant *Hypericum perforatum*. For centuries, extracts from the yellow *Hypericum* flower have been used to treat a variety of conditions, including psychological disorders, pain, and even malaria. More recently, the *Hypericum* extract has become available over the counter in tablet form.

St. John's Wort is widely proclaimed to be an effective antidepressant, and a number of studies seem to support its use for the treatment of mild to moderately severe depression. However, research comparing the effectiveness of St. John's Wort with traditional antidepressants and placebos is inconsistent at best. Recent analyses of large numbers of published studies (a meta-analysis) tend to conclude

© Jose B. Ruiz/Nature Picture Library

that St. John's Wort is effective for the short-term treatment of mild depression but not for the chronic treatment of severe depressive disorder. For instance, investigators have found St. John's Wort to be more effective than placebos and about as effective as traditional antidepressants (Kasper et al., 2006; Linde et al., 2005). Other research has suggested that St. John's Wort may be even more effective than traditional antidepressant medication. For instance, a recent study found that St. John's Wort was more effective than fluoxetine (Prozac) but not more effective than a placebo in decreasing symptoms of depression as measured by depression inventories (Fava et al., 2005). Knowing that the vast majority of studies find antidepressants to be more effective than placebos makes the interpretation of this study particularly difficult. And to further complicate this picture, evidence from long-term studies has found St. John's Wort to be ineffective for major depressive disorder when compared to traditional antidepressants (Gelenberg et al., 2004; Shelton et al., 2001). The National Institute for Health (NIH) also sponsored a large study of St. John's Wort by the Hypericum Depression Trial Study Group (Davidson et al., 2002). In this study, the effects of Hypericum, the SSRI sertraline, and an active placebo were compared. The results of this study are presented in Figure 3.8, which reveals that Hypericum is not as effective as sertraline when depression symptoms are measured by the Hamilton Rating Scale for Depression (HAM-D) (a widely used inventory to measure depression severity). The results

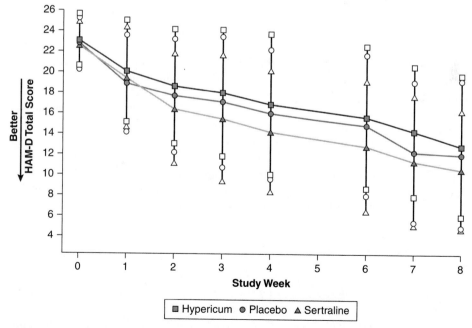

FIGURE 3.8   HAM-D total mean score by treatment week. Higher scores indicate greater severity of symptoms.   © Hamilton M. A rating scale for depression. J *Neurol Neurosurg Psychiatry* 1960; 23:56–62.

also reveal that all three groups improved over the eight-week treatment phase, including the placebo-treated patients. This observation is typical in studies of antidepressant effects, further illustrating the difficulty of separating placebo from treatment effects in clinical trials. These results are shown in Figure 3.8.

In animal studies, Hypericum appears to have effects similar to traditional antidepressants. That is, Hypericum decreases immobility time in forced swimming tasks and protects animals from the behavioral effects of acute stressors in learned helplessness and escape tasks (Butterweck, 2003; Zanoli et al., 2002).

Mechanisms of St. John's Wort Antidepressant Action   Evidence suggests that St. John's Wort increases serotonin and norepinephrine activity, but not by acting on reuptake transporters as do the SSRIs and SNRIs discussed above. Rather, it appears to inhibit the reuptake and vesicular storage of monoamine neurotransmitters, resulting in more being available in the synapse. Because the active ingredient of St. John's Wort, *Hyperforin,* does not appear to bind with the reuptake transporters or the vesicular transporter proteins, its mechanism of action may be to increase intracellular sodium concentrations, which in turn interfere with reuptake and contribute to a reserpine-like effect on storage vesicles (Müller, 2003; Roz et al., 2004). Hyperforin also increases the extra cellular concentrations of gamma-aminobutyricacid (GABA) and glutamate by the same mechanisms. The putative antidepressant effects of St. John's Wort are believed to be mediated by its effects on serotonin and norepinephrine availability (Müller, 2003; Roz et al., 2002; Zanoli, 2004).

In summary, St. John's Wort appears to be more effective than inert placebos for the short-term treatment of mild to moderately severe depression—an effect observed in numerous human and animal studies. Whether St. John's Wort is more effective than an active placebo for severe depression or for extended treatment is uncertain. Patients report fewer and less severe side effects with St. John's Wort compared to traditional antidepressants, the most common being gastrointestinal upset, sedation, restlessness, sexual dysfunction, and headache. The effects of St John's Wort appear to be mediated by enhanced neurotransmitter release and reuptake inhibition. Because St. John's Wort also enhances the synthesis of the liver enzyme CYP3A4, which is involved in the metabolism of most drugs, it can decrease the duration of action and the effectiveness of other medication. Finally, St. John's Wort can contribute to serotonin syndrome when it is combined with other antidepressant medication (Izzo, 2004).

Bipolar Disorders

Rick was a completely normal high school kid. He was class president during his senior year and a member of the basketball team. He graduated as the only male valedictorian that year and was looking forward to attending a small, prestigious liberal arts college in the fall. Like most other kids his age, Rick experienced a full range of emotions, including a bout of depression after a year-long relationship with his girlfriend ended. This depression disappeared quickly, and he began seeing someone else within a few months. During the summer following graduation, Rick experienced his first significant symptoms. While working for his father in a family-owned business, Rick made frequent trips for business purchases out of town. On this particular trip, he failed to return from his three-hour drive and ended up staying in an out-of-town hotel. For the next few days, he went on spending sprees, charging clothing and sports equipment on his father's business card. He returned a few days later after spending over $10,000. This first manic episode lasted a little over two weeks. During that time, he slept very little, demonstrated bouts of anger and hostility, and talked enthusiastically about his new plans to open a clothing store of his own. This episode revealed behavior that was so uncharacteristic of Rick that his parents made arrangements for a psychiatric evaluation. He was not diagnosed with acute mania at that time, however. Rather, his psychiatrist reasoned that his behavior was completely normal—he was simply displaying some anxiety about attending college in a few months.

Midway through his first semester at college Rick experienced his first severe depression. He stopped attending classes, slept for much of each day, rarely showered or changed clothes, and even attempted suicide by alcohol ingestion. On that occasion, he consumed nearly a fifth of vodka before blacking out. Fortunately, he was taken to the hospital before respiratory depression killed him.

Rick remained in a depressed mood for several more months and often self-medicated with marijuana. During Christmas break, he was prescribed Prozac, which appeared to help. Unfortunately, within a few months, he experienced another manic episode. During this episode, he became so euphoric and enthusiastic about finding religion that he did little else but publicly proclaim his religious faith and try to convince others of his special relationship with God. Rick would speak in the center of campus for hours at a time. After several days of exhibiting this behavior, he was asked by the administration to leave college.

His parents had him reevaluated, and he was finally diagnosed with bipolar disorder. His medication was switched to lithium, which may have helped to terminate this second manic episode. Rick stayed at his parents' home for the remainder of the year and worked intermittently at the family business. He stopped taking lithium after about six months and quickly returned to a severely depressed state. This episode of depression lasted about three months and was followed by about a month of a relatively normal mood. Just about the time his family thought they had seen the worst of his condition, Rick entered another manic state. As with his prior manic episode, he began to have delusions about his special relationship with God and used every opportunity to demonstrate his newly found religiosity. Rick was convinced to go back on lithium and antidepressants. However, after several months of intermittent use, he abandoned lithium for alcohol and marijuana. His life ended several months later in a fatal one-car accident that was suspicious of suicide.

Rick's case is not untypical. His first symptoms came as acute mania when he was 18 years old. This episode was followed within a few months by an episode of depression.

The diagnosis of depression and its treatment with an SSRI may have hastened his second manic episode during which he exhibited some psychosis. Also, noncompliance with lithium is common and can lead to an even more severe depression with an increased risk of suicide.

Defining and Diagnosing Bipolar Disorders

Bipolar disorders are distinguished from other depressive disorders by the presence of **manic** or **hypomanic episodes.** During a manic episode, a person experiences an excessive elevation in mood and euphoria often accompanied by extreme enthusiasm and energy. These manic episodes also may be characterized by psychotic features such as delusional beliefs and hallucinations. Hypomanic episodes are similar to but less severe than manic episodes. They are noticeable changes that impair social and occupational functioning but do not include psychotic features or require hospitalization. These mood changes must be present for at least four days to be diagnostic. The depression associated with bipolar disorders is essentially indistinguishable from major depressive disorder and may be confused with it until a manic or hypomanic episode appears. Unfortunately, misdiagnosis and treatment with antidepressants may promote manic symptoms and therefore worsen a patient's condition. As many as 30 percent of patients with bipolar disorders may be inappropriately treated with antidepressants without mood-stabilizing medication.

Bipolar disorders occur with equal frequency in men and women and typically present in late adolescence or early adulthood. As many as 6 million people (about 2.5 percent of the population) in the United States are diagnosed with a bipolar disorder each year. The lifetime prevalence of these disorders may be as high as 4.4 percent of the population when its various forms and severity are considered (Merikangas et al., 2007).

The diagnostic criteria for bipolar disorders are complicated by the presence or absence of manic and depressive features as well as their appearance and severity upon diagnosis. The disorders include bipolar I disorder, bipolar II disorder, and cyclothymia. The DSM-IV-TR criteria for bipolar I disorder require that a patient exhibit at least one manic or mixed episode. For a bipolar I diagnosis, major depressive episodes occur often, but they are not required. If a patient has not yet presented a major depressive episode, it is presumed that he or she eventually will. Most often the first manic episode immediately precedes or follows a period of major depression. The episodes of mania and depression can vary in duration, but typically the depressive episodes are shorter than a bout of unipolar depression, lasting three to four months. Manic episodes typically last from a few days to several weeks. If an individual experiences four or more episodes of depression or mania during a year, the condition is referred to as **rapid-cycling** bipolar disorder.

The distinctions between bipolar I disorder, bipolar II disorder, and cyclothymia are more of symptom severity than of the presence of symptoms.

A diagnosis of bipolar II disorder requires that at least one major depressive episode and one or more occurrences of hypomania have been presented. More prevalent than bipolar I disorder, bipolar II disorder does not require that a full-blown manic episode has occurred. Between periods of depression and hypomania, individuals with bipolar II disorder may function normally, whereas those with bipolar I disorder are more likely to experience continued social and occupational difficulties. Cyclothymia is characterized by the presence of hypomanic episodes intermixed with periods of mild to moderate depression, not meeting the criteria for a major depressive disorder. These bouts of depression and hypomania must be present for at least two years without remission. Cyclothymia and subthreshold bipolar disorder may be most prevalent, accounting for 2.4 percent of the 4.4 percent lifetime prevalence for these disorders (Merikangas et al., 2007).

DIAGNOSTIC CRITERIA FOR MANIC EPISODE   *The following criteria are used to diagnose a manic episode:*

1. *A distinct period of abnormally elevated, expansive, or irritable mood lasting at least one week.* During these periods, an individual may become more inspired and creative than normal. In fact, a large number of prominent scientists and writers claim much of their most productive work came during manic episodes. Compliance with medication schedules can become problematic as some patients prefer these manic episodes to more normal and less creative periods. It is not uncommon for an individual to switch from an enthusiastic euphoric mood to irritability, particularly when his or her wishes are frustrated or denied.

2. *During the mood disturbance, at least three of the following symptoms must have occurred:*

   - *Inflated self-esteem or grandiosity.* Characterized by an inflated sense of self-confidence, individuals may embark on huge unrealistic projects such as writing a novel or composing a symphony or profess expertise in areas in which they have no special knowledge. Grandiose delusions of identity are also common, including having a special relationship with God or some other religious figure.
   - *Decreased need for sleep.* Individuals may wake much earlier than normal or go for days without sleeping or feeling tired.
   - *Excessive talking.* Manic speech is typically loud, rapid, erratic, and difficult to interrupt. The speech may be dramatic or jovial with excessive gestures and movements. If the person is in an irritable mood, the speech may be critical or even hostile.
   - *Racing thoughts or ideas.* Along with excessive talking, an individual may describe his or her thoughts as racing and shifting among several simultaneous themes as if switching television channels rapidly. These racing and shifting thoughts contribute to the fast, erratic, and incoherent speech mentioned above.

- *Distractibility by irrelevant or unimportant stimuli.* For instance, an individual may become preoccupied with room furnishings or external noise, making concentration difficult. In some cases, it may be impossible to attend to relevant stimuli, further diminishing the person's ability to converse and attend to work.
- *Increase in goal-directed social, work-related, or sexual activity.* Increases in sexual interest and activity are quite common. In addition, individuals may become overly social with colleagues, friends, and family. Taking on considerably more work or obligation than normal also is characteristic of mania.
- *Excessive involvement in pleasurable activities that have potentially painful consequences. This includes buying sprees, sexual promiscuity, and irrational business decisions.* An individual's excessive self-confidence and grandiosity may lead to poor and irrational decisions about purchases and business without appropriate consideration of his or her financial consequences. In addition, an enhanced sexual drive may lead to promiscuous, frequent sexual activity with little regard for health or legal consequences.

3. *The mood disturbance is sufficient to cause marked impairment in occupational functioning or in usual social activities and relationships with others.* Most often bipolar disorders are recognized only by family, friends, and colleagues, and the disorders may be recognized only after considerable damage to relationships has occurred. In severe instances of mania, hospitalization may be required to prevent individuals from further harming others or themselves.

DIAGNOSTIC CRITERIA FOR MIXED EPISODE *The criteria are met for both manic and major depressive episodes if these symptoms occur nearly every day for at least one week.* The symptoms of a full-blown manic episode and major depression may alternate rapidly every few days, or symptoms of both may be present together. Mixed episodes are being recognized with more frequency and are now considered to be a relatively common expression of bipolar disorder. In fact, many patients present symptoms of depression during manic episodes even when the symptoms are not severe enough to be considered a mixed episode or major depression.

Pathology of Bipolar Disorders

Of all of the psychological disorders, perhaps least is known about the pathology underlying bipolar disorders. Because of the nature of the disorders, cycling between manic and depressive episodes, the pathology must embody dynamic perturbations in neural structures and function. And unlike the pathology of depression, which was largely revealed by an understanding of antidepressant drug action, relatively little has been learned about the pathology of bipolar disorders from mood-stabilizing drugs. Research continues to describe both genetic and structural correlations with bipolar disorders that may eventually reveal better clues to its evasive pathology.

GENETIC DETERMINANTS OF BIPOLAR DISORDER   It has long been known that there are strong genetic contributions to bipolar disorders. These disorders occur more frequently when there is a family history of the disease, and heritability studies suggest that the concordance rate among genetically identical (monozygotic) twins approaches 70 percent, compared to a rate of approximately 12 percent for dizygotic twins. Genetic studies have found evidence for bipolar genes on a number of chromosomes, but there is no consensus yet about how many genes are involved or about their locations (Cassidy et al., 2007; Hamet et al., 2005). Recent attention has focused on the genes responsible for coding the serotonin transporter (5-HTT), and BDNF may be implicated in both major depression and bipolar disorders. Specifically, polymorphisms resulting in decreased expression of the serotonin transporter gene have been shown to strongly correlate with suicide ideation and the incidence of major depression in individuals experiencing major life stress (Canli et al., 2006; Caspi et al., 2003). A number of other studies have found strong correlations between the expression of the BDNF gene and bipolar disorders, suggesting that decreased BDNF synthesis may predispose individuals for these diseases (Lohoff et al., 2005; Müller et al., 2006; Nakata et al., 2003). However, not all studies have replicated these findings, suggesting that it may be too early to conclude that a causal association exists between genotypes for the expression of serotonin transporters, BDNF synthesis, and the susceptibility to bipolar disorders (Kato, 2007).

ANATOMICAL DETERMINANTS OF BIPOLAR DISORDER   Bipolar disorders also are associated with structural abnormalities in several brain regions. As shown in Figure 3.9, individuals who have had the disease for longer periods of time and

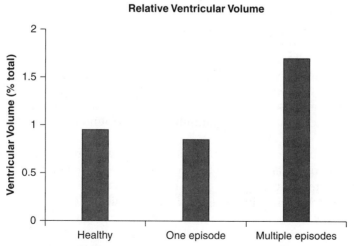

FIGURE 3.9   Ventricular volumes in bipolar disorder.   © Reprinted with permission from the *American Journal of Psychiatry.* (Copyright 2002). American Psychiatric Association.

have had recurrent episodes of mania have significantly enlarged lateral ventricles compared to individuals who have had only one episode or compared to healthy control subjects (Strakowski et al., 2002; Strakowski et al., 2005). Enlarged ventricles are believed to be indicative of the loss of neural tissue from surrounding brain structures. As neural degeneration occurs, ventricles gradually enlarge to occupy that space. Functional imaging studies suggest that the areas most afflicted in bipolar disease include the prefrontal cortex, the amygdala, and the striatum.

The structural degeneration observed in bipolar patients is consistent with the abnormalities in BDNF synthesis described earlier in the discussion of major depression. Decreases in BDNF levels also have been shown to be associated with the severity manic episodes in bipolar patients (Machado et al., 2007). Furthermore, treatment with antidepressants as well as several mood stabilizers increases BDNF synthesis and contributes to neurogenesis in the hippocampus as well as in other brain structures implicated in depression (Castren et al., 2007; Duman et al., 2006; D'Sa, et al., 2002; Laeng et al., 2004; Post, 2007).

In summary, genetic studies have strongly implicated several genes that control the expression of the serotonin transporter and BDNF synthesis in major depression and in bipolar disorders. While it may be premature to link the expression of specific genes to predispositions for bipolar disorders, pharmacological evidence is mounting to support this argument. Antidepressants and mood-stabilizing drugs do contribute to the expression of serotonin transporters and to increased levels of BDNF in animals and humans. These adaptations also have been associated with **neurogenesis** in affected neural structures and to improvements in the symptoms of these diseases. The following section examines several drugs used in the treatment of bipolar disorders.

Pharmacological Treatment of Bipolar Disorders

Perhaps one of the most intriguing events in the history of psychopharmacology was John Cade's discovery in 1948 of the **antimanic** properties of lithium. At that time, lithium was widely used as a substitute for salt in patients with high blood pressure and heart disease. Its medical use was quickly discontinued because it was toxic and occasionally lethal. Lithium also was found in several tonics used in Europe for a variety of ailments.

John Cade believed that mania was caused by an excessive amount of a normal by-product of metabolism. To test this idea, he collected urine from manic patients and injected it into guinea pigs. He reasoned that the excess by-product would be found in their urine. The urine from manic patients was certainly more toxic than that of normal people or from people suffering from other diseases, but it did not have manic effects. Cade isolated urea as the toxic compound in urine and continued to believe this to be the substance that caused mania despite the fact that his animals did not exhibit any signs of it. To determine urea's toxic levels, Cade needed to dissolve urea in different concentrations to test them for toxicity and manic-inducing properties. After many unsuccessful attempts to dissolve urea, he found it was most soluble as lithium urate. Unfortunately, the lithium urate solutions did not cause manic responses in his guinea pigs either. Still not dissuaded by lack of evidence supporting his urea hypothesis, Cade continued to believe that some substance excreted in the urine (most likely urea) caused manic episodes in his patients and the lithium subdued them. To evaluate the effects of lithium in his toxic compound, he also injected animals with lithium carbonate. This compound caused his animals to become lethargic for several hours. In Cade's own words, "It may seem a long way from lethargy in guinea pigs to the control of manic excitement, but as these investigations had commenced in an attempt to demonstrate some possibly excreted toxin in the urine of manic patients, the association of ideas is explicable." Cade was now in a position to test the effects of lithium on his manic patients. One of his patients was described as "a little wizened man of 51 who had been in a state of chronic manic excitement for five years . . . amiably restless, dirty, destructive, mischievous, and interfering." Several days after lithium treatment commenced, this patient was "more settled, tidier, less disinhibited, and less distractible." Other patients apparently responded similarly (Cade, 1949).

Although lithium carbonate treatment continued to gain support around the world, it was not approved by the FDA for the treatment of mania until 1970. One can wonder whether approval might have occurred much sooner had the simple compound been of any commercial value.

LITHIUM   Lithium (Li^+) is a light alkali metal with properties similar to those of sodium (Na^+), including its ability to substitute for sodium in ion exchange across neural membranes. Because sodium is highly reactive in air and water, it is rarely found in its elemental form. Lithium carbonate (Li_2CO_3), lithium's pharmacologically active form, is one of the most common natural compounds of lithium. However, lithium citrate and lithium sulfate also are available pharmacologically. These compounds are sold under several brand names, but they all have the same pharmacological properties.

Pharmacokinetics of Lithium   Lithium carbonate is easily absorbed into the bloodstream, but it crosses the blood-brain barrier relatively slowly. Because lithium is not metabolized by liver enzymes, it is excreted by the kidneys with its compound form intact. It has an elimination half-life of approximately 18–30 hours. The therapeutic dose of lithium falls within a very narrow index and is quite toxic and even lethal above these levels. Blood levels between 0.6 and 1.5 mEq/L (milliequivalents per liter of blood) are typically therapeutic. The higher range is typically used to treat acute mania, whereas blood levels between 0.6 and 1.0 mEq/L are used for maintenance.

Dosages causing blood levels to rise above 1.5 mEq/L are often toxic and can produce severe side effects, including nausea and vomiting, abdominal pain, ataxia, tremors, slurred speech, and cognitive difficulties. Lithium toxicity also can occur if there is a sudden loss of salt through excessive sweating or a decrease in dietary salt intake, as these may cause in an increase in the lithium/sodium ratio and hence blood levels of lithium. The long-term use of lithium also may contribute to significant weight gain, thyroid disease, skin rash, kidney dysfunction, and compromised immune function. Because of these troublesome side effects, patients often discontinue taking their medication. Suddenly suspending medication can have severe consequences by dramatically increasing one's risk of suicide or suicide attempts. A recent study reported a 16-fold increase in suicide attempts in patients who suddenly discontinued lithium therapy (Yerevanian et al., 2007).

Pharmacodynamics of Lithium   While lithium carbonate may be the simplest compound used to treat psychological disorders, its mechanisms of action remain paradoxically elusive. In normal individuals, lithium taken in pharmacological doses has few discernable effects beyond some occasional abdominal discomfort. In patients with bipolar disorder, it has remarkable effects on both the incidence and severity of manic and depressive episodes. It also is known to be an effective antidepressant and to decrease suicide ideation and attempts in patients with major depressive disorder (Guzzetta et al., 2007).

Evidence accumulated over the past several years supports an argument that bipolar disorders, as well as major depressive disorder, result from downregulated BDNF synthesis and the resulting cascade of neurodegenerative effects occurring in the hippocampus and frontal cortex (Brunello et al., 2003; Einat et al., 2003; Hashimoto et al., 2004). Lithium has been shown to increase BDNF activity in these brain regions and to reverse degeneration through gene activation of protein synthesis (Brunello, 2004; Mai et al., 2002). Furthermore, lithium reverses BDNF downregulation and a mania state induced in animals by d-amphetamine (Frey et al., 2006). Lithium also appears to increase serotonergic activity in the cortex and hippocampus by agonizing $5\text{-}HT_{1B}$ autoreceptors and $5\text{-}HT_{1B}$ heteroreceptors on dopaminergic neurons (Chenu et al., 2006). This latter effect is believed to mediate lithium's antimanic properties, perhaps by stabilizing the activity of central dopamine neurons. As a summary of these effects, lithium treatment appears to reverse the neural degeneration in the hippocampus and frontal cortex caused by downregulated BDNF synthesis. Increases in BDNF contribute to gene activation and to cellular adaptations, leading to increased cortical serotonergic and dopaminergic activity during the depressive phase of bipolar disorder and a stabilization of dopamine activity during the manic phase (Berk et al., 2007). Currently, these alterations are believed to mediate the antidepressant and antimanic properties of lithium.

Lithium continues to be regarded as the gold standard for the treatment of bipolar disorders despite its relative toxicity and high incidence of side effects. For these reasons, other drugs are replacing lithium as the principal drug for managing bipolar disorders. Many of these newer drugs also have been utilized as

anticonvulsants to treat seizure and anxiety disorders. These drugs may be used alone to treat acute mania or in combination with antidepressants to treat cycling bipolar disorders.

VALPROIC ACID (VALPROATE, DEPAKOTE)   Valproic acid was introduced in 1994 and approved as an anticonvulsant to treat seizure disorders, acute mania, and migraine headaches. While its mechanisms of action are not completely understood, valproic acid does stimulate BDNF synthesis and alters the activity of several neurotransmitters, including GABA and dopamine. In animal studies, valproic acid increases the number and synaptic growth of GABAergic neurons and inhibits GABA reuptake, thereby elevating its inhibitory effects (Eckstein-Ludwig et al., 1999; Laeng et al., 2004). Valproic acid also increases dopamine release in the prefrontal cortex but apparently not in the nucleus accumbens (Ichikawa et al., 2005). It also may protect and stimulate the neuronal growth of dopaminergic neurons through the neurotropic effects of BDNF (Chen et al., 2006; Wang et al., 2007). The anticonvulsant and antimanic actions of valproic acid also may be mediated by its inhibitory effects on the glutamate NMDA receptor. Excessive glutamate activity is believed to underlie both mania and seizures, and it can contribute to neuronal degeneration. Valproic acid inhibits NMDA receptor activity and therefore may protect against glutamate excitotoxicity (Chuang, 2005; Gobbi et al., 2006).

Patients typically tolerate valproic acid better than lithium, and valproic acid is often more effective for rapid cycling patients. Its most notable side effects include sedation, tremor, ataxia, nausea, and weight gain.

GABAPENTIN (NEURONTIN)   Gabapentin was approved in 1993 for the treatment of seizures, but it became a popular alternative to valproic acid and lithium for the *off-label* (non–FDA approved) treatment of mania associated with bipolar disorders. It also has been used to treat anxiety and has been found to be effective in the management of **neuropathic pain.** Gabapentin was designed to structurally and functionally mimic the neurotransmitter GABA. And although gabapentin increases levels of GABA in the brain, its direct effects on GABA neurons remain unclear. Several presumed mechanisms of action have been suggested, and these may contribute to its antiseizure and antimanic effects.

Gabapentin decreases the influx of calcium into neurons by inhibiting a subset of voltage-dependent calcium channels (Cheng et al., 2006; Rogawski et al., 2004). As a result, glutaminergic activity, which is known to mediate seizure and manic episodes, is decreased in the cortex (Cunningham et al., 2004; Czapinski et al., 2005). Gabapentin also increases GABA-mediated inhibition at $GABA_A$ receptors in the hippocampus as well as in other brain regions (Cheng et al., 2006). It is unknown whether these diverse effects share a common underlying mechanism. Gabapentin has a side effect profile that is similar to that of valproic acid. It may cause bothersome sedation, dizziness, ataxia, tremors, nausea, and weight gain.

A large number of antimanic and anticonvulsant drugs currently are available for treating bipolar disorders. Often these drugs are used in combination with other antimanic and antidepressant drugs. Most of these drugs are in the anticonvulsant category and are used to treat seizures; not all of them are approved by the FDA for the treatment of bipolar disorders. The off-label use of these drugs for treating mania associated with bipolar disorders is often controversial because of a lack of research demonstrating their effectiveness (Mack, 2003). The newest drug approved by the FDA for bipolar disorder is

TABLE 3.6   Mood Stabilizers and Anticonvulsants

Drug Name	Brand Name	Mechanism of Action	Half-Life	FDA-Approved Use
Lithium	Lithium Carbonate	Serotonin agonist, dopamine agonist	18–30 hours	acute mania
Valproic Acid	Valproate, Depakote	Glutamate antagonist, dopamine agonist	9–16 hours	acute mania, seizure disorders, migraine
Gabapentin	Neurontin	Glutamate antagonist, GABA agonist	5–7 hours	seizure disorders, neuralgia (pain)
Pregabalin	Lyrica	GABA agonist	5–7 hours	neuralgia (pain)
Lamotrigine	Lamictal	Glutamate antagonist	33 hours	bipolar disorders, seizure disorders
Oxcarbazepine	Trileptal	Glutamate antagonist	2–9 hours	seizure disorders
Topiramate	Topamax	Glutamate antagonist, GABA agonist	21 hours	seizure disorders, migraine
Quetiapine	Seroquel	Dopamine antagonist	6–7 hours	acute mania, schizophrenia
Carbamazepine	Tegretol	Glutamate antagonist	12–17 hours	acute mania, seizure disorders
Aripiprazole	Abilify	Dopamine D_2 agonist, serotonin 1_A agonist	75 hours	schizophrenia, acute mania, bipolar maintenance
Zonisamide	Zonegran	Sodium and calcium channel blockade, dopamine agonist (?)	63 hours	seizure disorders

aripiprazole (Abilify), which acts as a partial agonist at dopamine D_2 and serotonin 1_A receptors. Abilify also is approved for schizophrenia and acute mania. However, a recent study found it to be no more effective than a placebo, and it had rather severe side effects (Thase et al., 2008). At lower doses, aripiprazole may be used to augment antidepressant therapy (Philip et al., 2008). A number of drugs currently approved for bipolar disorder are presented in Table 3.6 with their common brand name, presumed mechanisms of action, half-life, and FDA-approved use.

4

Anxiety Disorders
Panic, Generalized Anxiety, and Obsessive-Compulsive Disorders

Susan began her day as she always had. She rose early before her husband, started the coffee, and headed to the shower. She was rehearsing how she would conduct her sales meeting later that morning when she began to feel as if someone or something had taken control of her body. In an instant, her heart rate jumped from a normal 65 to over 150 bpm. Her respiration was strained, and she could not get air into her lungs. She grabbed the bathroom counter as she began to lose her balance in a spinning room. Her skin felt cold and clammy, but at the same time, she felt as if she were burning alive. A terror like she had never experienced before overwhelmed her as she realized she must have had a heart attack and was dying. She tried to scream out to her husband, but she could not make a sound. She was paralyzed with fear knowing she was going to die in her bathroom. Susan felt as though an hour had passed when she realized that her breathing was now under her control. She took long deep breaths as her racing heart slowed back to normal. Susan got up from the floor not even remembering the fall. At that moment, her husband walked in carrying her morning coffee. She then realized that everything had occurred in just a few minutes. What she did not yet know was that this was only the first of many episodes to follow.

Susan had just experienced her first panic attack. Like over 6 million other Americans each year, her attack was not preceded by a warning or even noticeable anxiety. Another 7 million people suffer from generalized anxiety, an additional 8 million from post-traumatic stress disorder (PTSD), over 2 million from obsessive-compulsive disorder (OCD), and many others from various debilitating phobias. In all, over 40 million people in the United States suffer from some form of anxiety disorder, making it the most prevalent of all psychological disorders. This chapter will examine the pathology and pharmacological treatment of several of the most prevalent anxiety disorders. But the chapter begins with a review of the neurobiology of normal fear and anxiety.

BIOLOGICAL BASES OF FEAR AND ANXIETY

Fear is an adaptive emotional response that involves changes in behavior; autonomic reactivity; hormonal activity; and in humans, the body sensations of these changes. These components of fear are integrated by several neural structures and glands, and they provide animals with the ability to adapt to potentially life-threatening circumstances. In addition, specific changes to these structures enable animals to learn about stimuli that are predictive of danger, thus providing them with the ability to avoid situations that may be harmful. Several structures are critically important to elicit fear responses. These include the amygdala, the hypothalamus, the thalamus, and several areas in the cortex.

The amygdaloid nuclei, part of the limbic system, are located deep within the temporal lobes (see Figure 4.1). They (or more specifically, structures within the amygdaloid complex) receive sensory information about potentially threatening stimuli and initiate the various components of the fear response. The central nucleus of the amygdala sends information to other brain structures, including the hypothalamus, which controls the hormonal component of the fear response, and to the pons and medulla, which control various fear response such as the inability to move, facial expression, and heart and respiration rates. Other brainstem structures receive neural input from the amygdala and control autonomic and cortical arousal. Therefore, the amygdala is the most important brain structure for the integration of sensory information and for the initiation of fear responses to it. Damage to the amygdala has long been known to disrupt emotional behavior. In fact, bilateral destruction of the amygdala was used early on to control psychiatric patients who did not respond to pharmacological treatment.

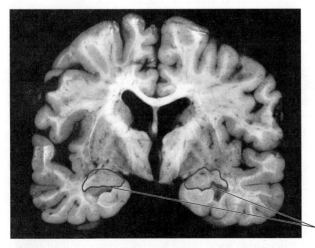

Amygdala

FIGURE 4.1 Coronal section of the human brain revealing the amygdaloid nuclei located deep within the temporal lobes.
© R. H. Ettinger

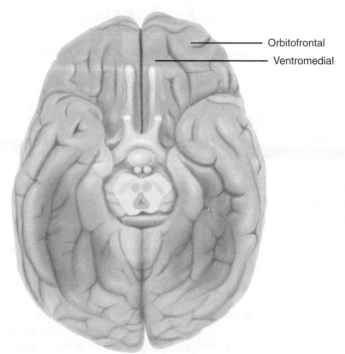

Orbitofrontal

Ventromedial

FIGURE 4.2   Ventral view of human brain. The ventromedial cortices lie adjacent to the midline on both halves of the brain. The orbitofrontal cortices lie above the eye orbits and adjacent to the ventromedial areas.   © Carlson, *Physiology of Behavior*, Fig (a) "The Ventral View, from the Base of the Brain." Copyright 2007. Reproduced by permission of Pearson Education, Inc.

Several cortical areas also are important for fear as well as for other emotional responses. Two areas in the prefrontal cortex—the ventromedial prefrontal cortex and the orbitofrontal cortex—are particularly important (see Figure 4.2). These prefrontal areas receive input from the thalamus, the ventral tegmentum, and the amygdala. They send output to the cingulate cortex and to the hypothalamus and inhibitory signals to the amygdala. These structures function to integrate emotional content from stimuli and to organize and guide a person's behavior in response to them. In humans, the prefrontal cortices also guide and control emotional behavior in social contexts. Damage to these areas severely affects judgment in social situations and the way an individual anticipates consequences of their behavior. Therefore, the prefrontal areas are involved in interpreting fear-producing stimuli and in regulating or inhibiting fear responses in nonthreatening contexts.

The prefrontal cortices also send input to and receive output from the cingulate cortex, which is located deep within the central fissure above the corpus callosum (see Figure 4.3). The cingulate cortex receives sensory information about

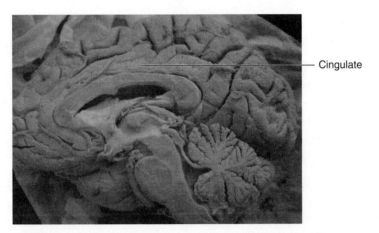

Cingulate

FIGURE 4.3   The cingulate cortex lies deep within the central fissure above the corpus callosum.   © R. H. Ettinger

body states during emotional responses. For example, the emotion of fear is represented as a set of physiological and behavioral responses including high heart rate and changes in respiration, posture, facial expression, muscle tension, and blood flow. All of these changes contribute to the sensory information that is essentially mapped into the cingulate cortex and perceived as the feeling of fear. Damage to the cingulate does not disrupt the physiological state of an emotion, but it does disrupt a person's subjective feeling and his or her awareness of it.

When we experience fear, a cascade of physiological events results in changes in posture, facial expression, heart rate and blood flow, respiration, and cortical arousal. These changes allow animals either to flee from or to confront the emotion-causing stimulus. When the emotional stimulus can be ignored, the prefrontal cortices send inhibitory signals to the amygdala, which in turn shuts off output to structures that cause these adaptive changes.

Anxiety differs from fear in that an emotion-causing stimulus does not need to be present for a person to experience the emotion. Anxiety occurs when someone perceives an expectation of a vague and uncertain threat as opposed to a specific danger. For instance, a student may experience anxiety when preparing for an important exam. Anxiety also persists for extended durations once it is initiated and no specific pattern of behavior is motivated to terminate it. And, unlike fear, anxiety is not accompanied by specific postures or facial expressions. However, the physiological components of anxiety are essentially identical to those of fear. Increases in autonomic activity lead to increased heart rate, blood pressure, muscle tension, and respiration. In addition, anxiety is characterized by increased cortical arousal and vigilance. Anxiety makes it difficult to concentrate on other tasks and activities and contributes to disturbances in normal sleep patterns.

Both fear and anxiety are normal adaptive responses to specific and diffuse threats to a person's well-being. These emotional responses consist of physiological and behavioral changes that enable animals to deal with threat and uncertainty more effectively. However, when fear begins to occur to nonthreatening stimuli or anxiety is excessive and persists for extended periods of time, these emotions can become debilitating and may contribute to cardiovascular diseases and compromised immunity. As you will see, the distinctions between normal fear and anxiety and pathological anxiety are not always clear. The following sections describe several of the most debilitating anxiety disorders.

PANIC DISORDER

The diagnosis of **panic disorder** requires the repeated and unexpected occurrence of panic attacks and at least one month of persistent worry about having other attacks or about the consequences of these attacks. Often an individual's persistent worry is whether he or she will die during an impending panic attack. According to the *Diagnostic and Statistical Manual of Mental Disorders*, Text Revision (DSM-IV-TR), panic attacks are discrete periods of intense fear during which four or more of the following symptoms occur:

- *Heart palpitations or accelerated heart rate.* Nearly everyone experiences the feeling of his or her heartbeat occasionally, but during a panic attack, these palpitations are intense sensations of accelerated heart rate. These palpitations may contribute to other symptoms and a fear of an imminent heart attack.
- *Sweating.* Sweating occurs in the absence of exertion or excessively high temperatures.
- *Trembling or shaking.* Feelings of trembling or shaking with fear may occur with the sensation of being immobile or frozen in place.
- *Sensations of shortness of breath or breathing restriction.* A person feels as if he or she cannot get enough air in each breath. Respiration rate may increase to compensate for a lack of sufficient oxygen, which can lead to dizziness and other symptoms of mild hypoxia.
- *Feelings of choking.* This sensation of shortness of breath also may be related to the sensations of choking or the feeling of tightening of the neck and airway.
- *Chest pain.* Chest pains or abnormal chest sensations may be associated with higher-than-normal heart rates and palpitations. These sensations also may contribute to fear of an imminent heart attack.
- *Nausea or abdominal distress.*
- *Dizziness, fainting, or lightheadedness.* These symptoms can be related to hypoxia caused by breathing difficulties.
- *Derealization or depersonalization.* A person experiences feelings of unreality or being detached from oneself.
- *Fear of losing control.* A person is unable to calm himself or herself or control the intensity of feeling. A person may feel as if he or she is going crazy or mad.

- *Fear of dying.* This common fear during panic attacks can be exacerbated or confirmed by other symptoms (e.g., high heart rate, palpitations, chest pain, and breathing difficulties).
- *Parasesthesia.* Numbness or tingling sensations are typical of the limbs and face.
- *Chills or hot flashes.*

Panic attacks can, and often do, happen without warning or without situational triggers, although after recurrence, they may occur in specific situations or places. For the diagnosis of panic disorder, however, the attacks must be unexpected or uncued, at least initially. Panic disorder also may be associated with a phobic avoidance that makes it difficult for people to be in crowded places, on public transportation, in theaters, or in places where escape might be difficult or embarrassing if and when a panic attack occurs. This phobia of experiencing a panic attack in inescapable situations is referred to as *agoraphobia.* Individuals with agoraphobia experience intense anxiety when they find themselves in situations (or even anticipate situations) where a panic attack might occur. As a result, they often develop a phobic avoidance of these situations. The phobic avoidance behavior may mitigate anxiety, but it often contributes significantly to other problems. In severe cases, agoraphobia can be so debilitating that an individual may find it impossible to leave the confines of his or her home or a room.

POST-TRAUMATIC STRESS DISORDER (PTSD)

A significant number of individuals who experience severe stress associated with a disaster, an accident, military combat, or rape or who witness a horrific crime may continue to experience stress and anxiety through intrusive memories or dreams of these traumatic events. After the 9/11 attacks on the World Trade Center in New York, about 11 percent of the rescue and recovery workers continued to be traumatized by their memories, and many of these people could not continue to live and work in New York City. About 8 percent of the population, over 24 million people, in the United States will experience PTSD at some point during their lifetime. The DSM-IV-TR lists the following criteria for a diagnosis of PTSD:

1. The person experienced, witnessed, or was confronted with an event or events that involved actual or threatened death or serious injury to them or others and the person's response involved intense fear, helplessness, or horror.
2. The traumatic event is persistently experienced as intrusive recollections, dreams, or feelings as if the event were recurring.
3. The person demonstrates a persistent avoidance of stimuli associated with the trauma indicated by avoiding thoughts, activities, places, or people associated with the event.

4. The person demonstrates persistent symptoms of increased arousal indicated as difficulties with sleep, outbursts of anger, difficulty concentrating, hypervigilance, or exaggerated startle responsiveness.

5. These disturbances have occurred for at least one month and cause significant distress or impairment in social, occupational, or other areas of functioning.

Pathology of PTSD

Stress causes profound changes to structures in the brain that regulate fear and anxiety. Among these changes are significant decreases in both hippocampal and prefrontal cortex volumes and an increase in dendritic density and activity in the amygdala. The decreases in hippocampal volume, particularly in the region of the dentate gyrus, are a result of increased glucocorticoid and catecholamine release during the stress response. Decreases in the volume of the medial prefrontal cortex also may be related to increased glucocorticoid and catecholamine activity. As a result, stimuli associated with traumatic events cause enhanced amygdala responsiveness that is not suppressed by cortical inhibition. Recent functional neuroimaging studies confirm that the medial prefrontal cortex is hypoactive in PTSD patients. In addition, PTSD patients demonstrate heightened responses in the amygdala following exposure to trauma-related stimuli (Karl et al., 2006; Miller et al., 2006; Shin et al., 2006). It is believed that heightened amygdala responsiveness to emotional stimuli and hypoactive inhibitory input from descending prefrontal cortical regions underlie PTSDs. Evidence for decreased gamma-aminobutyric acid (GABA) inhibitory activity in PTSD patients comes from a recent study comparing the ability of the $GABA_A$ antagonist flumazenil to bind to GABA receptors in PTSD patients compared to normal control subjects. Radioactively labeled (^{11}C) flumazenil was injected into subjects in both groups and was measured using positron emission tomography (PET) scans. Significantly decreased densities of $GABA_A$ receptors were found in PTSD patients (see Figures 4.4 and 4.5.)

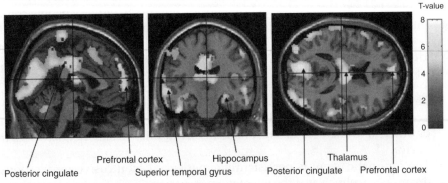

FIGURE 4.4 Areas with decreased GABAA receptor binding in PTSD patients are indicated in lighter shades of grey. © Geuze et al (2008). Reduced GABAa benzodiazepine receptor binding in veterans with post-traumatic stress disorder. *Molecular Psychiatry*, 13, 74–83. Reprinted by permission from Macmillan Publishers Ltd.

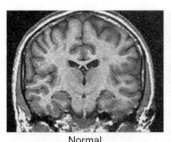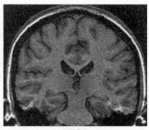

Normal   PTSD

FIGURE 4.5   Magnetic resonance image (MRI) comparing brain volumes of a patient with PTSD with those of a normal subject. Enlarged lateral ventricles in the image on the right correspond with decreases in hippocampal volume.   © Bremner, J. D. (1999). Does stress damage the brain? Reprinted from *Biological Psychiatry*, 45(7), 797–805 with permission from Elsevier.

Animal studies also confirm that stress hormones and the catecholamines contribute to neuronal atrophy and degeneration in the hippocampus, whereas stress manipulations cause enhanced dendritic branching and growth in the amygdala. These structural changes lead to enhanced emotionality in laboratory animals and seem to parallel changes observed in humans with PTSD (Bremner, 1999; Vyas et al., 2002).

Generalized Anxiety Disorder (GAD)

Mark is a first-year law student who recently sought help for insomnia. He complains that on most nights, he cannot "shut off his brain." His mind shifts rapidly between assignments and projects he has not yet completed and the constant worry about his financial and medical situations. Like many students, Mark has taken out several student loans, but his debt will not be unmanageable because he already holds the promise of a position at his father's law firm. This security, however, provides little respite from his fret about finances. Mark's medical concerns commenced when his father was diagnosed with prostate cancer several years ago. Now Mark has noticed that he too has every symptom of an enlarged prostate. While lying awake much of the night, he frequently makes bathroom visits that are pointless, and assurances from his doctors that there are no signs of enlargement convince Mark that they are missing something even more serious. Often Mark's anxiety seems unrelated to anything explicit. In these cases, the feelings of anxiety and dread are just as intense even though they have no particular focus.

While Mark had little trouble getting through college with his unrelenting worries, he is having difficulty in law school. More frequently he is finding that his anxiety interrupts his ability to pay attention during class and to concentrate while studying. On several occasions, he has been embarrassed when professors called on him to comment and he had no idea what the preceding discussion was about. Pushing aside the incessant worrying during his study time also is getting more difficult. Mark is now beginning to agonize about whether he will flunk out of law school and disappoint his parents even further.

It turns out that Mark has a much longer history of worrying about pleasing his parents than his latest academic concerns. While in high school, Mark was preoccupied with his athletic and academic competencies even though he was a good student earning an athletic scholarship in track. He fought his less-than-perfect performances and his fear of competition with countless hours of training. During his high school years, Mark was diagnosed with depression and was prescribed an antidepressant. After diligently following the prescription for almost a year, he discontinued it because it made him feel too lethargic. Mark claims he has never felt depressed—only anxious and concerned about his future.

Generalized anxiety disorder (GAD) typically emerges in early adolescence or adulthood, as it did with Mark, but it can occur in children. The lifetime prevalence of GAD is about 5 percent of the population, and about 7 million people suffer from it at any given time. It is not uncommon for GAD to disappear for several years and to reoccur during times of stress. The DSM-IV-TR criteria for a diagnosis of GAD are as follows:

1. *Excessive anxiety and worry occurring more days than not for at least six months.* The anxiety and worry are exaggerated far out of proportion for the perceived threat or peril. For instance, a child or an adolescent may worry about his or her athletic or academic performance when he or she is in fact doing quite well. An adult may worry unnecessarily about an illness that he or she or a family member may or may not have. During the course of the disorder, the focus of anxiety or worry often shifts from one concern to another or there may be no specific focus at all.

2. *Difficulty in controlling the worry.* The worry and anxiety repeatedly interrupt the person's daily activities and work. These interruptions are difficult or impossible to quell and may persist for hours at a time.

3. *The focus of the anxiety or worry is not about experiencing an impending panic attack, being embarrassed, or being alone or about any other phobia.* The anxiety is not associated with social phobia or agoraphobia. In addition, the anxiety is not related to a specific person, place, or activity. Rather, the anxiety is more general and often diffuse. In fact, intense anxiety can arise with no apparent focus.

4. *The anxiety, worry, or physical symptoms cause clinically significant distress or impairment in social or occupational functioning.* Anxiety and constant worry make normal social and occupational difficult if not impossible. Normal activities and concentration are interrupted frequently. Sleep disturbances, headaches, and gastrointestinal symptoms also are common.

Pathology of GAD

GAD does not appear to be heritable, and there is no identifiable gene linked with it. However, a number of studies have reported associations with genes for monoamine oxidase A (MAOA) (Tadic et al., 2003) and the serotonin transporter (Stein et al., 2006), but conclusions about the role of specific genes in the disorder are unwarranted at present. It also has been suggested that GAD and major depression share a common etiology, with some individuals being more prone to depression, some being more prone to anxiety, and others sharing features of both disorders. Researchers have found strong associations between the co-occurrences of major depression and generalized anxiety in large twin studies suggesting a common genetic risk (Kendler, 1996; Kendler et al., 2007). GAD also occurs with other anxiety disorders—particularly social phobias, PTSD, and panic disorder.

Several neurotransmitter systems also have been implicated in GAD, with particular interest focused on the inhibitory neurotransmitter GABA. A number of studies have found deficiencies in GABA receptor expression in patients with GAD. Researchers have further shown that messenger RNA (ribonucleic acid), which transcribes the GABA receptor, also is deficient and that these deficiencies can be restored following treatment with GABA agonist (Rocca et al., 1998). Furthermore, GABA has long been known to exert inhibitory effects on nuclei in the amygdala and the hypothalamus. Both of these structures are implicated in the regulation of anxiety.

Studies with laboratory animals provide additional support for the role of GABA. One animal model of generalized anxiety utilizes an **elevated maze** with two enclosed and two exposed (open) arms. Using animals, researchers measure the latency to leave an enclosed arm and enter an exposed arm to receive food (inhibitory avoidance) as a measure of anxiety (cf Graeff et al., 1998; Zangrossi et al., 1997). Experimental animals tend to prefer maze arms that have protective sides over the exposed arms and leave to explore or retrieve food only after some hesitation. Drugs that are known to reduce anxiety in humans also decrease the latency to leave enclosed arms and increase time spent in exposed arms in the elevated maze. Microinjections of GABA agonists directly into hypothalamic structures, which innervate the amygdala, also decrease latencies to leave enclosed arms. This suggests that both GABA activity in the amygdala and anxiety are regulated by the hypothalamus (Bueno et al., 2007). Animal models also have been useful in the identification and development of numerous anxiety-producing (**anxiogenic**) and anti-anxiety (**anxiolytic**) substances.

The neurotransmitters serotonin and norepinephrine have been implicated in generalized anxiety as well. However, because generalized anxiety and depression often can be difficult to disassociate, the specific roles these neurotransmitters play in anxiety has been difficult to corroborate even though antidepressants are often prescribed to alleviate generalized anxiety. Using animal models such as

FIGURE 4.6   Elevated plus maze used to measure anxiety in laboratory animals. Latencies to leave enclosed arms and the amount of time spent exploring open arms are measures of anxiety.

the elevated maze (Figures 4.6 and 4.7) may be a useful way to clarify the interaction between serotonergic and GABAergic systems in anxiety. Results from several such studies suggest that serotonergic neurons in the dorsal raphe nucleus, which project to the forebrain, are involved in the regulation of anxiety (Pobbe et al., 2005; Sena et al., 2003). These ascending neurons receive inhibitory input from GABA neurons in this region of the brainstem (Lemos et al., 2006).

To summarize, evidence from both human and animal studies suggests that GABA dysfunction underlies GAD. Several different mechanisms, including decreased GABA receptor expression, may be involved. Drugs that enhance GABA activity are effective in alleviating the symptoms of generalized anxiety and decrease latencies to leave enclosed arms of an elevated maze. Serotonin 5-HT$_{1A}$ agonists also are prescribed for GAD, but whether they act specifically on anxiety-regulating mechanisms or act indirectly by treating comorbid depression is unknown. In an animal model of anxiety, serotonin 5-HT$_{1A}$ agonists do decrease latencies to leave enclosed arms in elevated mazes, suggesting serotonin involvement in the dorsal raphe nucleus.

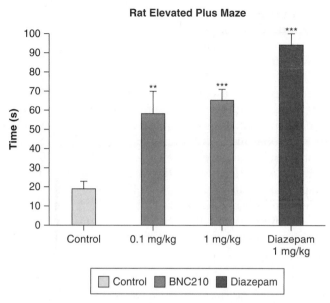

Rat Elevated Plus Maze

FIGURE 4.7 In an animal model of anxiety, GABA agonists increase time spent in exposed arms of an elevated maze. BNC210 is an experimental drug being developed as an anxiolytic. Diazepam is an anxiolytic and a GABA agonist. © Reprinted with permission from Dr. Sue O'Connor, Bionomics Ltd. (2007).

PHARMACOLOGICAL TREATMENT OF PANIC DISORDERS AND GADS

Based on the preceding discussion, it should come as no surprise that GABA agonists are effective in alleviating many of the symptoms of both panic and generalized anxiety. In fact, long before the discovery of the neurotransmitter GABA, pharmacologists had discovered a class of drugs known for their anxiolytic and sedative effects. Only much later would these drugs become known as GABA agonists. In 1903, several chemists working at the Bayer laboratories announced their discovery that barbital, a derivative of barbituric acid, had sedative properties in animals. This product, called barbital, was introduced a year later under the trade name Veronal. Veronal was the first among a long list of barbiturate drugs, including phenobarbital, that were widely used until the 1960s as anti-anxiety and sedative-inducing drugs.

Barbiturates

All of the barbiturate drugs are powerful central nervous system (CNS) depressants, and prior to their introduction, only a few substances were known to induce sedation and quell anxiety. These substances included the narcotic opium and various preparations of alcohol. Much later, in the mid 1800s, bromide and chloral hydrate were introduced to bring on sleep and to serve as anesthetics for surgery. With the discovery of barbiturates, a new era of psychopharmacology began. Drugs could now be developed to produce profound changes in neural functioning and behavior.

The barbiturates share a common molecular structure that contains the barbital nucleus shown in Figure 4.8. The main difference between these drugs is their half-life, which can range from several hours for Thiopental to over 100 hours with phenobarbital. The short-acting, highly fat-soluble barbiturates such as Thiopental can induce sleep or anesthesia within 20–30 seconds when administered intravenously. The longer-acting drugs have much lower fat solubility and may take up to an hour to produce an effect. The duration of action of the lower fat-soluble barbiturates such as phenobarbital can be as long as 12 hours. Several common barbiturates and their half-lives are presented in Table 4.1. Over 50 different barbiturates have been marketed; however, many are no longer available in the United States.

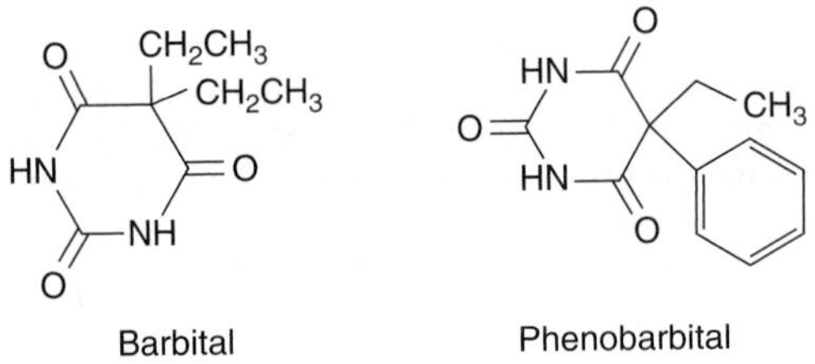

Barbital   Phenobarbital

FIGURE 4.8 All barbiturates share a common barbital nucleus.

TABLE 4.1 Several common barbiturates, their respective half-lives, and their present uses. Many different barbiturates were used to some extent to control anxiety before benzodiazepines and *selective serotonin reuptake inhibitors* (SSRIs) became available

Drug Name	Trade Name	Half-Life Hours	Present Use
Amobarbital	Amytal	10–40	Anesthesia, sedation
Butabarbital	Butisol	30–40	Sedation, seizures
Methohexital	Brevital	1–2	Short-duration anesthesia
Pentobarbital	Nembutal	20–50	Anesthesia, sedation
Phenobarbital	Luminal	25–120	Sedation, seizures
Secobarbital	Seconal	20–40	Anesthesia, sedation
Thiopental	Pentothal	2–5	Short-duration anesthesia

The barbiturates produce behavioral effects that can be indistinguishable from alcohol intoxication. At lower doses, they cause drowsiness and sedation in addition to disruptions in motor and cognitive abilities. At higher doses (or with barbiturates that are highly fat-soluble), they induce sleep or a state of anesthesia. The anxiolytic effects of barbiturates cannot be separated from these effects, thus limiting their usefulness during most daytime activities. Because barbiturates disrupt REM (rapid eye movement, or dream) sleep, their use in treating insomnia also is limited.

Barbiturates have a narrow therapeutic index, and when combined with other GABA agonists, such as alcohol, they can suppress respiratory centers in the brainstem and have lethal consequences. Suicide by barbiturate and alcohol consumption was not at all uncommon prior to their largely discontinued used in the late 1960s. In spite of these disadvantages, barbiturates were used extensively to treat anxiety disorders, insomnia, muscle spasms, and convulsions and to induce anesthesia before safer drugs became available. The barbiturate sodium amytal (amobarbital) was used in psychoanalysis to induce a hypotonic state during an **Amytal interview.** It was presumed that Amytal would increase a patient's ability to recall and verbalize repressed memories, making psychotherapy more effective. And in forensic science, Amytal has a long history of use as a truth serum to elicit confessions from crime suspects. This use was disputed when it was recognized that false memories could easily be coerced from drugged suspects. Nonetheless, amobarbital has allegedly been used on al Qaeda prisoners detained in Afghanistan and Cuba. However, evidence obtained with the use of drugs is not allowed in U.S. courts [*People v. Cox,* 271 N.W.2d 216 (1978)].

MECHANISMS OF BARBITURATE ACTION   The barbiturates bind effectively to a specific subtype of receptor on the $GABA_A$ receptor complex called the barbiturate site. The $GABA_A$ receptor is an ionotropic receptor that controls the influx of chloride (Cl^-) ions. This receptor has five membrane spanning regions that include two α, two β, and one γ subunits, with other configurations possible. These subunits make up the Cl^- ion channel illustrated in Figure 4.9. In addition to a site for the neurotransmitter GABA, four other distinct receptor sites are distributed on these subunits that selectively bind to GABA agonists: a barbiturate site, a benzodiazepine site, an alcohol site, and a steroid site. When any of these receptors are bound to a specific agonist, the neurotransmitter GABA binds to its receptor more effectively for longer durations, producing greater hyperpolarization of postsynaptic membranes. Hyperpolarization reduces the likelihood of postsynaptic cells producing an action potential, thus reducing the firing rate of receiving neurons. GABA antagonists (e.g., picrotoxin) bind effectively to other receptor sites and produce **convulsant** effects by inhibiting the binding of GABA. However, all barbiturates are presumed to act by binding to the barbiturate site on the $GABA_A$ receptor complex. Unlike other GABA agonists, however, barbiturates can open the Cl^- channel and hyperpolarize postsynaptic membranes in the absence of GABA.

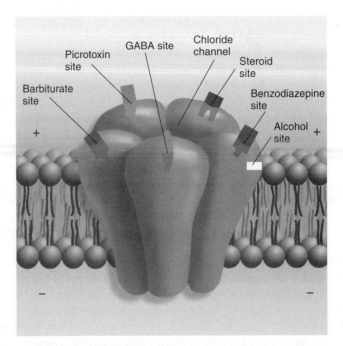

FIGURE 4.9 GABA receptor complex. Several drugs, including the barbiturates, benzodiazepines, and alcohol, act to facilitate GABA binding and chlorine influx.

One of many mysteries of psychopharmacology is why these receptor subtypes have evolved on the $GABA_A$ receptor. Although they were named after the drugs that have high affinities for them, it would certainly be presumptuous, if not mistaken, to assume that these receptor subtypes were waiting for the drugs to be discovered. Identification of a natural ligand called diazepam-binding inhibitor (DBI), which prevents benzodiazepine binding and produces anxiety-like effects, has only partially resolved this mystery. To date, other natural ligands for these receptors have not been identified.

SIDE EFFECTS OF BARBITURATES   The use of barbiturates to treat anxiety and insomnia has largely been discontinued because of severe side effects. At anxiolytic doses, barbiturates cause confusion, impaired judgment, retarded reflexes, loss of muscle coordination, and impaired speech—effects similar to those of alcohol intoxication. Because of these intoxicating effects, most normal activities, including driving, working, and studying, are greatly impaired.

When they are prescribed as sedatives to treat insomnia, the barbiturates disrupt normal sleep cycles, including REM sleep. A few nights of REM deprivation may produce symptoms such as irritability, aggressiveness, and poor concentration. After a week or more of REM deprivation, symptoms may escalate to delusions, hallucinations, and other symptoms of psychosis. When barbiturates are suddenly discontinued for sleep, REM rebound occurs, resulting in significantly increased durations of REM sleep.

Tolerance of and dependence on barbiturate use also occur rapidly. Tolerance is mainly a result of increased liver metabolism and GABA receptor downregulation. Both of these mechanisms also decrease the effectiveness of other GABA agonist drugs—a phenomenon referred to as **cross-tolerance.** In addition, tolerance to a barbiturate's sedating and anti-seizure effects occurs more rapidly than to its respiratory-suppressing effects. This difference in the rate of tolerance acquisition decreases the therapeutic index, making a barbiturate overdose more likely. Physical dependence on barbiturates makes discontinuation difficult for most long-term users and can lead to seizures caused by an excitable rebound of CNS activity.

The barbiturates have been linked to fetal abnormalities and cognitive impairments similar to those seen with **fetal alcohol syndrome (FAS).** Female patients using barbiturates to control seizures or other disorders should be advised to suspend medication early in their pregnancy. Other drugs with a lower risk of adverse fetal effects may be more appropriate. Finally, combining barbiturates with other GABA agonists, such as alcohol, can accidentally cause respiratory depression and death. The CO_2-sensitive respiratory center located in the medulla contains $GABA_A$ receptors that regulate respiration in response to increased carbon dioxide (CO_2) levels. Excessive GABA inhibition decreases medulla responsiveness to CO_2 and depresses respiration.

Benzodiazepines

The introduction of barbiturates in the early 1900s ushered the promise that drugs could be developed to alleviate symptoms of behavioral disorders by altering brain chemistry. For the first time, epileptic seizures, severe anxiety, debilitating insomnia, muscle spasms, and a variety of other ailments were treated effectively and humanely. Surgical anesthesia, which to this point was induced by vapors of ether or chloroform, also was dramatically improved with the introduction of barbiturates. For nearly 50 years, barbiturates were the choice of treatment for these disorders and for surgical anesthesia.

In the 1960s, however, the treatment of anxiety disorders was revolutionized by the introduction of the benzodiazepines, which were discovered in 1954 in laboratories at the pharmaceutical company Hoffman-La Roche. In 1960, the first benzodiazepine was released as Librium, which was quickly followed by Valium. Since then, more than 2,000 benzodiazepines have been synthesized and approximately 30 have been marketed for their anxiolytic and hypnotic properties. However, not all of these are currently available for use in the United States. Once the benzodiazepines became available, they rapidly replaced the older barbiturates and became the most widely prescribed psychoactive drugs in the world.

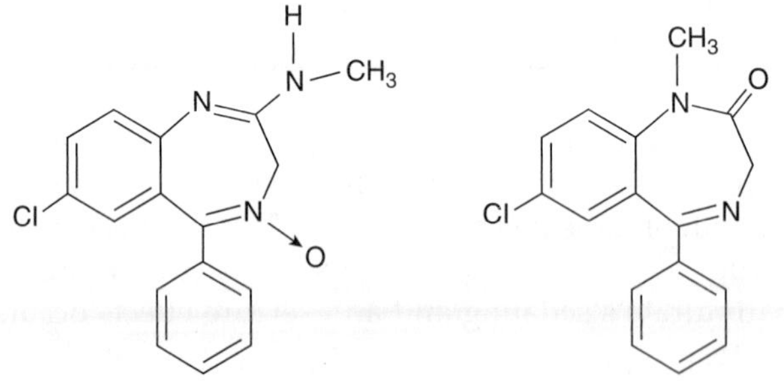

Librium (chlordiazepoxide)   Valium (diazepam)

FIGURE 4.10 The molecular structure of several common benzodiazepines. All of the pharmacologically active benzodiazepines share a common three-ring nucleus. Substitutions with hydrogen molecules at the CH_3 sites and NO_2 at the Cl site are common structural arrangements for many of the benzodiazepines.

The benzodiazepines all share a common three-ring molecular structure that largely determines their activity. The main differences are the specific molecules attached at the methyl (CH_3) sites and the Cl site on the rings, shown in Figure 4.10. Substitutions on the CH_3 sites are typically with hydrogen molecules (H or H_2) and at the Cl sites, typically nitrogen dioxide (NO_2). All of the benzodiazepines have the same mechanism of action regardless of their specific molecular structures. The major differences are their half-lives and their fat solubility, which determines how quickly they enter the brain.

The half-lives of benzodiazepines can range from a few hours with the ultra short-acting anesthetic Versed (midazolam) to several days with the longer-acting anxiolytic Valium (diazepam). The effective half-lives of Valium and most other longer-acting drugs are extended by their active metabolite nordiazepam. Several common benzodiazepines and their respective half-lives are presented in Table 4.2. The longer- and intermediate-acting benzodiazepines are typically prescribed for anxiety and seizure disorders, while the shorter-acting drugs are most often used for insomnia and surgical anesthesia.

MECHANISMS OF BENZODIAZEPINE ACTION Benzodiazepines bind to the benzodiazepine site on the $GABA_A$ receptor complex, as illustrated in Figure 4.9. As with the barbiturates, benzodiazepines alter the shape of the $GABA_A$ receptor protein; so GABA has a greater affinity for its site. When the inhibitory neurotransmitter GABA binds to its receptor, the chlorine channel opens and allows for the influx of Cl^- ions, thereby hyperpolarizing the cell and making it less likely to fire. The anxiolytic and sedative effects of the benzodiazepines are mediated by $GABA_A$ receptors in the frontal cortex, the hippocampus, and several limbic structures including the amygdala. Because the benzodiazepines

TABLE 4.2 Several common benzodiazepines and their half-lives. Long-acting drugs have an intermediate active metabolite, nordiazepam

₁g Name	Trade Name	Half-Life Hours	FDA-Approved Uses
Acting			
₁m	Valium	20–50	Anxiety, seizures, muscle spasms
iazepoxide	Librium	24–48	Anxiety, alcohol withdrawal
razepam	Rohypnol	16–35	Insomnia, but not approved in the U.S.
azepam	Klonopin	30–40	Panic disorder, seizures
ermediate			
razepam	Ativan	10–20	Anxiety, seizures
lprazolam	Xanax	12–15	Generalized anxiety, panic disorder
Short-Acting			
Midazolam	Versed	2–4	Sedation, preoperative anxiety
Oxazepam	Serax	3–21	Anxiety, alcohol withdrawal
Triazolam	Halcion	2–5	Insomnia
Antagonists			
Flumazenil	Romazicon	1–2	Overdose—reverses benzodiazepine effects

do not open chlorine channels on their own, as do the barbiturates, the amount of neural inhibition they can produce depends on the availability of GABA (see Figure 4.11).

Not all benzodiazepines function as agonists on the GABA$_A$ receptor complex. The benzodiazepine flumazenil is a potent antagonist of benzodiazepines in that it competitively binds to the benzodiazepine site. In cases of suspected benzodiazepine overdose, flumazenil effectively competes with and displaces other benzodiazepines at the receptor site. As a result, flumazenil reverses the anxiolytic, sedating, and motor effects caused by benzodiazepines. In large doses, flumazenil can produce anxiety, increases in muscle tone, and convulsions—effects opposite to those produced by other benzodiazepines.

SIDE EFFECTS OF BENZODIAZEPINES   Because the benzodiazepines cannot open Cl$^-$ channels on their own, as the barbiturates do, they are less likely to contribute to respiratory depression. Therefore, lethal overdose by benzodiazepines is quite rare unless combined with alcohol or another GABA agonist. In combination with alcohol, the benzodiazepines can cause a serious and sometimes fatal interaction by enhancing GABA neurotransmission. Other side effects of these drugs include marked sedation, cognitive impairments, retarded motor movements, and slurred speech—all effects observed with barbiturates and alcohol.

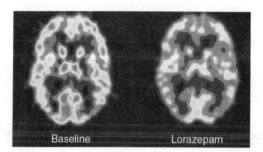

Baseline   Lorazepam

FIGURE 4.11 PET image showing decreased neural activity throughout the brain after benzodiazepine treatment. Lighter shading at baseline indicates more neural activity than grey shading after treatment. © American Psychiatric Publishing, Inc.

When combined with alcohol, the benzodiazepine Rohypnol (fluni-trazepam) produces euphoria, sedation, and amnesia. Because of these effects, Rohypnol allegedly has been used to facilitate date rape in a number of sexual assault cases. Prior to 1998, the drug Rohypnol, which is used in England and Mexico for the short-term treatment of insomnia, was colorless, was tasteless, and could rapidly be dissolved in drinks. Consuming this cocktail would bring about sedating and amnesiac effects within 15–20 minutes. Since 1998, a blue dye has been added to alert the presence of this drug in spiked beverages. Nevertheless, the FDA has not approved Rohypnol for use in the United States.

When used for the extended treatment of insomnia, the benzodiazepines disrupt normal sleep cycles and REM sleep. Discontinuation may cause rebounds in REM sleep, insomnia, and anxiety. These effects are mediated by benzodiazepine receptor downregulation. Tolerance and dependence, also mediated by the downregulation of benzodiazepine receptor sites, occurs rapidly and may make discontinuation difficult for many patients. Although long-term use may cause physical dependence, there is little evidence from human or animal studies that the benzodiazepines are addictive. This conclusion may be somewhat surprising because benzodiazepines and alcohol share similar mechanisms of action. Perhaps the addictive potential of GABAergic drugs depends on how rapidly they enter the brain and on their ability to significantly increase dopamine activity in the mesolimbic system. The benzodiazepines are absorbed relatively slowly when compared to alcohol. In support of this hypothesis, the self-administration of benzodiazepines by laboratory animals is both variable and nonrobust when compared to other abused drugs (Griffiths et al., 1991). A high rate of drug self-administration by animals is considered to be a reliable method of determining a drug's addictive potential.

In summary, the benzodiazepines represent a significant advance in the pharmacological treatment of anxiety disorders, seizures, muscle spasms, and insomnia compared with their predecessors, the barbiturates. All benzodiazepines agonize GABA neurotransmission by their activity on specific sites on the benzodiazepine receptor complex. Increases in inhibitory GABAergic activity decrease the firing rate of neurons in the frontal cortex, hippocampus, and limbic structures assumed to underlie anxiety disorders. The benzodiazepines are safer than their predecessors and are rarely lethal by themselves in overdose. Their side effects are essentially the same as alcohol intoxication and the barbiturates, including sedation, cognitive impairment, retarded motor activity, and slurred speech. Although the benzodiazepines can cause physical dependence with long-term use, they have little or no addictive potential.

Third-Generation Anxiolytics

PARTIAL GABA AGONISTS   In attempts to minimize the side effects of sedation and cognitive impairment associated with the benzodiazepines, a number of partial $GABA_A$ agonists have been investigated. A **partial agonist** has a high affinity for the $GABA_A$ receptor, but it has much less of an effect on the ability of GABA to bind than do full $GABA_A$ agonists. As you may recall, $GABA_A$ agonists alter the configuration of the $GABA_A$ receptor slightly, thus making it more structurally compatible for GABA. Partial agonists appear to produce even more subtle structural changes than do full agonists such as the barbiturates and benzodiazepines. Several partial $GABA_A$ agonists have been investigated but are no longer being pursued for use in the United States. These include etizolam, which is available in Europe; imidazenil; pazinaclone; and bretazenil. In both human and animal studies, these drugs appear to have similar anxiolytic effects but lower sedative and cognitive impairing effects than do the benzodiazepines. In addition, they appear less likely to induce tolerance and dependence (Mirza, 2006; Pinna et al., 2006; Sanna et al., 2005). The reasons for pharmaceutical companies not pursuing these alternatives aggressively may be due in part to the increased interest in SSRIs for treating anxiety disorders. However, interest in partial GABA agonists has continued with the development of several drugs used to treat insomnia. These drugs are discussed in the chapter on sleep disorders.

SEROTONIN 5-HT$_{1A}$ AGONISTS   Because serotonin receptors are located through the brain regions known to be involved in anxiety, it should not be surprising to learn that serotonin agonists have anxiolytic properties. Genetically engineered 5-HT$_{1A}$ knockout mice lacking 5-HT$_{1A}$ receptors in the hippocampus, the amygdala, and the frontal cortex demonstrate exaggerated fear and anxiety compared to normal mice when tested in an elevated maze (Overstreet et al., 2003). In addition to increased behavioral anxiety, these mice have elevated autonomic activity, including increased heart rate and body temperature, analogous to that observed in anxious humans. Injections of diazepam do not eliminate these stress responses, suggesting that interactions between GABAergic and serotonin 5-HT_{1A} receptors are involved in anxiolysis (Pattij et al., 2002). Although several 5-HT_{1A} agonists have been shown to have anxiolytic effects, buspirone is the only one approved for anxiety at this time.

Buspirone (BuSpar)   Buspirone is a member of the azapirone group of 5-HT_{1A} partial agonist drugs originally developed for their potential as antidepressants. And although buspirone is used occasionally for the treatment of depression, it has not been approved by the FDA for this use. However, buspirone is an effective anxiolytic, which has been established in numerous human and animal studies. In an extensive review of 36 clinical trials involving nearly 6,000 participants, buspirone was shown to be more effective than a placebo and as effective as benzodiazepines in treating GAD (Chessick et al., 2007).

The agonistic effects of buspirone on 5-HT_{1A} receptors result in downregulation or desensitization of these presynaptic autoreceptors and a corresponding increase in serotonin synthesis and release (Hensler, 2003). Typically, it takes two or three weeks for buspirone to become effective—a time course similar to the adaptive changes observed in serotonin receptors. Because of the delay in its therapeutic effects, buspirone is not as useful as the benzodiazepines for treating acute anxiety. Buspirone is typically better tolerated than benzodiazepines and causes less sedation and fewer cognitive- and motor-inhibiting effects. In addition, buspirone does not cause dependence and there is no evidence for an abuse potential.

GABA$_B$ AND GAMMA-HYDROXYBUTYRIC ACID (GHB) RECEPTOR AGONISTS

GHB   GHB is discussed here only because of its historical significance and the recent discovery of a GHB receptor, not because it is currently used as an anxiolytic drug. In the 1960s, GHB was used in general anesthesia, as an anxiolytic, and as a sedative for the treatment of insomnia. More recently, GHB has been used recreationally and athletics have used it to enhance muscle growth through increased synthesis of growth hormone. In some cases, GHB reportedly has been used as a potent hypnotic to facilitate rape. Because GHB is odorless and colorless, it is difficult to detect and could easily be dissolved in beverages and consumed without detection. GHB also is difficult to detect in urine samples. Thus, the incidence of its use as a date rape drug remains largely unknown. Because it is now restricted, GHB use to facilitate rape is presumed to be quite rare.

Gamma-Hydroxybutric Acid (GHB) is a naturally occurring metabolite of GABA found in small amounts in plant and animal tissues. Until quite recently, GHB was believed to exert its sedating effects solely through the GABA$_B$ metabotropic receptor—a less common form of the GABA receptor distributed throughout the brain and spinal cord. It is now known that GHB also binds to a separate and specific presynaptic G protein-coupled receptor (GHB$_R$) that regulates adenyl cyclase activity and ultimately neurotransmitter release (Snead, 2000; Ticku et al., 2008; Carter et al., 2009). At present, there is no consensus about whether the behavioral effects of GHB are mediated by GABA$_B$ receptor agonism, the newly identified GHB receptor, or a combination of both.

Alternatives to Drug Therapy for Anxiety Disorders

The treatment of anxiety disorders with nontraditional pharmacotherapy has a long and controversial history. Although dozens of herbal remedies for anxiety have been utilized, only valerian and inositol are discussed here because there is some scientific evidence for their effectiveness.

VALERIAN *(VALERIANA OFFICINALIS)*   The herb **valerian,** which is extracted from the root of the valerian plant, shown in Figure 4.12, has a history dating back to Hippocrates, who may have been the first to describe its sedating and anxiolytic properties. Controversy about the evidence for these effects continues today. This controversy will go on until research on valerian is replicated by well-controlled clinical trials. The majority of the literature on the effectiveness of valerian has been promoted by the herbal supplement industry or has been based on poorly designed studies or anecdotal evidence.

In a recent review of the research on the anxiolytic effects of valerian researchers, Miyasaka et al. (2007) found that only one study utilized random assignment of subjects into treatment conditions and included a placebo control. In this particular study, patients were randomly assigned to one of three treatment groups receiving valerian, diazepam, or a placebo. After four weeks of treatment, compared to the placebo group, the groups receiving valerian and diazepam scored lower on a subset of questions allegedly measuring the psychic symptoms of anxiety as measured by the Hamilton Anxiety Scale (Questions 1–6 in Figure 4.13).

FIGURE 4.12   Valeriana officinalis.   © Dorling Kindersley Media Library

HAMILTON ANXIETY RATING SCALE (HAM-A)

Classification of symptoms: 0 - absent; 1 - mild; 2 - moderate; 3- severe; 4- incapacitating.

HAM-A score level of anxiety: <17 mild; 18 - 24 mild to moderate; 25 - 30 moderate to severe

Symptoms   Date: _____

1. Anxious mood   0 1 2 3 4
   - worries
   - anticipates worst
2. Tension   0 1 2 3 4
   - startles
   - cries easily
   - restless
   - trembling
3. Fears   0 1 2 3 4
   - fear of the dark
   - fear of strangers
   - fear of being alone
   - fear of animal
4. Insomnia   0 1 2 3 4
   - difficulty falling asleep or staying asleep
   - difficulty with nightmares
5. Intellectual   0 1 2 3 4
   - poor concentration
   - memory impairment
6. Depressed Mood   0 1 2 3 4
   - decreased interest in activities
   - anhedonia
   - insomnia
7. Somatic complaints — Muscular   0 1 2 3 4
   - muscle aches or pains
   - bruxism
8. Somatic complaints — Sensory   0 1 2 3 4
   - tinnitus
   - blurred vision
9. Cardiovascular Symptoms   0 1 2 3 4
   - tachycardia
   - palpitations
   - chest pain
   - sensory of feeling faint

10. Respiratory Symptoms   0 1 2 3 4
    - chest pressure
    - choking sensation
    - shortness of breath
11. Gastrointestinal Symptoms   0 1 2 3 4
    - dysphagia
    - nausea or vomiting
    - constipation
    - weight loss
12. Genitourinary Symptoms   0 1 2 3 4
    - urinary frequency or urgency
    - dysmenorrhea
    - impotence
13. Autonomic Symptoms   0 1 2 3 4
    - dry mouth
    - flushing
    - pallor
    - sweating
14. Behavior at Interview   0 1 2 3 4
    - fidgets
    - tremor
    - paces

TOTAL SCORE

Rater's Signature _____

FIGURE 4.13 Hamilton Rating Scale (from Hamilton, 1959). According to Hamilton, questions 1–6 address psychotic anxiety, while questions 7–14 address somatic anxiety.

Source: Hamilton M. A rating scale for depression. *J Neurol Neurosurg Psychiatry* 1960; 23:56–62.

However, these results were confounded by the fact that Hamilton anxiety scores decreased overall in all three treatment groups (Andreatini et al., 2002), suggesting that valerian and benzodiazepines were no more effective than a placebo, at least in these patients. The relative lack of well-designed clinical trials, as well as reliable measures of anxiety in humans, continues to make conclusions about valerian's effectiveness difficult at best. In addition, few objective studies examine valerian's effects on inhibitory avoidance or forced swimming in experimental animals. As discussed earlier, animal studies are particularly useful in corroborating human studies when outcome measures are largely subjective.

The author's laboratory isolated several active compounds in the valerian root extract, including GABA and valerenic acid. The effectiveness of valerian was compared to the known anxiolytic diazepam and samples of the active compounds extracted from valerian root, using the elevated plus maze. In this study, female rats were randomly assigned to receive an injection containing valerian root extract, diazepam, or saline. Additional groups received valerenic acid or valerenic acid and GABA in the concentrations titrated from the valerian root extract. After 30 minutes, these animals were placed in the center of the plus maze suspended 4 feet above the floor. The time these animals spent exploring open arms of the maze is shown in Figure 4.14. In this experiment, valerian extract was as effective as diazepam in increasing exploration—a measure of a drug's anxiolytic effects (Murphy et al., 2010).

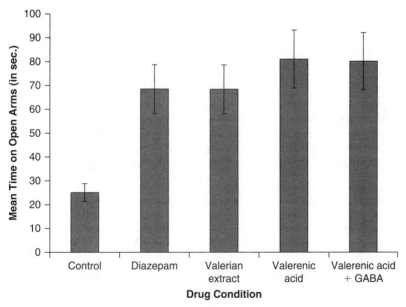

FIGURE 4.14 A comparison of the anxiolytic effects of valerian root extract, diazepam, valerenic acid, and valerenic acid with GABA in female rats using the elevated plus maze. (From author's laboratory, 2008.)

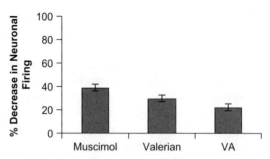

FIGURE 4.15 Percent decrease in neuronal activity in rat brainstem following treatment with the $GABA_A$ agonist muscimol, valerian, or valerenic acid. Based on Yuan et al., 2004.

Mechanisms of Valerian Action   Despite the fact that research on valerian's anxiolytic properties is fragile, evidence that the herb acts as a $GABA_A$ receptor agonist suggests that valerian at least has anxiolytic potential. Specifically, both valerian and its main constituent valerenic acid were shown to induce neuronal inhibition in experimental animals in a manner similar to, by slightly less potent than, the $GABA_A$ agonist muscimol (see Figure 4.15). Valerian apparently potentiates the inhibitory effects of GABA by binding to specific subunits on the $GABA_A$ receptor complex (Khom et al., 2007; Yuan et al., 2004). Whether the neuronal-inhibiting effects of valerian are sufficient to produce an anxiolytic effect in people remains to be demonstrated in clinical studies.

INOSITOL   Inositol, a natural isomer (a molecule made up of the same elements as another but in a different structural arrangement) of glucose, is a precursor to several of the phosphate-based second messengers (shown in Figure 4.16). Found in a variety of foods, including bran cereals, nuts, and fruits (e.g., oranges and melons), inositol (myo-inositol) is synthesized by the body and is a member of the vitamin B complex. Inositol has been reputed to treat panic disorders, generalized anxiety, OCD, and depression. Evidence of these effects is sparse relative to the abundance of research supporting the effectiveness of traditional anxiolytic drugs for the disorders listed.

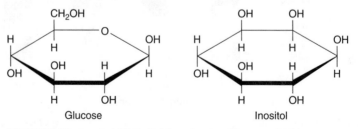

FIGURE 4.16 Inositol ($C_6H_{12}O_6$) is a structural isomer of glucose ($C_6H_{12}O_6$).

A few studies have shown inositol to be more effective than a placebo and as effective as fluoxamine (an SSRI) in treating panic disorder and in reducing the severity of anxiety as measured by the Hamilton Rating Scale (Benjamin et al., 1995; Palatnik et al., 2001). Why the researchers did not compare inositol with barbiturates or benzodiazepines is unclear. As with valerian, inositol research often lacks scientific rigor, which makes conclusions about its effectiveness speculative. Furthermore, the mechanisms of action that underlie the putative effects of inositol have yet to be described, although inositol is involved in second messenger systems in many neural pathways, including serotonin.

In summary, alternatives to drug therapy for anxiety disorders have been proposed and some experimental evidence supports their use. Both valerian and the glucose isomer inositol have limited experimental support for treating anxiety and panic disorder, but the mechanism of action of valerian on $GABA_A$ receptors is at least consistent with its alleged anxiolytic effects. However, the mechanisms of action of inositol remain elusive, although inositol does function in the second messenger systems of most neurons, including neurons that are known to underlie anxiety. Because neither of these substances causes significant side effects or interacts measurably with other anxiolytic or antidepressant drugs, their sensible use is not discouraged. In fact, as a first treatment attempt, they might be not only effective, but also better tolerated and cause appreciably fewer side effects than prescription anti-anxiety medication.

OBSESSIVE-COMPULSIVE DISORDER (OCD)

Obsessive-compulsive disorder (OCD) is an anxiety disorder characterized by recurrent unwanted thoughts (obsessions) and repetitive behaviors (compulsions). Obsessions may consist of thoughts of contamination or infection, repeated self-doubt, a need for order, aggressive impulses to hurt someone or to shout an obscenity, or sexual imagery. Compulsions, which may include hand washing, counting, checking, cleaning, or hoarding miscellaneous items, are often performed with the anticipation of preventing obsessive thoughts or making them go away. Performing these repetitive behaviors appears to provide only temporary, if any, relief. Not performing these behaviors, however, tends to increase the person's anxiety and obsessive thoughts. Patients with OCD recognize that their obsessions and compulsions are excessive and unreasonable, but this recognition does little to subdue their anxiety.

Obsessive Compulsive Disorder (OCD) typically emerges in early adolescence or adulthood, but it can occur in children. The lifetime prevalence of OCD is about 2.5 percent of the population, and over 2 million people suffer from it at any given time. The prevalence of OCD is about equal for males and females, but it may be more prevalent among males in the child population. The majority of patients with OCD experience cycling periods with and without symptoms and experience the most debilitating symptoms during times of stress.

The DSM-IV-TR criteria for a diagnosis of OCD are as follows:

1. *Either obsessions or compulsions.* Obsessions are recurrent persistent thoughts, impulses, or images that cause marked anxiety or distress. In addition, these obsessions are not simply worries about real-life problems and the patient realizes that the obsessive thoughts are a product of their own mind and are not imposed by another. Compulsions, which are repetitive behaviors the person feels driven to perform, are aimed at preventing or reducing distress or some dreaded event.
2. *The person recognizes that the obsessive thoughts and compulsive behaviors are excessive and unreasonable.*
3. *The obsessions and compulsions cause marked distress; are time-consuming; and significantly disrupt a person's normal routine, occupational functioning, and social activities.*

Carl, a 24-year-old college student, began seeing a psychologist at his girlfriend's request because of his persistent checking behavior. Once they began living together, she was shocked by his inability to sit through a television show, a complete dinner, or even a conversation without getting up to make sure the kitchen stove was off or the door to their apartment was locked. During the night, Carl would often get up to ensure that everything was turned off and secure. Carl even insisted that they leave the theater in the middle of a movie because he was certain they had left the door to their apartment open. Reassuring him that she had checked was of little use once he began obsessing about it.

Carl's obsessions appear to have begun in high school when he became obsessed with arranging and rearranging things in his room. At first, his parents encouraged his cleanliness and the order of his personal things. When he went off to college, they assumed that his behavior would change in the presence of roommates who would likely be much messier than he was. While Carl was not obsessed with the disorder of the dorm room he shared with a roommate, his obsessions about his own possessions persisted. Carl was meticulous about folding his clothes and maintaining their order in his small closet and drawers. He also became concerned about the shared sink in the room. He spent hours washing and disinfecting the shared area where his roommate shaved and brushed his teeth. Any amount of hair or toothbrush splatter in the sink or on the counter repulsed him.

After several months, Carl was granted a request to move into a single dorm room. In his room, Carl was aware that his excessive concern about order was unusual. He was even embarrassed when others commented about how clean and orderly everything was. At one point prior to friends coming to visit, he disorganized everything to make his dorm look "normal." Carl found this to be so distressing that he spent their entire visit rearranging things again rather than playing cards. Living in the shared space of dormitories was getting more difficult for Carl. His obsessions over the sanitary conditions of the showers, the many door knobs, and the shared kitchen space distracted him much of the time. He also was concerned about leaving his dorm room door unlocked and needed to check it frequently throughout the day. By his senior year, Carl had moved into a small but new apartment. Within a few months, his girlfriend joined him, only to be stunned by his unusual behavior.

After two visits to the university psychologist, Carl was referred to a psychiatrist at the university hospital for medication. Following a brief visit, Carl was prescribed Zoloft, which he continues to take today. His obsessive symptoms of anxiety have improved, but his ritualistic checking has not. Carl's symptoms seem to come and go and are most severe when he is under stress.

Assessment of OCD

One of the most common assessment tools for diagnosing the severity of OCD is the Yale-Brown Obsessive Compulsive Scale (Y-BOCS) (Goodman et al., 1989). This ten-item scale (shown in Figure 4.17) is presumed to measure both obsessive and compulsive symptoms. It is mentioned here because it is often used to evaluate the effectiveness of treatment medication as well as the effectiveness of cognitive behavioral therapy. Researchers also are interested in developing animal models of OCD to study its underlying pathology as well as to investigate drug effectiveness. Several animal models that have been proposed involve inducing OCD symptoms with drugs (e.g., quinpirole) that increase dopamine activity in the striatum and produce compulsive checkinglike and hoarding behaviors in animals (e.g., Fernandez et al., 2003; Joel, 2006; Szechtman et al., 1998). Drugs that effectively decrease OCD symptoms in human patients appear to diminish OCD-like symptoms in animals as well.

Pathology of OCD

Of all of the anxiety disorders, OCD has the clearest connection to abnormal neuroanatomy and function. The prevailing view of OCD argues that it is a biological disease involving neural dysfunction in circuitry between the orbitofrontal cortex, the cingulate gyrus, the caudate nucleus, the globus pallidus, and the thalamus. This neural circuit forms a loop where dopamine hyperactivity in the caudate nucleus inhibits the globus pallidus, which normally suppresses thalamic activity (shown in Figure 4.18). Excessive dopamine inhibition in the globus pallidus is presumed to disrupt the normal inhibitory control that the globus pallidus has over the thalamus. Increased activity in the thalamus of OCD patients produces increased activity in the orbitofrontal cortex via the cingulate gyrus. This proposal is supported by several neuroimaging studies (Saxena et al., 1998) and volumetric studies of these structures (Atmaca et al., 2007). Furthermore, OCD patients who had been successfully treated with SSRI medication showed normalized functioning in the caudate nucleus compared to patients treated for depression (Saxena et al., 2003). A number of patients with severe OCD have benefited from surgically disrupting the excitatory input from the cingulate gyrus to the frontal cortex through a procedure known as a **cingulotomy,** which severs this connection. Surgical intervention is an option only when patients do not respond to medication.

PSYCHIATRIC ASSOCIATES OF ATLANTA, LLC

NAME: _____

DATE: _____

PHYSICIAN: _____

Note: Scores should reflect the composite effect of all the patient's obsessive compulsive symptoms. Rate the average occurrence of each item during the prior week up to and including the time of interview.

Obsession Rating Scale (circle appropriate score)

Item	Range of Severity				
1. Time Spent on Obsessions	0 hr/day	0–1 hr/day	1–3 hr/day	3–8 hr/day	>8 hr/day
Score:	0	1	2	3	4
2. Interference From Obsessions	None	Mild	Definite but manageable	Substantial impairment	Incapacitating
Score:	0	1	2	3	4
3. Distress From Obsessions	None	Little	Moderate but manageable	Severe	Near constant, disabling
Score:	0	1	2	3	4
4. Resistance to Obsessions	Always resists	Much resistance	Some resistance	Often yields	Completely yields
Score:	0	1	2	3	4
5. Control Over Obsessions	Complete control	Much control	Some control	Little control	No control
Score:	0	1	2	3	4

Obsession subtotal (add items 1–5) _____

Compulsion Rating Scale (circle appropriate score)

Item	Range of Severity				
6. Time Spent on Compulsions	0 hr/day	0–1 hr/day	1–3 hr/day	3–8 hr/day	>8 hr/day
Score:	0	1	2	3	4
7. Inteference From Compulsions	None	Mild	Definite but manageable	Substantial impairment	Incapacitating
Score:	0	1	2	3	4
8. Distress From Compulsions	None	Mild	Moderate but manageable	Severe	Near constant, disabling
Score:	0	1	2	3	4
9. Resistance to Compulsions	Always resists	Much resistance	Some resistance	Often yields	Completely yields
Score:	0	1	2	3	4
10. Control Over Compulsions	Complete control	Much control	Some control	Little control	No control
Score:	0	1	2	3	4

Compulsion subtotal (add items 6–10)_____

Y-BOCS total (add items 1–10) [_____]

Total Y-BOCS score range of severity for patients who have both obsessions and compulsions:

0–7 Subclinical   8–15 Mild   16–23 Moderate   24–31 Severe   32–40 Extreme

COMMENTS: _____
_____

FIGURE 4.17 Y-BOCS. Psychological inventory used to measure the severity of obsessive and compulsive symptoms for OCD. From Goodman et al., (1989).   Source: Goodman et al., (1989). The Yale-Brown obsessive compulsive scale. *Archives of General Psychiatry*, 48(10), 1012–1018 (fig 1 on pg 1007).

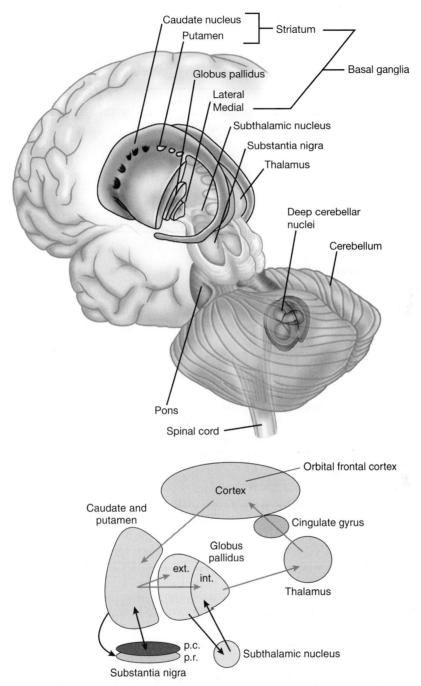

FIGURE 4.18 Neural structures implicated in OCD (top). Normally, thalamic activity suppresses activity in the orbitofrontal cortex via the cingulate gyrus. In OCD, hyperactivity in the caudate nucleus suppresses inhibitory input from the globus pallidus to the thalamus. This results in an increase in activity in the thalamus, cingulate gyrus, and orbitofrontal cortex (bottom). (Top)-The Basal Ganglia and the serial order of communicative signs. Robert N. St. Clair, Walter E. Rodriguez, and Irving Joshua, University of Louisville.

TABLE 4.3   FDA-approved medication for the treatment of OCD. Other serotonin agonists may be equally effective, but they are used off label

Drug Name	Trade Name	Class
Clomipramine	Anafranil	SNRI
Fluoxetine	Prozac	SSRI
Fluvoxamine	Luvox	SSRI
Paroxetine	Paxil	SSRI
Sertraline	Zoloft	SSRI

Pharmacological Treatment of OCD

The observation that symptoms of OCD are dissipated with serotonin agonists (SSRIs and SNRIs) has led to the hypothesis that serotonin dysfunction underlies this disorder. However, there is little evidence for serotonin dysfunction in OCD (Westenberg et al., 2007). Also, there is little agreement about which serotonin receptors may be involved when symptoms do improve (Lin, 2007). It does appear, however, that serotonin reuptake inhibition mediates the effectiveness of treatment even with the dual serotonin-norepinephrine reuptake inhibitors. A number of these drugs are described in Table 4.3. There is a growing consensus that serotonin agonists are initially effective in 50–60 percent of OCD patients. Nonresponders may eventually respond to another serotonin agonist or to combinations of drug and cognitive behavioral therapy.

Patients who respond to treatment with serotonin agonists also reveal decreases in blood flow to the thalamus compared to patients who do not respond to drug treatment—a finding consistent with thalamic hyperactivity contributing to OCD symptoms (Ho Pian et al., 2005). Treatment with the serotonin agonist fluvoxamine also has been shown to increase dopamine (D_2) receptor availability in the caudate nucleus. This secondary effect of serotonergic activity is presumed to normalize hyperexcitability in the caudate nucleus and the thalamus (Moresco et al., 2007).

In conclusion, OCD is a serious and debilitating condition that affects a significant portion of the population. Disruptions in neural circuits between the caudate nucleus, globus pallidus, and thalamus appear to cause increased activity in the cingulate gyrus and the orbitofrontal cortex. Evidence supporting this hypothesis comes from numerous imaging and surgical studies as well as animal models of OCD. While there appears to be evidence for a genetic contribution to OCD, there is little agreement on the details of its underlying pathology or on the details of serotonin involvement. However, drugs that increase serotonin activity effectively decrease symptoms in many patients and appear to normalize hyperexcitability in the caudate nucleus and the thalamus.

5

Psychotic Disorders
Schizophrenia

David was first diagnosed with schizophrenia when he was 26 years old. At that time, he was in his fourth year as an architect student at the University of Oregon. David's life prior to attending the university was not unusual. He had many high school friends, he was outgoing, and he was exceptionally bright. Any eccentricities in his behavior during these years were attributed to deep passion for everything he did, particularly drawing. While in college, David began to withdraw socially during his freshman year. He started college as an art major and he spent most of his time immersed in his drawings. At first, his artwork earned him praise because of his obsession with detail; but this fixation later began to take over, and he could not complete his assignments. He preferred spending time alone and often would be seen wandering aimlessly around campus, failing to recognize or respond to those who knew him. During David's third year, his adviser suggested architecture because David seemed more intrigued with drawings of buildings. David's sketches were becoming increasingly complex and not well suited to his assignments. Discussions with his mentors were getting more frustrating as his elaborations began to reveal his psychosis. David would talk enthusiastically about his design concepts only to be met with an outright rejection of his increasingly bizarre ideas. By this point, David was becoming convinced that his professors were concealing their real interest in plagiarizing his work by their rejection of it. Rather than continuing to work in the student lab in the architecture building, David found it necessary to do his work in secret because he believed his professors were spying on him. Within a few months, David was convinced that coconspirators of the plagiarism scheme were tapping his phone and following him everywhere. By now, he was having great difficulty sleeping and was spending time altering his drawings to conceal the innovations he had made.

After seeing and discussing his recent work, David's parents realized their son needed professional help. Several appointments later he was diagnosed with paranoid schizophrenia and given a prescription for clozapine. David's psychiatrist encouraged him to schedule monthly appointments and to return to school to finish his architecture degree. David remained on the medication for several months and was showing signs of improvement, but he believed the medication dampened his creativity and made it difficult to draw. His paranoia quickly returned when he discontinued the medication, forcing him to leave school altogether. During our initial visit, David's enthusiasm for architecture was easy to draw out—so too was his paranoia of members of the department at the university who were conspiring to steal his creations. It was not at all unusual for David to hear voices threatening him if he did not reveal his work. On numerous occasions, one familiar voice threatened, "We know where you live, David."

While David could respond sensibly to questions about his past, when discussing his future plans, he would lapse into an incoherent speech where sentences were only loosely connected. His thoughts also seemed to shift unpredictably, making it difficult to follow. If one did not know of his medical condition, he or she might be easily convinced of his architectural genius during a rant about building design.

Of all of the psychological disorders, schizophrenia may be the most serious and debilitating. It typically emerges in early adulthood, and although there may be periods of remission, schizophrenia is a chronic lifelong illness for most patients. The lifetime prevalence of schizophrenia worldwide is about 1 percent (1 in every 100 individuals during their lifetime), but it may be higher in some ethnic groups than others. For instance, there appears to be a greater incidence among African Caribbeans living in England compared to any other group. Schizophrenia also is known to run in families. Sons and daughters of schizophrenic parents have a tenfold risk of developing the disease. And although the concordance rates among monozygotic twins are significantly greater than those of dizygotic twins, there is no consensus on which gene or genes are involved. Schizophrenia does appear to have a strong genetic contribution, but environmental factors seem to play an even greater role in its etiology.

Schizophrenia is a complex collection of diseases that affect all aspects of human functioning. It causes disturbances in affect, cognitive functions, speech and language, perception, and even movement. However, the most distinctive (and diagnostic) features of schizophrenia are the presence of psychotic delusions and hallucinations.

This chapter discusses psychotic disorders, with an emphasis on schizophrenia. The chapter will examine its diagnostic criteria, its pathology, and the pharmacological approaches to its treatment. Other psychotic disorders, including schizoaffective disorder, delusional disorder, and schizophreniform disorder, are not discussed separately here because their pathology and treatment do not differ significantly from that of schizophrenia.

DEFINING AND DIAGNOSING SCHIZOPHRENIA

The DSM-IV-TR diagnostic criteria for schizophrenia require that two or more of the following symptoms be present for a significant portion of the time during the one month preceding its diagnosis.

1. *Delusions*. Delusions are strongly held beliefs that are clearly contradictory to external evidence. They often consist of misinterpretations of perceptions and everyday experiences. The most common theme in schizophrenia seems to be delusions of persecution where the individual feels as if he or she is being watched, followed, or ridiculed behind his or her back. Another common theme is delusions of reference that may include a person feeling as though other people's comments, song lyrics, comments made by television personalities, news reports, or passages from books are purposely directed at the person. Delusions also may be bizarre in that they are clearly impossible and not understandable by others who share the same religious and cultural experiences. For example, an example of a bizarre delusion is that someone inhabits the body of another individual or that parts of a person's body have been exchanged with those of another person. Sometimes bizarre delusions include themes of control, where a person's thoughts or behaviors are being manipulated by others, even aliens.

2. *Hallucinations*. Hallucinations are perceptual experiences that are not consistent with or that happen in the absence of external stimuli. Schizophrenic hallucinations may occur in any sensory modality (visual, olfactory, auditory, gustatory, or tactile), but auditory hallucinations occur most frequently. The most common theme for auditory hallucinations is familiar voices that are critical and judgmental. For example, upon passing a woman on the sidewalk, a patient may hear, "You raped her" or "You hurt that woman." Voices from God, the devil, or any other supreme being also can occur, but they are less frequent. Rarely do schizophrenic patients act on commands from auditory hallucinations. Magnetic imaging studies conducted while patients are experiencing auditory hallucinations suggest that they represent misattributed subvocal speech because they activate the same auditory structures as when speaking, not structures associated with hearing speech (Plaze et al., 2006).

3. *Disorganized speech*. Often the speech of a schizophrenic is so disorganized, fragmented, and incoherent it can be difficult to converse with them. Switching topics frequently, providing excessive detailed elaboration, and discussing grandiose ideas are common. This author spent four hours on a flight from Washington, D.C., to Portland listening to a schizophrenic describe the origins of matter and the universe. Frequently, he made up words to describe strange forces that have yet to be identified. Challenges to his theory only fueled his conviction and led to even greater fabrication. Occasionally, speech can be so disjointed that it is referred to as *word salad.* In

these cases, individual words are clearly spoken, but there is no coherent sentence structure or meaning to utterances.

4. *Disorganized or catatonic behavior.* The ability of schizophrenic patients to conduct normal activities also can be severely disrupted. Goal-directed behavior is often thwarted by distractions and changes in plan. Maintaining appropriate hygiene, dress, and manners in social settings also may deteriorate over time. In extreme examples, motor stereotypes and catatonia begin to emerge. Catatonia is a state of waxy flexibility where posture can be molded into or held in uncomfortable positions for extended periods of time.

5. *Negative symptoms.* Schizophrenic symptoms often are described as *positive* (excessive or distorted) or *negative* (in absence or deficit). The symptoms described in the preceding examples are **positive symptoms** because they represent exaggerations or distortions of behavior. Examples of **negative symptoms** include a flat or muted expression, lack of speech, avolition, and long periods of nonreactive immobility. A preponderance of negative symptoms tends to occur in later stages of the disease and may be associated with greater neural damage. Typically, the prognosis of patients displaying predominantly negative symptoms is not good.

Prior to the discovery of antipsychotic drugs in the 1950s, the majority of schizophrenic patients were housed in mental institutions and had few treatment options. Physical restraint was used for severely agitated patients, as was the administration of insulin to dramatically lower blood glucose levels and induce a state of **insulin shock**—a comatose state that was maintained for about an hour. **Electric shock therapy** (electroconvulsive therapy, or ECT) is still used to treat drug-resistant depression, but it is rarely used on schizophrenic patients except those who do not respond to drug treatment or who need immediate managment. Originally, the rationale behind electroconvulsive shock therapy was that seizures were never observed during acute schizophrenic states. Therefore, the induction of a seizure might prevent the occurrence of psychosis. None of these treatments affected the course of schizophrenia, and all were essentially replaced as pharmacotherapy gained prominence in the late 1950s.

The most widely used surgical procedure was a **frontal lobotomy,** which was introduced as a treatment in the late 1930s by the Portuguese physician Antônio Moniz. Moniz received the Nobel Prize in 1949 for refining this procedure at a time when there were no treatment options for severe schizophrenia. The lobotomy (or leucotomy) procedure involved separating the prefrontal areas from the remainder of the frontal cortex by knife cuts or by destroying these areas with ice picks inserted behind the eyes. About 40,000 lobotomies are believed to have been performed in the United States before it was banned in all states. The last lobotomies performed in the United States were conducted in the late 1980s.

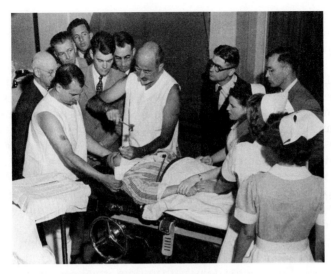

Dr. Walter Freeman performing a prefrontal lobotomy in the United States.   © Bettmann/CORBIS

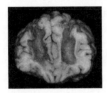

Brain section revealing the damaged frontal lobes after lobotomy.   © Erin A. Hazlett, Ph.D.

Pathology of Schizophrenia: Dopamine Hypothesis

The **dopamine hypothesis** of schizophrenia can be traced back to early research on the effects of antipsychotic drugs on animals (Carlsson & Lindqvist, 1963; Randrup & Munkvad, 1965) and to the discovery of the mechanism of action of the first effective antipsychotic drugs (van Rossum, 1966). This hypothesis proposes that schizophrenia is caused by excessive dopamine activity in the striatum and mesolimbic pathways and perhaps a decrease in dopaminergic activity in the prefrontal cortex. A number of observations provided early support for this hypothesis, including evidence that dopamine agonists such as cocaine and amphetamine induced psychotic symptoms. Large doses or prolonged use of these drugs can cause positive psychotic symptoms that appear indistinguishable from schizophrenic symptoms—a state referred to as amphetamine psychosis. In addition, the psychoses induced by amphetamine, methamphetamine, or cocaine are treated with traditional antipsychotic medication that block dopamine D_2 receptors. Finally, a number of postmortem studies revealed that psychotic patients had increased numbers of D_2 receptors, which may have contributed to hyperactive dopamine activity in the striatum and mesolimbic areas. However, not all studies have found increased numbers of D_2 receptors, particularly studies involving patients who have had schizophrenia for long periods of time.

Perhaps the most compelling support for the dopamine hypothesis comes from **amphetamine challenge** and **receptor competition** studies. Amphetamine challenge estimates dopamine release by scanning for radioactive markers of dopamine receptor occupancy following the administration of amphetamine. Amphetamine increases synaptic dopamine by blocking dopamine reuptake and vesicular transporters. When compared to matched controls, schizophrenic patients exhibit significantly greater dopamine release following amphetamine administration (Abi-Dargham et al., 2000; Laurelle, 1998). Schizophrenic patients also show greater D_2 receptor density than do normal control subjects. Both of these findings are consistent with the dopamine hypothesis. In addition, the only predictor of a drug's **antipsychotic** efficacy is its ability to block dopamine receptors. The ability of a drug to compete with dopamine for D_2 receptors is measured by its capacity to displace a radioactive dopamine ligand. Clinically effective doses of antipsychotic drugs are highly correlated with their ability to compete for and block D_2 receptors, as shown in Figure 5.1 (Seeman et al., 1998). Similar correlations are not observed for other receptors types even though additional neurotransmitters (e.g., serotonin) have been implicated in schizophrenia.

According to the dopamine hypothesis, the positive symptoms of the disease are associated with hyperdopamine activity in the striatum and the mesolimbic system, while negative symptoms and cognitive impairment result from hypodopominergic activity in mesocortical pathways to the prefrontal cortex. There appears to be a reciprocal relationship between mesocortical and mesolimbic dopaminergic activity such that hypodopaminergic functioning in the prefrontal cortex may lead to disinhibition of and therefore increased mesolimbic dopamine activity (Abi-Dargham et al., 2003; Joyce, 2003). Evidence from neuroimaging studies also suggests that schizophrenia is associated with hypoactive prefrontal cortices. There is a marked reduction in frontal lobe activity in schizophrenic patients when compared to normal controls. This reduction in activity seen in Figure 5.2 is believed to be associated with hypodopaminergic activity in these regions.

BEYOND THE DOPAMINE HYPOTHESIS: NMDA AND GABA DYSFUNCTION   While the dopamine hypothesis continues to be the most prominent theoretical explanation for schizophrenia, there is evidence that GABAergic and glutaminergic systems are involved. This evidence comes from two observations. First, the drugs phenylcyclidine and ketamine, both glutamate NMDA receptor antagonists, produce effects that mimic schizophrenia, including hallucinations, delusions, thought

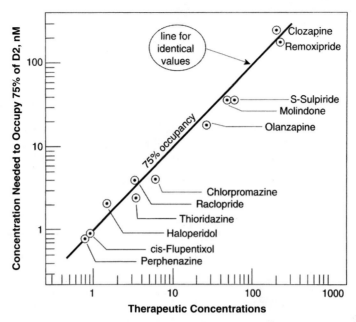

FIGURE 5.1 Drug concentration required to compete for D_2 receptors as a function of clinically effective dose. An antipsychotic's therapeutic dose is nearly identical to its concentration needed to occupy 75 percent of D_2 receptors. Drugs lower along the diagonal line bind more tightly than dopamine on D_2 receptors, while those higher along the line bind more loosely than dopamine. From Seeman et al., 1998. © Seeman et al. (1998). Antipsychotic drugs which elicit little or no parkinsonism bind more loosely than dopamine to brain D2 receptors, yet occupy high levels of these receptors. *Molecular Psychiatry*, 3(2), 123–134. Reprinted by permission from Macmillan Publishers Ltd.

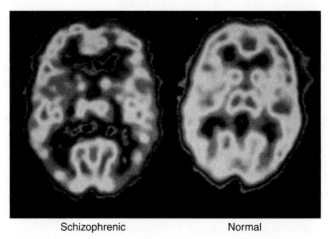

Schizophrenic   Normal

FIGURE 5.2 PET images of schizophrenic brain (left) and normal brain (right). The frontal lobes are at the top of each image. These images reveal decreases in frontal lobe activity in schizophrenics (top of each image) as well as enlarged ventricles. Lighter regions indicate more cortical activity. © Buschbaum, M. & Hazlett, E.A. (1998). Three-Dimensional Analysis With MRI and PET of the Size, Shape, and Function of the Thalamus in the Schizophrenia Spectrum.

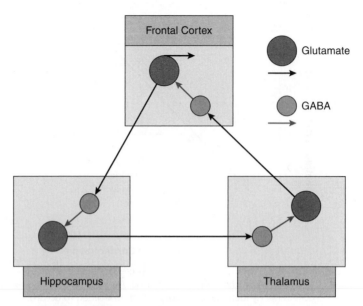

FIGURE 5.3 A simplified model for glutamate excitotoxicity. Hypoactive glutamate in the thalamus leads to decreased GABA inhibitory control over glutamate in the frontal cortex. Glutamate excitotoxicity causes damage to neurons receiving glutamate in the frontal cortex and to GABA neurons in the hippocampus. © After Stone et al., (2007). Routine Upstream Initiation vs. Deferred Selective Use of Glycoprotein IIb/IIIa Inhibitors in Acute Coronary Syndromes. *JAMA*. 2007; 297:591–602.

disorders, and (perhaps most interesting) negative symptoms. Repeated administration of these NMDA antagonists also produces structural changes that resemble those observed in schizophrenia. It has been proposed that the psychotic symptoms and neural degeneration seen following phenylcyclidine and ketamine administration result from a disruption of glutaminergic innervation of GABA neurons in the thalamus and basal forebrain. The effect of NMDA receptor blockade, as shown in Figure 5.3, would be disinhibition of GABA and an increase in cortical glutamate and acetylcholine activity. Neural degeneration (and the negative symptoms of schizophrenia) may result from cortical glutamate excitotoxicity (Olney et al., 1999; Stone et al., 2007). Excitotoxicity is a process whereby neurons are destroyed when glutamate neurons become depolarized for long durations. Prolonged depolarization leads to an excessive influx of Ca^{++}, which activates several cell-damaging enzymes.

Second, schizophrenic patients have depressed numbers of NMDA receptors in the thalamus and the hippocampus. It is presumed that glutamate dysfunction in these subcortical regions leads to excitotoxic glutamate activity in the cortex and the development of negative symptoms in later stages of schizophrenia. The next sections will review several antipsychotic drugs that may be utilized during early stages of schizophrenia to diminish cortical and hippocampal excitotoxicity and to prevent the development of negative symptoms of schizophrenia.

In summary, the dopamine hypothesis has received considerable support since its inception approximately 40 years ago. Evidence from the pharmacodynamics of antipsychotic drugs, amphetamine-induced psychosis, amphetamine challenge, and receptor competition studies are consistent with this hypothesis as an account for the positive symptoms of schizophrenia. Glutamate dysfunction arising from subcortical regions may lead to excitotoxic effects of elevated cortical and hippocampal glutamate neurons and contribute to the development of negative symptoms often observed during later stages of the disease. The following sections discuss the evolution of drug therapy for schizophrenia and other psychotic disorders.

Pharmacological Treatment of Schizophrenia and Psychotic Disorders

PHENOTHIAZINES   It was estimated that by the 1950s, over one-half million patients were hospitalized for schizophrenia in mental institutions in the United States. These patients had few nonsurgical treatment options and typically remained in these institutions for much of their adult lives. The serendipitous discovery of the antipsychotic effects of a class of drugs called phenothiazines in the mid 1950s literally changed the lives of most schizophrenic patients. The phenothiazine chlorpromazine (Thorazine) was originally used as an **antiemetic** (antinausea) agent, but it was quickly observed to have remarkable sedative properties. Chlorpromazine was used to sedate patients with severe burns or trauma as well as to sedate agitated patients prior to surgery. Its first use to treat psychotic patients may have occurred in France in 1952 when 38 patients were treated with daily injections (Turner, 2007). Chlorpromazine appeared to relieve the symptoms of psychosis in these patients without producing heavy sedation. Within a few years of its approval for treating psychosis, the number of hospitalized patients in the United States was reduced by at least half. Chlorpromazine is credited with liberating hundreds of thousands of patients from the harsh and often cruel conditions of mental institutions, but it also may have contributed to the simultaneous increase in the homeless population wandering the streets of bigger cities. Patients often discontinued the use of their medication as they developed troubling and often serious side effects. Once they discontinued medication, most of these patients found themselves unable to function outside an institution. Many of these schizophrenic patients were unmonitored and simply faded into the streets.

The mechanisms of action of chlorpromazine were not understood when it was first approved by the FDA in 1954. In fact, it was alleged to have predominantly sedative and antihistamine properties. It was becoming clear, however, that its antipsychotic effects were not related to its sedative effects. In other words, patients were not merely sedated out of their psychotic symptoms. Since the discovery of the antipsychotic effects of chlorpromazine, a number of other phenothiazines were introduced. All phenothiazines have similar mechanisms of action, but differ to some extent in their side effect profiles.

Mechanisms of Phenothiazine Action The antipsychotic effects of the phenothiazines are mediated by their antagonism of D_2 receptors, although they do have partial affinity for other dopamine receptor subtypes. Phenothiazines compete effectively with dopamine at these sites, thereby decreasing dopamine neural transmission. It is estimated that the phenothiazine dose required to obtain a therapeutic effect must be sufficient to occupy between 70 and 80 percent of D_2 receptors (Seeman et al., 1998). D_2 receptors are found postsynaptically and as presynaptic autoreceptors in the basal ganglia, mesolimbic system, hippocampus, and amygdala as well as throughout the cortex. The initial response to phenothiazine treatment is an increase in dopamine synthesis and release because of autoreceptor antagonism. Chronic blockade of the inhibitory D_2 autoreceptors leads to upregulation and a greater sensitivity to the inhibitory effects of the autoreceptors on dopamine synthesis and release. The time course of these neuronal adaptations corresponds with the lag time to the onset of their antipsychotic effects.

The phenothiazines also block norepinephrine α_1 and α_2 receptors, acetylcholine muscarinic receptors, and histamine H_1 receptors to different extents. In addition, many of the undesirable side effects of the phenothiazines are mediated by these receptors.

Side Effects of Phenothiazines The side effects of phenothiazines vary depending on the extent of receptor involvement. Blockade of norepinephrine α_1 and α_2 receptors results in hypotension, tachycardia, and sedation. Blocking muscarinic receptors causes dry mouth and eyes, dilated pupils, blurred vision, decreased sweating, and memory impairment. Competing with histamine at H_1 receptors contributes to its sedative effects.

The phenothiazines also cause serious and often debilitating motor effects by blocking D_2 receptors in the basal ganglia. These symptoms, referred to as **extrapyramidal symptoms,** resemble the motor impairments seen in Parkinson's disease. Extrapyramidal suggests that these symptoms are caused by disruptions to neurons outside the major pyramidal tracks descending from the medulla. Long-term treatment with phenothiazines can lead to a more serious motor disorder called **tardive dyskinesia.** Dyskinesia refers to involuntary movements and motor tics, often of the mouth and tongue; tardive, meaning slow or delayed, comes from the observation that these dyskinesias often continue long after the drug has been discontinued. Unfortunately, there is no treatment for tardive dyskinesia other than terminating the use of antipsychotic medication, and even then these disorders may persist. Because of the serious motor disorders caused by long-term treatment with phenothiazines, other drugs have been developed in attempt to minimize these effects. However, given that both antipsychotic and extrapyramidal effects are mediated by D_2 receptors, these efforts have, for the most part, been frustrated.

Nonphenothiazine Antipsychotics

Haloperidol (Haldol) was the first nonphenothiazine used for the treatment of psychotic disorders. Although introduced as an antipsychotic in the late 1960s, it was not approved for this use by the FDA until 1988. The pharmacodynamics of haloperidol are essentially identical to those of the phenothiazines even though the drugs are not structurally related. Haloperidol competes for and blocks D_2 receptors as effectively as most phenothiazines, which means it is an effective antipsychotic, but it also produces the severe extrapyramidal side effects mediated by its effects on D_2 receptors in the basal ganglia described previously. Haloperidol's effects on norepinephrine α_1 and α_2 and acetylcholine muscarinic receptors contribute to its autonomic effects, including blurred vision, dizziness, dry mouth and eyes, constipation, and hypotension. Haloperidol has less affinity for histamine H_1 receptors, so sedation is not as problematic as with the phenothiazines.

Several other nonphenothiazines were developed as alternatives to the phenothiazines and to haloperidol in the 1970s, including loxapine, molindone, and pimozide. These drugs are not discussed in detail here as their mechanisms of antipsychotic action are essentially the same as that of haloperidol except that loxapine also competes for and antagonizes serotonin 5-HT$_2$ receptors. Whether this contributes to its antipsychotic effects is unknown. Because their side effect profiles also are similar to those of the phenothiazines and haloperidol, these nonphenothiazines have remained relatively obscure.

New Generation (Atypical) Antipsychotics

The 1990s were celebrated as the *decade of the brain* because of rapid advances in the neurosciences and psychopharmacology. During this decade, a number of novel drugs were developed to treat psychotic disorders without causing serious extrapyramidal side effects. The mechanisms of action of these newer drugs also differed from their predecessors; for this reason, they are referred to as **atypical antipsychotics.** The first atypical antipsychotic introduced in 1990 was clozapine. This was quickly followed by the introduction of several others, which are listed in Table 5.1. All of the atypical antipsychotics differ somewhat in their mechanisms of action, but most antagonize dopamine D_2 and serotonin 5-HT$_{2A}$ receptors to varying extents. The following discussion will examine several atypical drugs in some detail. Table 5.1 includes several of the most common antipsychotic drugs.

CLOZAPINE (CLOZARIL)   Clozapine was the first antipsychotic that appeared to improve the symptoms of schizophrenia without causing severe extrapyramidal (Parkinsonian-like) effects. In addition, clozapine is effective in many patients who do not respond to phenothiazines. It is known to alleviate the negative symptoms and cognitive deficits that are often observed in schizophrenia.

TABLE 5.1 Three Major Classifications of Antipsychotic Drugs

Drug Name	Trade Name	Half-Life	Receptor Effects
Phenothiazines			
Chlorpromazine	Thorazine	8–33 hours	D_2 antagonism
Fluphenazine	Prolixin	15 hours	D_2 antagonism
Mesoridazine	Serentil	2–9 hours	D_2 antagonism
Perphenazine	Trilafon	9 hours	D_2 antagonism
Prochlorperazine	Compazine	4–6 hours	D_2 antagonism
Thioridazine	Mellaril	7–13 hours	D_2 antagonism
Trifluoperazine	Stelazine	12 hours	D_2 antagonism
Triflupromazine	Vesprin	5 hours	D_2 antagonism
Nonphenothiazines			
Haloperidol	Haldol	12–38 hours	D_2 antagonism
Loxapine	Loxitane	4 hours	D_2, 5-HT_2 antagonism
Molindone	Moban	1.5 hours	D_2 antagonism
Pimozide	Orap	55 hours	D_2 antagonism
New Generation (Atypical)			
Amisulpride	Solian	12 hours	D_2 antagonism
Aripiprazole	Abilify	75 hours	D_2, 5-HT_2 antagonism
Clozapine	Clozaril	5–16 hours	D_2, 5-HT_2 antagonism
Olanzapine	Zeprexa	21–54 hours	D_2, 5-HT_2 antagonism
Quetiapine	Seroquel	6–7 hours	D_2, 5-HT_2 antagonism
Risperidone	Risperdal	20–24 hours	D_2, 5-HT_2 antagonism
Ziprasidone	Geodon	6–7 hours	D_2, 5-HT_2 antagonism, 5-HT_{1A} agonist

Pharmacodynamics of Clozapine All antipsychotic drugs differ in their affinities for dopamine receptors, but specifically D_2 receptors. Drugs that bind more competitively than dopamine are not displaced when dopamine is present, while drugs that bind more loosely can be displaced by available dopamine. Furthermore, all drugs that bind tightly are associated with a greater incidence of extrapyramidal side effects compared to drugs that are less competitive. It appears that when drugs bind tightly to D_2 receptors, they disrupt dopamine transmission in the basal ganglia, causing these side effects. Drugs that are less competitive than dopamine in the basal ganglia cause far less disruption to dopamine neurotransmission and cause fewer motor side effects. Because relatively less dopamine is present in the mesolimbic system when compared to the basal ganglia, drugs that bind weakly to D_2 receptors can effectively antagonize dopamine in these structures and induce their antipsychotic effects (Seeman et al., 1998; Seeman et al., 2006).

Clozapine competes weakly with dopamine receptors even though it occupies 75–80 percent of D_2 receptors, at least transiently—a level comparable to the phenothiazines and haloperidol and illustrated in Figure 5.1. Therefore, clozapine can be an effective antipsychotic without causing extrapyramidal side effects (Seeman et al., 1998). In addition to antagonizing D_2 receptors, clozapine also antagonizes serotonin $5\text{-}HT_{2A}$ receptors. How antagonism at these receptors mediates its antipsychotic effects, if it does at all, remains unclear. What is known, however, is that dopamine neurons originating in the ventral tegmental area are regulated by excitatory serotonergic activity. Antagonizing these excitatory influences decreases downstream release of dopamine in the nucleus accumbens (Broderick, 1992). In addition to weak competition with dopamine at dopamine receptors, clozapine also may contribute to decreased dopamine release, thereby enhancing its dopamine antagonistic effects.

Side Effects Associated with Clozapine   Although clozapine remains one of the most widely prescribed antipsychotics, it is not without significant side effects, one of which can be fatal. Clozapine produces considerable sedation in a large proportion of patients. This effect is most likely the result of high occupancy of histamine receptors. In addition, dizziness, hypotension, high heart rate, dry mouth and eyes, and constipation are common. These effects are common with phenothiazines and haliperdol as well and are mediated by activity at noradrenergic α_1 and α_2, acetylcholine muscarinic, and histamine H_1 receptors. Clozapine also is associated with an increased risk of hyperglycemia and diabetes.

The most serious, but rare, side effect of clozapine is a condition known as agranulocytosis, which is a life-threatening deficiency of white blood cells. Agranulocytosis occurs in approximately 0.8 percent of patients taking clozapine. It may be caused by an intermediate metabolite of clozapine that causes excessive oxidative stress to white blood cells (Fehsel et al., 2005). Careful monitoring of white cell counts during the first year of treatment is an effective way to detect this condition early enough to avoid serious consequences to immune system function.

RISPERIDONE (RISPERDAL)   Risperidone was approved by the FDA in 1993 for the treatment of schizophrenia and more recently in 2007 for the treatment of schizophrenia and bipolar disorders in children and adolescents aged 10–18. It also has been approved to treat autism and disruptive behaviors in children. It has been used off label (non-FDA-approved uses) to treat depression, obsessive compulsive disorder, eating disorders, and anxiety disorders.

Pharmacodynamics of Resperidone   Resperidone, as with clozapine, competitively blocks both dopamine D_2 and serotonin $5\text{-}HT_{2A}$ receptors. In addition, it competes with noradrenergic α_1 and α_2 receptors. At relatively low therapeutic doses, resperidone competes weakly with dopamine and has a low risk of extraprymidal side effects. However, at higher therapeutic doses, resperidone

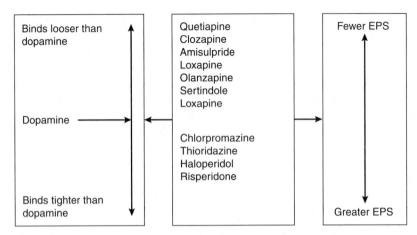

FIGURE 5.4 Antipsychotic drugs that bind more tightly to dopamine D_2 receptors tend to produce more severe extrapyramidal side effects (EPS) than do drugs that bind more loosely and for shorter durations. © Seeman et al. (1998, 2002) Antipsychotic drugs which elicit little or no parkinsonism bind more loosely than dopamine to brain D2 receptors, yet occupy high levels of these receptors. *Molecular Psychiatry*, 3(2), 123–134. Reprinted by permission from Macmillan Publishers Ltd.

binds tightly with D_2 receptors and can cause Parkinsonian motor symptoms (thus, its low position in Figure 5.4). For this reason, resperidone may be a first choice for treatment at lower doses or may be used in combination with clozapine for treatment-resistant patients.

In addition to extrapyramidal side effects, resperidone can cause dizziness, sedation, headache, hypotension, and high heart rate, which are mediated by its noradrenergic effects. Other side effects include weight gain, hyperglycemia, and an increased risk of diabetes. The mechanisms responsible for these later effects remain unknown.

AMISULPRIDE (SOLIAN)   While not yet approved by the FDA, amisulpride has been used in Europe and Australia to treat schizophrenia. Amisulpride has been shown to be as effective as other atypical antipsychotics (e.g., clozapine and olanzapine); it is not associated with hyperglycemia and other metabolic side effects, as are the other atypical drugs. In addition, compared to other atypical agents, amisulpride has been shown to be more effective in treating depression associated with psychotic symptoms (Kim et al., 2007; Vanelle et al., 2006).

Pharmacodynamics of Amisulpride   Amisulpride is discussed here because its mechanisms of action are unusual when compared to other atypical antipsychotics. Amisulpride is a potent blocker of both D_2 and D_3 receptors, but in low doses, it appears to act preferentially on presynaptic autoreceptors. Unlike other atypical antipsychotics, it does not block serotonin 5-HT_{2A} receptors. Blockade of D_2 autoreceptors causes an increase in dopamine synthesis and release in these neurons. Consequently, its antidepressant effects are believed to be mediated by increased dopamine activity, similar to bupropion (Wellbutrin). At low doses, Amisulpride is more effective than other antipsychotic drugs are in alleviating negative symptoms (Olié et al., 2006). Amisulpride binds relatively weakly with dopamine receptors in the basal ganglia; therefore, it produces fewer extrapyramidal side effects than do traditional antipsychotics (Seeman, 2002). In addition to fewer and less severe extrapyramidal side effects, amisulpride causes less weight gain, which is problematic with all other atypical antipsychotics.

Because amisulpride is as effective as other atypical antipsychotic drugs without antagonizing serotonin $5\text{-}HT_{2A}$ receptors, the role of serotonin in atypical antipsychotics remains allusive. In animal and human studies, no clear relationship has been shown between a drug's affinity for serotonin $5\text{-}HT_{2A}$ receptors and extrapyramidal symptoms. In fact, resperidone has a high affinity for serotonin $5\text{-}HT_{2A}$ receptors and is known to produce these symptoms (Nyberg et al., 1999). The most predictive feature of an antipsychotic's propensity to cause extrapyramidal symptoms is how tightly it competes for D_2 receptors (shown in Figure 5.4) in the basal ganglia (Kapur et al., 2000; Seeman et al., 1998; Seeman, 2002), not for its affinity for serotonergic or cholinergic receptors.

GLUTAMATE AND GLYCINE AGONISTS A large number of studies show that schizophrenic patients have depressed numbers of NMDA receptors in the thalamus and hippocampus. It is alleged that glutamate dysfunction in these subcortical regions leads to excitotoxic glutamate activity in the cortex and to the development of negative symptoms in later stages of schizophrenia. Therefore, drugs that enhance glutamate activity might be more effective in alleviating negative symptoms and cognitive impairment than dopamine antagonists by themselves (Javitt et al., 2004).

There are several ways to increase glutaminergic NMDA activity. One way is to directly increase NMDA activity with glutamate agonists. Although a number of these agonists are available for research, in general, increasing glutamate activity is likely to increase the rate of glutamate excitotoxicity by activating other glutamate receptors. Therefore, research has focused on specific NMDA receptor agonists and on glycine, which modulates glutamate effects on NMDA receptors. Both of these pharmacological approaches are being investigated as potential treatments to improve negative symptoms, with mixed results. In a review of recent research, Tuominen et al. (2006) reported that the NMDA receptor agonist D-cycloserine seemed ineffective in treating negative symptoms, but the glycine receptor agonists glycine and D-serine were just marginally effective. These conclusions were confirmed in the large Cognitive and Negative Symptoms in Schizophreniatrial recently sponsored by the NIH. In this trial, neither glycine nor D-cycloserine was consistently more effective than a placebo in improving negative symptoms in the 157 patients studied (Buchanan et al., 2007).

How Are the Effects of Antipsychotic Drugs Measured?

ANIMAL RESEARCH   In animal studies, several models of psychosis have been utilized to investigate the effectiveness of antipsychotic drugs. One of the earliest animal models, **amphetamine-induced psychosis,** was based on the observations of psychotic behavior in amphetamine users. The most prominent symptoms are those that mimic paranoid schizophrenia, which are typically treated in emergency rooms by administering phenothiazines. In animal studies, rats or mice are given repeated doses of amphetamine, which causes an increase in the incidence of stereotyped behaviors (repetitive motor movements). At high doses, catatonic states (a waxy flexibility) can be observed where animals will hold unusual postures for extended periods of time. Both of these behaviors are easily observed and measured in experimental animals. Drugs suspected of having antipsychotic properties can be administered to animals in amphetamine psychosis to test for their effects. All known antipsychotic drugs somewhat alleviate amphetamine-induced psychosis in laboratory animals.

Another animal model, referred to as **prepulse inhibition (PPI),** also is based on abnormalities in the reactions of schizophrenic patients. In this case, however, psychotic patients do not appear to filter extraneous stimuli as do normal subjects. This may reflect a deficit in sensorimotor gating, which is considered to be the brain's ability to close the gate on irrelevant sensory information. In a PPI experiment, a subject is presented with a warning stimulus (a prepulse, typically a loud sound) for several milliseconds before being presented with a more intense stimulus (the pulse). Presentation of the prepulse inhibits the startle response to the pulse in normal subjects, as shown in Figure 5.5. In animal studies, prepulse inhibition can be disrupted by drugs that agonize dopamine, such as amphetamine and cocaine. Disruptions in PPI are reversible with antipsychotic medication, making this a useful animal model for drug investigation.

HUMAN RESEARCH   Measuring the effects of antipsychotic medication in human experiments is typically done with clinical evaluation scales. For example, the Clinical Global Improvement (CGI) scale requires clinicians to rate the changes they observe from a baseline phase to a treatment follow-up stage in three categories: severity of illness, global improvement, and efficacy. A clinician rates each of these indices to obtain a total CGI score. Average CGI scores for different groups of treated patients are then compared to determine relative effectiveness of different treatment protocols. To avoid biases in both patient responses and clinician ratings, these studies are often conducted in a double-blind manner where neither the patient nor the clinician knows which medication (or placebo) a patient has received. A number of other scales, including the Positive and Negative Syndrome Scale (PANSS) for schizophrenia and the Brief Psychiatric Rating Scale (BPRS), are used in a similar manner. Each of these evaluation scales require clinicians to rate the severity of positive and negative symptoms as well as

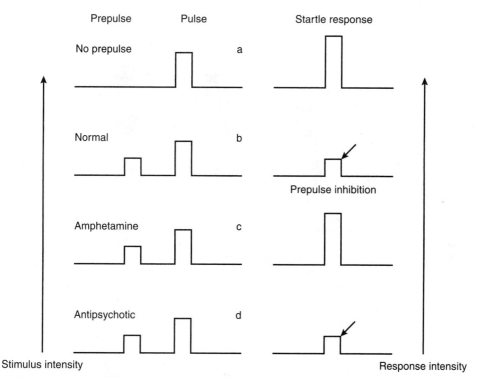

FIGURE 5.5   PPI. When normal subjects or animals are presented with a prepulse that predicts the pulse stimulus, the startle response is inhibited (b). Dopamine agonists such as amphetamine disrupt PPI, resulting in a larger startle response (c). Antipsychotic medication reinstates PPI (d).

side effects before and after treatment. Often researchers employ several of these evaluation scales as well as personal observations in their assessment of drug effectiveness.

Although most clinical research utilizes evaluation scales to rate changes in schizophrenic behavior, some studies are beginning to employ more objective measures, including startle responses and sensorimotor gating measured by the PPI test mentioned previously. In several recent studies involving schizophrenic patients, PPI deficits were found to be correlated with symptom severity. That is, patients with more severe symptoms or greater cognitive deficits also had greater deficits in sensorimotor gating (Hazlett et al., 2007; Swerdlow et al., 2006). Other studies are using PPI to compare the effectiveness of antipsychotic medication in schizophrenic patients (e.g., Kumari et al., 2002, 2007; Wynn et al., 2007). In many of these studies, atypical antipsychotics seem to be more effective than the phenothiazines or haloperidol in reinstating PPI. Figure 5.6 shows the results of a carefully conducted study that compared subjects who were taking phenothiazine

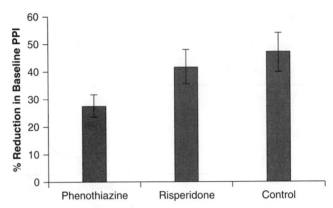

FIGURE 5.6 Comparison of the effects of risperidone and phenothiazine antipsychotic medication on PPI in schizophrenic patients. The bars represent the percentage reduction in eyeblink startle responses over baseline. Larger PPI values represents greater PPI. Risperidone restores PPI to levels observed in healthy control subjects. © Kumari et al. (2002). Prepulse inhibition of the startle response in risperidone-treated patients: comparison with typical antipsychotics. Reprinted from Schizophrenia Research, 44(1–2), 139–146 with permission from Elsevier.

antipsychotics (e.g., chlorpromazine) with subjects who were matched for age, duration of illness, and rating scores for the severity of negative symptoms and who were taking risperidone. The treated groups also were compared to an age-matched group of healthy control subjects. In this study, risperidone (an atypical antipsychotic) was more effective than phenothiazine treatment in restoring PPI to near-normal values. Researchers speculate that PPI restoration is a good predictor of cognitive improvements and decreases in the severity of negative symptoms and might therefore be a valuable test of the effectiveness of newly developed antipsychotic drugs.

How Effective Is Pharmacological Treatment

There is little doubt that the majority of schizophrenic patients improve with medication, particularly with the newer generation antipsychotics (or combinations of them) that have minimized the serious motor side effects and the sedation caused by the older phenothiazines. Nevertheless, a significant proportion of these patients do not receive additional psychological counseling and psychosocial intervention as recommended in the *Practice Guideline for the Treatment of Patients with Schizophrenia* 2nd edition, published by the American Psychiatric Association in 2004. Schizophrenia is a chronic, degenerative brain disease that, at present, can be managed only by the careful selection of medication and psychosocial training. While there is no cure for schizophrenia, early detection and pharmacological treatment may slow or even suspend its progression in many patients.

Drug therapy does not work for all schizophrenic patients, however. Estimates of the proportion of patients who will respond to pharmacological treatment vary from 60–85 percent depending on the drugs that were prescribed initially, the duration of illness, and the use of additional medication after an initial nonresponse to treatment. Eventually, 75–85 percent of schizophrenic patients do respond to medication, at least partially.

Few viable alternatives to drug treatment for schizophrenia are currently available. Patients who do not respond to pharmacological treatment or who need immediate intervention may respond to ECT alone or in combination with antipsychotic medication. ECT remains controversial, but it has been demonstrated to be effective, at least for the short term, for refractory or nonresponding patients (Braga et al., 2005).

CHAPTER

6

Attention and Developmental Disorders
Attention-Deficit Hyperactivity Disorder and Pervasive Developmental Disorders

The attention and developmental disorders cover a wide range of conditions that typically emerge during early childhood and in many cases continue throughout adolescence and adulthood. These disorders include attention-deficit hyperactivity disorder (ADHD) and the pervasive developmental disorders (PDD). They are discussed in this chapter because many of their symptoms are managed with medication. A number of other psychological disorders discussed in this text (including depression, anxiety, and schizophrenia) may appear during childhood, but they are not generally classified as attention or developmental disorders. Other developmental disorders, including mental retardation, learning disorders, and motor disorders, are not discussed in this text.

ATTENTION-DEFICIT HYPERACTIVITY DISORDER (ADHD)

Attention-deficit hyperactivity disorders (ADHDs) are characterized by a pervasive inability to attend to tasks and often are associated with disruptive and excessive motor activity and impulsivity. Children with ADHD have difficulty maintaining attention, following instructions, and completing tasks. Often they begin one task only to be quickly distracted by another task, making it difficult to complete or follow through on anything. Approximately 8 percent of the child population between the ages of 4 and 17 is diagnosed with ADHD at any given time. Attention disorders affect over 4.5 million children, of whom a substantial proportion (over 2.5 million) takes medication to alleviate symptoms. Attention disorders are typically first observed in young children as they begin to develop independent locomotion. However, a diagnosis of ADHD usually occurs in elementary school, where its symptoms begin to interfere with normal functioning. In many cases, ADHD symptoms dissipate in late adolescence or early adulthood. However, in as many as 50 percent of all cases, symptoms of inattentiveness may persist well into adulthood. Adulthood ADHD frequently co-occurs with other behavioral disorders, including depression, anxiety, conduct disorder, drug abuse, and/or antisocial behavior. Attention disorders also may co-occur with other developmental disorders (e.g., autism and Asperger's disorder). This chapter focuses on ADHD but includes the diagnostic criteria and pharmacological treatment of these developmental disorders as well.

Josh's parents suspected that their child was hyperactive when he was first learning to walk at age 2. Compared to other children his age, Josh was in constant motion and was little deterred by his numerous falls and altercations with furniture. Like other children, he liked toys, but rarely spent time with any particular one before moving on to the next. It was as if he were attempting to grab and relocate a toy rather than play with it. Josh was easily irritated with other children and rarely played with them. In first grade, Josh had difficulty attending to reading materials presented by his teacher and he appeared easily frustrated by the experience. He was passed on to second grade without knowing how to read, with the assumption that he was merely "slow." At home, Josh was becoming increasingly demanding of his parents' attention. He could not entertain himself, and he needed constant supervision to complete his schoolwork. And even though he was beginning to read in second grade, he would not do it on his own. Josh displayed behavioral problems and learning difficulties throughout elementary school. He ignored the demands of his teachers and behaved aggressively toward other students. His parents assumed that he was acting out his frustration and insecurity based on his family having relocated three times during these years.

The diagnosis of ADHD occurred midway through seventh grade when Josh's teacher recommended a psychological evaluation. His school psychologist referred him to a psychiatrist who, after a 20-minute visit, diagnosed him with ADHD and prescribed Ritalin. Josh has been on and off ADHD medication since then. Now in high school, Josh finds little relief from medication. It contributed significantly to insomnia, which only seemed to exacerbate his inattentiveness and ability to concentrate. Josh now worries whether he will earn good enough grades to attend college. He acts out his frustration with poor performance; he remains disorganized both at home and school, is easily distracted, and has few friends.

Based on the *Diagnostic and Statistical Manual of Mental Disorders*, Text Revision (DSM-IV-TR), for a diagnosis of an attention disorder to be made, symptoms of *inattention* or *hyperactivity-impulsivity* must be present for a period of at least six months prior to the diagnosis.

A. At least six of the following symptoms of *inattention* have been present to a point that they are disruptive and inappropriate for the child's developmental level:
   1. Often does not give close attention to details or makes careless mistakes in schoolwork, work, or other activities.
   2. Often has trouble maintaining attention on tasks or play activities.
   3. Often does not seem to listen when spoken to directly.
   4. Often does not follow instructions and fails to finish schoolwork, chores, or duties in the workplace (not due to oppositional behavior or failure to understand instructions).
   5. Often has trouble organizing activities.
   6. Often avoids, dislikes, or does not want to do things that take a lot of mental effort for a long period of time (such as schoolwork and homework).
   7. Often loses things needed for tasks and activities (e.g., toys, school assignments, pencils, books, or tools).
   8. Is often easily distracted.
   9. Is often forgetful in daily activities.
B. At least six of the following symptoms of *hyperactivity-impulsivity* have been present to an extent that they are disruptive and inappropriate for the child's developmental level:
   1. Often fidgets with hands or feet or squirms in seat.
   2. Often gets up from seat when remaining in seat is expected.
   3. Often runs about or climbs when and where it is not appropriate. (Adolescents and adults may feel very restless.)
   4. Often has trouble playing or enjoying leisure activities quietly.
   5. Is often "on the go" or often acts as if "driven by a motor."
   6. Often talks excessively.
   7. Often blurts out answers before questions have been finished.
   8. Often has trouble waiting one's turn.
   9. Often interrupts or intrudes on others (e.g., butts into conversations or games).
   10. Presence before age 7 of some symptoms that cause impairment.
   11. Presence of some impairment in two or more settings (e.g., at school/work and at home).
   12. Clear evidence of significant impairment in social, school, or work functioning.

Pathology of ADHD

While causes of ADHD remain elusive, there appears to be a consistent pattern of cortical **hypoarousal** and an increase in **theta activity** in ADHD patients when compared to normal children and adolescents. Electroencephalagraph

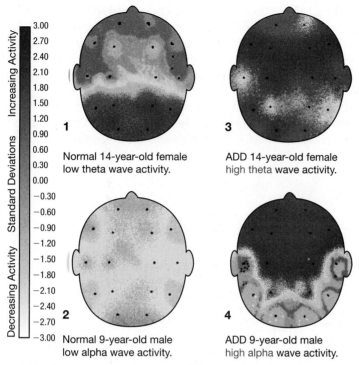

FIGURE 6.1 Quantitative EEG (Q-EEG) patterns from normal children and children affected by ADHD. Excessive slow wave activity (alpha and theta activity) is characteristic of ADHD. Higher theta (3) and alpha (4) activity are indicated by darker grey. © Reproduced with permission from Jay Gunkelman.

(EEG) studies, such as the one shown in Figure 6.1, typically find a higher theta/**beta activity** ratio among ADHD subjects than in normal subjects. This is consistent with cortical hypoarousal, particularly in the frontal and cingulate cortices (Dickstein et al., 2006; Rowe et al., 2005; Snyder et al., 2006; Zang et al., 2007). Cortical hypoarousal would account for poor attentiveness and concentration.

Imaging studies (fMRI) also find decreases in thalamic sensory activity, suggesting abnormalities in **reticular activating system.** Decreases in cholinergic input to the **sensory thalamus** and to the **thalamic reticular nucleus (TRN)** may contribute to cortical hypoarousal and an EEG pattern that is uncharacteristic of the normal beta pattern that is predominant during wakefulness (see Figure 6.2). Corticothalamic projections from the frontal cortex back to the TRN are believed to underlie **attentional regulation** (Zikopoulos et al., 2007) and may be hypoactive in ADHD. These findings may account for the difficulties ADHD patients have in attending to objects or tasks for extended periods of time. Stimuli or tasks that would normally arouse the cortex via the thalamocortical pathway are apparently inhibited by the TRN. During normal wakefulness, cholinergic input to the TRN disinhibits the **attentional gate,** allowing for cortical arousal. In ADHD, the attentional gate is essentially closed and the cortex remains under aroused (see Figure 6.2).

Research also indicates that children with ADHD may express delayed cortical maturation when compared to age-matched controls. In a large study conducted at the National Institute of Mental Health (NIMH), researchers using magnetic

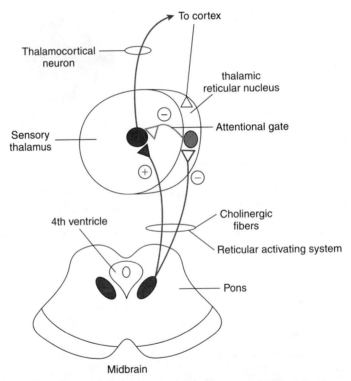

FIGURE 6.2 Cholinergic neurons originating in the pons project to both the sensory thalamus and the TRN. During normal wakefulness, projections to the sensory thalamus facilitate thalamocortical activity, while projections to the TRN disinhibit the inhibitory influence the TRN has over the sensory thalamus (inhibition of inhibition = facilitation). The effect is to open the attentional gate, allowing sensory input to reach and arouse the cortex. In ADHD, the reticular activating system is hypoactive, resulting in the inhibition of the sensory thalamus. Therefore, projections from the thalamus to the cortex are inhibited, contributing to cortical hypoarousal and a more synchronized EEG pattern characterized by abnormal theta activity.

resonance imaging compared cortical thickness in 223 children with ADHD to 223 normal controls. While these groups showed similar developmental patterns in their primary sensory cortices, there were significant differences in cortical thickness in remaining cerebral areas. These differences were most pronounced in the prefrontal regions (Shaw et al., 2007). What is presently unknown is whether delayed cortical maturation is a result of cortical hypoarousal or the cause of it.

Stimulant drugs appear to normalize cortical activity by increasing beta activity and decreasing slower wave alpha and theta activity in the frontal cortices (Loo et al., 2004; Pliszka, 2007; Song et al., 2005). These effects are most evident in ADHD subjects who respond well to stimulant medication. Stimulant drugs act directly on catecholamine pathways in the frontal and cingulate cortices by facilitating ascending cholinergic activity to the thalamus.

Decreased activity in the brain's arousal systems and their targets in cortical areas often appear contradictory to the hyperactive and impulsive symptoms observed with ADHD. That is, how could an individual with hyperactivity be underaroused? While it has been suggested that cortical hypoarousal is causally related to inattention and distractibility, hyperactivity and impulsivity, on the other hand, may be patients' attempts to increase neural arousal by engaging in ADHD-typical behaviors including self-stimulation and attention seeking (Antrop et al., 2000; White, 1999). The excessive appearance of these behaviors typifies ADHD.

DOPAMINE DEFICIT THEORY OF ADHD   The **dopamine-deficit theory** of ADHD proposes that depressed dopamine (DA) activity in the caudate nucleus and frontal cortices may contribute to cortical hypoarousal. Research from a variety of studies provides evidence for an increased expression of the dopamine transporter (DAT) in ADHD patients (Swanson et al., 2007; Volkow et al., 2007). Specifically, studies using radioactive ligands for the DAT have found increased DAT numbers in the caudate nucleus of ADHD patients when compared to matched control subjects. However, as illustrated in Figure 6.3, these differences were not observed in the putamen (Spencer et al., 2007). The **dopamine transporter (DAT)** plays a key role in regulating DA activity throughout the brain by determining synaptic DA availability. An increase in DAT expression in the caudate nucleus and frontal cortices is believed to diminish DA availability and receptor activity in ADHD. Depressed DA activity is presumed to contribute to cortical hypoarousal and inattention.

MEASURING ADHD SEVERITY AND IMPROVEMENT   Like other psychological disorders, ADHD cannot be objectively measured; so clinicians and researchers need to rely on psychological evaluation to determine its severity and the effectiveness of treatments. It is important that students and researchers alike understand how this research is conducted so they can better evaluate treatment effectiveness.

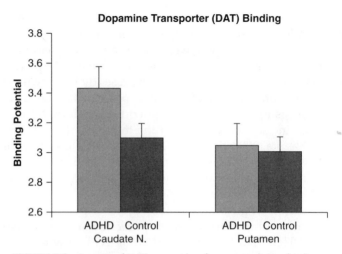

FIGURE 6.3 Increased DAT expression (means and standard errors) in the caudate nucleus but not in the putamen in 21 ADHD patients compared to 26 matched control subjects. Data derived from Spencer et al., 2007.

Perhaps one of the most widely used assessment scales for measuring treatment outcomes for ADHD is the Connor's Global Index (CGI) scale. The Connor's scale comes in several different forms, including assessments to be used by parents and teachers. A subscale of the Global Index (CGI-ADHD) is typically used to assess changes in ADHD specifically and is based on the DSM-IV-TR diagnostic criteria. Like psychological evaluations discussed in previous chapters, the CGI requires raters to judge the severity or frequency of an assortment of symptoms and behaviors. Figure 6.4 shows a representative comparison

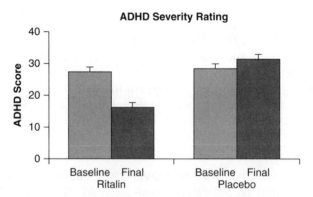

FIGURE 6.4 The effects of Ritalin versus placebo on Connor's ADHD rating scores (means and standard errors). From a pretreatment baseline to the final treatment at 14 days, Ritalin reduced symptom severity significantly. Scores worsened slightly for the placebo group. Data summarized from Biederman et al., 2003.

of treatment outcomes as measured by the Connor's ADHD subscale. In this study, 128 patients aged 6–14 years participated. These subjects were randomly assigned to receive Ritalin or a placebo for two weeks. Baseline ADHD scores were assessed by the Connor's ADHD scale before treatment commenced and again after the final treatment at 14 days. In this comparison, Ritalin reduced symptom severity significantly while the placebo had no discernable effect. Other psychological assessment scales used to evaluate ADHD tend to reveal similar results.

A more objective assessment involves fMRI or EEG to measure changes in cortical activity following treatment. However, the costs and limited availability of these methods often restrict their use to smaller research studies at major research institutions.

Pharmacological Treatment of ADHD

AMPHETAMINES AND METHYLPHENIDATE   In 1999, the NIMH published its findings from a 14-month study of treatment options for ADHD. A major conclusion from this study was that treatments that included stimulant medication were far superior to intensive behavioral treatment or community-based treatment alone. In addition, children treated with medication (alone or in combination with intensive behavioral therapy) showed greater improvements in academic performance and social skills compared to children in the nonmedicated comparison groups. The use of stimulant medication is now considered to be vital to an effective treatment program, even in young children. Concerns about the potential risks of stimulant abuse and increases in substance abuse appear to be unwarranted. In fact, drug abuse risk appears to decrease among stimulant-treated ADHD patients compared to their nontreated cohorts (Faraone et al., 2007). Because an increase in substance abuse risk is associated with ADHD, these findings are particularly noteworthy because they reveal that stimulant medication may protect against later drug abuse.

Amphetamines have been used for the treatment of ADHD since the early 1930s. These stimulant drugs include dextroamphetamine (Dexedrine), dextro/levoamphetamine (Adderall), and the most recently approved amphetamine for ADHD lisdexamfetamine (Vyvanse). The dextroamphetamine isomer is the main compound and active ingredient in Adderall and Vyvanse, which contain other amphetamine structural isomers.

Methylphenidate (Ritalin) and dexmethylphenidate (Focalin) are other stimulant drugs whose effects are virtually indistinguishable from those of the amphetamines. Daytrana, a methylphenidate, is available only as a skin patch to provide slower extended release as well as to reduce abuse potential. Research comparing the effectiveness of amphetamines and methylphenidates reveals little difference in their effectiveness and side effect profiles. Both classes of drugs are available in rapid- and extended-release formulations. At the time of this writing, methylphenidate and other amphetamine compounds accounted for over 90 percent of the prescription medication used to treat ADHD.

Mechanisms of Amphetamine and Methylphenidate Action Amphetamines (including methamphetamine to be discussed later) may have some of the most complex and wide-ranging synaptic effects of any psychoactive drug (see Figure 6.5). They increase synaptic concentrations of norepinephrine (NE) and

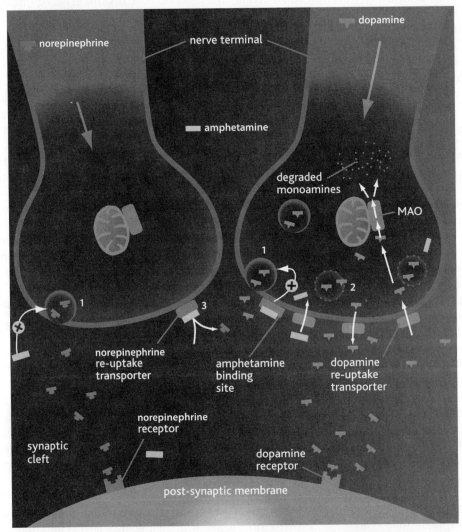

FIGURE 6.5 Amphetamines (including methamphetamine) increase the availability of DA in several distinct ways: (1) by binding to the presynaptic membrane of dopaminergic and noradrenergic neurons, thereby increasing the release of NE and DA from synaptic vesicles; (2) by causing the transporters for DA to act in reverse, transporting vesicular DA back into the terminal and transporting this "free" DA into the synaptic cleft; and (3) by blocking the reuptake transporter for NE. © CNSforum.com.

DA through several distinct mechanisms. First, amphetamines block **reuptake transporters** for NE and increase the amount of NE released into the synapse. Both of these effects contribute to enhanced NE activity in the brain and peripheral nervous system.

Amphetamines also contribute to increased DA activity through several different mechanisms. Amphetamines bind to the vesicular transporter and cause DA to be released from its storage vesicles into the cytoplasm of the terminal button. This "free" DA is then transported to the synaptic cleft by amphetamine-induced reversal of the DAT. Amphetamines also increase the amount of DA released from synaptic vesicles during neuronal signaling. These combined mechanisms significantly enhance extracellular concentrations of DA.

The mechanisms by which amphetamines contribute to cortical arousal in ADHD appear to be complex as well. DA contributes to cortical arousal via the mesocortical pathway originating in the nucleus accumbens (see Figure 6.6). Increased NE activity contributes to cortical arousal via the reticular activating

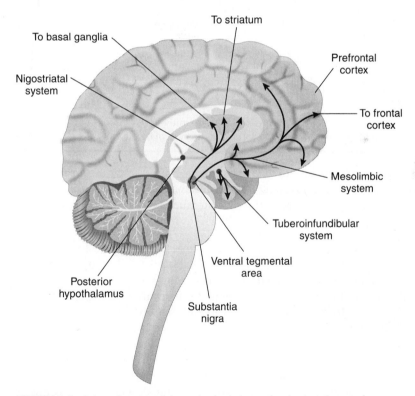

FIGURE 6.6   DA pathways originate in the substantia nigra and ventral tegmental area of the pons. The nigrostriatal system innervates the basal ganglia, and the mesolimbic-cortical system projects to the nucleus accumbens and to the frontal cortex.   © CNSforum.com.

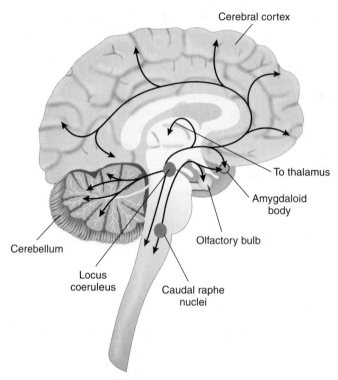

FIGURE 6.7 NE pathways originate in the locus coeruleus and project along the reticular activating system to the frontal cortex. © CNSforum.com.

system originating in the **locus coeruleus** (see Figure 6.7). The relative contributions of these systems to ADHD remains unknown. However, as discussed previously, depressed DA activity in the caudate nucleus and the prefrontal cortices are presumed to play important roles in ADHD symptoms. Amphetamines may act to increase and stabilize this activity.

Side Effects of Amphetamine and Methylphenidate   While amphetamines remain the treatment of choice for ADHD and narcolepsy, they are not without significant side effects. The most noticeable effects are insomnia, nervousness, irritability, weight loss, and dizziness. Because amphetamines enhance noradrenergic activity peripherally as well as centrally, they also may cause hypertension, tachycardia, and cardiac arrhythmias. In excessive doses or overdoses, amphetamines are known to induce psychotic states, seizures, and cardiac failure. While these effects may seem extreme, the most common side effects with prescribed doses are well managed by dosing early in the day and by using slower release formulations or transdermal patches.

In 2003–2005, several studies were released suggesting that methylphenidate (Ritalin) might be associated with an increase in cancer (El-Zein et al., 2005).

However, larger follow-up studies conducted in Germany found no such association (Walitza et al., 2007). Methylphenidate also was implicated in delayed growth in children, but researchers investigating this alleged side effect monitored 229 children for two years and found no evidence for delayed growth or maturation (Wilens et al., 2005). Methylphenidate continues to be the most widely prescribed drug for ADHD, but because of the stigma associated with stimulant use and its alleged potential for abuse, physicians and parents are seeking alternatives.

Alternatives to Amphetamine and Methylphenidate for ADHD   Several effective alternatives to amphetamines are now available for treating ADHD, including atomoxetine (Strattera) and modafinil (Provigil). While both of these drugs are promoted as nonstimulants, they resemble the amphetamines in that they block reuptake transporters for NE and DA and promote wakefulness and increases in activity (Madras et al., 2006). Specifically, modafinil appears to increase NE and DA activity in the brainstem and forebrain areas that regulate sleep and promote wakefulness (Wisor et al., 2005). Recent research suggests that modafinil may activate hypothalamic centers that regulate sleep-wake cycles by inducing orexin release (Kim et al., 2007; Rao et al., 2007). Orexin is an excitatory neuromodulator that regulates the activity of catecholamine brainstem nuclei involved in arousal. Modafinil appears to promote alertness by increasing histamine release in the **tuberomammillary nucleus** of the hypothalamus. Histamine activity in the hypothalamus is known to regulate sleep and wakefulness by activating hypothalamic nuclei involved in arousal. Increasing histamine activity contributes to wakefulness, while histamine blockade causes drowsiness and sedation. The potent sleep-promoting effect of antihistamines is well known.

Modafinil is approved for narcolepsy and excessive sleepiness associated with sleep apnea and shift work sleep disruptions. Its off-label use for ADHD is supported by several studies, including comparison studies with methylphenidate. For example, Amiri et al. (2008) found modafinil to be as effective as methylphenidate in reducing ADHD symptoms, with modafinil having fewer side effects. Subjects taking modafinil reported better appetites and fewer sleep difficulties than subjects taking methylphenidate. Other side effects associated with modafinil included headache, nervousness, agitation, dry mouth, and hypertension—all similar to the side effects of amphetamines and methylphenidate.

Atomoxetine is a catecholamine agonist that selectively blocks reuptake transporters for NE. It also may indirectly increase DA activity in the frontal cortex. Originally developed as an antidepressant, atomoxetine was tested for efficacy in ADHD patients because of its effects on NE transporters. A number of studies have found atomoxetine to be as effective as methylphenidate; well-designed studies have shown it to be more effective than placebos. A meta-analysis of research conducted prior to 2007 also concluded that atomoxetine was effective in treating ADHD (Cheng et al., 2007). While atomoxetine is promoted as a nonstimulant, its agonizing effects on NE activity, as well as its side effect profile, resemble those of

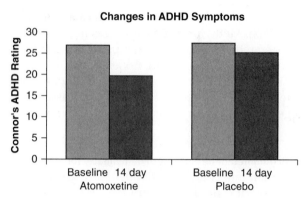

FIGURE 6.8 Comparison of atomoxetine and placebo treatment on Connor's ADHD evaluation scores. Atomoxetine significantly reduced ADHD symptoms relative to placebo controls. Data from Spencer et al., 2002.

amphetamine and methylphenidate. Its most notable side effects include gastrointestinal discomfort, decreased appetite, insomnia, agitation, increased heart rate, and hypertension. A comparison of 120 atomoxetine- and 114 placebo-treated patients using the Connor's ADHD rating scale is presented in Figure 6.8. As shown, atomoxetine significantly reduced ADHD symptoms after 14 days of treatment. Several commonly prescribed drugs for ADHD are described in Table 6.1.

TABLE 6.1 Commonly Prescribed Drugs for Treating ADHD. Other Drugs May be Used in Addition to Those Mentioned Here to Address Specific Symptoms that may Occur with ADHD. These Drugs Include Antidepressants; Anxiolytics; and, in Some Cases, Antipsychotics

Drug Name	Trade Name(s)	Mechanisms of Action
Amphetamine	Dexedrine, Adderall, Vyvanse	Increases both NE and DA availability in synapse by multiple mechanisms (see Figure 6.4)
Methylphenidate	Ritalin, Metadate, Concerta, Daytrana	Increases both NE and DA availability in synapse by blocking reuptake transporters
Dexmethylphenidate	Focalin	Increases both NE and DA availability in synapse by blocking reuptake transporters
Atomoxetine	Strattera	Increases NE activity by selectively blocking NE reuptake transporters
Modafinil	Provigil	Increases NE activity in hypothalamus by blocking reuptake transporter; increases orexin release in hypothalamus; increases histamine release in tuberomammillary neurons
Pemoline	Cylert	(discontinued in 2005 because of liver toxicity)

PERVASIVE DEVELOPMENTAL DISORDERS (PDD): AUTISTIC SPECTRUM DISORDERS

Autistic spectrum disorders are most prevalent of all of the **pervasive developmental disorders (PDD).** The autistic spectrum disorders include autistic disorder, Asperger's disorder, and Rett's syndrome (a rare condition that occurs only in females). Autistic and Asperger's disorders are presented as distinct disorders here because they are described with different diagnostic criteria in the DSM-IV-TR. However, considerable debate continues among clinicians and researchers about whether these are distinct conditions with different underlying pathologies or whether they represent an autistic continuum with Asperger's disorder being a less severe and more functional appearance of autism. Because describing Asperger's disorder as a distinct psychological condition is a relatively recent addition to the DSM, prevalence data for it are rather limited. It appears, however, that together PDD may affect as many as 90–110 in every 10,000 children (Kogan et al., 2009). Autism is most common of all of the PDD, with rates approaching 50–70 per 10,000 children and Asperger's disorder affecting as many as 20–30 per 10,000. Both of these disorders occur about four times more frequently in males than in females. The reason for the wide variation in prevalence estimates appears to be related to inconsistencies in survey methods and the use of different diagnostic criteria and whether children with low IQ are included in the estimate.

Autistic disorder was first named in 1943 when Leo Kramer used the term **early infantile autism** to identify a group of 11 children with the condition. At about the same time, Hans Asperger, an Austrian physician, used the term **autistic psychopath** in his description of what is now known as Asperger's disorder. Prior to the use of these modern terms, autistic and Asperger's disorders fell into categories of mental retardation and **infantile schizophrenia.**

The first symptoms of these disorders are most often observed by parents who notice their children's marked lack of responsiveness to others or objects, tendency to withdraw from social interaction, and lack of verbal and nonverbal communication. In many cases, these children engage in repetitive and self-abusive behaviors. While autistic spectrum disorders may co-occur with other developmental disorders, including mental retardation and growth abnormalities, these conditions are not required for a diagnosis.

Autistic Disorder

According to the diagnostic criteria (DSM-IV-TR), the following indicators must be present for a diagnosis of autistic disorder:

1. Qualitative impairment in social interaction, as manifested by *at least two* of the following:
   a. marked impairments in the use of multiple nonverbal behaviors such as eye-to-eye gaze, facial expression, body posture, and gestures to regulate social interaction

    b. failure to develop peer relationships appropriate to developmental level

    c. a lack of spontaneous seeking to share enjoyment, interests, or achievements with other people (e.g., by a lack of showing, bringing, or pointing out objects of interest to other people)

    d. lack of social or emotional reciprocity (e.g., not actively participating in simple social play or games, preferring solitary activities, or involving others in activities only as tools or "mechanical" aids)

2. Qualitative impairments in communication as manifested by at least one of the following:

    a. delay in, or total lack of, the development of spoken language (not accompanied by an attempt to compensate through alternative modes of communication such as gesture or mime)

    b. in individuals with adequate speech, marked impairment in the ability to initiate or sustain a conversation with others

    c. stereotyped and repetitive use of language or idiosyncratic language

    d. lack of varied, spontaneous make-believe play or social imitative play appropriate to developmental level

3. Restricted repetitive and stereotyped patterns of behavior, interests and activities, as manifested by at least one of the following:

    a. encompassing preoccupation with one or more stereotyped and restricted patterns of interest that is abnormal either in intensity or focus

    b. apparently inflexible adherence to specific, nonfunctional routines or rituals

    c. stereotyped and repetitive motor mannerisms (e.g., hand or finger flapping or twisting, or complex whole-body movements)

    d. persistent preoccupation with parts of objects

4. Delays or abnormal functioning in at least one of the following areas, with onset prior to age 3 years:

    1. social interaction

    2. language as used in social communication

    3. symbolic or imaginative play

Jeffery appeared to be perfectly normal until he was about 2½ years old. While other children his age were learning to speak, he was becoming more withdrawn. His parents assumed that he was having hearing problems because he reacted very little to their commands or attempts to engage him verbally. By 3 years of age, Jeffery's behavior was becoming more concerning. He would clutch a toy, showing no interest in others and rarely responding to attempts by his parents to play. Attempts by his brother, who was a year and a half older, to engage in play also were rejected through Jeffery's withdrawal or outbursts of anger. While his older brother could be entertained by television, Jeffery did not even appear to realize that it was on. He could sit for long periods, content to manipulate a moving part on a small toy while rocking back and forth. Abrupt noises or appearances of others would often cause Jeffery to react strongly, as if he were suddenly surprised anyone else was present. Tests of his hearing were conducted with great difficulty and were followed by a referral to a child psychiatrist. Jeffery was determined to have normal hearing, but he was diagnosed with autistic disorder at the age of 4.

Jeffery displays several characteristic abnormalities of autistic disorder. He shows a total lack of verbal communication, a deficit in emotionality, no ability to interact or connect with his peers, and stereotypy in his motor movements. The prognosis for Jeffery is poor, as he will likely present abnormalities in language usage and emotionality for much of his life. Treatment will include various attempts at behavior modification to teach him personal hygiene and minimal social skills. Medication for his agitation and bouts of depression also will be used. As Jeffery enters his teenage years, he will become increasingly aware of his condition and realize just how different he is from other children his age. The painful recognition that he is socially awkward as well as his developing sexuality will likely lead to a deterioration of his condition. Outbursts of aggression will increase to express his growing frustration and to combat the hurtful comments and gestures made by his classmates.

Asperger's Disorder

The past few years have seen a fairly dramatic rise in the number of Asperger diagnoses. Whether this increase represents a real increase in the prevalence of Asperger's disorder or the diagnostic criteria have become clearer is unknown. However, considerable debate exists about whether Asperger's disorder represents a clinically distinct PDD or whether it is on the high-functioning end of a continuum of autistic disorders. The DSM-IV-TR diagnostic criteria for Asperger's disorder are essentially identical to those for autistic disorder without the severe impairments in speech development.

A. Qualitative impairment in social interaction, as manifested by at least two of the following:
   1. marked impairment in the use of multiple nonverbal behaviors such as eye-to-eye gaze, facial expression, body postures, and gestures to regulate social interaction
   2. failure to develop peer relationships appropriate to developmental level
   3. a lack of spontaneous seeking to share enjoyment, interests or achievements with other people (e.g., by a lack of showing, bringing, or pointing out objects of interest to other people)

       4. lack of social or emotional reciprocity (e.g., not actively participating in simple social play or games, preferring solitary activities, or involving others in activities only as tools or "mechanical" aids)

  B. Restricted repetitive and stereotyped patterns of behavior, interests, and activities, as manifested by <u>at least one </u>of the following:

      1. encompassing preoccupation with one or more stereotyped and restricted patterns of interest that is abnormal either in intensity or focus

      2. apparently inflexible adherence to specific, nonfunctional routines or rituals

      3. stereotyped and repetitive motor mannerisms (e.g., hand or finger flapping or twisting, or complex whole-body movements)

      4. persistent preoccupation with parts of objects

  C. The disturbance causes clinically significant impairment in social, occupational, or other important areas of functioning.

  D. There is no clinically significant general delay in language (e.g., single words used by age 2 years, communicative phrases used by age 3 years).

  E. There is no clinically significant delay in cognitive development or in the development of age-appropriate self-help skills, adaptive behavior (other than social interaction), and curiosity about the environment in childhood.

CJ's mother first recognized problems with her 8-month-old son after an automobile accident in which he bruised his head. At about this time, he became increasingly withdrawn and isolated. He would sit for long periods watching his hands as he used them to make elaborate repetitive movements in front of his eyes. CJ also became more emotionally distant. He reacted very little to attempts by his parents to engage him, and he rarely made eye contact with anyone. CJ began to speak in single words before his second birthday and appeared fascinated by some words, repeating them over and over whenever he used them. For example, when his father left for work, he would say "bye-bye," then continue to repeat this word for 10–15 minutes after his father left the house. Throughout this recitation, he appeared completely distracted and did not display any emotion to his father's leaving. CJ appeared normal in his ability to learn and to use language. His vocabulary was far larger than any other child in his kindergarten, and he learned to read almost spontaneously. By first grade, he was reading third- and fourth-grade material easily, but apparently without much comprehension. He also learned numbers easily and would continue to draw them with perfection until he filled an entire page. If disrupted from this task, he would scream in protest. CJ's experiences in elementary school were not unlike most of his peers. He had difficulty socializing and preferred to be left alone with his drawing numbers and symbols.

His problems of socialization have been confounded by his inability to understand the implications of his unthoughtful actions on others. If someone has something CJ wants, he simply takes it; if a person is speaking, CJ interrupts. Furthermore, he appears unaware of another's personal space. He has been reprimanded on several occasions for inappropriately touching another person.

Because CJ is above normal intelligence and has no difficulty learning, he will likely lead a productive life, but one that is socially unfulfilling. Like Jeffery who was diagnosed with autism, in later school years, CJ will begin to recognize how different he is from others. And like Jeffery, as CJ's sexuality emerges in his teenage years, he will most likely be frustrated by his social incompetence and lack of friends. In addition, the teasing he now receives in fourth grade will likely be no comparison to what he will receive as he gets older. CJ will most likely suffer from depression as an adolescent and adult. If he is like other Asperger's children, he will experience the effects of a range of medication, including Ritalin, Prozac, Depakote, and Clozaril, as doctors desperately attempt to manage his array of symptoms.

PATHOLOGY OF AUTISTIC SPECTRUM DISORDERS While the causes of autistic spectrum disorders remain allusive, some of the most consistent pathological correlates of these disorders may be **cortical underconnectivity** and deficits in both function and volume of the anterior cingulate cortex. The theory of cortical underconnectivity proposes that autism is a result of deficits in **white matter** that makes up the cortical circuits that integrate intrahemispheric connections. These integrative circuits are essential for normal cognitive and social functioning, which require the integration of activity from a variety of cortical structures involved in social, language, problem-solving, and decision-making functions (Barnea-Goraly et al., 2004; McAlonan et al., 2004; Silk et al., 2006). For instance, a number of studies comparing people with autism with normal subjects have reported less connectivity and synchronized activity in left temporal areas involved in language comprehension. Using fMRI, Just et al. (2004) found that people with autism showed less activity in the left inferior frontal gyrus (Broca's area) but more activity in the left posterior superior temporal gyrus (Wernicke's center) while engaged in sentence comprehension tasks (Figure 6.9). For example, subjects were asked to read a sentence displayed on a computer monitor, after which they were asked to respond by identifying the recipient of action.

Example of sentence comprehension task:

The cook thanked the father.
Who was thanked? cook or father

In addition, these authors found that activation between the language areas was less temporally synchronized in the autistic group during comprehension tasks. That is, there was a significant delay in cortical activation during the comprehension

A Autism group

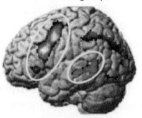

B Control group

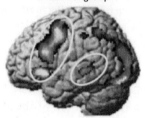

Sentence Comprehension

FIGURE 6.9 Brain activity measured by fMRI in autistic and normal control subjects during a sentence comprehension task. Autistic subjects (top) showed less activity in the left inferior frontal gyrus but more activation in the left superior temporal gyrus (circled areas) than control subjects (bottom). © Just et al., (2007). Function and anatomical cortical underconnectivity in autism: Evidence from an MRI study of an executive function task and corpus callosum morphometry. *Cerebral Cortex*, 17, 951–961.

tasks when compared to nonautistic control subjects. Functional underconnectivity is presumed to account for the wide range of deficits observed in autistic disorders, including language comprehension, judgment, and social cognition that require the integration and temporal synchronization of activity from several cortical areas. Deficits in the development of myelination throughout the corpus callosum and cortex are presumed to underlie autistic disorders.

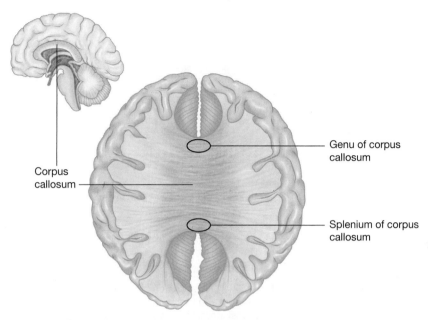

FIGURE 6.10   Horizontal section through the human brain, revealing the corpus callosum. The anterior genu and posterior splenium are significantly smaller in people with autism.   © Rhawn Joseph, Ph.D. Reprinted with permission.

In addition to underconnectivity, autistic disorders also are associated with abnormalities in the corpus callosum, which connects left and right cortical hemispheres. The **corpus callosum** is a band of approximately 200 million interconnecting myelinated axons that unite left and right cortical areas as well as intrahemispheric regions. A number of studies have reported reductions in the size of the corpus callosum in people with autism, particularly in the anterior (genu) and posterior (splenium) regions (see Figure 6.10) (Barnea-Goraly et al., 2004; Hardan et al., 2000; Hughes et al., 2007; Just et al., 2007). It has been proposed that this reduction constrains functional connectivity within and across cortical regions. A moderate correlation between genu area and functional connectivity between frontal and parietal areas supports this hypothesis (see Figure 6.11).

PHARMACOLOGICAL TREATMENT OF AUTISTIC SPECTRUM DISORDERS   Unlike other disorders discussed in this text, autistic disorders are not believed to be a consequence of abnormal synaptic activity or neuronal communication. Therefore, pharmacological intervention is not likely to improve the most prominent

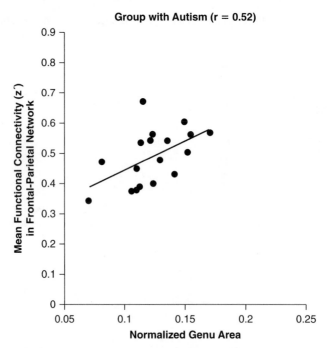

FIGURE 6.11 Moderate positive correlation between the size of genu of the corpus callosum and functional connectivity between frontal and parietal areas. From Just et al., 2007. © Just et al. (2007). Function and anatomical cortical underconnectivity in autism: Evidence from an MRI study of an executive function task and corpus callosum morphometry. Cerebral Cortex, 17, 951–961.

TABLE 6.2 Drugs Used Off-Label to Treat Symptoms Accompanying Autistic Spectrum Disorders

Drug Name	Trade Name	Behavioral Symptoms	Classification
methylphenidate	Ritalin	inattention, hyperactivity	stimulant
lorazepam	Ativan	hyperactivity, anxiety	anxiolytic, hypnotic
diazepam	Valium	hyperactivity, anxiety	anxiolytic, hypnotic
fluoxetine	Prozac	pediatric depression, anxiety, obsessive-compulsive disorder (OCD)	antidepressant
fluvoxamine	Luvox	depression, anxiety, OCD	antidepressant
sertraline	Zoloft	depression, anxiety, OCD	antidepressant
clomipramine	Anafranil	OCD, anxiety, depression	antidepressant
haloperidol	Haldol	psychosis, behavioral agitation, tics	antipsychotic
risperidone	Risperidal	psychosis, behavioral agitation, mania	antipsychotic
olanzapine	Zyprexa	psychosis, behavioral agitation, mania	antipsychotic
carbamazepine	Tegretol	bipolar depression, seizures, mania	antimanic, antiseizure
lamotrigine	Lamictal	bipolar depression, seizures, mania	antimanic, antiseizure
topiramate	Topamax	pediatric seizures, migraine	antiseizure
valproate	Depakote	seizures, migraine	antiseizure

symptoms of autistic disorders. However, autistic spectrum disorders commonly co-occur with symptoms of depression, anxiety, hyperactivity, seizures, and/or severe behavioral agitation. These conditions are often managed with drugs that have been approved for other psychological disorders; therefore, they are used off-label (a non-FDA-approved use) for autistic disorders. A list of commonly prescribed drugs, along with the behavioral symptoms they effectively manage, is presented in Table 6.2. Because all of these drugs are described in some detail in other chapters, their mechanisms of action is not discussed here.

7

The Pharmacology of Opiates and Analgesia

THE OPIATES (OPIUM, MORPHINE, HEROIN, AND CODEINE)

The use of **opium** (Figure 7.1) can be traced back to at least 4500 BC, when early Egyptian images and Sumerian texts depicted its use as medicine and for religious or ritualistic purposes. Its use as a potent analgesic is described in several early medical texts, including the original Egyptian text, the *Papyrus,* written in approximately 1600 BC. The use of unprocessed opium as an analgesic continued throughout the world through much of the 19th century. Opium was largely discontinued only after **morphine,** its main active compound, was isolated in 1805 by the German chemist Wilhelm Sertürner, who named it after Morpheus, the Greek god of dreams. With its isolation and the invention of the hypodermic syringe in the mid-1800s, morphine quickly emerged as a popular and effective analgesic for surgical pain, as a cough suppressant, and as a treatment for fevers and diarrhea. Even 150 years after its commercial introduction, morphine continues to be the most valuable postsurgical analgesic available in spite of efforts to identify even more effective and less addictive compounds. One such attempt resulted in the compound diacetylmorphine, which Bayer pharmaceuticals marketed heavily in 1898 under the brand name **Heroin** (see Figures 7.2 and 7.3)

The availability of opium and heroin in the late 1800s and early 1900s led to a significant increase in opiate addiction worldwide. In 1914, the **Harrison Narcotics Act** was passed as an attempt to begin regulating the manufacture and distribution of opiates and cocaine, which were mischaracterized as narcotics by this legislation. The Harrison Narcotics Act effectively eliminated any legal source for opiates for all nonmedical uses. In fact, in its original interpretation, the act even prohibited prescribing controlled amounts of heroin to patients who were in treatment programs. However, neither the Harrison Narcotic Act nor its successor, the **Controlled Substances Act**, has done much to curtail the illicit importation and distribution of heroin in the United States.

FIGURE 7.1   Pink flowers of the opium poppy *Papaver somniferum*, which is grown mainly in Afghanistan, India, and Mexico. The milky latex sap (opium) extracted from immature seed pods contains morphine and codeine, which can be easily transformed into heroin.   © Jerry Mason/Photo Researchers, Inc.

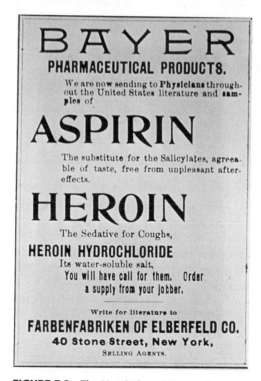

FIGURE 7.2   The Heroin brand name of diacetylmorphine marketed by the German pharmaceutical company Bayer.   © United States Drug Enforcement Agency

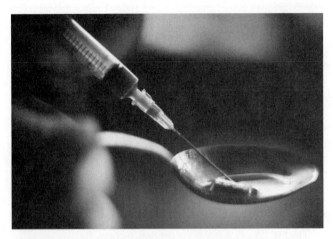

FIGURE 7.3 A small block (about 250 mg) of brown heroin is typically heated in a spoon with citric acid and water until it dissolves. Citric acid is commonly used as a buffering agent to increase heroin's water solubility. The liquid form of heroin can then be injected intravenously. © Everynight Images / Alamy.

Pharmacology of the Opiates

The pharmacologically active compounds in opium are principally morphine, codeine, and the baine alkaloids. **Alkaloids** are nitrogen-containing natural compounds produced by a variety of plants. In fact, most of the psychoactive compounds discussed in this chapter and the next are alkaloids or are derived from them. The relationships between the natural alkaloids of opium are illustrated in Figure 7.4. In addition to natural opiate alkaloids, a number of synthetic opiate compounds have been produced as potent analgesics (see Table 7.1). This text will refer to **opiates** as substances derived from opium and the term **opioid** as analgesics produced synthetically.

Morphine and heroin are typically administered by intravenous injection, while codeine and the synthetic opioids are most often taken orally. Once administered, opiates readily cross the blood-brain barrier and reach all bodily tissues fairly rapidly. The structural modification to heroin (see Figure 7.5) makes it more lipid-soluble, and it reaches the brain within seconds of an injection—a property that gives heroin the ability to produce an intense rush or high. In addition, because morphine and codeine also are water-soluble, only 20–30 percent of the administered dose is available to reach the brain; the rest is rapidly excreted. In the liver, morphine and heroin (heroin is converted to morphine during its metabolism) are metabolized into morphine-6-glucuronide (M6G), which is a potent active metabolite. Both morphine and its metabolite have half-lives of approximately 1–3 hours, so the duration of analgesia produced by morphine is extended significantly.

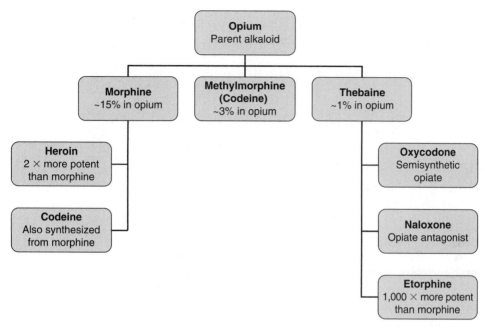

FIGURE 7.4 Relationships between common natural opiate derivatives.

TABLE 7.1 Several Common Natural Opiate and Synthetic Opiate Compounds and their Half-lives

Drug Name	Trade Name	Origin	Half-Life
morphine	Morphine	opium	1–3 hours*
diacetylmorphine	Heroin	opium	10–20 minutes*
methylmorphine	Codeine	opium, morphine	2–3 hours
hydrocodone	Vicodin	codeine	1.5–3 hours
oxycodone	OxyContin, Percocet	thebaine	2–3 hours
methadone	Dolophine	synthetic	15–22 hours
levomethadyl	Orlaam	synthetic	48–72 hours**
buprenorphine	Suboxone	synthetic	36–73 hours
pethidine	Demerol	synthetic	3–4 hours
propoxyphene	Darvon	synthetic	6–12 hours
pentazocine	Talwin	synthetic	2–3 hours
fentanyl	Actiq	synthetic	13–22 hours

*active metabolite

**discontinued in 2003

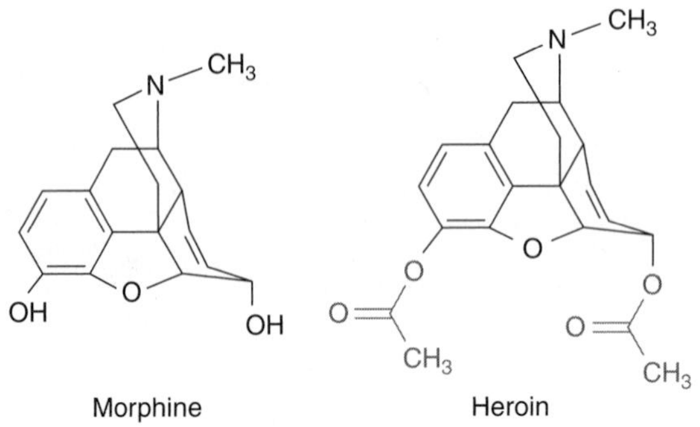

FIGURE 7.5 Molecular structures of morphine and heroin. The two acetyl groups (in grey) increase heroin's lipid solubility and, compared to morphine, allow it to pass through the blood-brain barrier more rapidly.

MECHANISMS OF OPIATE ANALGESIC ACTION The opiates have a complex spectrum of effects on neural activity that include analgesia, euphoria, and respiratory depression. This chapter will examine these mechanisms of action separately. The first topic of discussion will be the neural pathways for pain sensation and analgesia.

Pain sensations arise from several sources, including intense pressure, extremes in hot or cold temperature, inflammation caused by tissue injury or infection, chemical irritation, and assaults or damage to skin or bone tissues. These sources of stimulation activate pain receptors called **nociceptors,** which transduce stimulation into neural activity along pain-transmitting neurons. Pain signals travel along myelinated **Aδ fibers and unmyelinated** C fibers. Myelinated Aδ fibers transmit "fast" pain signals, which are perceived as sharp localized pain, whereas unmeylinated C fibers transmit delayed or slow, dull pain. It is common to experience dull or throbbing pain after the initial sharp piercing pain caused by tissue damage. These distinct perceptions are transmitted and processed along different neurons and pathways to the brain. The perception of pain is highly variable among people and can be affected by psychological states as well as by drugs. For example, many people are familiar with the powerful analgesia caused by an extreme emotion or the excitation that often occurs after an accident. Depression, on the other hand, has long been known to increase the perception of pain.

Nociceptors have their cell bodies in the dorsal root of the spinal cord called the dorsal root ganglia (ganglia for cell bodies). These neurons terminate in the dorsal horn of the spinal cord and release the excitatory neurotransmitter **substance P.** The origin of the name *substance P* is unclear, but it was first isolated in powder form, it is a peptide, and it signals pain messages. Its name could be derived from any or all of these anecdotes. From the dorsal horn, signals ascend via the **spinothalamic pathway** to the thalamus, somatosensory cortex, and

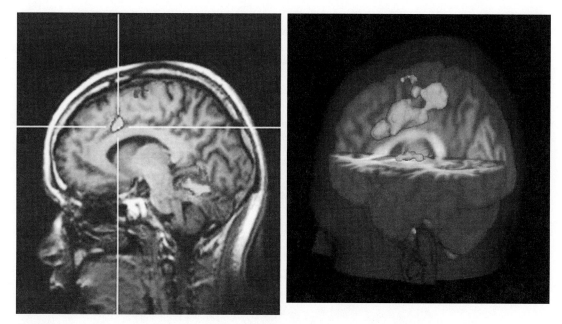

FIGURE 7.6   (a) Pain caused by extreme heat is perceived in the anterior cingulate gyrus as well as the somatosensory cortex.   © Control over brain activation and pain learned by using real-time functional MRI. R. Christopher deCharms, Fumiko Maeda, Gary H. Glover, David Ludlow, John M. Pauly, Deepak Soneji, John D. E. Gabrieli, and Sean C. Mackey. Proceedings of the National Academy of Sciences, December 14, 2005. (b) Pain-induced activation of the thalamus, the somatosensory cortex, and the anterior cingulate cortex.   © Dr. Robert Coghill

anterior cingulate cortex (Figure 7.6). The cingulate cortex is believed to be involved in the feeling, or body representation, of the pain sensation. Damage to the anterior cingulate does not eliminate pain signaling or the reflexive responses to pain, but it does disrupt feelings of pain.

Ascending information from the spinothalamic pathway and information originating in the hypothalamus project to the periaqueductal gray area (PAG) of the pons, where the descending pain pathway originates. The PAG projects to the locus coeruleus and to the raphe nucleus of the medulla. Excitatory adrenergic neurons (yellow) from the locus coeruleus and inhibitory serotonergic neurons (green) from the raphe nucleus converge in the dorsal horn of the spinal cord, where they inhibit the release of substance P (Figure 7.7). In addition, endogenous opiates and their receptors throughout the descending pathway modulate pain signaling. The involvement of endogenous opiates in the spinal cord to modulate pain is as follows:

1. Opiates modulate the activity of serotonergic and noradrenergic neurons in the medulla that project to the dorsal horn.
2. Small interneurons in the dorsal horn release opiates that inhibit the release of substance P (Figure 7.8). These interneurons are activated by descending noradrenergic neurons.

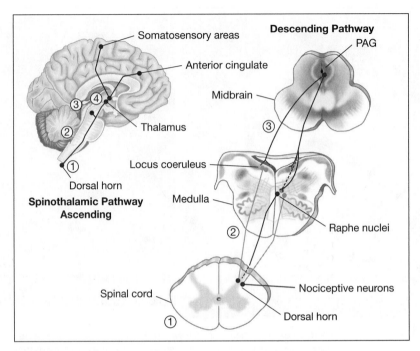

FIGURE 7.7   Ascending (left) and descending (right) pain pathways.
Nociceptive pain neurons carry information from pain and temperature
receptors to the dorsal horn of the spinal cord to the thalamus forming the
spinothalamic pathway (left). The descending pathway (right) begins at the
PAG of the pons (3) and terminates on serotonergic cell bodies in the Raphe
nucli and enkephaline cell bodies in the locus coeruleus in the brain stem (2).
Serotonergic and enkephalin neurons project to the dorsal horn (1), where
they activate inhibitory opiate interneurons. Numerous opiate receptors
are located in the PAG, raphe nucleus, and the dorsal horn of the spinal
cord.   © Schema of the pain inhibitory pathway from Bear, MF, Connors BW,
Paradiso, MA, 2001. *Neuroscience*. Exploring the Brain, 2nd edition. Baltimore
Lippincott, Williams and Wilkins.

In addition to opiate receptors in the brainstem and spinal cord, opiate receptors in the cingulate cortex, thalamus, striatum, nucleus accumbens, and amygdala are involved in modulating pain perception as well as the emotional
components of pain.

OPIATE RECEPTORS AND ENDOGENOUS LIGANDS   The identification and distribution of opiate receptors and their endogenous ligands began in the early 1970s
with the work of Candace Pert and Solomon Snyder, who first identified opiate
receptors using radioactively labeled opiate drugs. Since their discoveries, three
different receptor subtypes (μ, δ, and κ) and their ligands have been identified.

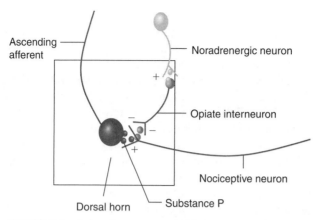

Ascending afferent

Noradrenergic neuron

Opiate interneuron

Nociceptive neuron

Dorsal horn

Substance P

FIGURE 7.8   Opiate interneurons inhibit the release of pain-signaling substance P in the dorsal horn of the spinal cord. (Also see Figure 7.9.)

These receptor subtypes have distinct functions and distributions throughout the brain and spinal cord.

The **μ (mu) receptor** is widely distributed throughout the brain and spinal cord and is presumably the most important of the opiate receptors for pain analgesia. Morphine and related opiates have a high affinity for μ receptors, while **naloxone,** a drug that competes for and blocks these receptors, disrupts drug-induced analgesia. μ receptors also contribute to the regulation of respiration in the ventral medulla. High doses of opiates acting on these receptors can cause **respiratory depression** by inhibiting respiratory responses triggered by carbon dioxide. A second receptor subtype, the **δ (delta) receptor,** is most abundant in the striatum and the nucleus accumbens. The δ receptor is believed to play important roles in analgesia and opiate-induced euphoria and in reinforcement. The third receptor subtype, the **κ (kappa) receptor,** is found predominantly in the amygdala, the hypothalamus, and the pituitary gland. These receptors also are involved in analgesia, but perhaps contribute most importantly to **dysphoria** and thermoregulation. Dysphoria is an emotional state characterized by depression, anxiety, and restlessness—a state opposite that of euphoria. Dysphoria may be caused by κ antagonism of μ receptors. The κ receptor subtype will be discussed in greater detail in later sections about opiate-induced euphoria and dependence.

Endogenous ligands for the opiate receptors were discovered soon after the receptors were described. These ligands were called **endorphins,** after *endo* for endogenous and *orphan* for morphine. The endorphins are a class of opiate peptides produced from the breakdown of larger peptides in the cell's soma. These opiates include two **enkephalin** peptides, leu- and met-enkephalin, and **dynorphin,** which are stored in and released from synaptic vesicles.

All of the opiate receptor subtypes are metabotropic G-coupled receptors that have inhibitory effects on receiving neurons. Several of these inhibitory effects have been described. First, opiate receptors can hypopolarize postsynaptic membranes by increasing K^+ conductance at axoaxonal synapses. As K^+ flows out of the neuron, the membrane becomes hyperpolarized, making it less likely to fire. Opiate synapses in the dorsal horn inhibit the release of substance P in this way (Figures 7.7 and 7.8). Second, opiate activation of presynaptic heteroreceptors decreases the amount of neurotransmitter synthesized and released from these neurons. For example, in the nucleus accumbens, dopamine release is regulated by inhibitory gamma-aminobutyricacid (GABA) heteroreceptors on dopamine-releasing neurons. Opiates bind to heteroreceptors on GABA neurons, thereby inhibiting the release of GABA. Dopamine release is increased by inhibition of inhibition (disinhibition) (see Figure 7.9). The anesthetic and reinforcing effects of opiates appear to result from these and perhaps other inhibitory mechanisms. The euphoric and reinforcing effects of opiates will be discussed later in this chapter.

OPIATE AGONISTS AND ANTAGONISTS   Drugs that bind to opiate receptors can exert a variety of effects depending on their molecular structure. The natural opiates heroin, morphine, and codeine bind to opiate receptors with high affinity and exert the same effects as the endorphins on opiate receptors. That is, they contribute to neural inhibition. Drugs that mimic the effects of endogenous ligands are called **pure agonists.** Several of the synthetic opiates also are pure agonists, including methadone, pethidine (Demerol), and fentanyl (Actiq). Drugs that have a lower affinity for receptors compared to a natural ligand or are selective in their affinity for specific receptor subtypes are called **partial agonist.** Several partial synthetic opiate agonists are available, but they have relatively little clinical significance. Finally, several synthetic opiate drugs exert agonist effects on some receptors and antagonistic effects on others. These drugs are referred to as **mixed agonist-antagonists.** For example, it may be clinically desirable to activate κ receptors for their analgesic effects while inhibiting μ receptors to blunt the euphoric effects of an opiate. Several mixed agonist-antagonist drugs have been synthesized, including pentazocine (Talwin). Partial and mixed agonists are less effective than pure agonists for analgesia. In fact, morphine remains the most effective opiate for postoperative pain even after 50 years of research and drug development.

Drugs also may block or diminish the effects of endogenous opiates or any of the opiate agonists. A **pure antagonist** has a high affinity for receptors, but it does not exert any physiological effect on the receptor or the receiving cell. Antagonists compete with agonists as well as with natural ligands for receptor sites and may even displace an agonist that is occupying a receptor. **Naltrexone** (Revia), the prototype opiate pure antagonist, is often administered to heroin overdose victims in attempts to reverse life-threatening respiratory depression. An intravenous injection of naltrexone can reverse a serious heroin overdose

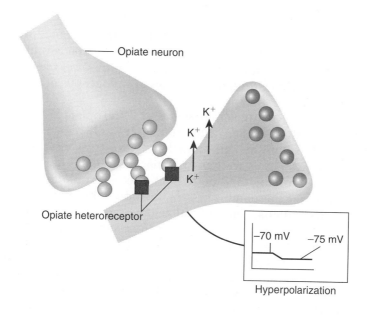

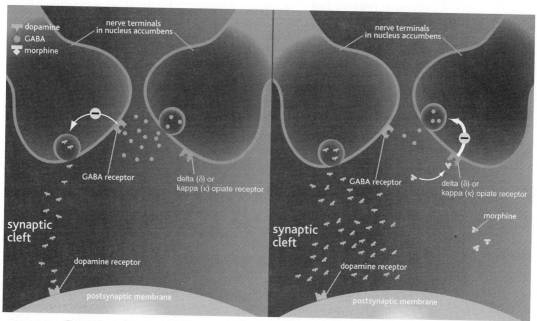

Dopamine release is inhibited.   Dopamine release is disinhibited.

FIGURE 7.9 Opiate receptors cause neural inhibition in two ways: an increase in K⁺ conductance, which results in the cell becoming hyperpolarized (top), and disinhibition of catecholamine neurotransmitter release (bottom).   © CNSforum.com

within minutes. Naloxone (Narcan), also a pure opiate antagonist, is typically used to treat opiate dependence. Although naltrexone or naloxone can be used to augment treatment for opiate dependence, naloxone is preferred because it is longer-acting. In addition to their clinical significance, these opiate antagonists have been useful in elucidating the roles of endogenous opiates in behavior.

MECHANISMS OF OPIATE REINFORCEMENT   The opiate heroin may be one of the most powerfully addictive drugs known. It rapidly enters the brain because of its high lipid solubility and immediately exerts its effects on synapses in the mesolimbic system as well as on synapses throughout the brain and spinal cord. The reinforcing (and addictive) effects of opiates take place in several structures of the mesolimbic system, including the **ventral tegmentum** and the **nucleus accumbens**. The ventral tegmentum of the midbrain is rich with dopaminergic cell bodies that project their axons to several limbic structures, including the nucleus accumbens. Axons from the nucleus accumbens project via the globus pallidus to the dorsal medial nucleus of the thalamus, which then projects to the prefrontal cortex. Most of the neurons that comprise the nucleus accumbens are GABAergic. This area also is rich with dopamine and opiate receptors.

Increases in dopamine activity in the nucleus accumbens mediate the reinforcing effects of opiates and other drugs. As illustrated in Figure 7.9, opiates bind to autoreceptors at GABAergic synapses and exert inhibitory effects on GABA release. This in turn results in decreased GABA inhibition of dopamine release in the nucleus accumbens. Just how increased dopamine activity in the mesolimbic system contributes to reinforcement is less clear. It is speculated, however, that a major function of this pathway is to amplify stimulus salience and to motivate motor activity. From an evolutionary perspective, stimuli associated with palatable foods and sexual behaviors, for example, should become highly valued for their predictive significance. Likewise, these stimuli should excite motor activities that lead to appetitive behaviors. Research from several types of experiments supports this hypothesis. For example, in animals that have been surgically prepared for the recording of electrical activity in mesolimbic structures, increased activity occurs when the animals are given opportunities to eat palatable food or to engage in sexual behavior. Furthermore, similar increases in electrical activity take place in contexts in which these behaviors regularly occur. Therefore, stimuli associated with feeding or engaging in sexual behavior can control dopamine activity in the mesolimbic system. As a result, these activities (and the stimuli associated with them) become highly valued.

Certain drugs, as well as stimuli associated with the onset of drug effects, also become highly valued and therefore reinforcing. Numerous experiments report the powerfully reinforcing effects of opiates on the operant behavior of animals. For example, rats will lever-press at high rates for opiate infusions into the nucleus accumbens or the ventral tegmentum (see Figure 7.10). The reinforcing

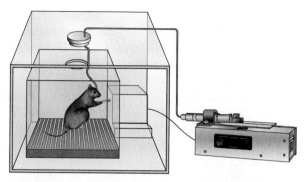

FIGURE 7.10   Laboratory rats fitted with a cannula lever press for opiate reinforcement delivered by an infusion pump into the nucleus accumbens. Response rates for opiate reinforcement typically far exceed those for food or water reinforcement and can be maintained for several hours.

effects of opiates also can be blunted by the administration of naloxone—a powerful opiate antagonist. The topic of drug **self-administration** will be discussed further in the section on opiate dependence. As you will see, research on the reinforcing properties of drugs, as well as on the properties of drug-associated stimuli, have contributed significantly to the understanding of addiction.

OPIATE TOLERANCE   Chapter 2 defined drug tolerance as a shift to the right in the dose response curve. That is, after repeated drug exposure, it takes larger doses to produce an effect (illustrated in Figure 7.11). Although tolerance to opiate drugs develops quickly, the rate of tolerance development is not the same for all opiate

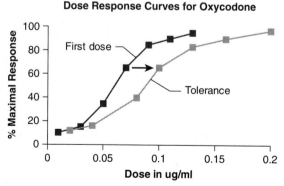

FIGURE 7.11   Tolerance can be observed as a shift to the right in the dose response curve. After repeated exposure, larger drug doses are required to produce the same magnitude of effect.

effects. For instance, tolerance to the analgesic and reinforcing effects of opiates occurs more rapidly than it does to respiratory depressant effects. Because of this fact, overdose to opiates can be a significant concern when doses are increased over time to sustain analgesia or when heroin patients use increasing amounts to thwart withdrawal symptoms.

Tolerance to opiates is complex, as described in some detail in Chapter 2, and it involves several distinct mechanisms. The primary metabolic enzyme for morphine is UGT2B7 (UDP-Glucuronosyltransferase-2B7), which converts morphine into M3G (morphine-3-glucuronide) and M6G. These metabolic by-products account for about 70 percent of administered morphine; the remaining 30 percent is excreted unchanged or is converted into other minor metabolites. The active metabolite of morphine, M6G, is about 2–4 times more potent than morphine, while M3G metabolite appears to have little pharmacological activity. These products are further metabolized and eventually excreted by the kidneys. After repeated opiate administration, the concentration of UGT2B7 in the liver increases and morphine is metabolized more quickly. This increased rate of drug metabolism is referred to as **metabolic tolerance.**

However, with regard to opiate tolerance, adaptive changes to opiate-receiving neurons may be even more important. While the details of these mechanisms have not been completely resolved, several adaptive changes have been described and evidence is accumulating for others. For example, chronic use of opiates is known to inhibit cyclic AMP (cAMP) production initially, which is later offset by compensatory mechanisms that return cAMP levels to normal. As you may recall, cAMP is an essential second messenger for metabotropic receptors. Therefore, compensatory production of cAMP appears to be an important mechanism underlying opiate **cellular tolerance.** When opiate use is suddenly terminated, upregulated cAMP may contribute to a rebound in noradrenergic cell activity in the locus coeruleus and to withdrawal symptoms (Ivanov et al., 2001; Punch et al., 1997; Rasmussen et al., 1990).

Metabolic tolerance and upregulation of cAMP alone cannot completely account for opiate tolerance. As discussed in Chapter 2, tolerance often depends on prior exposure to drug-associated cues. That is, tolerance may be expressed in contexts where drugs were administered, but not in another unfamiliar context. This **associative tolerance** results from the acquisition of a Pavlovian association between salient drug cues (conditioned stimuli) and drug onset cues (unconditioned stimuli). Because this kind of tolerance can be expressed immediately in the appropriate context, additional dynamic cellular adaptations must be involved. At this point, all that is known is that this mechanism is likely to be mediated by the NMDA receptor. Evidence from a number of studies, including those conducted by the author of this text, indicate that associative tolerance can be both disrupted and reversed by the administration of an NMDA receptor antagonist such as **dextromethorphan.**

This research has important implications for drug addiction treatment. First, it illustrates why recidivism may be so high for drug addiction, as drug treatment

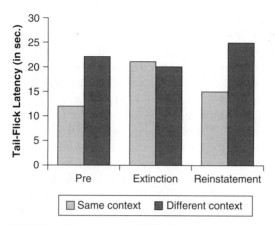

FIGURE 7.12 Average tail-flick latencies in response to thermal pain for animals receiving morphine in the same context in which tolerance developed versus receiving morphine in a different context. The first panel shows associative tolerance that develops to the drug administration context (shorter latencies). Panel 2 shows the extinction of tolerance following a two-week period of no drug administration. Panel 3 shows the reinstatement of associative tolerance following the single administration of 3 mg/kg morphine in context. Data from author's laboratory.

often involves controlled abstinence in a clinical setting away from drug-associated cues. Once the user returns to places or contexts where drug use occurred, conditioned responses associated with drug use (e.g., cravings and drug seeking) are elicited. Furthermore, exposure to a single dose may completely reinstate the addiction and tolerance. In the author's laboratory, after a single low dose of morphine, rats demonstrated the reinstatement of tolerance and drug-seeking behaviors after several months of abstinence, but only when the morphine was administered in the original drug context. Rats given morphine after abstinence in their home cages did not show reinstatement (Figure 7.12). Clearly, more research on the cellular mechanisms underlying associative tolerance is needed before effective drug treatment programs can be developed.

Pharmacological Treatment of Opiate Dependence and Addiction

The Centers for Disease Control and Prevention (CDC) estimates that approximately 1 million people in the United States are currently dependent on heroin or other opiates, including oxycontin and hydrocodone. These opiate users are at risk for HIV, hepatitis, and liver disease as well as a host of other disorders. As many as 10,000 of these users die from drug overdose each year. The financial costs of opiate dependence and addiction, although impossible to determine, are estimated to exceed $20 billion annually.

From the preceding discussion, it is clear that successful programs for opiate dependence must involve more than detoxification in a clinical setting. Drug-associated contextual cues can and often do elicit cravings and withdrawal symptoms even after months of abstinence. And, as illustrated in Figure 7.12, these drug-related behaviors can be reinstated after extinction when drug use reoccurs in familiar drug contexts. Therefore, successful programs must employ both behavioral and pharmacological approaches to minimize the probability of recidivism, which occurs in as many as 80 percent of treated opiate users.

Most opiate treatment programs begin with a period of **methadone maintenance,** where methadone is substituted for heroin or another opiate. Methadone is the preferred substitute for heroin for several reasons. First, it has a very long half-life (15–22 hours) compared to other opiates. For most patients, once-daily methadone administration may be sufficient to reduce withdrawal symptoms and maintain abstinence. Methadone can be administered orally, which does not produce the rush or high associated with intravenous (IV) drug use. Most patients require between 60 and 120 mg of methadone each day for at least one year, often for a period of several years to life, at a cost of about $4,000 per patient per year. Every day more than 100,000 patients take methadone as part of a drug treatment program.

Other synthetic opioids have been developed for opiate maintenance, including **levomethadyl** (Orlaam), which was discontinued in 2003 because of adverse cardiac side effects, and **buprenorphine** (Suboxone), which was approved by the FDA in 2002. Both of these synthetic opioids have long half-lives of about 2½ days, requiring dosing only 3 times per week. Suboxone contains buprenorphine, the synthetic opioid, and naloxone to deter illicit intravenous use. When administered intravenously, naloxone antagonizes buprenorphine effects and precipitates withdrawal symptoms. When taken orally, the naloxone does not cross the blood-brain barrier and has little or no antagonistic effect.

Methadone (or buprenorphine) by itself is not sufficient as a treatment for opiate addiction, but space in comprehensive residential treatment facilities is limited and expensive. Often methadone maintenance is initiated in an outpatient setting while the patient is awaiting space in a residential facility. Unfortunately, in these cases, many patients return to using heroin or other drugs. The success of methadone maintenance is difficult to assess because definitions of success vary widely. Critics of methadone maintenance programs argue that these programs merely substitute one addiction for another and that success should be defined as complete abstinence from all drugs. Applying this definition, these programs fail. Advocates, on the other hand, argue that success should be measured in terms of social cost, and methadone programs do decrease the costs of crime and disease associated with illicit drug use. Regardless of definition, methadone is not a cure for opiate addiction.

8

Substance Abuse and the Neurobiology of Addiction

The most recent national surveys on drug abuse estimate that the lifetime prevalence of substance abuse and dependency is approaching 15 percent of the U.S. population (Kehoe, 2008; Kessler et al., 2005). If tobacco products are included in this estimate, the number increases dramatically to over 45 percent of the population (Hatsukami et al., 2008). These numbers have remained relatively stable over the past 10–20 years since accurate surveys and criteria from the *Diagnostic and Statistical Manual of Mental Disorders* (DSM-IV-TR) have been employed. While not all of these individuals are drug-addicted, clearly many are. This chapter will examine the diagnostic criteria for substance abuse disorders and explore the neurobiology of drug addiction. As you will see, the term *addiction* has often been used synonymously with *dependence.* Not all drugs that cause dependence will be defined here as addictive. While drug addiction implies a dependency, **addiction** is a consequence of specific neural adaptations resulting from the use of drugs that affect dopamine activity in the mesolimbic and mesocortical systems. Not all drugs that cause a dependency produce these types of neural adaptations. The drugs listed in Figure 8.1, among others, do.

Carl remembers his first drink at age 12. His parents had a liquor cabinet in their dining room where he found a well-used bottle of gin. After consuming about 8 ounces, he immediately became ill and vomited in his bedroom. Hours later Carl was punished by his parents, and they locked the cabinet to prevent another occurrence. However, the last thing Carl wanted was another drink. The illness and subsequent hangover were sufficient to deter his drinking for almost a year. While in middle school, Carl befriended a young boy who was more experienced with alcohol than Carl was. As a son of an alcoholic father, Carl's friend had unfettered access

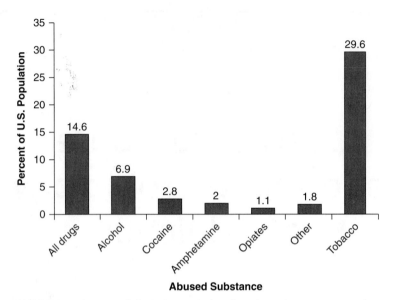

FIGURE 8.1 Percent of the U.S. population that abuse drugs at some point during their lifetime. The category "All drugs" does not include tobacco products or marijuana (8.5 percent lifetime prevalence). The category "Cocaine" includes crack, "Amphetamine" includes methamphetamine, "Opiates" includes prescription and nonprescription narcotics, and "Other" includes inhalants and sedatives. Compiled from Cotter, 2007; Hatsukami et al., 2008; Keohe, 2008; Kessler et al., 2005.

to alcohol. Carl remembers drinking at all times with his friend, even in the morning on the way to school. By the time Carl graduated from high school, he was drinking most days. He stole wine from a local grocery store or from the parents of his friends. Although Carl knew a few alcoholics, including the father of his friend, he did not think of himself as one. He simply enjoyed the feeling of intoxication and was quite good at hiding it from his parents and teachers. Carl looked forward to attending college, where he anticipated the parties and binge drinking he had often heard about.

Soon after his freshman year in college began, Carl was involved in an automobile accident. He was charged with driving under the influence (DUI), was sentenced to a night in jail, and had his driver's license suspended for a year. In addition, Carl was required to attend weekly meetings with other alcohol users, where they discussed the symptoms and ramifications of abuse and addiction. Carl was not convinced he had an alcohol problem, but he played along to meet the requirements of his sentence. After a dismal academic performance his first year, Carl decided college was not for him and accepted a sales position at a local car dealership where he had worked the previous summer. Selling cars was easy for Carl. He enjoyed meeting people and found that working at the dealership provided numerous opportunities to meet for drinks with other salespeople. Carl believed that his performance was actually enhanced with a few drinks because it made conversation and sales talk much easier.

Within a year at the dealership, Carl began drinking at work. After several reprimands, his position was changed from a salaried one to one paid solely on sales commissions. The increased stress of earning a livable wage and being newly engaged precipitated even more drinking. By now, Carl had developed tolerance to large amounts of alcohol. He also found that abstaining from drinking was increasingly difficult. When confronted about alcohol by his fiancée, Carl would become enraged in denial. He claimed that he needed the alcohol to relax from the pressures of work. After they were married, Carl promised to quit and he found a new job as an insurance adjuster. Quitting drinking, however, was just a promise.

After a mere three months, Carl was fired from his new job. The reasons for his dismissal were never stated, but it was clear to his wife that drinking was the problem. Carl began each day with a glass of vodka. For lunch, he would have a few drinks with a sandwich or fries. After work, Carl would have a few martinis before dinner and a scotch or two immediately after dinner. Because he never felt drunk, Carl was still convinced alcohol was not a problem. He knew he could quit if he wanted to—he just did not want to quite yet.

Within a year of marriage, Carl and his wife sought counseling as a last resort to save their marriage. Carl had become increasingly aggressive after drinking and was having difficulty finding work. Their social life also had deteriorated; according to his wife, this too was because of his excessive drinking. After a few drinks, Carl was prone to become belligerent and aggressive. It was during his first counseling session that Carl agreed to alcohol treatment and to attend Alcoholics Anonymous meetings. Carl abstained from alcohol for nearly three months before he resumed drinking. During this time, he had suffered through his first bout of alcohol withdrawals, delirium tremens, and severe alcohol cravings. This was not to be his last bout, however.

After Carl began drinking again, his wife filed for divorce and moved back with her parents. Carl moved into a small apartment because he could not afford the house payments on his intermittent salary. With another car accident and DUI, Carl was sentenced to 30 days in a residential treatment facility. Carl is anticipating completing his treatment at this time.

Carl's story is neither unusual nor typical of alcohol addiction. Addiction to alcohol can occur abruptly or develop gradually over many years. It may begin in adolescence, as it did with Carl, or it may begin later in life. What appears to be a common thread in substance abuse is the pattern of destruction it renders to personal and family lives. Substance abusers are often in denial about the pain they cause those individuals who are close to them. In addition, they are in denial about the severe health and financial consequences of substance abuse to themselves. Alcohol addiction is more common in individuals with other comorbid psychological disorders, including depression, bipolar disorder, and anxiety disorders. Perhaps alcohol addiction is a form of self-medication for these preexisting conditions. Another possibility is that alcohol abuse potentiates the development of other psychological disorders.

Substance abuse treatment is rarely successful on the first attempt and is seldom complete. Recovered alcoholics often rightly claim that addiction is "just a drink away." Carl's story provides an effective introduction to substance abuse disorders. His case clearly meets the criteria for **substance dependence disorder.**

The *Diagnostic and Statistical Manual of Mental Disorders,* Text Revision (DSM-IV-TR), does not make a distinction between drug dependence and addiction. Rather, it classifies substance abuse disorders by the degree of impairment caused by drug use and whether tolerance and/or withdrawal symptoms are present. According to these distinctions, an individual may be dependent on a substance without having a disorder. For example, most individuals addicted to nicotine are not considered to have a substance dependence disorder even though they may meet the minimal diagnostic criteria for this disorder.

The diagnosis of substance dependence disorder supersedes a substance abuse disorder and requires that the additional symptoms of drug tolerance and/or withdrawal be present. This diagnosis presumes that the drug use has persisted long enough for these symptoms to develop.

The DSM-IV-TR criteria for substance dependence disorder are as follows:

A maladaptive pattern of substance use, leading to clinically significant impairment or distress, as manifested by three, or more, of the following occurring at any time in the same 12-month period:

1. tolerance, as defined by either of the following:
   a. a need for markedly increased amounts of the substance to achieve intoxication or the desired effect
   b. markedly diminished effect with continued use of the same amount of the substance
2. withdrawal, as manifested by either of the following:
   a. the characteristic withdrawal syndrome for the substance
   b. the same or a closely related substance is taken to relieve or avoid withdrawal symptoms
3. the substance is often taken in larger amounts over a longer period than was intended
4. there is a persistent desire or unsuccessful efforts to cut down or control substance use
5. a great deal of time is spent in activities necessary to obtain the substance, use the substance, or recover from its effects
6. important social, occupational, or recreational activities are given up or reduced because of substance use
7. the substance use is continued despite knowledge of having a persistent or recurrent physical or psychological problem that is likely to have been caused or exacerbated by the substance

Carl's condition clearly meets most of those criteria. He has developed a tolerance to large amounts of alcohol, he suffers withdrawals with abstinence, and alcohol use has caused severe disruptions to all areas of his life. If he is like many recovering alcoholics, he will be in and out of treatment for much of his life. During periods of abstinence, he will be tempted to drink and will experience alcohol cravings when in the presence of others using alcohol. These symptoms may diminish, but they will never completely disappear, even after many years of abstinence.

If the diagnostic criteria of tolerance and withdrawal symptoms are not present (most likely because the condition is too recent and the symptoms have not yet appeared), a diagnosis of substance abuse disorder may apply. The DSM-IV-TR criteria for **substance abuse disorder** are as follows:

A maladaptive pattern of substance use leading to clinically significant impairment or distress, as manifested by one (or more) of the following, occurring within a 12-month period.

1. recurrent substance use resulting in a failure to fulfill major role obligations at work, school, or home
2. recurrent substance use in situations in which it is physically hazardous
3. recurrent substance-related legal problems continued substance use despite having persistent or recurrent social or interpersonal problems caused or exacerbated by the effects of the substance

Carl also meets the criteria for a substance abuse disorder. However, since the symptoms of tolerance and withdrawal were experienced, this diagnosis was superseded by substance dependence disorder. A diagnosis of substance abuse disorder may be appropriate for an individual who uses marijuana frequently. As the next chapter will discuss, tolerance to marijuana is modest if it occurs at all and withdrawal symptoms during abstinence are mild compared to those experienced with other drugs that cause dependence. However, marijuana use may contribute to disruptions at work or school as well as to the user's social obligations.

NEUROBIOLOGY OF ADDICTION

As stated earlier, certain drugs cause not only dependency after repeated use, but also addiction. While addiction does imply a dependency, behavioral and neurobiological features of addiction are not present in all case of drug dependency. Among the most remarkable features of drug addiction is the intense desire or motivation to take a drug, even in the face of serious adverse consequences including arrest and imprisonment, termination of employment, and an increased risk of serious disease. Equally sinister is the enduring craving for the drug after many years of abstinence, making drug relapse a likely occurrence for most addicts. How can a substance produce such powerful control over a person's behavior that the person risks everything, including family, employment, freedom, and health? To understand how drugs can produce such powerful effects on behavior, you need to explore how addictive substances change the brain. Over the past 20 years, both human and animal experiments have provided a great deal of information about the neurobiological adaptations resulting from the use of certain drugs. It is these adaptations that form the critical distinction between drug dependence and its more insidious form, drug addiction.

Reward Pathways

The brain's response to addictive substances may be a mere coincidence of a drug's effects on the brain's **reward pathway.** This pathway is an evolutionary adaptation that assists organisms in assigning hedonic value to stimuli. For instance, the reward pathway ensures that organisms find certain foods more appealing than others based on their caloric value. It also ensures that organisms are motivated to seek out sexual partners and reproduce. This survival-enhancing system motivates animals to seek out and repeat whatever activities activated the reward pathway.

The essential neural structures that comprise the brain's reward pathway include the ventral tegmental area (VTA) of the midbrain and the nucleus accumbens. Even simple organisms such as the earthworm *Caenorhabditis elegans* have a rudimentary version of these dopamine-containing structures. Deactivation of these neurons disrupts the worm's ability to identify food. In the laboratory, rats can be trained to lever-press to receive small amounts of a dopamine-stimulating drug (e.g., cocaine) in their nucleus accumbens. Blocking the activity of these drugs or destroying dopamine-containing cells in these structures can severely disrupt lever pressing and drug administration. Addictive drugs tap into and modify the brain's reward pathway, ensuring that the motivation to seek and use drugs persists.

The investigation of reward pathways originated in 1954 with James Olds and his student Peter Milner. In their experiments, rats were implanted with electrodes in the **septum** to determine whether electrical stimulation would enhance maze learning. The septum is located centrally, deep below the basal ganglia and adjacent to the nucleus accumbens. In fact, in Latin, the complete name of the nucleus accumbens is *nucleus accumbens septi,* which means "nucleus leaning against the septum." To Olds's and Milner's surprise, after stimulating a rat when it was in a particular corner of the maze, the rat quickly returned for more. After a few applications of electrical stimulation, the animals were *"indubitably coming back for more"* (Olds & Milner, 1954). While the exact location of their electrode is unknown, numerous other experiments have replicated the findings with electrodes located in various areas, including the septum, the **medial forebrain bundle** (the bundle of axons projecting from the VTA to the nucleus accumbens)**,** and the nucleus accumbens. These structures, which are illustrated in Figure 8.2, are part of the reward pathway and comprise the mesolimbic system.

Since the discovery by Olds and Milner, neuroscientists have learned that electrical stimulation, like cocaine, causes an increase in the availability of dopamine in the VTA and the nucleus accumbens (see Figures 8.2 and 8.3). In addition, natural reinforcers such as palatable food, sucrose solution, and the availability of a sex partner stimulate the availability of dopamine in this region (see also Figure 8.4). Therefore, it appears that certain drugs activate the same brain regions as do natural reinforcers and this activation is well correlated with positive feelings in humans (Cooper & Knutson, 2008; Knutson et al., 2001). Addiction may not be solely dependent upon a drug's ability to increase

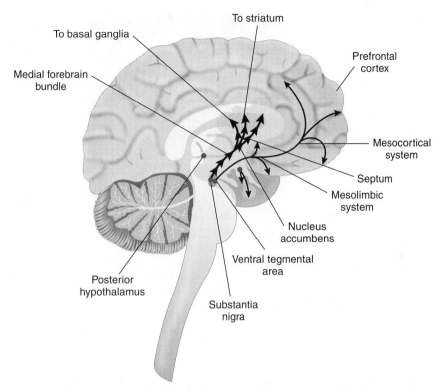

FIGURE 8.2 Mesolimbic and mesocortical dopamine systems. The mesolimbic system originates in the VTA and projects along the medial forebrain bundle to the amygdala, lateral hypothalamus, and nucleus accumbens. The mesocortical system also originates in the VTA but projects to the prefrontal cortex. Increased activity of dopamine in these reward systems is believed to underlie reinforcement as well as drug addiction. © CNSforum.com

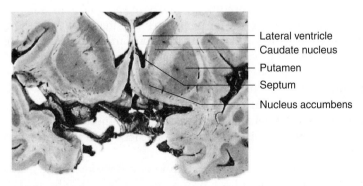

FIGURE 8.3 Transverse section through a human brain revealing structures of the basal ganglia and mesolimbic system. Note the close proximity of the septum and the nucleus accumbens.

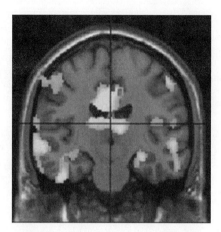

FIGURE 8.4 Functional MRI scan showing activity in the nucleus accumbens. Activation of the nucleus accumbens is correlated with positive subjective feelings. © Knutson et al. (2001). Anticipation of increasing monetary reward selectively recruits nucleus accumbens. *The Journal of Neuroscience*, 21(16), RC159.

dopamine activity in these mesolimbic structures, but on how quickly it does so. Drugs such as cocaine, heroin, and nicotine are more addictive when smoked or administered intravenously than when ingested orally because of how rapidly these routes of administration reach the brain.

DRUGS AND REWARD PATHWAYS   Drugs that directly (e.g., cocaine) or indirectly (i.e., heroin) increase dopamine activity in the VTA and nucleus accumbens are powerfully reinforcing and can maintain high rates of lever pressing in experimental animals. In addition, disrupting neurons in these regions (or the pathways connecting them) greatly diminishes the reinforcing effects of these drugs. The strong correlation between a drug's ability to maintain **self-administration** through high rates of lever pressing and its addictive potential makes animal self-administration a useful tool for evaluating a drug's liability for addiction (Figure 8.5). However, increasing dopamine activity in these mesolimbic structures in itself is not sufficient to cause addiction. If it were, addictions to all sorts of activities and foods would easily occur.

Why might the rate of drug administration determine its addictive liability? Several hypotheses have been proposed. The first hypothesis argues that the more rapidly a drug enters the brain, the more euphoric it is. Support for this comes from early studies comparing the subjective effects of cocaine when administered at different rates. At all doses investigated, cocaine and heroin produce greater

FIGURE 8.5 A self-administration experiment where a laboratory rat is fitted with a drug-delivery cannula. Lever presses result in small infusions of drug directly into specific regions of the brain.

euphoria when administered intravenously compared to similar doses delivered intranasally (Comer et al., 1999; Resnick et al., 1977). These results are depicted in Figure 8.6.

While this argument seems compelling, only a weak relationship exists between a drug's subjective euphoric effects and its reinforcing effects. For example,

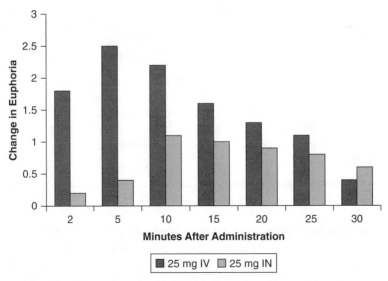

FIGURE 8.6 The subjective effects of 25 mg of cocaine depend on route of administration. Cocaine administered intravenously (IV) produces greater changes in euphoria than do intranasal (IN) doses. Data from Resnick et al., 1977.

nicotine produces little change in euphoria in smokers, but it is both reinforcing and highly addictive. In fact, intravenous nicotine produces few if any pleasurable subjective response in smokers even though it is effective in reducing nicotine cravings (Rose et al., 2000). Therefore, it appears that euphoria may be important in drug-taking behavior, but something other than euphoria must contribute to a drug's reinforcing and addictive potential.

The second and more recent hypothesis of addictive liability poses that a drug's psychomotor and incentive sensitization effects are more closely associated with its addictive potential than with its ability to induce euphoria. **Psychomotor sensitization** refers to a drug's potential to increase motor activity and drug-seeking behaviors after repeated administration. These behavioral effects are easily conditioned and elicited by contexts in which drugs were administered. On the other hand, **incentive sensitization** is an increase in the incentive value of the drug as well as drug-associated cues. For example, an animal previously exposed to nicotine, amphetamine, or cocaine demonstrates an increase in the rate of drug self-administration (increase in incentive value) and an increase in preference for drug-associated cues and contexts (as a result of conditioning) (Bradberry et al., 2000; Crombag et al., 2001). Both psychomotor and incentive sensitizations are observed in humans with a history of drug use.

The ability of drugs to induce psychomotor and incentive sensitization appears to depend on neurological adaptations in mesolimbic areas resulting from rapid rates of drug administration. It has been well established, for example, that the consequences of acute cocaine administration depend on its route of administration. Changes in neural activity measured by glucose utilization occur primarily to the nigrostriatal system following intraperitoneal administration as compared to increased activity in the mesolimbic and mesocortical systems following intravenous administration. The author of this report concluded that

> cocaine activates different neuronal circuitry depending on the route by which it is administered. Furthermore, the absence of metabolic activation in the mesolimbic system following acute intraperitoneal cocaine was not the result of the specific dose chosen or the length of time between cocaine administration and measuring glucose utilization (Porrino, 1993).

Since this study, other studies have been conducted to examine the cellular adaptations resulting from rapid drug administration.

NEUROLOGICAL ADAPTATIONS RESULTING FROM RAPID DRUG DELIVERY   Because drug addiction is characterized by long-lasting behavioral changes, including drug cravings and drug seeking that can be reinstated after long periods of abstinence, the neural adaptations underlying addiction must be enduring as well. The most likely candidates for these adaptations include drug-induced changes to gene expression in dopaminergic neurons in the mesolimbic and mesocortical pathways. Other neuronal adaptations such as long-term potentiation (LTP) are too short-lived to adequately account for addiction. How then do drugs initiate gene expression in specific neurons? In attempts to answer this question, researchers have focused on a class of regulator proteins called **immediate early genes (IEGs).** IEGs are proteins activated by stimuli that activate intracellular signaling. While many of the signaling pathways activated by IEGs may be regulatory or homeostatic, the IEGs activated by certain drugs may have profound influences on dopaminergic cell functioning. One IEG that has received considerable attention because it is activated by addictive drugs is **c-FOS.** c-FOS is a protein expressed in response to a variety of extracellular signals including drugs such as cocaine, amphetamine, nicotine, and morphine. As cellular activity in response to a drug increases, c-FOS protein is expressed in greater amounts (Harlan et al., 1998; Thomas et al., 2008; Zhang et al., 2006).

Figure 8.7 shows how receptor activation by a neurotransmitter (e.g., dopamine) leads to activation of the **second messenger** cyclic AMP (cAMP), which in turn activates protein kinase (PKA). PKA enters the cell nucleus, where it activates a cAMP response element-binding (CREB) protein. The **CREB protein** binds to a specific binding element on DNA, allowing it to turn on the gene for the synthesis of the **c-FOS protein.** c-FOS proteins are transcription factors that promote the synthesis of messenger RNA (mRNA) under the direction of DNA. These

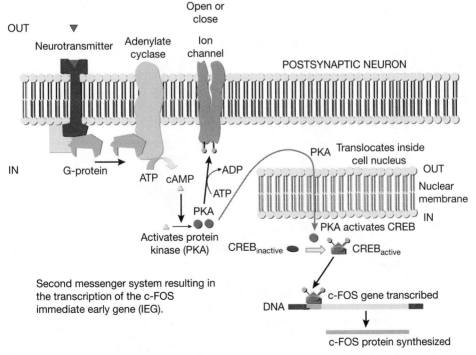

FIGURE 8.7 c-FOS gene transcription in response to neurotransmitter-activated second messenger system and CREB activation.   © Henry Jakubowski. Reprinted by permission.

proteins are essential for construction of the cellular adaptations resulting from drug use.

Drug addiction is a result of lasting neural adaptations that alter the brain's response to dopamine. The mechanism underlying this alteration appears to be CREB-activated c-FOS. c-FOS appears to coordinate the response of dopamine D_1 receptors to repeated drug exposure by increasing the density of dendritic branching and growth. The D_1 receptor is believed to mediate the psychomotor and incentive sensitization that follows addictive-drug use.

As mentioned, the rate of drug administration is critical to these neuronal adaptations. To illustrate this fact, rats were exposed to doses of cocaine or saline infused through intravenous catheters. The infusion rate of intravenous cocaine was varied over 5, 25, and 100 seconds. The researchers measured the density of c-FOS protein by a radioactive marker in several brain regions, including the medial prefrontal cortex and the nucleus accumbens. As shown in Figures 8.8 and 8.9, the rapid infusion of cocaine (delivered within 5 seconds) produced the greatest change in c-FOS expression. Rapid rates of cocaine and nicotine delivery also induced the greatest amount of locomotor activity (psychomotor sensitization) in these animals (Ferrario et al., 2008; Samaha et al., 2004, 2005).

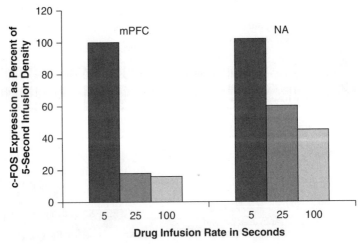

FIGURE 8.8 Cocaine-induced c-FOS expression in the medial prefrontal cortex (mPFC) and the nucleus accumbens (NA) following 5-, 25-, and 100-second drug infusion rates. Bars represent the percentage of c-FOS expression following a 5-second infusion rate. c-FOS density was greatest following a 5-second infusion and was approximately 18 percent of the 5-second density in the mPFC and about 50 percent of the 5-second density in the NA with 25- and 100-second infusion rates. © Samaha, A.-N., & Robinson, T.E. (2005). Why does the rapid delivery of drugs to the brain promote addiction? Reprinted from *Trends in Pharmacological Sciences*, 26(2), 82–87 with permission from Elsevier.

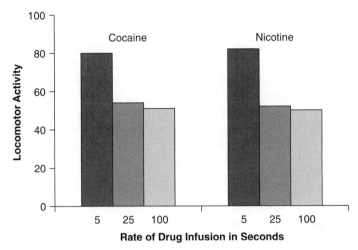

FIGURE 8.9 Locomotor activity of rats exposed to different rates of cocaine and nicotine administration. The rate of drug delivery influences the expression of psychomotor sensitization. © Samaha, A.-N., & Robinson, T.E. (2005). Why does the rapid delivery of drugs to the brain promote addiction? Reprinted from *Trends in Pharmacological Sciences*, 26(2), 82–87 with permission from Elsevier.

In summary, drug addiction is characterized by powerful and long-lasting behavioral changes, including drug cravings and drug seeking, that can be reinstated after long periods of abstinence. Addiction occurs to a wide range of drugs; and although the drugs have no common structural features, all of them contribute to increased dopamine activity in the nucleus accumbens as well as in other structures of the mesolimbic pathway. After repeated use, these addictive substances begin to alter the structure of dopamine-receiving neurons by upregulating the proteins CREB and c-FOS. Although not essential, a rapid rate of drug delivery and availability to the brain enhances CREB and c-FOS upregulation. These proteins contribute to increased dendritic branching, increased numbers of D_1 receptors, and increased sensitivity to dopamine. In addition, changes to mesocortical structures occur, allowing for drug-associated stimuli to elicit drug-seeking behaviors.

Addiction is a complex set of neural adaptations leading to the development of tolerance, dependence, and a life-disrupting pattern of drug-related motivations and behaviors. The menacing fact that these changes are enduring and susceptible to reinstatement makes addiction particularly difficult to treat.

Treatment of Drug Addiction

Addiction's toll on society is estimated to exceed $300 billion each year, making it one of the most urgent social problems. A better understanding of the neurobiology of addiction is critical to the development of new treatment methods. The treatment options available today are largely unsuccessful for most addicts, and those who do recover are at a continued risk of recidivism. Treatment for addiction includes drug therapy as well as behavioral therapies such as the popular 12-step program. Behavioral programs tend to target problematic patterns of behavior and the social and environmental contributions to drug use. These programs also can provide support as an addict grapples with the pain of withdrawal. Current drug therapies, on the other hand, attempt to mimic the effects of the abused drug and to dampen cravings associated with withdrawal. Several of these approaches, including bupropion and nicotine replacement, are covered in the discussion of nicotine in Chapter 10. It is important to emphasize that there are presently no cures for drug addiction. However, there are several promising lines of research.

IMMUNIZATION AGAINST ABUSED DRUGS One of the most promising approaches to drug treatment research is to prevent the drug from entering the brain altogether. Two avenues of research along this line have been explored. One approach involves **passive immunization** with **catalytic antibodies** capable of rapidly degrading cocaine (Landry, 1997; Landry et al., 1993). Whether passive immunization with catalytic antibodies can effectively degrade cocaine over long periods of time has yet to be demonstrated. Passive immunization does not stimulate the production of new antibodies; thus, resistance to cocaine would be expected to diminish over time, requiring repeated immunization.

Another approach involves **active immunization** with a cocaine-protein conjugate that stimulates the formation of cocaine-specific antibodies (Ettinger et al., 1997; Johnson & Ettinger, 2000). In these experiments, cocaine molecules were attached to a large immunogenic protein and injected into laboratory animals. The reason for conjugating cocaine to a large protein is that organisms do not typically produce antibodies to small compounds. If they did, they (including humans) would develop antibody responses to all drugs and foods that enter the blood supply. Attaching cocaine to a protein that is known to stimulate an immune response essentially tricks the immune system into recognizing the cocaine molecule as a foreign protein. After immunization with the cocaine-protein conjugate, antibodies are produced, which attach to both the protein and cocaine molecule. Presumably, cocaine that is bound to a large antibody is unable to cross the blood-brain barrier, thereby resulting in lower levels of cocaine actually reaching the brain.

Figure 8.10 shows a typical Western dot blot assay. Strips of assay paper are pretreated with drops of cocaine solution. Later, blood from an immunized animal is applied to the paper. If cocaine antibodies are present in the blood, they will attach to the cocaine and be revealed by dark dots over the cocaine.

Research in the author's laboratory has shown that immunization with a cocaine-protein conjugate inhibits cocaine's reinforcing and analgesic properties as well as an animal's ability to discriminate cocaine from saline injections. Figure 8.11 shows the results of an experiment in which laboratory rats were trained to discriminate cocaine from saline injections. After the animals learned the discrimination, they were immunized against cocaine with the cocaine-protein

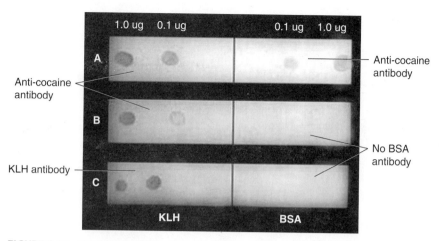

FIGURE 8.10 Western dot blot assays for anti-cocaine antibody. Two dilutions (1.0 ug and 0.1 ug) of cocaine-KLH were placed on the left side of strips A–C. Two dilutions of cocaine-BSA (1.0 ug and 0.1 ug) were placed on the right side of strips A and C. The right side of strip B contains two dilutions (1.0 ug and 0.1 ug) of BSA alone. Strips A and B were incubated with serum from an animal immunized with cocaine-KLH. Binding of antibodies to the strips is indicated by stain. Binding of antibody to cocaine-KLH (A and B, left side) and cocaine-BSA (A, right side, indicated by arrows) but not to BSA alone (B, right side) indicates the presence of anti-cocaine antibodies in this animal. Strip C was incubated with serum from an animal immunized with KLH alone. Binding of antibodies to cocaine-KLH (C, left) indicates the presence of anti-KLH antibody. The absence of binding to the cocaine-BSA (C, right) indicates the lack of anti-BSA or anti-cocaine antibody in this animal. From Ettinger et al., 1997.

conjugate. The ability of animals to accurately discriminate cocaine from saline decreased from nearly 100 percent before immunization to approximately 50 percent (chance levels) after immunization. High doses of cocaine could overwhelm the antibody, however, and reinstate cocaine discrimination. Evidence from other laboratories also suggests that immunization reduces the levels of cocaine in the brain even following rapid routes of delivery such as intravenous and intranasal administration (Fox, 1997).

Other laboratories have demonstrated effective immunization against the effects of heroin (Bonese et al., 1974), nicotine (LeSage et al., 2006; Pentel et al., 2000), and methamphetamine (Byrnes-Blake et al., 2001) in laboratory animals. Several clinical trials evaluating the effectiveness of cocaine immunization with humans have been conducted, but the results are mixed. In a clinical trial with 18 cocaine-dependent subjects, anti-cocaine vaccination apparently decreased the subjective euphoric effects of cocaine, but most patients relapsed to cocaine use during or immediately following treatment in spite of their high levels of anti-cocaine antibodies (Martell et al., 2005). Several additional clinical trials involving cocaine and nicotine vaccines are presently underway with the hopes of developing more effective immunization methods. Presently, there are no commercially available vaccines for addictive drugs.

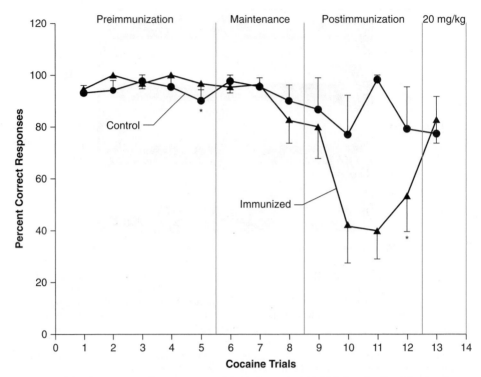

FIGURE 8.11   Percentage of correct responses during cocaine trials for the final five sessions prior to immunization, the three postimmunization maintenance sessions, and all five sessions after immunization. Points to the right of the third vertical line mark the increase in cocaine dose from 5.0 mg/kg to 20.0 mg/kg for the final cocaine trial.   © Johnson, M. W., & Ettinger, R.H. (2000). Active immunization attenuates cocaine's discriminative properties. *Experimental and Clinical Psychopharmacology*, 8, 163–167.

TARGETING NEURAL MECHANISMS TO PREVENT DRUG RELAPSE   As mentioned previously, a particularly sinister characteristic of addiction is its reinstatement following long periods of abstinence from drugs. The reinstatement of cravings and drug-seeking behavior can occur during periods of stress or upon exposure to drug-associated environmental cues. While it has long been suspected that projections from cortical neurons to the nucleus accumbens must be involved in reinstatement, these speculations have only recently been confirmed. In a series of studies, evidence for glutaminergic neurons projecting from the prefrontal cortex to the nucleus accumbens have been established (Bossert et al., 2007; Engblom et al., 2008; Kalivas et al., 2003; LaLumiere et al., 2008; Ping et al., 2008). These glutamate neurons project to and regulate the release of dopamine in the nucleus accumbens.

   During stress or in the presence of drug-associated cues, increased activity in the glutaminergic pathway from the prefrontal cortex to the nucleus accumbens results in increases in glutamate release, which contributes to increased dopamine

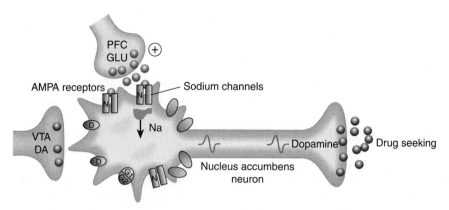

FIGURE 8.12   Glutaminergic involvement in the reinstatement of drug-seeking behavior following abstinence. Drug-associated cues can lead to the reinstatement of cravings and drug seeking via glutamate projections from the prefrontal cortex (PFC) to the nucleus accumbens, where they regulate the release of dopamine. Blockade of the glutamate AMPA receptor prevents reinstatement.

activity. A disruption of this activity caused by a dampening of prefrontal glutamate neuronal activity or the blockade of glutamate AMPA receptors in the nucleus accumbens prevents the reinstatement of drug-seeking behavior in animals (LaLumiere et al., 2008). Glutamate AMPA receptors control sodium channels and consequently the excitability of dopamine neurons (see Figure 8.12). These AMPA receptors are upregulated during drug use and are part of the set of complex neural adaptations contributing to and maintaining drug addiction.

Given what is now known about the neural circuitry involved in drug relapse, the development of pharmacological methods to dampen this activity may be on the horizon. The blockade of glutamate AMPA receptors in the nucleus accumbens or the activation of inhibitory glutamate autoreceptors prevent cue-induced reinstatement of drug seeking in animals. The development of drugs to target these receptors is in progress.

Are Video Games, Gambling, and Sex Addictive?

The term *addiction* is often used to describe compulsive (and occasionally destructive) behaviors such as excessive video gaming, gambling, and hypersexuality. But are those behaviors really addictions? According to the definition of *addiction* laid out here, to label them addictions would require establishing a pattern of neural adaptations similar to those resulting from repeated drug use. While there is evidence that video gaming, gambling, and sexual activity increase dopamine activity in the mesolimbic pathway, this by itself does not meet the preceding definition of addiction. Dopamine activity in the mesolimbic pathway is involved in numerous activities, including eating, drinking, sexual behavior, behavior reinforcement, attention, and the kind of sensory motor integration involved in video game playing (Koepp et al., 1998). Furthermore, cues associated with highly palatable foods, opportunities for reinforcement, a sexual partner, video games, and gambling can increase arousal and dopamine activity. As discussed in the previous section, the effectiveness of a substance as a reinforcer is not by itself useful in defining addiction.

In a recent study comparing the neural activity of casual video game players with excessive players, the researchers did find a difference in amplitude of electrical potentials induced by video game cues compared to those induced by neutral cues in one of nine brain areas investigated in excessive players (see Figure 8.13). While the authors concluded that this represents sensitization of dopaminergic neurons in the mesolimbic pathway, they provide no compelling evidence of sensitization mediated by neural adaptations resulting from excessive game playing. In fact, the only electroencephalograph (EEG) recording that revealed differences between casual and excessive game players was recorded above the midline (Thalemann et al., 2007). Whether these recordings represent activity differences in mesolimbic structures cannot be determined by the EEG procedure.

A number of other studies have reported differences in dopaminergic activity between compulsive and noncompulsive gamblers (e.g., Bergh et al., 1997). For example, there is evidence that compared to nongamblers, gamblers more frequently carry an allele for the dopamine receptor gene (D_2A_1) (Comings et al., 1996; de Silva Lobo et al., 2007). This may indicate a genetic disposition toward gambling. Similar results have been found with excessive video game players (Koepp et al., 1998). Again, however, an increase in dopamine activity is not evidence of a predisposition for addiction. In fact, increased densities of dopamine receptors do not appear to predispose individuals for substance abuse

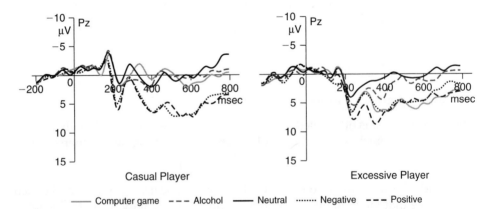

FIGURE 8.13 EEG recordings from the midline of brains in casual versus excessive video game players. The light grey shows the pattern of electrical potentials evoked by video game visual cues. The black trace was evoked by neutral cues; the grey-dashed line, by alcohol-related cues. These EEG records were recorded from electrodes placed along the midline of the head. Source: Thalemann et al (2007). Specific cue reactivity on computer game-related cues in excessive gamers. *Behavioral Neuroscience*, 121(3), 614–618.

or addiction. A considerable amount of research is currently being conducted to uncover possible genetic contributions to addiction. (See Agrawal et al., 2008, for a recent review.) While much of this research suggests associations with genes, there is still no consensus on which genes might be involved.

In summary, compulsive gaming, gambling, and sexual behavior may share common diagnostic criteria with substance abuse disorders, but evidence that they share common patterns of neural adaptations that underlie drug addiction remains controversial. Labeling compulsive and sometimes life-disruptive behaviors as addictions neither advances an understanding of their causal factors nor elevates their status as a disease. Until science can describe patterns of neural adaptations in the mesolimbic pathway that accompany these compulsions, there is little evidence that they are addictions. Compulsive video game play, gambling, and sexual activity are maintained by a complex set of reinforcer expectations and learned consequences that may make them more difficult to fully describe than drug addictions.

The following chapters will examine the pharmacology and abuse liability of some of the most common drugs of abuse. Chapter 9 will review the stimulants cocaine and amphetamine, the psychedelics LSD and psilocybin, and marijuana. Chapter 10 will discuss alcohol, nicotine, and caffeine.

9

The Pharmacology of Scheduled Psychoactive Drugs
Psychostimulants, Psychedelics, and Marijuana

This chapter and the next examine the pharmacology of a range of drugs that have both clinical and recreational significance. These drugs range from the mild psychostimulant caffeine, which is found in coffee, tea, and chocolate, to some of the most addictive and destructive substances known, including crack cocaine and methamphetamine. The pharmacology of the opiates will be described in a separate chapter.

Katherine had a relatively normal childhood. She grew up in a family of four. He father was a successful real estate broker in Seattle, and her mother, who was an elementary school teacher before she had children, remained at home during the early years before Katherine and her twin brother started school.

Late in elementary school, Katherine discovered that she could easily influence those around her by using her popularity and good looks. She matured more quickly than other girls her age and took advantage of the attention she drew. By middle school, Katherine was attracted to older boys and enjoyed the thrills of occasional cigarettes and alcohol they would provide. She was able to evade most of the trouble her risky lifestyle taunted until she became pregnant during her junior year of high school. Her gothic style of dress kept this fact a secret from her friends and parents through the first four months of pregnancy.

The secret ended when Katherine developed a serious infection from gonorrhea and needed medical attention. Because of the advanced stage of infection, Katherine was encouraged to have an abortion.

After this, Katherine's life began to change in significant ways. Her relationship with her parents deteriorated quickly, and she no longer attended school. Katherine found the company of an older boy who afforded a nice downtown apartment by selling marijuana, methamphetamine, and crack cocaine whenever it was available. It was not long before Katherine was using meth regularly and assisting her friend in its distribution. By the time she was 18, Katherine was addicted and was no longer a desirable partner to her companion and business partner. Once their relationship ended, Katherine found it more and more difficult to obtain the meth she craved. She returned home for a few weeks and convinced her father that she needed a loan to begin cosmetology school and to secure an apartment near its campus. With $8,000, Katherine moved back downtown and quickly reestablished a source for meth. Her stint at school lasted less than a month, and it became clear that $8,000 would not last much longer.

At this point, Katherine's life was consumed by methamphetamine. Most of her days began late, after she had shrugged off a drug hangover and was trying to locate methamphetamine or crack cocaine. Even though Katherine knew the streets well, her drug cravings often pushed her for miles in the rain to locate a seller. On days drugs were unavailable, Katherine returned to her apartment to fight off the severe headaches and nausea of withdrawals and, she hoped, to sleep. To keep her apartment—and the drug supply that now cost almost $100 per day—Katherine turned to petty theft and prostitution. At first, she found it easy to attract high-paying clients through an agency in Seattle. However, as the meth began to takes its toll, her appearance deteriorated quickly and her agency and once-easy clients were no longer interested. Predictably, Katherine, along with several other young girls, was arrested late one night in a prostitution sting. Not knowing who else to call, she woke her mother who was able to secure her release. Shocked by Katherine's appearance and stuporous condition, her mother rushed her to a hospital. Katherine had lost over 30 pounds from her previously healthy weight, her forearms had scars from numerous injections and scratching, and she had hepatitis from contaminated needles and unprotected sex. In the course of just over 18 months, Katherine had transformed from an attractive and popular high school student to a young woman hovering near death with a methamphetamine addiction.

Katherine was admitted to a private recovery clinic in Seattle where she spent the next 30 days living at the facility with few opportunities to leave. The exceptions were brief excursions with her parents for dinner or a quick shopping spree. After her in-house stay, Katherine was allowed to move back to her parents' home and attend college part-time. She is now in her second semester with plans to study psychology. During our interview, Katherine admitted that, although she had not used drugs since her release, she still felt the intense urge. While recently driving the streets she had once walked in search of meth, the frightening and exhilarating anticipation of seeing a seller rushed back to her. The next few hours were filled with the confusion of racing thoughts and the severe temptation to use just one more time.

In all likelihood, Katherine's addiction will win out within a year, as it unfortunately does with most drug addicts. The recidivism rate for meth addiction is over 80 percent within the first year of abstinence. Most recovered addicts will have sought help several times before finally quitting meth for good.

Katherine's case is neither surprising nor typical, as there is no characteristic course or set of experiences that leads a person to drug addiction. Katherine flirted with risky behavior from early in middle school, but other drug addicts may begin using at a much older age even after they have started a career and family. This chapter begins with a review of the pharmacology of a wide range of drugs with potential for abuse and discusses their significant clinical importance.

The use of drugs by youth in the United States had been rising at an alarming and steady rate prior to 1999. At that time, approximately 42.1 percent of high school seniors had used an illicit drug the previous year. Since 1999, however, illicit drug use by teenagers has gone down slightly each year. The most recent statistics from the National Survey on Drug Use and Health estimates the annual prevalence of illicit drug use to be just under 36 percent—a decline of about 1 percent a year (Figure 9.1). The same descending trend during these years has been observed with alcohol and tobacco use (Figure 9.2). The only upward trend has

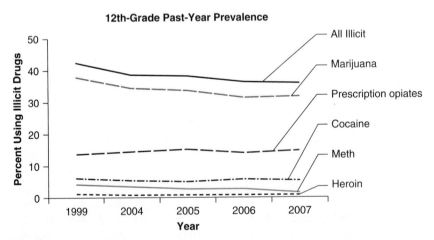

FIGURE 9.1 Annual prevalence of drug use by twelfth-graders from the highest prevalence rates recorded in 1999 through 2007. Since 1999, there has been a very slight decline in all illicit drug use with the exception of opiate prescription drugs (Vicodin and OxyContin), which increased slightly. From the National Survey on Drug Use and Health, 2007.

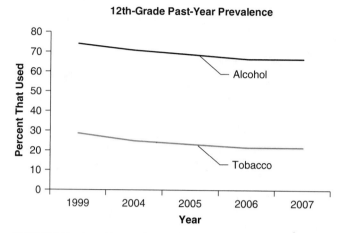

FIGURE 9.2   Annual prevalence of alcohol and tobacco use by twelfth-graders. Both alcohol and tobacco use has declined about 1 percent a year for the past eight years. From the National Survey on Drug Use and Health, 2007.

been a gradual increase in the illegitimate use of prescription pain medication. About 15 percent of high school seniors used Vicodin or OxyContin without a prescription the past year, which represents an increase of about 1.5 percent over the past eight years.

The use of psychoactive drugs is not a recent phenomenon, as many of the drugs discussed in this chapter have uses dating back hundreds—even thousands—of years. Caffeine, nicotine, cocaine, opium, psychedelic mushrooms, marijuana, and alcohol have uses that can be traced back to ancient times. Other more modern drugs are derivatives of these ancient substances or they have been discovered or synthesized more recently. For example, amphetamines were more recently extracted from the ephredra plant, LSD from the ergot fungus (which grows on grain), and morphine from opium. For convenience, these psychoactive drugs will be separated into two categories: scheduled drugs and unscheduled drugs and substances.

The term **drug schedule** refers to a drug classification based on its potential for abuse as described by the **Controlled Substances Act** of 1970. The Controlled Substances Act identified five schedules, or classifications, of drugs ranging from Schedule I to Schedule V. Schedule I drugs, for instance, include those drugs that have little or no clinical significance but have great potential for abuse. Included in Schedule I are LSD, marijuana, and heroin. Schedules II–V classify drugs with decreasing abuse potential and with some clinical importance. The drug schedules created by the Controlled Substances Act are summarized in Table 9.1, with a few examples provided in each classification. The use of scheduled drugs is highly regulated by the **Drug Enforcement Administration (DEA),** and they are

TABLE 9.1 The Classification of Controlled Substances by the Controlled Substances Act of 1970. A Complete List of Scheduled Drugs is Available from the DEA (http://www.usdoj.gov/dea).

Schedule	Description	Examples of Drugs and Substances
I	Drugs have a high potential for abuse, have no accepted medical use, and lack safety information regarding their use.	heroin, LSD, mescaline, psilocybin, marijuana
II	Drugs have a high potential for abuse, have accepted medical uses, but their use may lead to severe dependence.	morphine, codeine, cocaine, amphetamine, methamphetamine, nabilone (synthetic THC)
III	Drugs have a potential for abuse, have accepted medical uses, and may lead to low or moderate dependence.	anabolic steroids, pentobarbital, Marinol (synthetic THC)
IV	Drugs have a low potential for abuse, have accepted medical uses, and have a lower risk of dependence than do Schedule III drugs.	benzodiazepines, phenobarbital, Ambien and similar sleep aids
V	Drugs have a low potential for abuse, have accepted medical uses, and have a lower risk of dependence than do Schedule IV drugs.	Codeine and opiate preparations for cough or diarrhea

available only by prescription from a licensed practitioner or through a special license issued by the DEA to scientists and laboratories for the purpose of conducting research.

SCHEDULED PSYCHOACTIVE DRUGS

The scheduled drugs discussed in this section include cocaine, amphetamines, marijuana, and psychedelic drugs. All of these drugs fall into Schedule I or II for controlled substances. Keep in mind that the assignment of a drug schedule may be more influenced by politics than by pharmacology. Marijuana and LSD are two such examples. Neither drug has been shown to have a high abuse potential, and marijuana, arguably, has medical benefits. The barbiturates and benzodiazepines, which fall into Schedules III and IV, were described in Chapter 4 on anxiety disorders; the opiates, in Schedules I and II, were described in Chapter 7.

Psychostimulants: Cocaine

Cocaine is extracted from the coca plant (*Erythroxylum coca*), which readily grows in the mountainous regions of South America. Although most of the illicit cocaine comes from Columbia and Peru, significant amounts also are grown in Bolivia and Ecuador. Coca plants grown in South America are shown in Figure 9.3.

FIGURE 9.3 Coca shrubs grow readily in mountainous regions throughout South America. The coca leaves from these shrubs can be harvested several times a year.   © Dr. Morley Read/Science Photo Library/Photo Researchers, Inc.

Coca leaves have been used by the indigenous people of South America for thousands of years. When chewed, these leaves produce a sense of well-being and confidence as well as relief from fatigue. The practice of chewing coca leaves appears to have been widespread in South America, and evidence for its use has been found in ancient Peruvian tombs. While chewing coca is still popular in some South American regions, most cocaine is exported as cocaine sulfate or cocaine hydrochloride.

Cocaine compounds are extracted from the coca leaf by crushing the leaves in a solvent such as kerosene, benzene, or alcohol to extract the cocaine. Traditionally, the leaves were crushed by stomping them in large vats, but mechanical crushing has replaced stomping because it is a quicker, more efficient way to macerate the leaves for cocaine extraction. The resulting liquid mixture is processed with heat and sulfuric acid to isolate the cocaine alkaloids and remove the waxy residue from the leaf extract. This process results in a cocaine sulfate paste that may contain as much as 60 percent cocaine. Cocaine paste can be further processed with dilute hydrochloric acid to produce a water-soluble crystalline compound called cocaine hydrochloride shown in Figure 9.4.

Besides providing cocaine to customers around the world, large cocaine processing facilities in South America have begun to devastate the ecology of streams and rivers, where these solvents are dumped after cocaine extraction. Many formerly pure streams in Columbia and Peru are now polluted with extraction solvents such as kerosene, gasoline, and benzene as well as sulfuric and hydrochloric acids.

As shown in Figure 9.1, the use of cocaine among high school seniors has been essentially stable for the past eight to ten years. However, in 2006, it was estimated that more than 35 million Americans over the age of 12 had used cocaine at least once and that there are about 2 million regular users of cocaine. In the United States, a gram of cocaine hydrochloride (about 60–70 percent pure) costs just over $100, but the price can vary widely depending on location. This is enough cocaine to provide about 5–10 doses of snorted (or 10–15 doses of intravenous) cocaine to users who have not developed significant tolerance.

While the amount of cocaine produced in South America is difficult to determine, the Office of National Drug Control Policy estimates that 970 metric tons were produced in 2006, most of which was bound for the United States. In that year, more than 150 metric tons were seized by law enforcement agencies in the United States.

HISTORY OF COCAINE USE   The stimulant effects of coca were recognized and well described long before cocaine was identified as its active ingredient. The cocaine alkaloid was first isolated in 1855 by the German chemist Friedrich Gaedcke, who named it erythroxyline. It was another German scientist, Albert Niemann, who actually named it cocaine after carefully describing its extraction and purification process. Soon after its isolation, cocaine became widely used as a local anesthetic, particularly for surgeries of the eyes and nose. Cocaine also was added to tonics and beverages because of its stimulating effects. In 1863, the wine tonic Vin Mariani was marketed in the United States; soon after that, cocaine was added to the original Coca-Cola recipe, thus its name. By the early 1900s, cocaine could be purchased in local drugstores and was included in a variety of tonics and remedies.

Sigmund Freud's interest in cocaine began in the early 1880s after he had read scientific reports about its effects. Freud claims to have used cocaine frequently during this period:

> I take very small doses of it regularly against depression and against indigestion, and with the most brilliant success.

His experiences as well as recommendations for its uses were soon published in a series of scientific papers and letters called the *Cocaine Papers*. The first of this sequence, *Über Coca (About Cocaine)*, was published in 1884. The following selection from this work describes some of Freud's experiences:

> The psychic effect of cocaïnum muriaticum in doses of 0.05–0.10g consists of exhilaration and lasting euphoria, which does not differ in any way from the normal euphoria of a healthy person. The feeling of excitement which accompanies stimulus by alcohol is completely

lacking; the characteristic urge for immediate activity which alcohol produces is also absent. One senses an increase of self-control and feels more vigorous and more capable of work; on the other hand, if one works, one misses that heightening of the mental powers which alcohol, tea, or coffee induce. One is simply normal, and soon finds it difficult to believe that one is under the influence of any drug at all.

Freud enthusiastically promoted the use of cocaine to his friends and his fiancée in spite of concerns by those close to him that he may have become addicted to it. Freud continually denied that cocaine had any harmful effects, and whether he was addicted during this time remains unknown.

It seems to me noteworthy—and I discovered this in myself and in other observers who were capable of judging such things—that a first dose or even repeated doses of coca produce no compulsive desire to use the stimulant further; on the contrary, one feels a certain unmotivated aversion to the substance.

Not until the passage of the **Harrison Narcotic Tax Act** in 1914 was cocaine prohibited in all of its forms and mistakenly described as a dangerous narcotic. After its prohibition, cocaine was available only to licensed practitioners for medicinal and research uses. Its use as a local anesthetic continues although other local anesthetics such as lidocaine (Xylocaine) and procaine (Novocaine) are more commonly used.

PHARMACOLOGY OF COCAINE   Cocaine hydrochloride (cocaine HCl) is a water-soluble compound that once administered, readily separates into cocaine-H^+ and Cl^- ions in the blood. The protonated (positively charged) cocaine ion (cocaine-H^+) quickly passes through cell membranes and enters the brain. How rapidly cocaine enters the brain depends on its route of administration. Snorted and orally ingested cocaine enter the brain more slowly and incompletely than do intravenous administration or the inhalation of vaporized cocaine. For example, peak levels of cocaine are reached within five minutes of an intravenous injection compared to nearly an hour after intranasal administration.

Crack Cocaine   Beginning in the 1980s, cocaine users began converting cocaine hydrochloride (an acid) to a base by dissolving it in mild ammonia (NH_3) solution. This results in the compound **methylbenzoylecgonine** shown in Figure 9.4, which could be vaporized for inhalation. During the production process, a cracking sound is made—thus the name **crack**. Crack cocaine also can be manufactured by heating cocaine hydrochloride in water and sodium bicarbonate (baking soda). The cocaine rocks (called freebase cocaine) produced by these methods are then heated until they vaporize. Inhaling the vapors of freebase cocaine is an efficient and rapid method of cocaine delivery. By inhalation, peak plasma levels are reached within five minutes (see Figure 9.5).

FIGURE 9.4 Crack (freebase) cocaine (methylbenzoylecgonine) is produced by heating cocaine hydrochloride in water and sodium bicarbonate. Further heating then vaporizes the crystals, or "rocks" for inhalation. © United States Drug Enforcement Agency

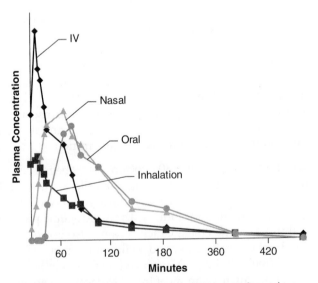

FIGURE 9.5 Cocaine concentrations in plasma depend on route of administration. The highest concentrations follow intravenous administration or inhalation in about five minutes.

Cocaine is widely distributed throughout bodily tissues and is metabolized quickly by both blood and liver enzymatic hydrolysis. The metabolic half-life of cocaine varies between 1 and 1.5 hours. The principle metabolites of cocaine are **benzoylecgonine** and **ecgonine,** both of which can be detected in the blood and other tissues for several weeks. Benzoylecgonine also can be detected in the hair of regular users for the life of a particular hair cell or until it is cut and only sections grown since the last drug use are exposed. When cocaine is used with alcohol, the active compound **cocaethylene** is formed, which is believed to be an even more potent euphoric than cocaine. Cocaethylene has a half-life of approximately 2.5 hours, nearly doubling the duration of the toxic and psychoactive effects of cocaine. Cocaethylene is particularly toxic to cardiac functioning. It causes severe hypertension, ventricular arrhythmia, and decreased blood flow—any of which can have unpredictably fatal consequences to otherwise healthy individuals (Wilson et al., 2002).

MECHANISMS OF COCAINE ACTION Cocaine readily passes through cell membranes in the brain and acts by binding to the **dopamine transporter (DAT)** on the presynaptic membrane. Because of its high affinity for the transporter protein, cocaine blocks the normal reuptake of dopamine from the synaptic gap, resulting in prolonged dopamine activity on postsynaptic receptors (Figure 9.6). Cocaine has similar effects on transporters for norepinephrine and serotonin. However, cocaine's effects on the DAT are believed to be most important for psychostimulating and reinforcing effects. In human studies, the subjective euphoric effects of cocaine appear to be directly related to its degree of DAT binding. At least 47 percent of DATs need to be blocked before subjects perceive the euphoric effects of cocaine, and doses that typically induce euphoria in cocaine users occupy between 60 and 80 percent of DATs (Volkow et al., 1997).

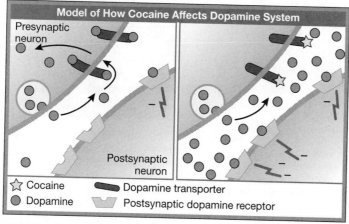

FIGURE 9.6 Cocaine acts by blocking the reuptake transporters for dopamine, serotonin, and norepinephrine on the presynaptic terminal.

However, DAT blockade by itself is not sufficient to account for cocaine's euphoric effects. The drug methylphenidate (Ritalin), which was described in the chapter on attention and developmental disorders, also blocks DATs to an extent similar to that of cocaine. The critical difference between methylphenidate and cocaine is how rapidly DAT blockade occurs after administration. Cocaine quickly enters the brain and blocks DATs, while orally administered methylphenidate does so slowly (Volkow et al., 1999). A rapid increase in dopamine activity in the **mesolimbic system** is believed to be critical for the euphoric and reinforcing potential of cocaine and other addictive substances. Addiction and dependence were discussed in greater detail in Chapter 8.

As stated previously, cocaine also blocks norepinephrine and serotonin transporters and these systems may contribute to cocaine's reinforcing and euphoric effects. To examine this, mice with genetic deletions of the DAT gene (knockout mice) have been tested for cocaine's reinforcing effects. If cocaine reinforcement is mediated solely by DAT blockade, DAT knockout mice are not expected to demonstrate cocaine-reinforcing effects. A popular method to investigate drug reinforcement is to repeatedly administer cocaine to animals in the same side of a dual-chambered apparatus (see Figure 9.7). Later, animals are given a choice as to which of two chambers to explore; the time animals spend on each side is a measure of their conditioned place preference. This procedure is referred

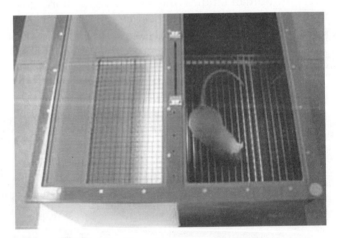

FIGURE 9.7 PPC apparatus used to investigate the reinforcing effects of drugs. Animals tend to prefer spending time in the chamber associated with cocaine administration. PPC is a demonstration of Pavlovian conditioning where context cues serve as conditioned stimuli (CSs) and drug onset serves as an unconditioned stimulus (US). Conditioned responses (CRs) are increases in motivation and arousal expressed as preferences for the drug-associated context.   © R. H. Ettinger

to as **place preference conditioning (PPC).** Typically, animals prefer spending time in the chamber associated with cocaine administration.

DAT knockout mice retain cocaine's reinforcing effects despite the fact that they do not express the DAT. It is believed that in these mice, cocaine effects on serotonin neurons in the **ventral tegmental area (VTA)** contribute to enhance dopamine activity in the mesolimbic system, particularly in the **nucleus accumbens** (Hnasko et al., 2007; Mateo et al., 2004; Sora et al., 2001; Thanos et al., 2008). This interaction is illustrated in Figure 9.8.

In summary, cocaine's euphoric and reinforcing effects are mediated primarily by enhanced dopamine concentrations in synapses in the nucleus accumbens and in the basal ganglia. In DAT **knockout animals,** these effects appear to be mediated downstream of the nucleus accumbens, in the VTA of the midbrain where these dopamine neurons originate. Serotonin in the VTA appears to regulate dopamine activity and may contribute to increased dopamine release in the nucleus accumbens.

Cocaine as a Local Anesthetic and Na$^+$ Channel Blockade   Cocaine has a long history of use as an **anesthetic** for surgery of the eyes, mouth, and nose (Figure 9.9). Its ability to dull pain as well as to constrict local blood flow makes it ideal for these uses. Cocaine disrupts the propagation of action potentials by blocking voltage-gated Na$^+$ channels. As action potentials propagate along an axon, voltage-gated sodium channels open as the membrane depolarizes, allowing Na$^+$ influx and a continuation of the action potential. When cocaine enters these channels, it effectively blocks Na$^+$ influx and prevents further depolarization. Because protonated cocaine (cocaine-H$^+$) more easily enters a sodium channel when it is open, the anesthetic effects of cocaine are greatest when local pain-transmitting

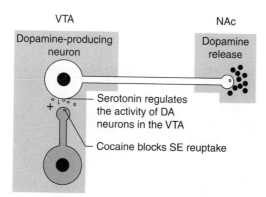

FIGURE 9.8   Serotonin-dopamine interactions in the VTA. Serotonin (and perhaps norepinephrine) regulate the activity of dopamine neurons in the VTA and can contribute to increased dopamine release in the nucleus accumbens (NAc).

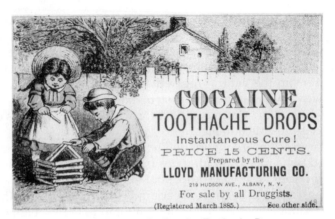

1885 Advertisement for Cocaine Toothache Drops

FIGURE 9.9 Cocaine was widely used as a local anesthetic before 1914, when it was prohibited in tonics and remedies.
© National Library of Medicine

neurons are firing rapidly. Cocaine is most often used as a **local anesthetic** whenever its actions are to be restricted to its site of administration. In surgery of the eye, for example, cocaine may be applied directly to the eye or injected in tissues surrounding the eye. Cocaine does have **analgesic** properties when administered systemically (an intravenous injection, for example), but these effects are not considered local anesthetic effects even though the anesthetic effects are still mediated by Na^+ channel blockade (Figure 9.10).

Occasionally, cocaine use is associated with cardiac toxicity, including myocardial infarction, arrhythmias, and occasional sudden death. Na^+ channel blockade in neurons controlling cardiac functioning may be a contributing factor in these abnormalities. Cocaine's respiratory depressant effects also are believed to be mediated by Na^+ channel blockade in neurons in the chemosensitive sites of

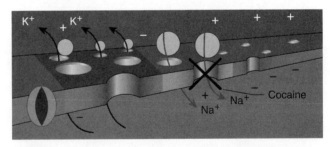

FIGURE 9.10 Cocaine's anesthetic effects are mediated by sodium channel blockade, thereby disrupting the propagation of action potentials. Protonated cocaine (cocaine-H^+) readily enters Na^+ channels when pain-transmitting neurons are firing.
© CNSforum.com. Reprinted by permission.

the medulla. Normally, these neurons respond to decreases in blood pH by triggering ventilatory responses. Cocaine, as well as the opiates, the barbiturates, and alcohol, can inhibit respiratory responses, although by different means, and can lead to respiratory failure and sudden death.

Psychostimulants: Amphetamine and Methamphetamine

The amphetamines are a collection of closely related compounds whose chemical structures are similar to those of the neurotransmitter dopamine (see Figure 9.11). The first of these compounds used was ephedrine, which is extracted from the *Ephedra sinica* plant, also known as ma huang from ancient Chinese medicine. For at least 5,000 years, ma huang has been used as an herbal remedy to treat a variety of ailments, including asthma and allergic reactions as well as congestion resulting from the common cold.

More recently, **ephedra** has been marketed as a diet aid for weight loss, as a way to increase wakefulness, and as a performance enhancer. Its effectiveness as a weight loss and performance-enhancing supplement remains controversial; nevertheless, it has been banned by many sports organizations as well as by the

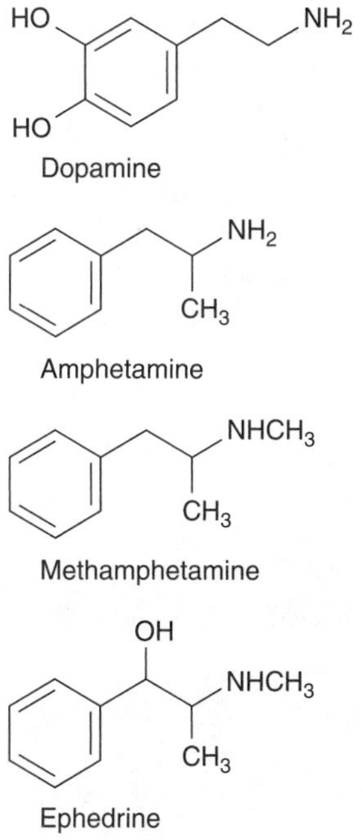

FIGURE 9.11   Molecular structures of dopamine, amphetamine, methamphetamine, and ephedrine. All of these compounds share a similar core structure.

International Olympic Committee. Because of several highly publicized fatalities related to ephedra in the late 1990s, the Food and Drug Administration (FDA) finally banned it altogether in 2004.

Amphetamine was first synthesized in by the Romanian chemist Lazăr Edeleanu in 1887. However, not until the mid 1930s was amphetamine finally marketed as an inhalant antihistamine under the trade name Benzedrine. Soon after, the structurally related amphetamine **dextroamphetamine (Dexedrine)** was introduced to treat narcolepsy, attention disorders, nasal congestion, and obesity. By the late 1940s, amphetamines were used to treat nearly 40 different disorders, including depression, fatigue, obesity, narcolepsy, drug addiction, and even hiccups. In addition, the U.S. military used dextroamphetamine during both World Wars to thwart fatigue and sleepiness in combat. By the 1960s, amphetamine production surged as it was mass-marketed as a weight loss aid. During this time of easy availability, many college students used it in lieu of caffeine to facilitate long study sessions. Endurance athletes, particularly competitive cyclists, found amphetamines useful to enhance training and competition. Sadly, use of amphetamines in sports led to a number of unfortunate deaths related to cardiac toxicity. In the early 1970s, amphetamine production reached its all-time high of over 10 billion tablets. Because of the widespread abuse of amphetamines, Benzedrine was replaced with propylhexedrine as the active ingredient in the Benzedrex inhaler and Dexedrine became more restricted as it was classified as a Schedule II drug with high abuse potential and limited medical use. Dexedrine, shown in Figure 9.12, and other amphetamines are still prescribed to treat narcolepsy and some attention disorders.

As amphetamines became less available and users demanded an even more powerful drug, illicit amphetamine sales and the manufacture of methamphetamine surged. **Methamphetamine** was first synthesized from ephedrine in 1893, but its popularity in the United States emerged in the 1980s as users quickly

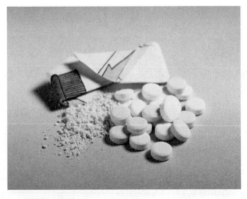

FIGURE 9.12   Dexedrine, dextroamphetamine sulfate, is available in tablet or capsule form.
© Alamy

discovered its powerful euphoric effects. The name methamphetamine comes from its chemical name methyl-amphetamine (**desoxyephedrine**). Methamphetamine is easily produced by the chemical reduction of ephedrine (loss of the hydroxyl group shown in Figure 9.11). Clandestine laboratories perform this reduction through various methods requiring chemicals that are easily obtained. Methamphetamine differs structurally from amphetamine by the additional methyl group (CH_3), which increases its lipid solubility, allowing it to cross the blood-brain barrier within seconds of an injection. As the illustration in Figure 9.13 shows, pure methamphetamine is in a crystal form, thus the name **crystal meth.**

PHARMACOLOGY OF THE AMPHETAMINES   Amphetamines can be administered by various methods, including the oral ingestion of pill form, nasal inhalation (snorting), smoking, or intravenous injection. Peak plasma levels are reached about two to three hours after oral administration and within five minutes of an intravenous injection or smoking. Once administered, amphetamine is rapidly distributed to body tissues, including the brain. Because of its greater lipid solubility, methamphetamine crosses the blood-brain barrier more quickly than other amphetamines allowing larger concentrations to enter the brain. For this reason, methamphetamine produces a greater high and users prefer it over other forms of amphetamine.

The metabolic half-life of the amphetamines varies between 10–15 hours. Amphetamine is metabolized into p-OH-amphetamine and norephedrine, both of which are inactive. Methamphetamine is metabolized into amphetamine before it is more completely metabolized and excreted by the kidneys.

FIGURE 9.13   Methamphetamine (desoxyephedrine) is derived from several precursor compounds, including ephedrine and pseudoephedrine. This crystalline form is typically called crystal meth.   © United States Drug Enforcement Agency

MECHANISMS OF AMPHETAMINE ACTION Amphetamines, including methamphetamine, may have some of the most complex and wide-ranging synaptic effects of any other psychoactive drug (see Figure 9.14). They increase synaptic concentrations of norepinephrine and dopamine by several different mechanisms. First, amphetamines block the **reuptake transporters** for norepinephrine as well as increase the amount of norepinephrine released into the synapse during neuronal firing. Both of these effects contribute to enhanced norepinephrine activity in the brain and the peripheral nervous system.

Amphetamines contribute to increased dopamine activity through several mechanisms. First, they bind to the vesicular transporter and cause dopamine to be released from its storage vesicles into the cytoplasm of the terminal button. This "free" dopamine is then transported to the synaptic cleft by amphetamine-induced reversal of the DAT. Amphetamines also increase the amount of dopamine released from synaptic vesicles during neuronal signaling. These combined mechanisms significantly enhance extracellular concentrations of dopamine.

The mechanisms by which the amphetamines contribute to behavioral stimulation, euphoria, and cortical arousal appear to be complex as well. Dopamine agonism contributes to euphoria and increased cortical arousal via the **mesolimbic-mesocortical pathways** originating in the VTA. Dopamine projects from the VTA to the nucleus accumbens as well as to several other limbic structures including the amygdala and hypothalamus. It is believed that the euphoria caused by amphetamine is mediated in these regions of the brain. Dopamine neurons from the VTA also project to the frontal cortex. In addition, amphetamines increase dopamine activity and release in the **nigrostriatal system,** which originates in the substantia nigra and projects to regions of the basal ganglia. The motor-stimulating effects of amphetamines are mediated by increased dopamine activity in these regions. At high doses, amphetamines can induce **stereotyped behavior** and hallucinations resembling behaviors observed in some schizophrenic patients. In fact, drawing on this observation, researchers have used amphetamine to induce psychotic states in animals to investigate the effectiveness of novel antipsychotic medication. The psychotic symptoms caused by toxic doses of amphetamine, referred to as **amphetamine psychosis,** are believed to involve structures in the basal ganglia.

In summary, amphetamines cause a wide array of effects mediated by enhanced dopaminergic activity in the brain's three major dopamine pathways. These effects include enhanced or stimulated cognitive abilities, increased motor activity, and states of euphoria and well-being.

As illustrated in Figures 9.15 and 9.16, amphetamines cause increased norepinephrine and dopamine activity, which also contribute to cortical arousal via the **reticular activating system** originating in the brainstem. Increased activity in the reticular activating system increases cortical arousal, vigilance, and attention. These neurotransmitters also contribute to amphetamines anorectic (decreased appetite) effects. Amphetamines increase the expression of the appetite-suppressing peptide **cocaine and amphetamine-regulated transcript (CART)** in the **arcuate nucleus** of the hypothalamus. CART is believed to play a significant role in the hypothalamic

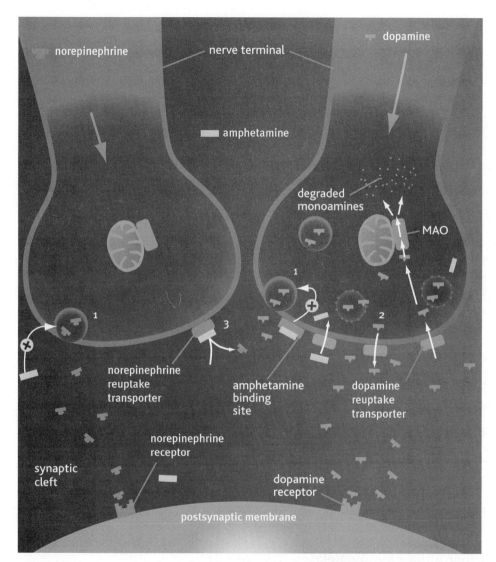

FIGURE 9.14   Amphetamines (including methamphetamine) increase the availability of norepinephrine and dopamine in several ways: (1) by binding to the presynaptic membrane of dopaminergic and noradrenergic neurons to increase the release of norepinephrine and dopamine from synaptic vesicles; (2) by causing the transporters for dopamine to act in reverse, transporting vesicular dopamine back into the terminal and to transport this "free" dopamine into the synaptic cleft; and (3) by blocking the reuptake transporter for norepinephrine.

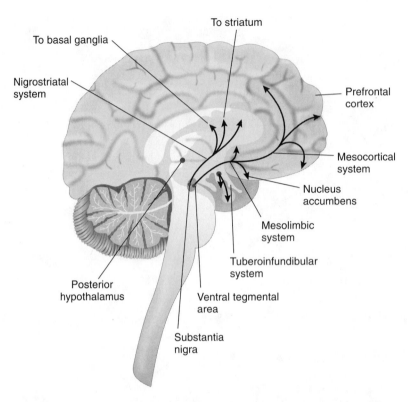

FIGURE 9.15 Dopamine pathways originate in the substantia nigra and VTA of the midbrain. The nigrostriatal system innervates the basal ganglia, while the mesolimbic-cortical system projects to the nucleus accumbens and to the frontal cortex.

regulation of feeding and satiety. Certainly, CART is partially involved in the appetite-suppressing effects of both cocaine and amphetamine.

Other Amphetamine-Related Compounds

A number of other compounds that are structurally related to the amphetamines have powerful euphoric effects as well (Figure 9.17). Perhaps the best known of these is **ecstasy,** or methylenedioxymethamphetamine (**MDMA**). Another but less familiar compound is 3,4 methylenedioxyamphetamine (**MDA**).

MDMA, also referred to as ecstasy, first gained popularity in the 1970s as a drug used to assist psychotherapy (Figure 9.18). Therapists who promoted its use claimed that it facilitated communication and allowed patients to more directly experience their inner self. MDMA quickly spread to recreational use before it was banned by the FDA in 1985. MDMA is now listed as a Schedule I drug with no

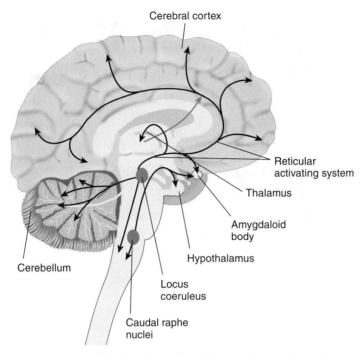

FIGURE 9.16 Cell bodies of norepinephrine neurons are located predominantly in the locus coeruleus and project along the reticular activating system to the hypothalamus, the thalamus, and the frontal cortex.

accepted medical use and a high potential for abuse. The use of MDMA peaked in the early 2000s as its popularity as a club drug soured. By 2003, an estimated 15 percent of 18–25 year olds had used ecstasy. Since 2003, there has been a slight decline in MDMA use.

Users of MDMA report that it produces euphoria, increased self-perception, and enhanced sensations and that it promotes intimacy with others. Ecstasy also produces some troubling side effects, including increased heart rate and blood

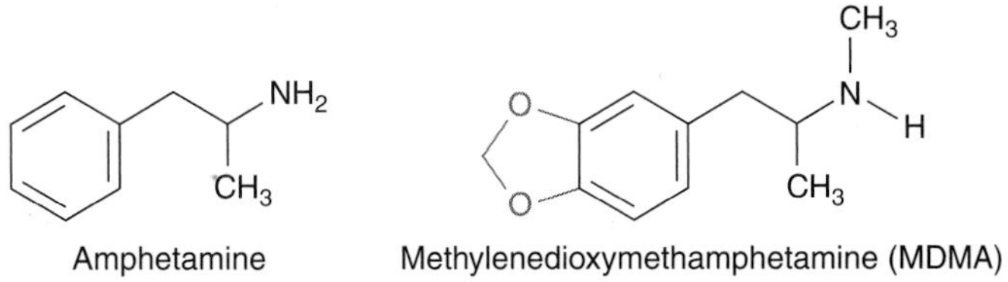

Amphetamine   Methylenedioxymethamphetamine (MDMA)

FIGURE 9.17 MDMA, also referred to as ecstasy, is structurally similar to amphetamine.

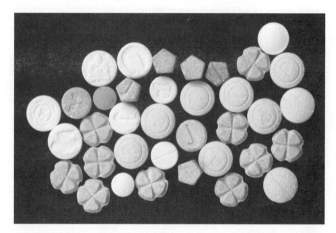

FIGURE 9.18 Tablets of MDMA, used as a club drug, have been banned since 1985. © Scott Houston/Corbis - NY

pressure, intense sweating, and teeth grinding so forceful that broken teeth are not uncommon. To prevent tooth damage, users often chew on baby pacifiers. Perhaps the most troubling effect of MDMA, however, is its powerful neurotoxic effects.

In animal studies, short-term MDMA administration is known to cause significant damage to cortical serotonergic and dopaminergic neurons (Hatzidimitriou et al., 1999; Mechan et al., 2006; Ricaurte et al., 2002). These degenerative effects shown in Figure 9.19 appear to persist for many years after acute MDMA use. By all indications, the use of MDMA by humans also is associated with neurotoxicity. Two recent reviews of research studies that examined the effects of MDMA use on cognitive functions concluded that even low to moderate drug use was associated with decrements in a number of cognitive domains, including attention, concentration, and memory (Kalechstein et al., 2007; Zakzanis et al., 2007).

MDMA is a potent serotonin and dopamine agonist. It directly increases serotonin activity by enhancing serotonin release during neuronal signaling and preventing its reuptake. MDMA appears to enhance dopamine activity in the nucleus accumbens by blocking DAT and may increase dopamine activity indirectly by activating serotonergic neurons, which regulate dopamine activity in the VTA (Amato et al., 2007; Federici et al., 2007). MDMA is predominantly a serotonin agonist, but dopamine activity plays a significant role in its euphoric and behavior-stimulating effects. Dopamine also is believed to mediate MDMA's reinforcing effects in animal self-administration studies (Daniela et al., 2006).

Psychedelic Drugs: LSD and Psilocybin

Of all psychotropic drugs, **lysergic acid diethylamide (LSD)** causes the most astonishing psychological effects. Most notable are LSD's powerful hallucinogenic effects. Hallucinations, which are profound distortions of a person's perceptual experiences, can occur in any sense modality. The most striking hallucinations caused by LSD are visual. These hallucinations typically involve color and movement elaboration. For

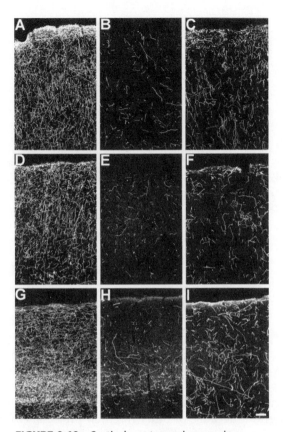

FIGURE 9.19 Cortical serotonergic axons in a squirrel monkey after saline (control) or 5 mg/kg MDMA twice daily for four days. Animals were sacrificed and examined after two weeks or after seven years. Some cortical regeneration can be seen after seven years. Hatzidimitriou et al. (1999). Altered serotonin innervation patterns in the forebrain of monkeys treated with (+/−) 3, 4-methylenedioxymethamphetamine seven years previously: factors influencing abnormal recovery. *The Journal of Neuroscience*, 19(12), 5096–5107.

example, while observing clouds, a person under the influence of LSD may see complex distortions in their color and movement. Sounds or music may be heard with greater intensity and complexity. For instance, because of sound exaggeration, a person may describe hearing a piece of music for the first time when in fact they have heard it on many occasions. Some LSD users describe their hallucinations as **synesthesia,** where sensations in one modality are experienced or mixed with another. For instance, visual hallucinations may occur to the sound of music. Users of LSD typically describe their perceptual experiences as pleasurable and amusing, but some users find these hallucinations disturbing.

FIGURE 9.20 Albert Hofmann (1906–2008). Discoverer of LSD and advocate of its responsible use.
© Bettmann/Corbis

LSD was first synthesized in 1938 by Dr. Albert Hofmann (1906–2008), who was working as a chemist for the Swiss pharmaceutical company Sandoz laboratories. Hofman, shown in Figure 9.20, was investigating the pharmacological properties of variety of alkaloids extracted from plants and the ergot fungus, which grows on grain. Because of other research projects, Hofmann placed the LSD on a shelf, only to return to it five years later.

In 1943, Hofmann began investigating the properties of his previously synthesized LSD, known as LSD-25 because it was the 25th lysergic acid compound synthesized in his laboratory. Hofmann reported in his journal that after working with LSD-25, he became "remarkably restless, combined with a slight dizziness." He returned home, where he further reported "fantastic pictures, extraordinary shapes with intense, kaleidoscopic play of colors." Hofmann believed that he must have absorbed a small amount of LSD through his skin. Several days later he ingested 250 micrograms of LSD to experiment with it further. Soon after ingesting this dose, Hofmann began to get dizzy again. He found it difficult to speak, but managed to get his assistant to escort him home on his bicycle.

> On the way home, my condition began to assume threatening forms. Everything in my field of vision wavered and was distorted as if seen in a curved mirror. I also had the sensation of being unable to move from the spot

Once home, Hofmann found his surroundings both unfamiliar and frightening. He believed that no other known substance evoked such profound psychic effects.

Everything in the room spun around, and the familiar objects and pieces of furniture assumed grotesque, threatening forms. They were in continuous motion, animated, as if driven by an inner restlessness.

Albert Hoffman continued taking LSD (usually on his birthday) for the remainder of his life. He remained an advocate of its responsible use and founded a nonprofit foundation dedicated to furthering the investigation of **psychedelic** substances.

PHARMACOKINETICS OF LSD AND PSILOCYBIN LSD is rapidly absorbed after oral administration and peak plasma levels are reached in about two hours. LSD readily crosses the blood-brain barrier and is quickly distributed to tissues throughout the body. The half-life of LSD ranges between 2 and 3 hours after oral administration, but its effects may last as long as 12 hours. LSD is the most potent of all psychoactive drugs. A popular method to distribute and consume LSD was to apply small amounts of the drug to paper stamps like the ones illustrated in Figure 9.21. Effective doses begin at approximately 25 micrograms (25 millionths of a gram) which is about 1,000 times more potent than amphetamine or cocaine, which have effective doses of approximately 25 milligrams (thousandths of a gram). Ironically, even though LSD is extremely potent, there appears to be no confirmed lethal dose. In 1977, a case of possible overdose was reported, where it was estimated upon autopsy that the user had ingested 320 milligrams (320,000 micrograms) of LSD. However, no cause of death was reported (Griggs et al., 1977). Other estimates for lethal overdose in humans range between 50,000 and 100,000 micrograms, or between 2,000 and 4,000 doses.

FIGURE 9.21 A popular way to deliver and administer LSD is on small stamps that contain 50–100 micrograms of LSD. These stamps are placed on the tongue, where the drug is rapidly absorbed.
© Sinclair Stammers/Photo Researchers, Inc.

FIGURE 9.22 Psilocybin mushroom (*Psilocybe semilanceata*). A common species of psilocybin mushroom found in the Pacific Northwest and in the northeastern United States. © Duncan Shaw / Photo Researchers, Inc.

Psilocybin, shown in Figure 9.22 is a psychedelic compound found in a variety of mushrooms in the *Psilocybe* genus. One common North American species is *Psilocybe semilanceata,* which can be found in cattle and sheep pastures in the Pacific Northwest as well as in several northeastern states. Because the pharmacological properties of LSD and psilocybin are so similar and because the majority of research conducted with psychedelic substances involves LSD, the focus here is on LSD.

LSD Toxicity and Side Effects LSD is characterized by its remarkable hallucinogenic effects, but several noticeable side effects are common as well. These include increased body temperature, heart rate, and blood pressure; pupil dilation; dizziness; and occasional nausea. The psychological side effects can include confusion, acute panic, and noticeable distortions in both space and time. Occasionally, LSD users report that their experience was disturbing or frightening and that their experience was a "bad trip." In addition, a few users report that they experience flashbacks of these disturbing experiences. While there is no known pharmacological mechanism that could cause flashbacks, these unpleasant perceptual experiences more likely correspond to memories of the experiences, not to some residual drug effect. Nevertheless, because a number of LSD users have reported flashbacks that persisted long after drug use, a separate category for **Hallucinogen Persisting Perception Disorder (HPPD)** was created in the *Diagnostic and Statistical Manual of Mental Disorders, Text Revision (DSM-IV-TR)*.

The DSM-IV-TR criteria for HPPD require that a person has not recently used a hallucinogenic drug and shows no present signs of drug intoxication. The following diagnostic criteria must be met:

A. The re-experiencing, following cessation of use of a hallucinogen, of one or more of the perceptual symptoms that were experienced while intoxicated with the hallucinogen (e.g., geometric hallucinations, false perceptions of movement in the peripheral visual fields, flashes of color, intensified colors, trails of images of moving objects, positive afterimages, halos around objects).

B. The symptoms cause clinically significant distress or impairment in social, occupational, or other important areas of functioning.

C. The symptoms are not due to a general medical condition (e.g., anatomical lesions and infections of the brain, visual epilepsies) and are not better accounted for by another mental disorder.

A recent review of the literature on HPPD (flashbacks) concluded that while the disorder is likely to be genuine and can persist for months after LSD use, it is an uncommon occurrence with no known pathology. In addition, there is no consensus on how or whether HPPD should be treated (Halpern et al., 2002).

PHARMACODYNAMICS OF LSD AND PSILOCYBIN   LSD and psilocybin are partial serotonin (5-HT) agonists that bind with high affinity to a number of 5-HT receptor subtypes. As you may recall from Chapter 2, agonists increase or facilitate neural transmission by various mechanisms. **Partial agonists** are drugs that have an affinity for a receptor site, but may exert less of an effect on the receptor than an agonist or the endogenous ligand—in this case serotonin. The affinity of LSD and psilocybin for 5-HT receptors is believed to be a consequence of their similar molecular structure. All three of these substances share a common indole structure, which is illustrated in Figure 9.23.

Research using laboratory animals suggests that the hallucinogenic effects of LSD are mediated specifically by the 5-HT_{2A} receptor subtype. For example, drugs that block 5-HT_{2A} receptors also disrupt the ability of laboratory animals to discriminate between LSD and saline administrations (Appel et al., 2004). Blocking other serotonin receptors does not disrupt the discriminative properties of LSD. Animals lacking the serotonin transporter gene (SERT knockout animals) also fail to discriminate LSD from saline, providing further support for the role of 5-HT_{2A} receptors in LSD's effects (Krall et al., 2008).

Understanding the action of LSD or psilocybin on serotonin receptors only partially explains their profound perceptual effects. What is needed is a better understanding of how serotonergic systems in the brainstem and the cortex modulate sensory information and perception. Several lines of research are beginning to elucidate the cause of hallucinations. One approach is to evaluate

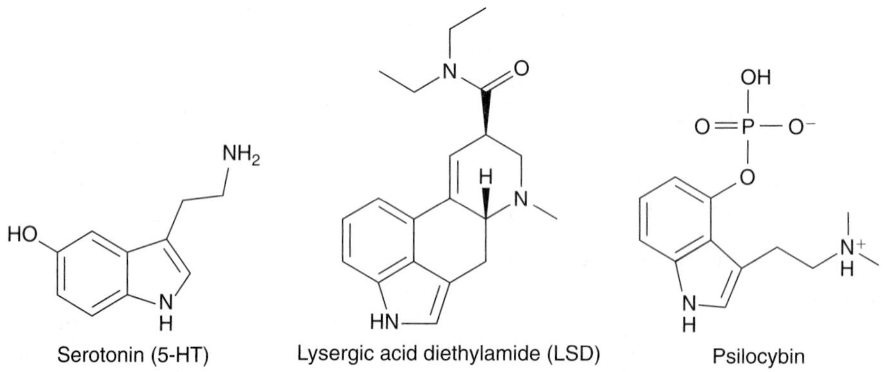

FIGURE 9.23 LSD and psilocybin share a common indole molecular structure with serotonin.

how serotonin systems regulate sensory information projected from the brainstem to the thalamus and then to cortical sensory areas. LSD may disrupt the normal filtering of extraneous sensory information, resulting in overstimulation of cortical sensory areas. LSD does increase the activity of sensory neurons—most notably those in the visual system (Aghajanian et al., 1999). In addition, LSD may also alter the activity of several cortical areas, including the medial prefrontal cortex and the anterior cingulate, by agonizing 5-HT$_{2A}$ receptors there. To demonstrate this, researchers have investigated the increased activity of cortical neurons in response to LSD administration (Gresch et al., 2002). More recent research has shown that LSD effects are mediated by specific pathways in the somatosensory cortex that express the 5-HT$_{2A}$ receptor. Activating these signaling pathways may be sufficient to induce hallucinations independently of sensory input via the thalamo-cortical pathways (González-Maeso et al., 2007).

In summary, LSD and psilocybin hallucinogenic effects are believed to be mediated by partial agonism of 5-HT$_{2A}$ receptors in the brainstem and in several cortical areas including the medial prefrontal cortex, the anterior cingulate, and the somatosensory cortex. How alterations in 5-HT$_{2A}$ activity in these brain regions cause hallucinations remains unknown, but several possibilities have been proposed. First, 5-HT$_{2A}$ agonism in the brainstem appears to disrupt normal filtering of sensory information to the thalamus and cortex, resulting in sensory overload. Second, increased cortical activity by 5-HT$_{2A}$ receptor agonism independent of sensory stimulation may cause hallucinations. Research on the neurophysiological and behavioral effects of hallucinogens is typically done with laboratory animals. Whether the patterns of neuronal signaling induced by these substances in animals resemble the hallucinations reported by humans may never be known.

Marijuana (Cannabinoids)

Marijuana is the common name for the hemp plant **Cannabis sativa.** Archeological evidence for the use of cannabis by the Chinese dates back about 10 thousand

FIGURE 9.24 Marijuana plant (top) and dried mature flower (bottom). © (top) United States Drug Enforcement Agency; (bottom) United States Drug Enforcement Agency

years BC. From China, cannabis apparently spread to India and other regions of the Middle East, where its resin, known as hashish, was and still is widely used. From Egypt, cannabis use spread throughout Europe and then to the United States. During the colonial period, the hemp plant was considered a valuable agricultural commodity, used primarily for the production of rope (Figure 9.24). Whether the colonists were aware of the intoxicating effects of cannabis is still not known for sure. Certainly, by the mid-1800s, cannabis was being used for its pharmacological effects in the United States. In the mid-1800s, a number of popular European writers were describing their experiences with cannabis, including the French authors Victor Hugo and Pierre Gautier, who established the then-famous Club des

Hashischins in Paris. In the early 1900s, cannabis was being touted for its medicinal properties in Western medicine and an assortment of cannabis products was available. In the 1930s, at least 28 different cannabis products were available to American physicians, including a variety of pills, syrups, and even drug mixtures. However, further investigations into the pharmacological properties and uses of cannabis were cut short by the **Marihuana Tax Act** of 1937, which essentially banned cannabis through an elaborate code of costly tax provisions. Legal historians have argued that had it not been for numerous unfounded claims that cannabis caused insanity, murder, and death, the act may not have passed. Cannabis was further regulated by the Controlled Substances Act of 1970, which listed cannabis as a Schedule I drug. Since 1970, a number of states have attempted to decriminalize marijuana use, but all legal efforts to reschedule it for medicinal purposes have failed. A few states, however, do allow patients with specific medical conditions to grow or purchase small amounts of marijuana for medicinal use.

PHARMACOKINETICS OF MARIJUANA (Δ^9-TETRAHYDROCANNABINOL, OR THC)   With two Israeli chemists' isolation of the active compound in marijuana in 1964 and its synthesis a year later, the pharmacological properties of cannabis were quickly pursued (Gaoni & Mechoulam, 1964; Mechoulam & Gaoni, 1965). Prior to the isolation of **Δ^9-tetrahydrocannabinol (THC)** (molecular structure shown in Figure 9.25) by Gaoni and Mechoulam, the assumption was that the psychoactive properties of cannabis were due to a combination of cannabinols that had first been extracted from marijuana in 1846 by the Smith brothers in Edinburgh Scotland. The Smiths were pioneers of modern pharmacology who produced a variety of plant extracts for medicinal purposes. Using traditional methods of the time, they tested their cannabis extract on themselves and reported the following:

> . . . two thirds of a grain of this resin acts upon ourselves as a powerful narcotic, and one grain produces complete intoxication.

(From Iversen, 2000; 1 grain is approximately 65 milligrams.)

Smoking marijuana may be the most effective method of administration. Upon heating, the THC in marijuana is vaporized and readily passes through the

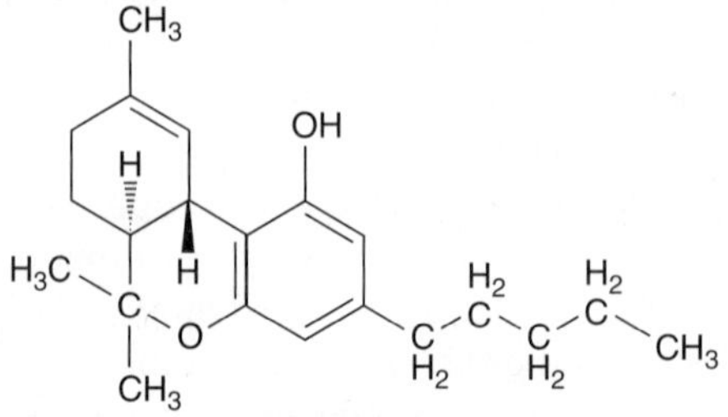

FIGURE 9.25   Molecular structure of THC.

surface of the lungs into the blood. Within seconds of inhalation, THC passes through the blood-brain barrier and enters the brain. Peak plasma levels are typically reached within a few minutes of smoking. While plasma concentrations vary depending on the amount administered, typical doses in experienced users result in concentrations between 100 and 200 ng/mL of plasma. The THC concentration of marijuana is highly variable depending on what variety of cannabis is used and how it is grown. Concentrations of THC in the dried flowering top of the plant average about 8.5 percent but can range from about 3 percent to as high as 25 percent for some varieties that have been developed through selective breeding. If a typical marijuana cigarette contains about 0.5 gram of plant material with a THC content of about 8.5 percent, it would contain approximately 42.5 milligrams of THC. The amount of this dose that is actually inhaled may only be as high as 10–20 percent, with the remaining going up as sidestream smoke or exhaled before complete absorption. Thus, the bioavailability of THC in a cigarette may be only about 5 milligrams.

After administration, TCH is rapidly metabolized in the liver into the active metabolite 11-hydroxy-THC and then into the inactive metabolite 11-nor-9-carboxy-THC before excretion. Relatively small amounts of THC are excreted unchanged. The subjective effects of THC peak at about the same time as plasma levels and persist for one to two hours or when plasma levels decline below about 5.0 ng/mL. The elimination half-life of THC ranges between 24 and 72 hours.

Orally ingested marijuana is absorbed more slowly and incompletely and can depend heavily on what else is in the stomach and digestive system since THC can be absorbed by dietary fats. In addition, orally ingested THC must first pass through the liver where much of it is metabolized by liver enzymes. Peak plasma levels are reached between 1 and 4 hours after consumption. Because THC and its metabolites remain in the body for such long periods sensitive drug tests can detect a single use for up to 2 weeks after exposure. Frequent users of marijuana may have detectable levels of metabolites for 3 to 4 weeks after abstinence as the THC that had accumulated in tissues is gradually metabolized.

PHARMACODYNAMICS OF MARIJUANA (THC) Before THC was isolated, the assumption was that cannabis acted on nerve cells in some nonspecific way that interrupted normal cell functioning. For example, an active substance might enter and distort the cell's membrane and thereby alter cell firing. You will learn in Chapter 10 that alcohol can exert these kinds of nonspecific effects. After the discovery of THC, however, it became clear that THC must interact directly with neuronal signaling systems. One clue to this hypothesis is that doses of THC that produce noticeable effects are extremely small. If an average marijuana cigarette delivers about 5 milligrams of THC, only a very small fraction of this amount actually enters the brain. Therefore, to exert its effects, THC must be acting directly on cell receptors rather than some unknown nonspecific effect taking place (e.g., the conformation of cell's membrane being altered).

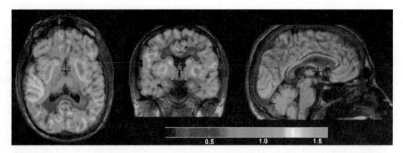

FIGURE 9.26 Positron emission tomography (PET) images of a brain following the injection of a radioactive CB_1 receptor ligand. High densities of cannabinoid receptors are expressed in the cerebral cortex, cerebellum, caudate nucleus, putamen, globus pallidus, substantia nigra, and hippocampus. Lighter regions indicate greater CB1 receptor density. © Burns et al., 2007.MK-9470, a positron emission tomography (PET) tracer for in vivo human PET brain imaging of the cannabinoid-1 receptor. PNAS, June 5, 2007, vol. 104, no. 23. © 2007 National Academy of Sciences, U.S.A.

In 1988, researchers using a radioactive labeling technique identified **cannabinoid receptors** in the brains of laboratory rats. In these experiments, radioactive tritium was attached to the synthetic cannabinoid compound CP-55,940 (Devane et al., 1988). By labeling cannabinoid receptors with a radioactive marker, scientists could locate the distribution of these receptors throughout the brain (see Figure 9.26). Numerous cannabinoid receptors (CB_1 receptors) are now known to be located in the basal ganglia, cerebellum, hippocampus, amygdala, thalamus, and cortex. The distribution of these receptors accounts at least partially for many of marijuana's behavioral effects. A second type of cannabinoid receptor has since been found outside the brain in lymphatic tissues of the immune system. These receptors are classified as CB_2 receptors to distinguish them from the CB_1 receptors located in the brain.

Cannabinoid CB_1 receptors are located on the presynaptic terminals of several types of neurons. All of these receptors are metabotropic G-protein coupled receptors that regulate the formation of cyclic AMP (cAMP). In fact, it is believed that CB_1 receptors are the most widely expressed G-protein coupled receptors in the brain. THC's activation of the G-protein inhibits cAMP formation, inhibits voltage-dependent Ca^{++} channels, and facilitates K+ efflux, all of which contribute to neural inhibition. In the hippocampus, THC binds to CB_1 receptors on gamma-aminobutyricacid (GABA) neurons, which exert inhibitory control over glutamate activity (Figure 9.27). The activation of these CB_1 receptors in the hippocampus disinhibits glutamate activity in hippocampal pyramidal cells, allowing them to fire more readily. Similarly, in the VTA, THC binds to CB_1 receptors on GABA neurons, which exert inhibitory control over dopamine activity (Szabo et al., 2002). This form of neuronal suppression appears to be a common type of short-term neuronal plasticity where depolarization of a neuron causes a decrease in GABA-mediated neural inhibition.

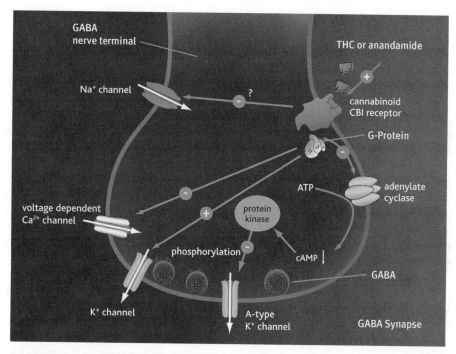

FIGURE 9.27 CB$_1$ G-protein coupled receptors on GABA presynaptic nerve terminal. The binding of THC or anandamide to the CB$_1$ receptor inhibits GABA release by preventing Ca^{++} influx.

Following the discovery of cannabinoid receptors in 1988, the search for endogenous ligands intensified. In 1992, William Devane (the discoverer of the cannabinoid receptor) and his colleagues in Israel also isolated an endogenous cannabinoid, arachidonoyl ethanolamine. They named this substance **anandamide** after the Sanskrit word *ananda*, which means "bliss." Anandamide is enzymatically synthesized on demand by neurons from a precursor fatty acid, arachidonic acid. Scientists now recognize that anandamide plays an important role in regulating neural activity that mediates memory formation, appetite, pain signaling, motor activity, and reward. Other endogenous ligands for the cannabinoid receptor have yet to be found. The euphoric effects of marijuana are believed to be mediated in part by disinhibition of dopamine activity in the mesolimbic system (Fadda et al., 2006; Lecca et al., 2006; Solinas et al., 2008). It remains unclear whether cannabis use is sufficient to cause the kinds of adaptations to dopaminergic neurons that underlie addiction.

MEDICINAL USES FOR CANNABINOID COMPOUNDS In the past decade, a number of states have attempted to pass legislation to allow the use of marijuana for medicinal purposes. Presently, only about a dozen states permit physicians to prescribe marijuana, and even in those states, it may be difficult to get a prescription. Also, a number of unsuccessful attempts have been made to reclassify marijuana as a Schedule II drug.

Drug manufacturers have created several synthetic THC drugs that are available by prescription. Dronabinol (Marinol) is a synthetic THC extracted from marijuana. Originally listed as a Schedule II drug, Marinol was recently rescheduled as a Schedule III drug. Marinol has been approved by the FDA to treat nausea and vomiting associated with cancer chemotherapy and radiation therapy as well as appetite loss in patients with AIDS. However, advocates for the medicinal use of marijuana claim that Marinol is not as effective as marijuana, perhaps because synthetic drugs lack the nearly 60 other cannabinoids that are present in marijuana. In addition, users of Marinol often complain about its delayed onset and its excessive intoxicating effects that are more difficult to regulate compared to marijuana that is smoked.

Nabilone (Cesamet) is an entirely synthetic THC that was approved by the FDA in 1985 but not marketed until 2006. It was approved to treat nausea and vomiting related to cancer therapy as well as to treat anorexia and weight loss associated with AIDS. Nabilone is presently a Schedule II drug.

A number of other medical conditions may respond well to marijuana treatment. These include the vision-threatening increase in ocular pressure associated with glaucoma; chronic and phantom limb pain; withdrawal symptoms associated with opiate and alcohol addictions; and muscle spasms in patients with multiple sclerosis, Huntington's disease, and Parkinson's disease. Marijuana also may be useful in treating bronchial constriction in asthmatics and in treating certain kinds of cancer by inhibiting cell proliferation and metastasis (Kogan, 2005; Preet et al., 2008). Clearly, more research is needed on the potential therapeutic benefits of marijuana.

PHARMACOLOGICAL EFFECTS OF MARIJUANA, DRONABINOL, AND NABILONE (THC)

Memory and Cognition Marijuana and synthetic THC compounds exert significant effects on the central and the peripheral nervous systems. The central effects of THC include mild euphoria, anxiolysis, and distortions in the perception of time. In some users, THC can cause confusion and a heightened sense of anxiety, but these effects tend to dissipate after repeated administration or use. In addition, THC impairs both cognitive and motor functioning—effects that do not typically persist beyond the period of intoxication. The deleterious effects of marijuana on memory have long been known, and recent research has revealed that these effects are mediated, at least in part, by cannabinoid CB_1 receptors in the hippocampus. Cannabinoids act by suppressing glutamate activity and **long-term potentiation (LTP)** in hippocampal neurons (Hoffman et al., 2007; Kang-Park et al., 2007; Nowicky et al., 1987; Ranganathan et al., 2006).

Motor Control and Coordination Cannabinoids also are known to disrupt motor control and performance. These effects appear to be mediated by two distinct mechanisms. First, there is an abundance of cannabinoid receptors on glutamate neurons in the basal ganglia. High doses of THC inhibit the release of glutamate in afferent neurons in the basal ganglia, causing disrupted movement and even

FIGURE 9.28 Roto-rod treadmill test for motor coordination. Rats or mice are placed on a rotating rod. Time spent on the rod is a measure of motor coordination. Accessed at: http://web .med.harvard.edu/sites/RELEASES/html/11_1Sinclair.html.

cataplexy. Animals administered high doses of THC exhibit immobility as well as symptoms characteristic of Parkinson's disease (Gerdeman et al., 2001). Second, cannabinoids disrupt normal cerebellar control of movement independently of central dopamine motor pathways (DeSanty et al., 2001; Patel et al., 2001). Taken together, cannabinoids have the potential to disrupt movement and coordination by activating CB_1 receptors in the cerebellum and the nigrostriatal dopamine system (see Figures 9.28 and 9.29). Paradoxically, activation of these cannabinoid receptors seems to have therapeutic effects for individuals with degenerative motor diseases, including multiple sclerosis, Parkinson's disease, and Huntington's disease. Cannabinoids also may offer protection from further neurodegeneration associated with these diseases by inhibiting the cytotoxic effects of excessive Ca^{++} influx into neurons in the motor pathways (Battista et al., 2006; Sagredo et al., 2007).

Antiemetic Effects: Nausea and Vomiting Nausea resulting from chemotherapy and radiation therapy remains a significant problem for most patients undergoing treatment for cancer. While several **antiemetic** (antinausea) drugs, including benzodiazepines, are often useful, a significant number of patients prefer marijuana over the alternatives. Beside the fact that cannabinoids may be more effective than benzodiazepines for nausea, the side effects of cannabinoids often are more tolerable to patients. Nausea and vomiting are triggered as toxic drugs and cellular debris stimulate receptors in the **area postrema** of the brainstem. Cannabinoids appear to act directly on CB_1 receptors in the area postrema, inhibiting the vomiting reflex (Sharkey et al., 2007; Slatkin et al., 2007; Van Sickle et al., 2001).

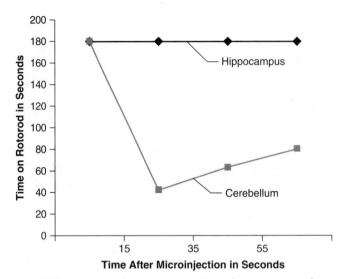

FIGURE 9.29 Time mice spent on a roto-rod as a measure of motor coordination after a microinjection of the CB_1 agonist CP55,940 into the hippocampus (control) or the cerebellum. Cerebellar injections of the CB_1 agonist sharply disrupted performance. Redrawn from DeSanty, 2001.

Cannabinoids also have significant peripheral effects, including effects on the cardiovascular and immune systems. In addition, cannabinoids exert a significant effect on the intraocular pressure associated with glaucoma.

Cardiovascular Effects   The cannabinoids have notable effects on both heart rate and blood pressure. While initial use may cause an increase in blood pressure as well as heart rate in some users, repeated use typically produces a significant decrease in blood pressure as a result of vasodilatation. This vasodilating effect is mediated peripherally through CB_1 receptors located on the heart and blood vessels. As blood pressure drops, heart rate increases moderately to compensate for a drop in blood flow. This increase in heart rate may be problematic for some users with severe cardiovascular disease, but there is no evidence that cannabis use is associated with adverse cardiovascular events. In fact, cannabinoids may protect the heart against ischemia, a restriction in blood supply to the heart, which can lead to a heart attack (Lépicier et al., 2006, 2007).

Immune System Effects   As noted earlier, cannabinoids interact with both CB_1 and CB_2 receptor types. While CB_1 receptors are expressed on central and peripheral neurons, CB_2 receptors appear to be localized almost exclusively on cells of the immune system. The role of these cannabinoid receptors in immunoregulation remains obscure. However, recent research has revealed that cannabinoids (and CB_2 agonists specifically) inhibit immune responses and inflammation (Lombard et al., 2007; McKallip et al., 2002). Therefore, the development of specific CB_2 agonists may prove useful in treating a variety of inflammatory and autoimmune disorders. As of yet, the immunosuppressive properties of cannabis have not been demonstrated to be a significant concern for patients or users. There is no evidence that cannabis use is associated with an increased risk of infectious disease or the progression of cancer.

Tolerance and Dependence   In laboratory animals, repeated administration of high doses of THC can produce tolerance to the cardiovascular and behavioral responses of THC. For example, in a recent study with mice, researchers administered THC twice a day for seven days on an escalating dose schedule from 10 mg/kg to 60 mg/kg. Animals on the increasing dose schedule developed tolerance to THC's locomotor and analgesic effects, while mice treated with 10 mg/kg twice each day did not. The mechanism underlying tolerance in these animals was a decrease in cannabinoid receptor activation in several brain regions including the hippocampus, cingulate cortex, periaqueductal gray area, caudate nucleus, nucleus accumbens, and cerebellum (McKinney et al., 2008). Other researchers have shown that cannabinoid receptor internalization may mediate this decrease in CB_1 receptor activation during tolerance (Wu et al., 2008). Changes in the rate of THC metabolism also may contribute to cannabis tolerance, but this alone is not sufficient to account for tolerance to such high THC doses.

While tolerance to THC has been demonstrated in humans and in animals that have been given extremely high doses of THC, tolerance may not occur to the doses most users and patients receive. A typical dose of Marinol, for example, is approximately 5–20 mg/day for a patient being treated for nausea or glaucoma, and as stated previously, a typical marijuana cigarette may contain about 5 milligrams of THC. The doses required to demonstrate tolerance in mice would be equivalent to approximately 300–500 milligrams of THC for a person.

Chronic use has been reported to produce dependence in some cannabis users, and abstinence can cause symptoms of withdrawal. These symptoms may include cravings, depressed mood, aggressiveness, and irritability—symptoms associated with other drug dependencies including nicotine and caffeine. Because not all users experience withdrawals upon abstinence, whether cannabis causes dependence or addiction remains controversial. Proponents of marijuana use argue that it neither causes dependence nor contributes to addiction; however, those who oppose marijuana use argue that it does. Research with animals may partially resolve this controversy. One way researchers investigate a drug's abuse potential is to determine whether animals will administer the drug or substance to themselves. Typically, such **self-administration** experiments involve training animals to press levers to receive small injections of a drug.

Self-Administration of THC   Drugs that have a high abuse potential (e.g., cocaine, heroin, amphetamine, and nicotine) easily maintain lever pressing by animals when these drugs are injected as reinforcers. In a self-administration experiment, animals are trained to lever-press for drug administration intravenously or directly into the brain via a cannula upon each completion of the schedule requirement. For example, on a fixed-ratio 10 (FR-10) schedule, a small amount of drug is administered after each tenth lever-press response. Each drug administration is typically followed by a brief delay before lever presses are counted for a successive trial. Over the course of an experimental session, an animal may earn 20–30 microinjections of a particular drug. In one such study, researchers trained squirrel monkeys to self-administer 4.0 µg/kg of THC per injection on an FR-10 schedule. Over the course of a one-hour experimental session, animals received between 40 and 50 injections of THC. After five 1-hour sessions, the reinforcer was switched from THC to a saline vehicle solution for another five sessions and then again to THC for the final five sessions (Justinova et al., 2003). The results of this experiment are presented in Figure 9.30. Clearly, THC maintained high levels of self-administration in this experiment, suggesting that TCH does have abuse potential.

To illustrate how complicated interpreting the research on the abuse potential of cannabis can be, consider an alternative method for evaluating a drug's abuse potential. It is widely accepted that addictive drugs produce sensitization to dopamine neural circuits in the mesolimbic reward system. These adaptations can be observed as behavioral sensitization and increased locomotor activity. In a

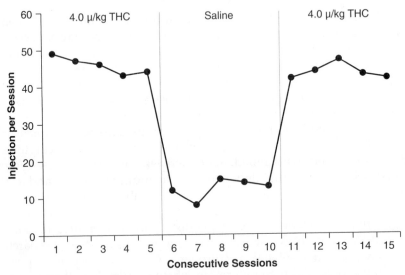

FIGURE 9.30 Number of THC or saline vehicle injections per training session on an FR-10 schedule for squirrel monkeys self-administering THC. THC maintained high rates of self-administration when compared to the saline vehicle solution. Redrawn from Justinova et al., 2003.

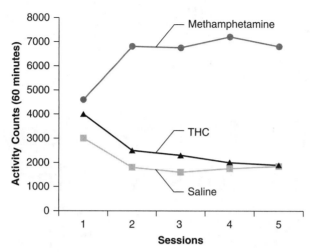

FIGURE 9.31 Behavioral sensitization as measured by activity in mice observed following methamphetamine treatment but not after THC or saline treatment. Redrawn from Varvel et al., 2007.

recent experiment, the behavioral sensitizing effects of THC after repeated administration in mice were compared to those following methamphetamine administrations. As shown in Figure 9.31, methamphetamine produced behavioral sensitization while THC did not (Varvel et al., 2007). Whether the lack of behavioral sensitization is a consequence of THC's motor-depressing effects in the basal ganglia is not known.

In summary, cannabinoids can, under certain conditions, produce tolerance and dependence in both animals and humans. Tolerance appears to be mediated by receptor internalization and a subsequent decrease in receptor activity. The controversy about the abuse and addictive potential of cannabis and the synthetic THC compounds remains unresolved at the time of this writing. It has been estimated that about 4 percent of regular cannabis users develop a substance abuse disorder as defined by the DSM-IV-TR (Chen et al., 2005), a number far lower than the frequency of dependency to other drugs of abuse. If cannabis use does lead to dependence, this risk is much lower than it is for other abused drugs.

10

The Pharmacology of Nonscheduled Psychoactive Drugs
Alcohol, Nicotine, and Caffeine

ALCOHOL

Alcohol is the most widely abused drug in the United States and throughout the world. By the time U.S. students graduate from high school, over 80 percent will have used alcohol and nearly 30 percent of those students will have used it heavily. Because alcohol is so readily available and is used by such a large proportion of the population, it is no wonder that it leads to the most prevalent of all substance abuse disorders. According to the National Institute on Alcohol Abuse and Alcoholism, approximately 6 percent of the population over 18 years of age has an alcohol abuse problem and alcohol continues to contribute to nearly 25 percent of all automobile fatalities.

While no one may ever know when alcohol was first produced and consumed, it was most likely the fortuitous result of fruit or grain fermentation. The earliest evidence of the intentional fermentation of an alcoholic beverage comes from the discovery of large Stone Age jugs used to make beer about 12,000 years ago. Wine production in China may be dated back more than 9,000 years, and wine making is depicted in Egyptian pictographs dating back as far as 6,000 years. Clearly, the production of alcoholic beverages from the fermentation of grains and fruits has a long history.

The distillation of alcohol from grains appeared much later during the second millennium BC in the region now known as Iraq, while large-scale distillation of alcohol for *spirits* probably did not occur until the first century AD in Greece. The modern distillation of spirits began in the early 1400s in Ireland, where whiskey making was first described by monks. Soon after, a variety of drinks, including gin, vodka, and rum, were produced by distillation in different regions around the world. Prior to modern distillation, the alcohol content of alcoholic beverages remained between 3 and 15 percent. With the wide implementation of distillation processes, the alcohol concentration in beverages increased dramatically, as did its abuse potential.

Distillation is essentially a separation process rather than a chemical process. In alcohol distillation, alcohol is separated from other fermentation products through heating. Because alcohol has a lower boiling point, it evaporates early in the heating process. This alcohol vapor is then cooled as purified alcohol. Although distillation can result in pure **ethyl alcohol (ethanol)**, most hard liquors and spirits are about 40–50 percent alcohol. Typically, the alcohol content of hard liquors is represented as **proof** alcohol. The term *proof* may have originated in the 18th century when British sailors were paid with provisions of rum. To prove that the rum was not diluted with water, it was mixed with gunpowder and ignited. If the mixture burned, this was proof that the alcohol content was at least 50 percent (actually closer to 57 percent). Thus, rum that was at least 57 percent alcohol was 100 percent proven to be undiluted. Today alcohol proof is exactly 2 times the alcohol percent by volume. For example, a spirit that is 40 percent alcohol is considered 80 proof.

Pharmacology of Alcohol

ABSORPTION   Alcohol (ethanol, illustrated in Figure 10.1) is both water- and fat-soluble and readily diffuses across all cell membranes. Once ingested, ethanol rapidly passes through the blood-brain barrier, allowing neural tissues to reach blood alcohol levels quickly. Peak blood levels are typically reached between 30 and 60 minutes depending on alcohol concentration and other substances present in the stomach and digestive track. Higher alcohol concentrations (stronger drinks) diffuse more rapidly than lower concentrations, and the availability of food in the stomach and intestines delays distribution because most alcohol (about 80 percent) is absorbed through the walls of the small intestine while the rest is absorbed by the stomach or excreted through sweat, respiration, and urine immediately after absorption. Because alcohol is so readily absorbed by all tissues, including the placenta, a pregnant woman exposes her fetus to the same blood levels she has.

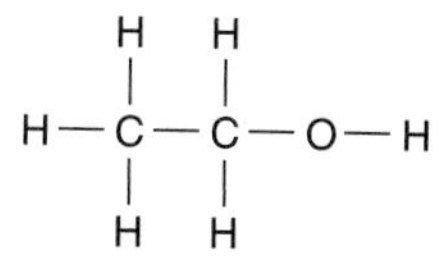

FIGURE 10.1   Molecular structure of ethanol (CH_3CH_2OH or C_2H_5OH).

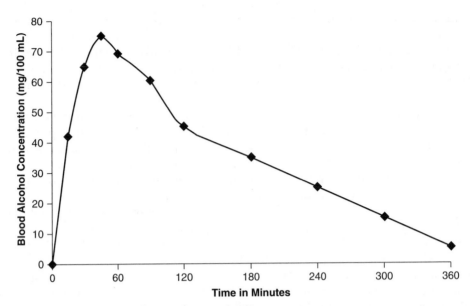

FIGURE 10.2 BACs are typically measured in milligrams of alcohol per 100 mL of blood. In this example, after the consumption of 100 mL of a 90 percent alcohol (180 proof) solution, peak blood levels are reached within 45 minutes. A BAC of 80 mg/100 mL is the same as 0.08 percent (.08 grams per 100 mL), which is the legal limit for intoxication in most states.

Blood alcohol concentration (BAC) is typically expressed as grams of alcohol in 100 milliliters (mL) of blood. For example, 80 milligrams (mg) of alcohol in 100 mL of blood is equivalent to 0.08 grams per 100 mL. Sometimes this is expressed as a percent of alcohol by weight in blood (see Figure 10.2). The somewhat arbitrary legal limit for intoxication in most states is 0.08 or 0.08 percent. Rather than measure the alcohol content of blood directly, most sobriety tests rely on the strong correlation between blood alcohol and the alcohol expired through respiration. A breathalyzer can immediately estimate BAC by analyzing a sample of a person's breath, which contains alcohol passed from the bloodstream into the lungs. A common misconception is that this alcohol can be concealed by eating breath mints that mask the odor of alcohol.

The level of intoxication an individual experiences at a particular BAC varies significantly. While one person may be considerably impaired at a BAC of 0.04 percent, another person may function quite normally. Table 10.1 describes some of the effects typically observed at different BACs in percent.

METABOLISM OF ALCOHOL The metabolism of alcohol begins immediately after consumption. Approximately 90–95 percent of ingested alcohol is metabolized by the enzyme **alcohol dehydrogenase;** the remaining 5–10 percent is excreted through perspiration and respiration or is metabolized by another liver enzyme, **P450.** P450, or cytochrome P450, is an enzyme found in most biological systems that is essential to oxidative reactions involved in metabolism. Some alcohol is

TABLE 10.1 **Common Behavioral and Cognitive Effects of Different Levels of Alcohol Intoxication**

BAC %	Common Behavioral and Cognitive Effects
.01–.05	Increased heart and respiration rates
	Moderate detrimental effects on cognitive and motor tasks
	Mild sense of euphoria and anxiolysis
	Reinforcement
.06–.10	Moderate sedation
	Decreases in attention, increased reaction time, impaired motor coordination
	Significant cognitive impairment
	Depression and irritability
.10–.15	Significant increases in reaction time and impairment in cognition and judgment
	Agitation and irritability (aggressiveness)
	Significant impairment of balance and movement
	Impaired vision
	Slurred speech
	Nausea and vomiting
.16–.29	Severe sensory impairment, including reduced awareness of external stimulation
	Severe motor impairment (e.g., frequently staggering or falling)
.30–.39	Nonresponsive stupor and loss of consciousness
	Significant anesthesia
	Respiratory depression and possible death
.40 and up	Unconsciousness
	Respiratory depression
	Death for most individuals at these levels

metabolized by this oxidative reaction. Only a small fraction of alcohol is excreted in the urine unmetabolized. Small amounts of alcohol dehydrogenase in the stomach begin to metabolize alcohol immediately. If the stomach is full, alcohol absorption is delayed and more of it is metabolized in the stomach. Once alcohol enters the small intestine, it is quickly absorbed into the blood supply, which carries it to the liver, where the remaining portion (80–85 percent) is metabolized by liver alcohol dehydrogenase. Alcohol that is metabolized by stomach and liver enzymes before it has had a chance to enter tissues is called **first-pass metabolism.** Approximately 25–30 percent of ingested alcohol is metabolized before or during its first pass through the liver. Once tissue and blood levels have equilibrated, metabolism continues at a slower rate. On average, about 17 mg of alcohol per 100 mL of blood is metabolized each hour. This is essentially equivalent to the amount of alcohol in a shot of 40 percent alcohol (whiskey), a 4-ounce glass of 12 percent wine, or a 12-ounce bottle of beer. The amount of alcohol

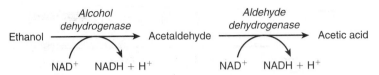

FIGURE 10.3 The metabolism of alcohol into acetaldehyde and further into acetic acid depends on the availability of the enzymes alcohol dehydrogenase and aldehyde dehydrogenase and the coenzyme NAD⁺.

metabolized each hour depends on the availability of alcohol dehydrogenase and its coenzyme **nicotinamide adenine dinucleotide (NAD)**. NAD is considered a rate-limiting enzyme because its availability determines the rate of alcohol metabolism. As a coenzyme in alcohol metabolism, NAD⁺ (positively charged) facilitates a reduction reaction (the transfer of an electron) that results in the release of energy. In alcohol metabolism, NAD⁺ is reduced to NADH during the production of adenosine triphosphate (ATP), which is a source of cellular energy.

Because men and women have different levels of alcohol dehydrogenase, they metabolize alcohol at different rates. Women have less stomach alcohol dehydrogenase than men do and may metabolize 50 percent less alcohol in their stomach compared to men. In addition, women typically have a greater fat-to-muscle ratio than men do, meaning that women have less blood for a proportional body weight, as fat has a lower blood supply than muscle. Both of these factors contribute to greater blood concentrations in women than in men for equivalent doses of alcohol.

During its first phase of metabolism, alcohol is converted to acetaldehyde, which is highly toxic. Acetaldehyde is quickly metabolized into acetic acid by the enzyme **aldehyde dehydrogenase** (Figure 10.3). Genetic variations in the expression and form of aldehyde dehydrogenase have profound effects on alcohol metabolism. For example, a small proportion of the Asian population codes for an inactive form of aldehyde dehydrogenase, meaning that in these individuals, acetaldehyde is not further converted to acetic acid. Even small amounts of alcohol result in toxic levels of acetaldehyde, which causes nausea, vomiting, sweating, dizziness, and severe headaches—more severe forms of the symptoms many be experienced as a hangover. The drug **disulfiram (Antabuse)** inhibits aldehyde dehydrogenase and causes these same symptoms in alcoholics who use it to discourage drinking. Acetic acid is oxidized into carbon dioxide and water.

Mechanisms of Alcohol Action: Pharmacodynamics

Although alcohol is a simple molecule, its pharmacodynamics are far from simple. As mentioned previously, alcohol is both water- and fat-soluble, and because of this, it exerts effects on a wide range of cellular functions and systems. To describe the pharmacodynamics of alcohol, this chapter will consider both its nonspecific and specific effects on neuronal functioning.

Alcohol's nonspecific effects include its effects on all cellular membranes. By its ability to dissolve in the lipid cell membrane, alcohol disrupts several cell

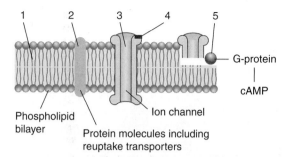

Phospholipid
bilayer

Protein molecules including
reuptake transporters

Ion channel

FIGURE 10.4 Specific and nonspecific effects of alcohol on neuronal membranes. (1) Fluidization alters lipid composition and distorts cell membrane. This affects the conductance of membrane potentials. (2) Fluidization interacts with proteins imbedded in cell membrane. Altering the function of membrane proteins disrupts internal cell processes, including synthesizing and storing neurotransmitters and disrupting neurotransmitter reuptake. (3) Fluidization interacts with ion channel. It interferes with the movement of ions across cell membranes. (4) Fluidization binds to receptor sites on receptor complex. Alcohol acts as an acetylcholine antagonist, a glutamate antagonist, and an agonist at GABA receptors. (5) Fluidization stimulates the G protein that regulates the activity of the second messenger cyclic adenosine monophosphate (cAMP).

processes. In the past, it was believed that alcohol's main mechanism of action was membrane **fluidization.** Alcohol was presumed to act as a neuronal depressant and as an anesthetic by dissolving in cell membranes and making them more fluid. This fluidization disturbs several membrane processes, including the movement of ions through channels, the conductance of membrane potentials, and the release and storage of neurotransmitter substances (Figure 10.4, 1–3). Membrane fluidization seems to account for many of alcohol's generalized depressant and analgesic effects at higher doses.

However, fluidization does not account for many other effects of alcohol. These effects, typically at lower doses, include cognitive and motor disruptions, euphoria, anxiolysis, and reinforcement. To account for these effects, the discussion will examine how alcohol specifically alters the synaptic activity of several neurotransmitter systems.

EFFECTS OF ALCOHOL ON NEUROTRANSMITTER SYSTEMS

Gamma-Aminobutyricacid (GABA)   Perhaps the most important of alcohol's specific actions is its agonistic effect on GABA receptors, specifically the GABA_A receptor. It has long been known that many of alcohol's behavioral effects are mediated by enhanced GABA activity. Early evidence for this comes from studies

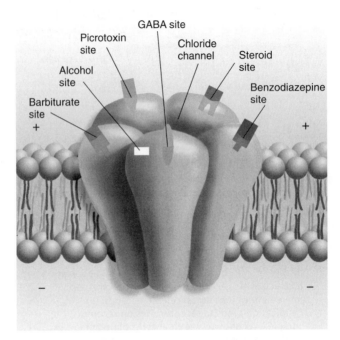

FIGURE 10.5 GABA$_A$ receptor complex controls an ion channel for Cl⁻. Several distinct receptor subtypes on the GABA$_A$ complex have been identified. These include receptor subtypes for barbiturates, benzodiazepines, steroids, and perhaps alcohol. The drug Ro15-4513 and alcohol appear to binds to the delta (Δ) receptor.

showing that alcohol's effects depend on increased GABA binding to its receptors and the influx of Cl⁻, which the GABA$_A$ receptor controls. What is not well understood is whether alcohol binds to a specific receptor site, as the barbiturates and benzodiazepines do, or whether it acts in some other facilitative way. Because GABA synapses control the activity of many neuronal systems, including glutamate, dopamine, and the opioids, a description of alcohol's effects on GABA receptors is essential for a complete understanding of alcohol's behavioral effects.

Recent evidence suggests that alcohol may bind to specific GABA$_A$ receptors, including the delta (Δ) receptor (see Figure 10.5). Some of the strongest evidence for alcohol's specificity for delta receptors comes from studies using the drug **Ro15-4513,** which is a powerful competitive antagonist for alcohol's effects. When Ro15-4513 is administered to intoxicated animals, the behavioral effects of alcohol intoxication are immediately reversed (see Figure 10.6). Because Ro15-4513 is known to competitively bind to the delta receptor, it is presumed that alcohol also has an affinity for this receptor subtype (Olsen et al., 2007; Santhakumar et al., 2007).

Chronic exposure to alcohol during pregnancy has long been known to cause damage to developing brains and to cause **fetal alcohol syndrome (FAS).** One

FIGURE 10.6 Two adult female rats 20 minutes after an injection of ethanol with or without the alcohol antagonist Ro15-4513. One rat received ethanol only and is lying down. The other rat received Ro15-4513 with ethanol show no signs of visible intoxication.   Suzdak (1986). A selective imidazobenzodiazepine antagonist of ethanol in the rat. Photograph Courtesy of National Institute of Mental Health, Bethesda, MD.

contribution to these deleterious effects of prenatal alcohol exposure is an upregulation of fetal GABA$_A$ receptor expression in the cerebral cortex and the hippocampus. Chronic alcohol exposure typically leads to the downregulation of specific GABA$_A$ receptor subtypes and the upregulation of others. (See "Alcohol Tolerance and Dependence," which follows.) Alterations in GABA$_A$ receptor expression have been shown to contribute to cognitive and behavioral deficits in experimental animals (Iqbal et al., 2004). In addition, alcohol consumption during pregnancy can lead to disruptions in normal GABAergic cell migration in fetal brains because of increased GABA availability in the cerebral cortex (Cuzon et al., 2008). A characteristic symptom of FAS is abnormal cortical morphology and development.

Glutamate   At high concentrations, alcohol is a powerful antagonist of the **N-methyl-D-aspartate (NMDA)** subtype of glutamate receptors. These receptors are widely distributed throughout the brain and spinal cord and play important roles in learning and memory as well as the general excitability of cortical neurons. The activation of NMDA receptors results in the opening of ion channels for Na$^+$ and Ca^{++} influx and K$^+$ efflux, all of which produce excitatory postsynaptic potentials in receiving neurons. NMDA receptors are all **ligand-gated receptors**, meaning that ion flow occurs only when a neurotransmitter is bound to it.

Alcohol's antagonism of NMDA receptors contributes to its impairment of learning and memory as well as to its amnesiac effects during intoxication at moderate doses and memory *blackouts* at higher doses. Chronic exposure to alcohol use contributes to NMDA receptor upregulation and appears to account for intensified central nervous system (CNS) activity and seizures often observed in alcoholics during abstinence and alcohol withdrawal.

Dopamine   Alcohol has a powerful effect on dopamine activity in the mesolimbic system. Injections of alcohol directly into the ventral tegmental area (VTA) increases dopamine release in the nucleus accumbens (NA) (Doyon et al., 2004; Rodd et al., 2004). In addition, alcohol ingestion at intoxicating doses increases dopamine release in these regions. It is widely accepted that alcohol's euphoric and reinforcing effects are mediated by increased mesolimbic dopamine activity. Drugs that block dopamine binding also disrupt the self-administration of alcohol in laboratory animals (Cowen et al., 2005; Gonzales et al., 2004). The mechanisms by which alcohol increases dopamine release remain unknown.

Dopamine neurons in the VTA are regulated by a large population of GABAergic neurons in this region. Therefore, increasing GABA release by alcohol would inhibit dopamine activity in the VTA and the subsequent release of dopamine in the NA. Indeed, $GABA_A$ receptor blockade in the VTA results in increased mesolimbic dopamine activity. Recent evidence by Theile et al. (2008) suggests that alcohol causes a biphasic effect on dopamine activity. Initially, alcohol causes an increase in dopamine excitability in the mesolimbic system, followed by GABA-mediated inhibition. Therefore, the effects of alcohol on mesolimbic dopamine release may be limited by neural inhibition in the VTA. It also is quite possible that there are two distinct populations of VTA dopamine neurons with different sensitivities to GABA inhibition, as there appear to be for opioid neurons in the same brain regions (Ford et al., 2006).

Although alcohol does alter dopamine activity, at least initially, and it does support limited self-administration by animals, its abuse and addictive potential is certainly less than that of the psychostimulants (e.g., cocaine and the amphetamines). A significant proportion of the population uses alcohol frequently, yet only a small fraction of these people become addicted.

Opioids   Acute alcohol administration also is known to increase opioid activity in several brain regions, including the VTA. As described in Chapter 7, opioids contribute to increased dopamine activity in the VTA by inhibition of GABAergic inhibitory control over dopamine release (inhibition of inhibition). At least part of alcohol's effects on dopamine neurons is mediated by opioid suppression of GABAergic inhibition (Job et al., 2007; Kang-Park et al., 2007; Xiao et al., 2007). Drugs such as the opiate antagonist naloxone significantly blunt alcohol-induced dopamine release while opiate agonists enhance it. This indirect mechanism of enhanced mesolimbic dopamine activity appears to contribute significantly to alcohol's reinforcing properties.

In summary, alcohol affects the activity of most major neurotransmitter systems directly as it does with GABA and glutamate and/or indirectly as it does with dopamine and the opiates. Because of alcohol's widespread nonspecific effects on these systems, exactly how alcohol exerts its behavioral effects remains somewhat unclear. To complicate this already confusing picture, long-term exposure to alcohol contributes to a host of cellular adaptations, including receptor downregulation. These adaptations appear to play roles in alcohol tolerance as well as dysphoria and seizures associated with abstinence.

Alcohol Tolerance and Dependence

The development of tolerance to alcohol depends on a person's pattern of drinking (sporadic binge drinking versus frequent drinking) as well as the amount of alcohol consumed during a drinking bout (one or two drinks versus numerous drinks leading to heavy intoxication). Individuals who sporadically consume a few drinks develop little or no tolerance to alcohol, while heavy, frequent drinkers develop tolerance quite rapidly. Another factor that influences alcohol tolerance is the use of other drugs in the sedative or anti-anxiety class. For example, the use of barbiturates or benzodiazepines can contribute to alcohol tolerance by a process referred to as **cross tolerance.** Cross tolerance occurs when drugs share similar mechanisms of action. In this case, $GABA_A$ agonism is the common mechanism. Individuals who have developed tolerance to benzodiazepines, for example, demonstrate tolerance to alcohol even when they have no history of alcohol use. Tolerance to alcohol (and other drugs) develops with contributions from several mechanisms.

METABOLIC TOLERANCE   **Metabolic tolerance** occurs as the liver produces compensatory increases in alcohol dehydrogenase and P450. Because over 90 percent of all alcohol is metabolized by these enzymes, even small increases in their availability can significantly increase alcohol metabolism. It is estimated that metabolic tolerance contributes to about 25 percent of all tolerance to alcohol. The remaining mechanisms for tolerance include cellular tolerance and behavioral tolerance.

CELLULAR TOLERANCE   **Cellular tolerance** includes several distinct adaptations to neuronal functioning, including receptor and cAMP downregulation. Chronic exposure to alcohol contributes to excessive GABAergic activity followed by receptor internalization (downregulation). Tolerance appears to result as specific $GABA_A$ receptor subtypes are no longer expressed on cell surfaces. $GABA_A$ receptors fall into several subunit classes, including alpha, beta, gamma, and delta subtypes. Each of these subtypes has several additional forms that traditionally are numbered (e.g., 1–4). Chronic alcohol intake appears to contribute to significant internalization of the alpha 1 $GABA_A$ receptors (Kumar et al., 2003, 2004; Liang et al., 2007). Alpha 1 $GABA_A$ receptors are widely expressed in the cortex and mesolimbic system, which may account for tolerance to alcohol's cognitive and motor effects as well as its reinforcing effect. Not all $GABA_A$ receptors are downregulated by chronic alcohol exposure. In fact, alpha 4 subtypes in the hippocampus appear to increase with chronic exposure. These differences in $GABA_A$ receptor expression may account for different symptoms observed during a person's abstinence from alcohol after chronic exposure.

BEHAVIORAL TOLERANCE   Animals and humans demonstrate significant motor impairment during alcohol intoxication. However, when animals are allowed to practice difficult motor tasks under the influence of alcohol, they develop tolerance to these disruptive effects. Tolerance to these motor effects of alcohol is called **behavioral tolerance,** which can be distinguished from cellular, metabolic, and associative tolerance in animal experiments. For instance, in one experiment, a group of rats under the influence of alcohol was trained to run on a treadmill to avoid small electric foot shocks while other rats were given the same amount of alcohol *after* the training sessions. During testing, all animals performed the avoidance task under the influence of alcohol, but only the group of animals that were trained under the influence of alcohol demonstrated good avoidance. Experiments like this one show that behavioral tolerance to alcohol can be learned (Wenger et al., 1981). This learning appears to involve adjustments to motor coordination (operant conditioning) in the presence of alcohol onset cues.

Another term for behavioral tolerance is **state-dependent learning** because animals tend to perform better when tested under the same physiological or drug state they were in while being trained (see Figure 10.7). In this case, performance is dependent upon the animal's alcohol state during training.

Associative Tolerance

Behavioral tolerance (a learned behavioral adaptation to alcohol's motor effects) is not the same as the **associative tolerance** discussed in previous chapters. Associative tolerance refers to Pavlovian conditioned responses elicited by drug onset cues—often the context of drug administration. It is presumed that these

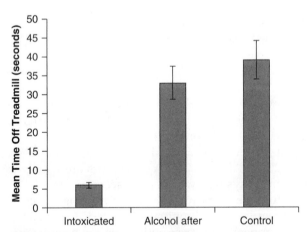

FIGURE 10.7 Avoidance performance as measured by time off the treadmill under the influence of alcohol. Intoxicated animals received alcohol before daily training sessions, the "alcohol after" group received the same amount of alcohol after daily training sessions, and the control group received saline. All animals were tested under the influence of alcohol. Data from Wenger et al., 1981.

elicited responses include the rapid internalization of receptors, making fewer available for drug or neurotransmitter binding. Associative tolerance to the effects of alcohol has been demonstrated by Siegel and his colleagues (Siegel, 1987). The details of synaptic adaptations that underlie associative tolerance have not been completely worked out, but they do seem to involve glutamate NMDA receptors.

Dependence

Dependence on alcohol is expressed by a pattern of symptoms typically observed during abstinence after chronic alcohol use. The duration and severity of these symptoms depends on several factors including the duration of heavy alcohol use, the amount of alcohol used, and genetic factors that control for the neuronal adaptations that occur during alcohol exposure. The symptoms of dependence include nausea and vomiting, headache, sweating, tremors, and seizures during alcohol abstinence. In severe cases of long-term alcohol (or benzodiazepine or barbiturate) abuse, **delirium tremens** (DT) can occur. Symptoms of DT include confusion, agitation, fever, tachycardia, and hypertension. If left untreated, DT can be fatal in as many as 35 percent of cases. DTs are typically managed by sedation with benzodiazepines, which can be gradually tapered off over the course of treatment. It is believed that the symptoms of dependence are the result of neural adaptations to $GABA_A$ receptor expression that occur during chronic alcohol use. In the absence of alcohol, these adaptations (primarily $GABA_A$ receptor downregulation) cause perturbations in the regulation of a variety of physiological systems.

Pharmacological Treatment of Alcohol Dependence   The prevalence of severe alcohol dependence and addiction in the United States is from 5–7 percent of the population, but as high as 10 percent among young adults between the ages of 18 and 29. The pharmacological treatment of alcohol dependence begins during the early stages of withdrawal by managing the symptoms with benzodiazepines. Because of the similarity in mechanism of action, benzodiazepines can diminish the severity of symptoms as neuronal systems begin to revert back to prealcohol states. In addition to benzodiazepine treatment, a number of other drugs have been used to diminish cravings that occur during alcohol withdrawal. The opiate antagonist naltrexone seems to be the most effective. Table 10.2 summarizes several common drugs used to treat alcohol dependence and addiction. Although several of these drugs appear to withstand rigorous treatment outcome studies, many have limited value in treating alcohol abuse.

A promising new line of research is investigating the role of the cannabinoid (CB1) receptor in substance abuse. A number of animal studies suggest that the CB1 receptor plays a significant role in alcohol preference. For example, CB1 knockout mice that lack the CB1 receptor show increased sensitivity to alcohol and a diminished alcohol-reinforcing effect. In addition, deleting the CB1 receptor gene eliminates voluntary alcohol intake by laboratory animals. The CB1 receptor antagonist **Rimonabant (SR141716)** also reduces voluntary alcohol intake in both

TABLE 10.2 Pharmacological Treatment Options for Alcohol Dependence and Addiction

Drug	Mechanism of Action	Effectiveness (recent reviews)
Diazepam (Valium)	$GABA_A$ receptor agonist, benzodiazepine	Effective in reducing the severity of withdrawal symptoms (Lejoyeux et al., 1998).
Naltrexone	Opiate antagonist	Effective in reducing the severity of cravings. Does not reduce recidivism rates (Richardson et al., 2008; Snyder et al., 2008).
Acamprosate	$GABA_A$ agonist, NMDA antagonist	Limited effectiveness in reducing cravings and recidivism rates (Richardson et al., 2008; Snyder et al., 2008).
Fluoxetine (SSRIs)	Selective serotonin reuptake inhibitor	Limited effectiveness when alcohol abuse is comorbid with depression or anxiety (Cornelius et al., 2008).
Disulfiram (Antabuse)	Inhibits conversion of acetaldehyde into acetic acid; causes nausea and vomiting when used with alcohol	Effective in compliant patients but compliance is low unless supervised (Suh et al., 2006).
Bupropion (Wellbutrin)	Dopamine agonist, antidepressant	Limited effectiveness (Torrens et al., 2005).
Rimonabant (SR141716)	Cannabinoid (CB1) antagonist	Effective in a limited number of studies (Le Foll et al., 2008; Soyka et al., 2008).

humans and experimental animals (Basavarajappa, 2007). The use of experimental CB1 antagonists in further research will be needed to substantiate these findings and to demonstrate its clinical effectiveness in treating substance abuse.

NICOTINE

Nicotine is a pharmacologically active alkaloid produced by the tobacco plant *Nicotiana tabacum,* shown in Figure 10.8. The tobacco plant appears to have been indigenous to the Americas but spread around the world. Evidence for its first cultivation and use date back at least 5,000 years by the natives of South America. Tobacco use played an important role in the culture and medicinal practices of indigenous Americans. Europeans were first introduced to tobacco after the return of Columbus, who received dried tobacco leaves as gifts from the inhabitants of the West Indies. By the early 1500s, tobacco was being planted and cultivated in Europe, where it had a great appeal. Shortly after tobacco's arrival in Europe, North American Indians, who smoked tobacco in small pipes, introduced it to American settlers. By the 1700s, tobacco use had spread around the world.

In 2006, the Centers for Disease Control and Prevention (CDC) estimated that the prevalence of smoking in the United States was 20.8 percent in adults over

FIGURE 10.8 A field of tobacco plants (*Nicotiana tabacum*) growing in North America. © Bill Barksdale/AG Stock Images/Corbis–NY

the age of 18. This is approximately 46 million smokers. Smoking contributes directly to about 438,000 deaths each year in the United States and to annual healthcare costs of over $167 billion dollars. Each year about 60 percent of smokers attempt to quit, but fewer than 5 percent are successful. On the bright side, nearly half of all American smokers eventually quit and the prevalence of smoking in the United States continues to decline from its all-time high of just over 50 percent of adults 40 years ago to fewer than 21 percent now. However, cigarette sales continue to increase in many countries and smoking is now considered to be the second major cause of death—and the leading preventable cause—in the world. Thirty percent of the world's smokers live in China, where smoking is promoted by the government, which produces, controls, and profits from cigarette sales. Over 350 million Chinese citizens smoke tobacco, which is more than the entire U.S. population. The World Health Organization (WHO) considers smoking tobacco to be a global epidemic.

Pharmacology of Nicotine

ABSORPTION The typical cigarette contains between 0.5 and 2.0 milligrams of nicotine. Only a small percent of this nicotine reaches the bloodstream, as the rest goes up in sidestream smoke, is captured by filters, or is destroyed through

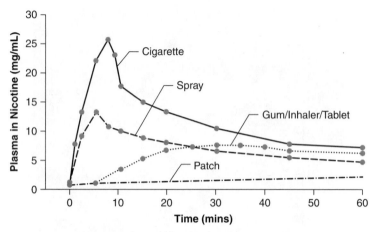

FIGURE 10.9 Time course of blood plasma levels of nicotine after several different routes of administration. Cigarette smoking yields the highest plasma levels.

burning. Nicotine is highly lipid-soluble and readily enters the circulatory system through the linings of the mouth and lungs as well as all skin and mucosal surfaces. Once in the blood, nicotine easily crosses the blood-brain barrier. The inhalation of smoked tobacco produces the highest plasma levels of nicotine, which begins to enter the brain within 5–10 seconds of inhalation (see Figure 10.9). Other routes of administration, including intravenous injections, produce substantially lower peak levels, but within 30–45 minutes, the blood levels of nicotine are essentially the same for all methods of administration. The metabolic half-life of nicotine is approximately 90–120 minutes in adults. However, in a fetus or newborn exposed to maternal nicotine, the half-life can be 3–4 times longer. Chronic smokers regulate their blood levels by adjusting the interval between cigarette smoking. During long periods of abstinence, as during sleep, blood levels drop and symptoms of withdrawal may begin to emerge. Regular smokers experience the most severe cravings upon waking during the night or early in the morning.

Most nicotine is metabolized by the P450 liver enzyme **CYP2A6** and aldehyde oxidase during first-pass metabolism. About 80 percent of nicotine is metabolized into **cotinine,** which is excreted along with several other minor metabolites in the urine. (Refer to Figure 10.10.)

A genetic variation in the gene that codes for the expression of CYP2A6 has been identified in about 20 percent of the population. Because most nicotine is metabolized by CYP2A6, this deficit decreases the rate of nicotine metabolism. Interestingly these individuals tend to smoke less and have a lowered risk of tobacco dependence and tobacco-associated disease (Pianezza et al., 1998; Siu et al., 2008). Presumably this decreased risk of dependency is a consequence of more

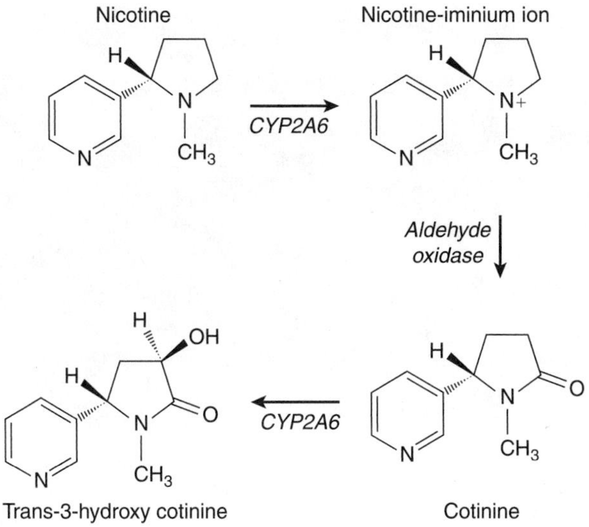

FIGURE 10.10 The metabolism of nicotine into its principal metabolite cotinine by the P450 enzyme CYP2A6.

stable but lower blood levels of nicotine, similar to wearing a nicotine patch. This conclusion is supported by animal studies showing that the rate of nicotine self-administration is positively associated with increased rates of nicotine metabolism (Siu et al., 2006).

Mechanisms of Nicotine Action: Pharmacodynamics

Nicotine has a high binding affinity for a subtype of the ionotropic acetylcholine receptor. This receptor subtype was in fact named the **nicotinic acetylcholine receptor** (nAChR) because of nicotine's binding affinity. The nAChR is constructed from a number of subunits referred to as alpha 2 through 10 and beta 2 through 4 (shown in Figure 10.11). These subunits are arranged around a central ion channel that controls the influx of positively charged ions. While some nAChR configurations control K^+ and Ca^{++} channels, the majority control an ionotropic Na^+ channel. Once nicotine or acetylcholine binds to the receptor complex, the ion channel opens rapidly. The ion channel returns to its closed configuration after nicotine diffuses away. Typically, nicotine remains bound to the nAChR for only 1–2 milliseconds. However, high doses of nicotine can have prolonged receptor-activating effects when high levels of the drug remain in proximity to the receptor. These nAChRs can be found both pre- and postsynaptically. Presynaptic nAChRs cause an increase in the release of neurotransmitter from the receiving neuron. When nicotine binds to a receptor controlling the influx of Ca^{++}, it activates a Ca^{++}-dependent second messenger system. These metabotropic synapses are much slower and their actions longer-sustained than ionotropic receptors. These

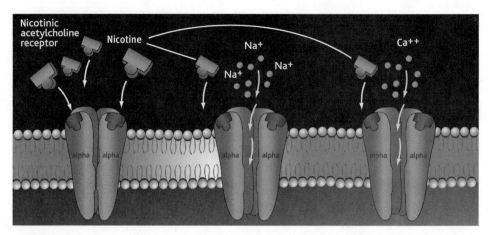

FIGURE 10.11   Nicotine binds to nAChRs, which control ion channels for Na⁺, K⁺, or Ca⁺⁺ influx. Source: How drugs act: molecular aspects. In: Pharmacology, 3rd edition. Rang HP, Dale MM and Ritter JM.   © CNSforum.com

metabotropic receptors have been found presynaptically where they function to increase the synthesis and release of neurotransmitters.

Nicotinic acetylcholine receptors are widely distributed throughout the central and peripheral nervous systems. In the peripheral nervous system, nicotinic receptor sites are located in neuromuscular junctions of voluntary muscles. Nicotine stimulates these receptors and can cause muscle tremors. Nicotine also increases heart rate and blood pressure, decreases body temperature, stimulates the release of epinephrine from the adrenal glands, increases muscle contraction and activity of the bowel, and causes a constriction of blood vessels in the skin. This latter effect may be what causes premature wrinkling of the skin in smokers and why facial wrinkles associated with aging can be diminished with acetylcholine antagonists (e.g., **Botox**). In the central nervous system nAChRs are found in the cerebral cortex, the thalamus, the hippocampus, the VTA, and regions of the basal ganglia. Nicotinic receptors also are located in the brainstem raphe nuclei and in the locus coeruleus.

Because of the wide distribution of nicotinic receptors, the presumption that nicotine has significant effects on a variety of behavioral and physiological functions would be correct. For example, nicotine increases arousal and cognitive functioning in humans and in laboratory animals. These effects are observed as increased cortical arousal measured by electroencephalograph (EEG), decreases in motor reaction time, and improved recall memory. Because of these effects, nicotine and other cholinergic drugs have been used to treat the cognitive deficits associated with Alzheimer's disease and other forms of dementia (Hernandez et al., 2005; Levin et al., 1998; Murray et al., 2002). Nicotine also may be used to improve symptoms in individuals with attention-deficit hyperactivity disorders (ADHDs). In a recent study of young nonsmoking ADHD adults, nicotine administered by a skin patch was shown to decrease excessive behaviors and improve several cognitive and reaction time measures (Potter et al., 2008).

NICOTINE TOLERANCE AND SENSITIZATION   Tolerance to nicotine is both complex and incomplete. Tolerance to several of nicotine's physiological and behavioral effects is observed following repeated nicotine administration to humans and animals. In fact, tolerance may need to occur to its aversive effects before nicotine's reinforcing effects may be experienced. For instance, early exposure to nicotine produces dizziness and nausea, which quickly disappear following repeated administration. Smokers would likely cease smoking if tolerance to these effects did not occur quickly. These effects also may occur in laboratory animals. Nicotine self-administration is often difficult to obtain in experimental animals and depends on the procedures for administration. The most effective method for establishing self-administration in animals is to initially force-administer nicotine. After a period of forced consumption, animals will respond to injections of nicotine on intermittent schedules of infusion. The initial period of forced administration may be sufficient to induce tolerance to nicotine's aversive effects.

Nicotine's effects are complicated by the fact that both tolerance and **behavioral sensitization** occur following repeated exposure. Numerous studies have demonstrated that repeated nicotine exposure contributes to tolerance to its behavior-activating effects. While initial treatment causes decreases in locomotor activity, chronic treatment produces behavioral sensitization. Tolerance to nicotine is typically lost after several days of abstinence (e.g., Stolerman et al., 1973). In an experiment conducted by Collins et al. (1990), rats were given subcutaneous infusions of either saline or nicotine for seven days. After chronic nicotine or saline administration, all of the animals were given nicotine and were exposed to an open field to measure locomotor activity. Control animals given prior exposure to saline demonstrated behavioral suppression, while nicotine-treated animals developed behavioral sensitization. As tolerance develops to nicotine's behavior-suppressing effects, animals show increased locomotor activity. These results are depicted in Figure 10.12.

Tolerance and sensitization to nicotine occur in two stages. The first stage is referred to as acute tolerance, which occurs rapidly during or immediately following the course of administration. **Acute nicotine tolerance** appears to result from rapid nAChR desensitization, resulting in a closing of the cation channel. This desensitization essentially attenuates further nicotine effects on its receptor. After repeated administration, the second stage of sensitization develops, which is represented by upregulation of specific subtypes of nAChRs (see Figure 10.13). This effect of nicotine appears paradoxical because repeated administration of most receptor agonists leads to receptor downregulation while repeated nicotine administration appears to lead to upregulation. A widely expressed subtype of

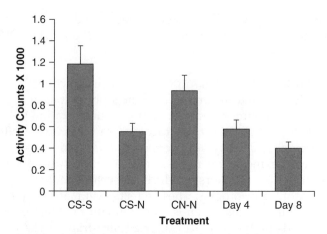

FIGURE 10.12 Tolerance to nicotine's behavioral depressant effects. Animals received chronic saline treatment followed by saline during open field testing (CS-S), chronic saline treatment followed by nicotine before testing (CS-N), or chronic nicotine treatment followed by nicotine before testing (CN-N). The effects of nicotine on activity in the open field also were examined four (Day 4) and eight (Day 8) days after nicotine abstinence. Tolerance to nicotine is observed as an increase in activity (behavioral sensitization) in the nicotine-treated animals (CN-N) but not in the saline pretreated animals (CS-N). Tolerance was lost after four days of abstinence.   Collins et al. (1990). Dissociation of the Apparent Relationship Between Nicotine Tolerance and Up-Regulation of Nicotinic Receptors. Reprinted from Brain Research Bulletin, 25, 373–379 with permission from Elsevier.

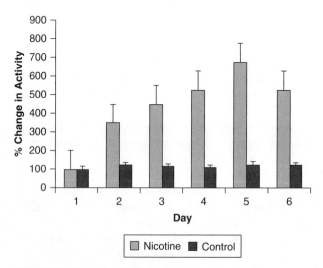

FIGURE 10.13 Behavioral sensitization expressed as increased activity to single and repeated nicotine injections in rats. Data from Li et al., 2008.

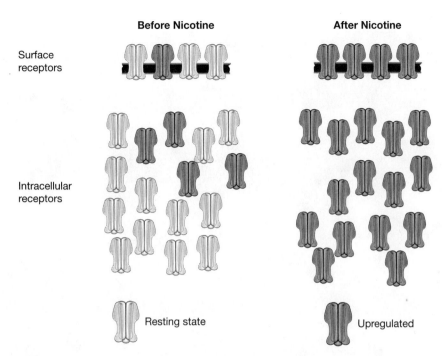

FIGURE 10.14 Exposure of the α4β2 nicotinic receptors to nicotine changes their state from a low-affinity resting state (white) to an upregulated high-affinity state (gray). Because nicotine readily crosses cellular membranes, both surface and intracellular receptors undergo structural changes. © Vallejo, Y. F., Buisson, B., Bertrand, D., & Green, W.N. (2005). Chronic nicotine exposure upregulates nicotinic receptors by a novel mechanism. *Journal of Neuroscience*, 25(23), 5563–5572.

nAChR that undergoes upregulation is the alpha 4 beta 2 (α4β2) receptor type. The α4β2 receptor exists in two activational states. In its resting state, nicotine binds only with low affinity to the α4β2 receptor, but in an upregulated state, nicotine binds with a much higher affinity (see Figure 10.14). Nicotine exposure appears to induce structural changes to α4β2 receptors on the cell's surface as well as to the intracellular receptors that may become expressed on the surface. Once in the upregulated state, these receptors have an increased affinity for nicotine (Sallette et al., 2004; Vallejo et al., 2005; Walsh et al., 2008). Other nicotinic receptor subtypes also may undergo similar structural changes.

Nicotine's behavioral sensitization effects may be mediated by upregulation of nAChRs in the VTA and its projections to the NA, in the prefrontal cortex (the mesolimbic-cortical system), and in the striatum and by nicotine's agonistic effect on dopamine release in these regions (Buisson et al., 2001; Li et al., 2008; Tapper et al., 2004; Vann et al., 2006). Imaging studies like the one shown in Figure 10.15 show upregulation and sensitization after repeated nicotine use. Upregulation of the α4β2 receptors in the mesolimbic system may underlie dependence and addiction.

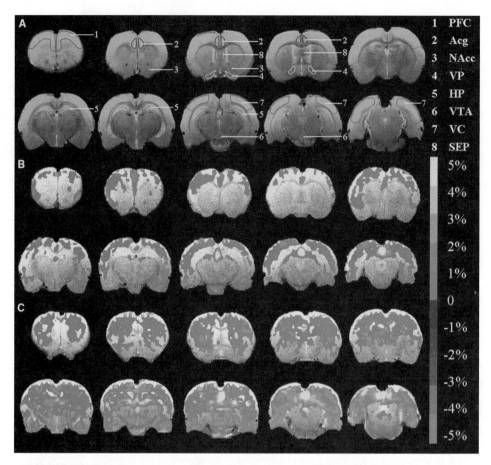

FIGURE 10.15   (A) MRI images showing eight brain regions. (1) PFC = prefrontal cortex; (2) Acg = anterior cingulate gyrus; (3) NAcc = nucleus accumbens; (4) VP = ventral pallidum; (5) HP = hippocampus; (6) VTA = ventral tegmental area; (7) VC = visual cortex; (8) SEP = septum. (B) Activation in many brain structures in response to a single dose of nicotine. (C) Increased activation in response to the fifth dose of nicotine shows upregulation and sensitization. © Zhixin Li.   © AP Wide World Photos

NICOTINE DEPENDENCE   From the preceding discussion, it is clear that even brief exposure to nicotine induces structural changes to the nicotinic α4β2 receptor. These changes to nicotinic α4β2 receptors underlie behavioral sensitization and nicotine dependence. In some individuals (with presumably different genetic propensities for these structural changes), upregulation and sensitization may occur after smoking one or two cigarettes (DiFranza, 2008; Scragg et al., 2008). Upregulation of nicotinic receptors has been shown to occur within minutes of nicotine exposure (Walsh et al., 2008).

Upregulation of nicotinic receptors induces increased dopamine release from neurons in the mesolimbic-cortical system. Prolonged nicotine exposure causes downregulation of these dopamine receptors and is believed to underlie nicotine dependence and the cravings associated with withdrawal. Like other drugs of abuse, including cocaine, the amphetamines, the opiates, and alcohol, nicotine stimulates dopamine release, which contributes to its dependence and addictive potential. During abstinence and cravings, neural activity in a number of brain regions, including the orbital frontal cortex, the prefrontal cortex, the cingulate cortex, and the NA, is increased. Increased activity of these mesolimbic-cortical structures mediates cravings to smoke and maintain nicotine addiction (Fehr et al., 2008; Wang et al., 2007).

Pharmacological Treatment for Nicotine Dependence   The health consequences of using tobacco products are well known and numerous (in spite of what Figure 10.16 depicts). Some of the most common risks include lung, esophageal, pancreatic, kidney, and oral cancer; pulmonary disease; heart disease; increased risk of stroke; and numerous complications to pregnancies. Although the numerous mechanisms by which tobacco products cause these diseases are not the topic of this text, some of the treatment options are.

As stated in the outset of this section, of the 46 million tobacco users in the United States, about 60 percent attempt to quit each year. Of these, only about 5 percent are successful for a full year or more. The good news is that about half of the individuals who have used tobacco will eventually be successful at quitting, but typically after many unsuccessful attempts.

FIGURE 10.16   Even though there has been little debate among scientists about the addictive potential of nicotine since the early 1950s, executives from major tobacco companies testified before Congress in 1994 that nicotine was not addictive.   © AP Wide World Photos.

Several pharmacological alternatives are available to assist those who want to stop smoking but need help. These aids include **nicotine replacement therapy (NRT)**, bupropion (Zyban), varenicline (Chantix), and potentially nicotine immunization.

Nicotine Replacement Nicotine replacement therapies include over-the-counter (OTC) nicotine transdermal patches (Nicoderm, Habitrol, and Nicotrol), nicotine gum (Nicorette and Polacrilex), and nicotine lozenges (Commit). Because these products contain doses of nicotine, the cravings associated with tobacco abstinence are blunted. The idea behind NRT is to transfer the delivery of nicotine from tobacco products to a method of administration that a person can gradually eliminate. In addition, many of the health hazards associated with tobacco use can be avoided. However, smokers find that NRT is not always effective. The slower absorption of nicotine from these products is not a substitute for the rapid absorption of nicotine inhalation. Furthermore, smokers find it more difficult to regulate nicotine doses with these products than with smoking.

Several prescription nicotine supplements are available, including nicotine sprays (Nicotrol, NicoNovum) and nicotine inhalers (Nicotrol). Unlike transdermal nicotine patches, these methods were designed to deliver nicotine more quickly and in a manner similar to smoking. When compared to placebos in randomized clinical trials, all NRTs are more effective. In some studies, NRT nearly doubled the success rate of quitting (Burns et al., 2008; Eisenberg et al., 2008).

Bupropion (Zyban) Bupropion was briefly discussed as a treatment for depression in Chapter 3. As you may recall, for an antidepressant, bupropion has an unusual mechanism of action. Rather than block the reuptake of serotonin and/or norepinephrine, bupropion preferentially blocks the reuptake of dopamine. Increasing dopamine activity by reuptake blockade appears to decrease the severity of cravings associated with nicotine abstinence. A long-acting form of bupropion (Zyban) has been approved for smoking cessation.

Varenicline (Chantix) The newest drug approved for smoking cessation, varenicline (Chantix), is a partial agonist for the nicotine α4β2 receptor. It appears to weakly agonize other nicotinic receptors as well. Varenicline has a half-life of about 24 hours. In clinical trials, varenicline has been demonstrated to be as effective as NRT and bupropion in reducing the severity of cravings and in maintaining abstinence from smoking (Eisenberg et al., 2008; Niaura et al., 2008). However, the Food and Drug Administration (FDA) recently issued an alert suggesting that varenicline may be associated with an increased risk of psychiatric symptoms. The Federal Aviation Administration (FAA) also announced that varenicline was not approved for pilots and air traffic controllers for the same reasons. Whether varenicline remains approved for treating symptoms of smoking cessation remains to be seen.

Nicotine Immunization Although nicotine immunization still has not been approved by the FDA, animal studies and clinical trials indicate that it may be a promising therapy for nicotine dependence. At present, two approaches to nicotine vaccination are being investigated. One approach is to immunize with a catabolic antibody that increases the rate of nicotine metabolism. This method of immunization is referred to as **passive immunization** because it does not recruit the production of antibodies by the body, but rather works by significantly increasing nicotine's enzymatic metabolism. Another approach is to use **active immunization** against the nicotine molecule itself. In active nicotine immunization, the nicotine molecule is conjugated with an immunogenic protein and administered by injection. This conjugate stimulates the production of antibodies against the protein as well as nicotine. Nicotine-specific antibodies attack nicotine in the blood and prevent its passage through tissue membranes into the brain. Both active and passive immunization have been shown to be effective in eliminating self-administration of nicotine in animals (LeSage et al., 2008) and to decrease nicotine-induced dopamine release in the NA (de Villiers et al., 2002).

A major difference between immunotherapy for nicotine dependence and drug treatment for nicotine withdrawal is that immunization only prevents the drug from entering the brain; it does not thwart withdrawal. In fact, immunization alone would precipitate withdrawal symptoms. Whether nicotine vaccination can be used to effectively treat smoking dependence remains to be seen. A potential problem with all immunotherapies against drugs (cocaine, amphetamine, and nicotine) is that users can overwhelm the antibody with increased doses of the drug (Johnson & Ettinger, 2000).

CAFFEINE

Caffeine, an alkaloid found in a variety of plants including coffee shrubs (Figure 10.17), tea plants (Figure 10.18), and cocoa plants, is the most widely used psychoactive drug in the world. While caffeine is consumed primarily in naturally caffeinated beverages such as coffee and tea, it is added to a number of other beverages, to OTC analgesics such as Excedrin and Anacin, and to alertness-promoting drugs such as NoDoz and Vivarin. (Refer to Tables 10.3 and 10.4.) A small amount of caffeine also is found in products containing chocolate.

Pharmacology of Caffeine

ABSORPTION AND METABOLISM   Caffeine (Figure 10.19) is readily absorbed by the stomach and small intestine within 30–60 minutes of ingestion. After absorption, it is distributed to all bodily tissues, including the brain. Because of its water solubility, caffeine is freely distributed throughout all body fluids. Peak plasma concentrations are reached within two hours. Caffeine is metabolized by the hepatic enzyme P450 into two active metabolites and one inactive metabolite. Caffeine is eliminated from the body after metabolism, and its metabolites are excreted through the urine. Only about 2 percent of caffeine is excreted unchanged.

FIGURE 10.17   Coffee (*Coffea*) is a genus of small trees and shrubs native to Africa and Southern Asia. Of the more than 90 species of *Coffea, Coffea arabica* is considered most suitable for making fine coffee. The fruits or beans of the *Coffea* plant are dried and roasted for brewing.   © Greg Vaughn/Pacific Stock

FIGURE 10.18   Tea plants are evergreens of the *Camellia* family native to China, Tibet, and northern India. The two main varieties of the tea plant are *Camellia sinensis,* which is grown in the mountainous regions of central China and Japan, and *Camellia assamica,* which grows in tropical climates of Northeast India and the Szechuan and Yunnan provinces of China.
© Gavin Thomas/Rough Guides Dorling Kindersley

The half-life of caffeine is approximately three to four hours. Its half-life is increased to about ten hours in women who are taking oral contraceptives or who are pregnant. Caffeine readily crosses the placental barrier and reaches comparable levels in a fetus, where its half-life may be much longer. In newborns and

TABLE 10.3 Approximate Caffeine Amount in Several Common Caffeinated Beverages. The Amount of Caffeine in Coffees, Teas, and Espresso Drinks Varies Widely and Depends on Variety and Preparation Methods

Beverage	Caffeine in Milligrams
Red Bull (8.2 oz)	80.0
Jolt (12 oz)	71.2
Coca-Cola (12 oz)	34.0
Brewed Coffee (8 oz)	100–200
Espresso (2 oz)	100–150
Tea (8 oz)	40–60
Hot Chocolate (8 oz)	10–15

TABLE 10.4 Caffeine Amount in Several Common OTC Remedies

Product (1 tablet)	Caffeine in Milligrams
Vivarin	200
NoDoz	200
Excedrin	65
Anacin	32

infants, the half-life of caffeine is as long as 80 hours. This can lead to significant blood levels in infants of mothers who drink caffeinated beverages while breast-feeding.

PHARMACOLOGICAL EFFECTS OF CAFFEINE   Consumers of caffeinated beverages are familiar with many of caffeine's physiological effects, which include CNS stimulation (increased alertness and insomnia), increase in heart and respiratory rates, and diuretic effects. Caffeine also is a powerful constrictor of cerebral blood

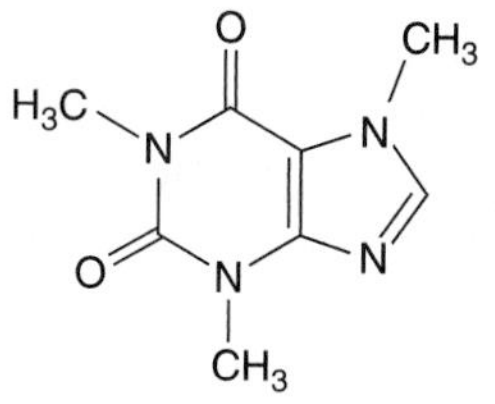

FIGURE 10.19
Molecular structure of caffeine.

vessels, making it a useful remedy for the treatment of some types of headaches, including migraines. For this reason, it is added to several OTC analgesics (Table 10.4). Caffeine and its active metabolite **theobromine** also are effective antiasthmatics because they relax bronchial muscles, allowing for greater airflow into the lungs. Caffeine and theobromine are mild ergogenic aids because they increase cardiac contractility and output and dilate coronary arteries, allowing for greater levels of oxygen to reach the heart. Many sports organizations, including the Olympics, listed caffeine as a banned substance until 2004, when it was finally removed from the list. However, it is still banned by the National Collegiate Athletic Association (NCAA). Whether caffeine increases athletic performance is debatable, but numerous studies using a variety of testing protocols have found significant improvement in endurance sports (e.g., Cox et al., 2002). In addition to caffeine's effects on cardiac functioning, caffeine also may increase carbohydrate metabolism and facilitate muscle glycogen replacement during and after prolonged exercise (Pedersen et al., 2008).

People suffering from anxiety are typically sensitive to caffeine's CNS-stimulating effects and may experience heightened anxiety following its administration. Therefore, individuals with anxiety disorders are advised to abstain from caffeinated products entirely. Anxiety also may be precipitated in normal individuals who consume more than 500 milligrams of caffeine over a period of several hours. Caffeine overdose, referred to as **caffeinism,** causes anxiety, irritability, muscle tremors, and insomnia, which are often referred to as caffeine jitters. Extreme caffeinism may precipitate mania, disorientation, delusions, and even temporary psychosis. Caffeine overdose also may cause cardiac arrhythmia, high heart rate and blood pressure, and gastrointestinal distress. The lethal dose of caffeine is considered to be approximately 150–200 milligrams per kilogram of body weight. This would be approximately 10,000 milligrams of caffeine, or about 100 cups of coffee. Because of the large amount of caffeinated beverage a person would need to consume, lethal overdoses are extremely rare. However, caffeine overdose can occur with abusers of caffeine tablets. Death by caffeine overdose typically follows ventricular fibrillation.

MECHANISMS OF CAFFEINE ACTION: PHARMACODYNAMICS Caffeine exerts its effects through several mechanisms, including its effects on receptors as well as its effects in cells on cAMP metabolic pathways. However, caffeine's principal mechanism of action is antagonism of the neuromodulator **adenosine.** Perhaps because of the structural similarity of caffeine and the **purine** component (circled in Figure 10.20) of the adenosine compound, caffeine easily binds to adenosine receptors and inhibits adenosine effects. Adenosine is a product of normal cellular activity. It is formed during the breakdown and synthesis of adenosine monophosphate (AMP), which is a nucleotide found in all forms of ribonucleic acid (RNA) and deoxyribonucleic acid (DNA). Therefore, adenosine monophosphate is a by-product of cellular activity. As cells become more active, as a result of stimulation, adenosine is produced and released by the activated cell and acts on

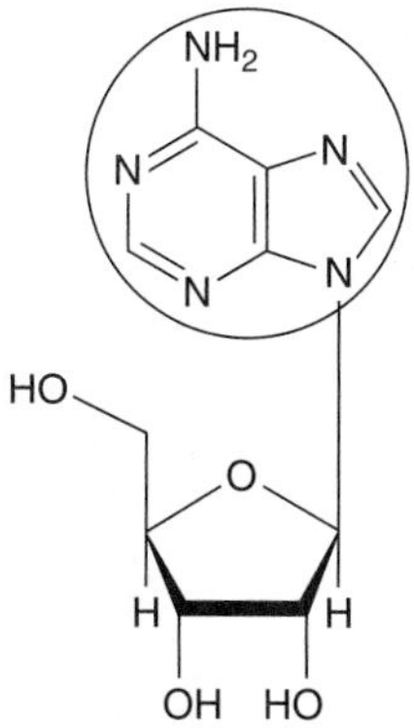

FIGURE 10.20
Molecular structure
of adenosine. The
circled purine
segment resembles
the structure of
caffeine.

the presynaptic cell to inhibit neurotransmitter release. Because of its backwards-acting effect, adenosine is referred to as a **retrograde neuromodulator.** Adenosine acts on presynaptic cells and inhibits their release of neurotransmitter, thereby turning down the activity of the adenosine-releasing cell's activity (see Figure 10.21.) You are correct if you see similarities here with autoreceptor and heteroreceptor modulation. The difference here is not in the inhibitory effect, but in the origin of the inhibiting modulator. In the case of retrograde neuromodulation, the modulation of transmitter release comes from the neuron that was activated initially. High rates of cell activity increase the rate of adenosine accumulation, resulting in a decrease in its firing rate.

Adenosine receptors are present in almost all brain areas, with highest concentrations in the hippocampus, cerebral cortex, cerebellum, and thalamus. Adenosine receptors are also found on dopaminergic cells within the striatum. Four distinct G protein-coupled adenosine receptor subtypes have been described—A_1, A_{2A}, A_{2B}, and A_3—but the A_1 and A_{2A} subtypes are considered most important for understanding caffeine action. The A_{2B} and A_3 receptors appear to regulate internal metabolic pathways. The A_1 and A_{2A} subtypes modulate neurotransmitter release. Specifically, adenosine on these receptors acts to inhibit the release of the neurotransmitters dopamine, serotonin, norepinephrine, and glutamate. Caffeine appears to increase the release of these neurotransmitters by competitively blocking adenosine receptors and by reversing adenosine inhibition of intracellular cAMP-phosphodiesterase activity (Daly et al., 1998). cAMP-phosphodisterase is an essential enzyme for the cAMP second messenger pathway. Caffeine also is known to block intracellular Ca^{++} activity and to block $GABA_A$ receptors at even

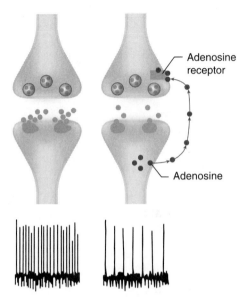

FIGURE 10.21 Adenosine acts as a retrograde neuromodulator inhibiting the release of neurotransmitter from presynaptic neurons, which in turn decreases the firing rate of the adenosine-releasing neuron.

higher doses (see Figure 10.22). It is the increase in neural activity resulting from these effects that is believed to underlie caffeine's effects on arousal, cognitive performance, and motor activity as well as on peripheral systems.

Caffeine Tolerance and Dependence   Tolerance to caffeine's sleep-disruptive, cardiovascular, respiratory, and motor-stimulating effects occurs quickly and can be observed after one to two weeks of moderate (400 mg/day) caffeine consumption. Other caffeine effects, including those on cognitive performance and mood, show little evidence of tolerance. Therefore, the degree of tolerance to caffeine depends on which caffeine effect is being investigated. Tolerance to caffeine is believed to be mediated by the upregulation of adenosine receptors, which corresponds well with the development of tolerance. All CNS and peripheral adenosine receptors do not undergo upregulation at the same rate, so tolerance across different caffeine effects is variable when it does occur.

Consumers of caffeinated beverages are well aware of the consequences of skipping their daily measure of caffeine. Abstinence on the part of regular caffeine users often leads to mild to moderate withdrawal symptoms that include headache, irritability, depression, drowsiness, and fatigue. These effects can begin within a few hours of abstinence but typically peak in severity between 24 and 48 hours. Withdrawal symptoms usually disappear in three to five days, corresponding to the time course of downregulation of adenosine receptors. The

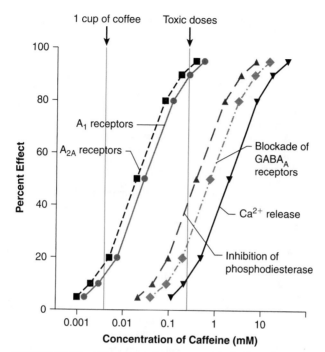

FIGURE 10.22 Effects of caffeine on adenosine and GABA$_A$ receptors and on intracellular messenger systems depends on concentration. At low doses equivalent to one or two cups of coffee, caffeine primarily blocks adenosine A$_1$ and A$_{2A}$ receptors. At higher toxic doses, caffeine blocks GABA$_A$ receptors, inhibits intracellular Ca^{++} release, and disrupts cAMP-phosphodiesterase activity. © Daly, J. W., & Fredholm, B.B. (1998). Caffeine-an atypical drug of dependence. Reprinted from Drug and Alcohol Dependence, 51, 199-206 with permission from Elsevier.

symptoms of withdrawal are caused in part by vasodilatation and an increase in blood flow. An increase in cerebral blood flow can cause severe headaches and is the reason caffeine is added to several common headache remedies. A decrease in norepinephrine, dopamine, and serotonin release following the upregulation of adenosine receptors may contribute to irritability, depression, lack of motivation, and fatigue. As most people know, the annoying symptoms of caffeine withdrawal are quickly relieved by caffeine consumption.

The health hazards, if any, of regular caffeine consumption are negligible even though caffeine is considered to be a dependence-producing substance. Therefore, the widespread and extensive use of caffeinated beverages does not appear to be a significant threat to the consumer or to society. Unlike the other substances covered in this chapter, caffeine is not addictive.

GLOSSARY

Δ^9-tetrahydrocannabinol (THC) the psychoactive compound in marijuana.

action potential a complete depolarization of the neuronal membrane from -70 mV to approximately $+40$ mV.

active immunization immunization that results in the stimulation of specific antibodies by the organism's immune system. Immunization against flu viruses is active immunization. Active immunization also may be used against specific drugs, such as cocaine.

active placebo a psychologically inactive drug that has some peripheral side effects that patients may recognize and thereby assume that they are receiving actual treatment. For example, a placebo may cause minor dry mouth, dizziness, or blurred vision.

acute nicotine tolerance the first stage of nicotine tolerance resulting from rapid internalization of nACh receptors.

addiction a debilitating form of dependence resulting from exposure to drugs that rapidly increase dopamine activity and induce synaptic adaptations in the mesolimbic system.

adenosine an inhibitory neuromodulator and a product of normal cellular activity. Formed during the breakdown and synthesis of adenosine monophosphate.

agonist a substance that facilitates or increases neural transmission.

agoraphobia fear of being in open places where a panic attack may occur and from which it would be difficult to escape or help would be unavailable.

alcohol dehydrogenase the principal metabolite of alcohol.

aldehyde dehydrogenase the principal enzyme involved in alcohol metabolism. See also nicotinamide adenine dinucleotide (NAD).

alkaloids nitrogen-containing compounds produced by a variety of plants. Many psychoactive compounds are alkaloids.

alpha activity defined as electroencephalograph activity between 8 and 12 Hz characteristic of a relaxed or meditative state.

AMPA an ionotropic glutamate receptor that controls a Na^+ channel. The formation of new AMPA glutamate receptors occurs during long-term potentiation.

amphetamine a class of stimulant drugs (including methamphetamine) that act by increasing catecholamine activity. Primarily used to treat ADHD and narcolepsy.

amphetamine challenge a test that scans for radioactive markers of dopamine receptor occupancy following the administration of amphetamine. A measure of dopamine activity in the brain.

amphetamine psychosis a psychotic state induced by the stimulants amphetamine and cocaine. Symptoms include paranoid delusions and hallucinations.

amphetamine-induced psychosis a psychotic state similar to schizophrenia induced by amphetamine overdose.

Amytal interview an interrogation of a witness after the administration of sodium amytal (truth serum). Evidence obtained under the influence of such drugs is not admissible in court.

analgesic a class of drug that blocks ascending pain signals in the spinal cord and brainstem.

anandamide an endogenous ligand for the cannabinoid receptor.

anesthetic a class of drugs used for anesthesia. Anesthetics produce a lack of awareness of body sensations and are used to sedate patients for surgery.

antagonist a substance that inhibits or decreases neural transmission.

anticonvulsants drugs used to treat seizure disorders. Occasionally used to treat symptoms of bipolar disorder.

antiemetic a class of drug used to treat nausea.

antimanic a drug used to treat bouts of mania or hypomania.

antipsychotic a drug used to treat symptoms of schizophrenia and other psychotic disorders.

anxiogenic a drug or substance that induces or exacerbates anxiety.

anxiolytic a drug or substance that is used to treat anxiety.

arcuate nucleus a structure in the hypothalamus implicated in feeding regulation.

area postrema an area of the brainstem that controls the vomiting reflex. The area postrema has a relatively weak blood-brain barrier, so it can detect toxins in the blood.

associative tolerance a form of Pavlovian conditioning where drug onset cues elicit cellular adaptations contributing to drug tolerance.

attentional gate the inhibitory influence of the thalamic reticular nucleus to regulate sensory information along the thalamocortical pathway.

attentional regulation the process whereby cortical input to the thalamus filters and allows attention to specific sensory information.

attention-deficit hyperactivity disorders (ADHDs) disorders characterized by difficulty in attending to tasks, excessive motor activity, and impulsivity. Often diagnosed in early childhood but may persist into adulthood.

atypical antidepressant anantidepressant that differs significantly in its mechanism of action compared to earlier antidepressants.

atypical antipsychotics antipsychotic drugs that differed in their mechanism of action from their predecessors, the phenothiazines. Clozapine was the first atypical antipsychotic to be widely used.

autistic psychopath the term first used by Hans Asperger to describe what is now known as Asperger's disorder.

autistic spectrum disorders a group of disorders that include autistic disorder, Asperger's disorder, and Rett's disorder.

autoreceptors receptors located on the terminal button or cell body that receive neurotransmitter released from the terminal button. Autoreceptors control neurotransmitter synthesis and release.

axon hillock the point on the cell body where both the axon and the electrical signal originate.

behavioral sensitization an increase in motor behavior following chronic exposure to certain stimulant drugs.

behavioral tolerance a form of operant conditioning or behavioral adaptation where training under the influence of a drug enhances performance later when under the influence of the same drug. *See* state-dependent learning.

benzoylecgonine a principle metabolite of cocaine.

beta activity desynchronized electroencephalograph activity ranging between 13–30 Hz typical of the normal aroused state.

bipolar disorder a severe mood disorder characterized by depressive and manic episodes.

blood alcohol concentration (BAC) the amount of alcohol in blood. Expressed as grams per milliliter of blood or as a percent weight. The legal limit for intoxication in most states is 0.08 percent. BAC can be estimated by a breathalyzer, which measure the amount of alcohol excreted in breath.

blood-brain barrier (or BBB) a relatively impermeable membrane forming and surrounding capillaries in the brain that prevents most substances from leaving the circulatory system and entering the brain.

Botox an acetylcholine antagonist derived from botulism toxin used in dermatology to decrease facial wrinkles.

brain-derived neurotropic factor (BDNF) a nerve growth factor essential for normal cell survival, receptor growth, and growth of new neurons.

brand names the names of drugs given by their manufacturers and used in advertising the drugs. Drug brand names are protected by patents.

buprenorphine a synthetic opiate used for the treatment of opiate dependence.

caffeine an alkaloid found in a variety of plants including coffee shrubs, tea plants, and cocoa plants.

caffeinism a consequence of caffeine overdose that causes anxiety, irritability, muscle tremors, and insomnia. Extreme caffeinism may precipitate mania, disorientation, delusions, and even temporary psychosis. Caffeine overdose also may cause cardiac arrhythmia, high heart rate and blood pressure, and gastrointestinal distress.

cannabinoid receptors a class of receptors specific for endogenous cannabinoids such as anandamide. There are two distinct forms of the cannabinoid receptor: CB_1 and CB_2.

Cannabis sativa a variety of hemp plant commonly known as marijuana.

CART *see* cocaine and amphetamine- regulated transcript.

catalytic antibodies antibodies used in passive immunization that facilitate the degradation of specific molecules or drugs.

cellular tolerance a decrease in drug effectiveness as a consequence of compensatory adaptations within receiving neurons.

cellular tolerance tolerance that develops as a result of cellular adaptations that decrease or downregulate cell activity.

central nervous system (CNS) consists of the entire brain and the spinal cord.

c-FOS a protein expressed in response to a variety of extracellular signals, including drugs such as cocaine, amphetamine, nicotine, and morphine.

c-FOS protein a protein transcription factor that promotes the synthesis of messenger RNA under the direction of DNA.

chemical name a drug's name that reveals its chemical composition and molecular structure.

cingulotomy surgically disrupting the excitatory input from the cingulate gyrus to the frontal cortex. Occasionally used to treat drug-resistant obsessive-compulsive disorder.

cocaethylene a compound that results from mixing the administrations of cocaine and alcohol.

cocaine a powerful stimulant drug extracted from the coca plant (*Erythroxylum coca*).

cocaine and amphetamine-regulated transcript (CART) a peptide neurotransmitter found in the arcuate nucleus of the hypothalamus. Believed to be involved in feeding.

codeine a less potent narcotic than morphine extracted from opium or synthesized from morphine.

Controlled Substances Act the present U.S. drug policy passed in 1970 that regulates the manufacture, importation, possession, and distribution of certain drugs.

convulsant a drug or substance that can induce seizures or convulsions in subjects.

corpus callosum a band of approximately 200 million interconnecting myelinated axons that unite left and right cortical areas as well as intrahemispheric regions.

cortical underconnectivity deficits in white matter that make up the cortical circuits that integrate inter- and intrahemispheric connections.

cotinine the primary metabolite of nicotine.

crack a cocaine product that is produced by dissolving cocaine hydrochloride in ammonia or a solution of sodium bicarbonate.

CREB (cyclic adenosine monophosphate [or cAMP] response element binding protein) a second messenger activated by metabotropic receptors responsible for transcribing brain-derived neurotropic factor from a cell's DNA.

CREB protein cyclic AMP response element-binding protein. Binds to an element on DNA, thereby activating a gene for the synthesis of a specific protein.

cross tolerance tolerance to a drug that occurs as a consequence of tolerance developed to a similarly acting drug. Benzodiazepine tolerance can contribute to alcohol tolerance without prior alcohol exposure.

crystal meth a crystalline form of methamphetamine.

CYP2A6 the P450 liver enzyme that metabolizes nicotine into cotinine.

deaminate an enzymatic reaction that deactivates a neurotransmitter by removing an essential amine chemical group from its molecular structure.

delirium tremens (DT) a state characterized by confusion, agitation, fever, tachycardia, and hypertension that occurs during abstinence from chronic alcohol abuse.

delta δ receptor an opiate receptor located predominantly in the cortex, nucleus accumbens, substantia nigra, and olfactory areas.

dependence a physiological state resulting from long-term exposure to certain drugs. Symptoms of dependence can include nausea, vomiting, delirium tremens, headache, sweating, nervousness, and agitation. *See also* addiction.

depot binding drug binding to inactive sites.

desoxyephedrine *see* methamphetamine.

dextroamphetamine (Dexedrine) an amphetamine compound used to treat narcolepsy, attention disorders, and obesity.

dextromethorphan a drug that acts as an NMDA receptor antagonist.

disulfiram (Antabuse) a drug that inhibits the aldehyde dehydrogenase metabolism of acetaldehyde. Causes illness and can discourage drinking.

dopamine deficit theory a theory proposing that depressed dopamine activity in the caudate nucleus and frontal cortices may contribute to cortical hypoarousal in ADHD.

dopamine hypothesis the hypothesis proposing that excessive dopamine activity in the mesolimbic-cortical systems of the brain underlie schizophrenia and its symptoms.

dopamine transporter (DAT) proteins on the presynaptic membrane that selectively transport extracellular dopamine back into the terminal button. Responsible for dopamine reuptake.

dose response curve the relationship between a drug dose and it physiological effects. Often this relationship is sigmoidal.

double-blind in a double-blind experiment, neither the patients nor the physician know which patient group receives the placebo or the actual medication. This experimental design can eliminate subject and researcher biases, which may affect the outcome of drug trials.

downregulation a process that results in a decrease in synaptic activity caused by decreasing neurotransmitter synthesis, its release, and/or its receptor availability.

Drug Enforcement Administration (DEA) an agency in the Department of Justice that oversees and enforces the Controlled Substances Act.

drug schedule a drug classification based on its potential for abuse as described by the Controlled Substances Act of 1970. Drugs with the highest abuse potential and lowest medicinal value are Schedule I drugs. There are five drug schedules (I–V).

dynorphin an endorphin neurotransmitter that binds to the kappa opiate receptor.

dysphoria an unpleasant or uncomfortable state that is opposite of euphoria.

dysthymic disorder a moderately severe mood disorder that is characterized by lengthy episodes of depression (at least two years).

early infantile autism the term first used by Leo Kramer in 1943 to describe what is now known as autism.

ecgonine a principle metabolite of cocaine.

ecstasy *see* MDMA.

electric shock therapy the induction of a severe seizure in a patient by delivering electric shocks to the head. Used as a treatment for drug-resistant schizophrenia and depression.

elevated maze an apparatus used to evaluate the effects of drugs on anxiety responses in laboratory animals. Designed with two enclosed and two open arms and suspended about 3 feet above the ground. The proportion of time spent in open arms is a measure of a drug's anxiolytic effect.

endorphins a class of endogenous opiate peptides.

enkephalin an endorphin. May be leu- or met-enkephalin.

ephedra a mild stimulant that is extracted from the *Ephedra sinica* plant.

ethyl alcohol (ethanol) alcohol produced during fermentation of sugars in fruits or grains.

excitatory postsynaptic potentials (EPSPs) graded membrane potentials that depolarize the neuron, bringing it closer to its firing threshold.

excitotoxicity a consequence of a high rate of presynaptic activity on a neuron, resulting in excessive Ca^{++} influx and eventual cell death.

extrapyramidal symptoms severe motor impairment following disruptions to neurons outside the major pyramidal tracks descending from the medulla. These symptoms are often caused by long-term use of phenothiazine drugs.

fetal alcohol syndrome (FAS) a severe developmental disorder caused by fetal exposure to alcohol or other similar-acting drugs.

first-generation drug the first class of drugs used to treat a particular psychological disorder.

first-pass metabolism metabolism during which ingested drugs are partially metabolized by stomach and liver enzymes before the remaining unmetabolized drug enters the bloodstream.

fluidization an increase in the fluids (alcohol) in cell membranes. Fluidization disrupts membrane processes and the ability of ions to pass through them.

frontal lobotomy a procedure that separates the prefrontal areas from the remainder of the frontal cortex by making knife cuts or by destroying these areas with ice picks inserted behind the eyes. Used as an early treatment for severe psychosis.

generalized anxiety disorder (GAD) chronic worry about events with no specific threat. Characterized by restlessness, fatigue, difficulty with concentration, and sleep disruptions.

generic drug drugs that must contain the same active ingredients as the original brand name drug and must be pharmacologically equivalent. Because several manufacturers may compete to produce and market generic drugs, their cost is often considerably less than their equivalent brand name drug

graded potential small changes in a membrane's resting potential. Graded potentials may be excitatory and depolarize the membrane from −70 mV to −60 mV, or they may be inhibitory and hyperpolarize the membrane to −75 or −80 mV. *See also* excitatory and inhibitory postsynaptic potentials.

half-life the amount of time it takes for a drug's blood level to be decreased by metabolism and elimination by 50 percent (one-half of its peak blood level).

Hallucinogen Persisting Perception Disorder (HPPD) A DSM-IV-TR disorder characterized by the reexperience of hallucinogenic effects caused by psychedelic drugs long after drug intoxication.

Harrison Narcotic Act the act passed by Congress in 1914 to regulate the manufacture and distribution of opiates and cocaine.

Harrison Narcotic Tax Act enacted in 1914 to control the manufacture, distribution, and use of certain drugs with abuse potential. Superseded by the Controlled Substances Act of 1970.

heroin a potent narcotic derived from morphine. Because of its abuse potential, it is no longer used as an analgesic.

heteroreceptors receptors located on the terminal button or cell body that receive neurotransmitter released from another neuron. Heteroreceptors control neurotransmitter synthesis and release.

hypoarousal a decrease in cortical arousal characterized by an increase in slow wave alpha and theta activity observed with an electroencephalograph.

hypomanic episode a period of elevated, expansive, or irritable mood lasting at least four days. Less severe than a manic episode.

immediate early genes (IEGs) proteins activated by stimuli that activate intracellular signaling. IEGs also may be activated by certain drugs.

incentive sensitization an increase in the incentive value of a drug as well as drug-associated cues.

infantile schizophrenia a term used under the original classification scheme proposed by Eugen Bleuler to characterize autism.

inhibitory postsynaptic potentials (IPSPs) graded membrane potentials that hyperpolarize polarize the neuron, making it less likely to fire.

inositol a derivative of the glucose molecule with putative anxiolytic properties.

insulin shock a comatose state induced by severe hypoglycemia following an injection of insulin. Used as an early treatment for schizophrenia.

interneurons reside only in the central nervous system and function to bridge communication between sensory and motor neurons.

ion channel a protein embedded in the cell membrane that controls the movement of charged ions across the cell membrane.

ionotropic receptor a receptor that directly controls an ion channel on the cell membrane.

kainate receptor an ionotropic glutamate receptor that controls Na^+ channels. Named after the artificial ligand that can stimulate it.

kappa κ receptor an opiate receptor with limited distribution found predominantly in the hypothalamus, pituitary, and the amygdale.

knockout animals experimental animals that have been genetically altered not to express certain genes.

lag time the delay of about 10–14 days between the onset of medication and observations of symptom relief in depression.

levomethadyl a synthetic opiate used for the treatment of opiate dependence.

ligand-gated receptors receptors where ion flow occurs only when the receptors are activated by a neurotransmitter or pure agonist.

limbic system is the portion of the brain most closely associated with emotional expression and motivation. Its structures also play a significant role in learning and memory.

local anesthetic a drug for surgery that blocks the conduction of nerve signals in a localized area.

locus coeruleus a nucleus of noradrenergic cell bodies located in the pons near the fourth ventricle.

long-term potentiation (LTP) a change in a neuron's ability to depolarize because of the ejection of Mg^{++} ions that previously prevented ion flow into the neuron. Long-term potentiation occurs on postsynaptic membranes when they are depolarized by a strong stimulus at the same time a presynaptic neuron is releasing a neurotransmitter. Long-term potentiation is believed to be the neural mechanism for associative (Pavlovian conditioning) learning.

lysergic acid diethylamide (LSD) a potent psychedelic drug that produces visual hallucinations. Discovered by Dr. Albert Hoffman.

major depressive disorder a severe mood disorder during which a person experiences depressive episodes without intermittent bouts of mania.

manic episode a period of at least one week of excessively elevated mood, euphoria, or enthusiasm that may be interrupted by outbursts of anger or irritability.

Marihuana Tax Act enacted in 1937 to regulate the distribution and use of marijuana by taxation.

marijuana the common name for the hemp plant *Cannabis sativa.*

MDA 3,4 methylenedioxyamphetamine. A compound structurally related to amphetamine and similar to MDMA. Produces a state of euphoria.

MDMA methylenedioxymethamphetamine. A compound structurally related to amphetamine with euphoric effects. Also known as ecstasy.

medial forebrain bundle the bundle of axons projecting from the ventral tegmental area to the nucleus accumbens.

mesocortical system dopamine neurons that originate in the nucleus accumbens and project to the cortex. *See also* mesolimbic-cortical system.

mesolimbic system a pathway of dopaminergic neurons originating in the ventral tegmentum projecting to the nucleus accumbens.

mesolimbic-cortical system dopamine neurons that originate in the ventral tegmental area of the pons and pass through the nucleus accumbens, where they are routed to the frontal cortex.

mesolimbic-mesocortical pathways neural pathways originating in the ventral tegmental area of the midbrain and projecting to the nucleus accumbens and the prefrontal cortex.

metabolic tolerance an increase in availability of metabolic enzymes that break drugs into water-soluble compounds after being repeatedly exposed to a drug. This results in more rapid metabolism as more enzymes are available for degradation.

metabotropic receptor a receptor that controls a variety of internal cell processes mediated by second messengers in the cell.

methadone maintenance a treatment program for opiate dependence that substitutes methadone for heroin or another opiate.

methamphetamine an amphetamine compound that can be produced by the reduction of ephedrine.

methylbenzoylecgonine a compound produced by dissolving cocaine hydrochloride in ammonia. Also known as crack cocaine.

mixed agonist-antagonists drugs that exert agonistic effects on some receptor subtypes and antagonistic effects on other receptor subtypes.

monoamine hypothesis the proposal that deficiencies in the monoamine neurotransmitters dopamine, norepinephrine, and/or serotonin cause depression.

monoamine oxidase inhibitors (MAOIs) antidepressants that block the activity of the degrading enzyme monoamine oxidase in the synaptic gap of monoamine neurotransmitters.

morphine the major active compound of opium. Used as a potent analgesic.

morphine-6-glucuronide (M6G) an active metabolite of morphine and heroin.

mu μ receptor an opiate receptor that is widely distributed throughout the brain and spinal cord. The μ receptor has a high affinity for morphine and other opiate drugs.

naloxone a pure opiate antagonist often used to treat opiate dependence.

naltrexone a pure opiate antagonist used to treat opiate overdose.

negative symptoms symptoms of schizophrenia characterized by features removed from normal behavior and functioning. They include lack of affect, social withdrawal, cognitive impairment, and muscle rigidity.

neocortex *neo* is Latin for "new cortex" because it was the last part of the brain to develop during evolution. It consists of the outer layers of the cerebral cortex.

neurogenesis the cellular process that contributes to neuronal growth.

neuromodulator a substance produced and released by neurons or glia that alter cell functioning. Neuromodulators may alter the effects of neurotransmitters at synapses and, unlike neurotransmitters, may act at greater distances from the releasing cell.

neuropathic pain pain associated with damage to or overuse of nerves. Neuropathic pain may be associated with certain types of cancer, autoimmune disorders, or trauma.

neurotransmitter reuptake the process of removing neurotransmitter substance from the synaptic gap back into the terminal button by a transporter protein.

nicotinamide adenine dinucleotide (NAD) a rate-limiting coenzyme involved in alcohol metabolism. *See also* alcohol dehydrogenase.

nicotine a pharmacologically active alkaloid produced by the tobacco plant *Nicotiana tabacum.*

nicotine replacement therapy (NRT) a form of treatment for nicotine dependence where controlled doses of nicotine are administered through gums, lozenges, or transdermal patches.

nicotinic acetylcholine receptor a subtype of the acetylcholine receptor constructed from a number of subunits referred to as alpha 2 through 10 and beta 2 through 4. The nicotinic receptor controls channels for Na^+, K^+, and Ca^{++}.

nigrostriatal pathway dopamine neurons that originate in the substantia nigra of the brainstem and project to the striatum or basal ganglia.

nigrostriatal system a system of brain structures and neurons originating in the substantia nigra and projecting to the striatum of the basal ganglia.

NMDA receptor an ionotropic glutamate receptor that controls both Na^+ and $Ca2^+$ channels. The NMDA receptor is involved in long-term potentiation.

N-methyl-D-aspartate (NMDA) a subtype of the glutamate receptor. Believed to be involved in long-term potentiation.

nociceptors pain receptors that transducer stimulation into activity in pain-signaling neurons.

node of Ranvier   a small gap in the myelin the surrounds the axon of a neuron. The membrane of the axon is exposed to the extracellular environment at these gaps.

nucleus accumbens   an area of the forebrain located adjacent to the head of the caudate nucleus and the putamen and below the lateral ventricles. Most of the neurons in the nucleus accumbens are GABAergic. Dopamine neurons from the ventral tegmentum terminate in the nucleus accumbens.

obsessive-compulsive disorder (OCD)   a severe psychological disorder characterized by the persistence of unwanted thoughts or disturbing images. Compulsive, often ritualistic behaviors also may occur in attempts to mitigate the obsessive thoughts.

opiate   a narcotic alkaloid found in, or derived from, the opium poppy plant. The term also applies to the neurotransmitter released from endorphin neurons and their receptors.

opioid   a partially or completely synthesized narcotic drug that binds to opiate receptors.

opium   a potent narcotic extracted from the poppy plant *Papaver somniferum*

orexin   a peptide neurotransmitter produced by cells in the lateral hypothalamus. Orexin is a powerful appetite stimulant and plays a significant role in sleep-wake cycles.

P450   cytochrome P450, the liver enzyme that is essential in oxidative metabolic reactions. Many drugs are metabolized by P450.

panic disorder   an anxiety disorder in which the individual experiences repeated and unexpected panic attacks as well as anxiety about impending attacks.

partial agonists   drugs that have an affinity for a receptor site but may exert less of an effect on the receptor than the endogenous ligand.

passive immunization   an immunization method that does not result in the formation of antibodies, but rather relies on the transfer of antibodies from one organism to another. It could also include the administration of enzymes or other substances that inactivate a pathogen or drug.

peripheral nervous system (PNS)   transmits and receives information to and from muscles, glands, and internal organs to the skin.

pervasive developmental disorders (PDD)   a group of developmental disorders characterized by deficits in language, social interaction, and motor development.

pharmacodynamics   the science of the mechanisms of drug action, or how drugs affect target cells and induce pharmacological effects.

pharmacokinetics   the science of how drugs are absorbed, distributed to body tissues, and eliminated from the body after metabolism.

pituitary gland   attached to the base of the hypothalamus by the pituitary stalk. The pituitary gland is responsible for the production and secretion of a variety of essential hormones.

place preference conditioning (PPC)   an experimental procedure in which animals are tested for their preference for an area in an experimental apparatus where drugs have been administered over other areas in the apparatus. A form of Pavlovian conditioning where a place becomes associated with drug effects.

placebo   a pharmacologically inert substance administered under the guise of medication.

positive symptoms   symptoms of schizophrenia that are characterized by features that are added to normal behavior and functioning. They include delusions, hallucinations, motor symptoms, and emotional turmoil.

post-traumatic stress disorder (PTSD)   a severe stress disorder brought about by an extreme traumatic experience.

prepulse inhibition (PPI)   the ability to inhibit a startle response to a strong stimulus if given a warning signal, or prepulse stimulus. Schizophrenic patients show deficits in prepulse inhibition.

presynaptic facilitation   the action of an axon-to-axon synapse that results in greater depolarization and more neurotransmitter being released.

proof   a measure of the amount of alcohol in a beverage or spirit. Proof alcohol is twice the percent of alcohol. Thus, 50 percent alcohol is 100 proof.

psilocybin   a psychedelic compound found in a variety of mushrooms in the *Psilocybe* genus.

psychedelic   a class of drug that causes disturbances in perception.

psychomotor sensitization   refers to a drug's potential to increase motor activity and drug-seeking behaviors after repeated administration.

psychostimulant   a drug that increases or stimulates cortical activity and arousal. Cocaine and amphetamines are psychostimulants.

pure agonists   drugs that mimic the effects of an endogenous neurotransmitter.

pure antagonist a drug that has a high affinity for receptors but does not exert any physiological effect on the receptor.

purine a structural component of the adenosine molecule that resembles the form of caffeine.

rapid-cycling a condition where periods of depression and mania in bipolar disorder cycle at least four times in a year.

reactive depression a period of depression associated with a significant life event such as loss of a spouse or significant other, loss of financial resources, or severe stress.

receptor competition the ability of a drug to compete with a neurotransmitter for receptor binding is measured by its capacity to displace a radioactive ligand. Used to predict drug effectiveness against schizophrenic symptoms.

respiratory depression a decrease in respiratory depth and frequency caused by inhibition of respiratory centers in the brain stem. Often the cause of death from drug or alcohol overdose.

resting potential the state of a neuron when the ionic electrostatic and diffusion forces are at equilibrium. The resting potential may vary between −60 and −70 millivolts depending on the neuron and its location.

reticular activating system a system of neurons originating in the brainstem and projecting to the thalamus. Involved in behavioral arousal and crucial for maintaining consciousness.

retrograde neuromodulator a neuromodulator that is produced and released by an activated neuron that acts backwards to inhibit the activity of the activating neuron. Adenosine is a retrograde neuromodulator.

reuptake a process where neurotransmitter substances are removed from the synaptic gap and returned to the terminal button of the transmitting neuron. Reuptake decreases the availability of the neurotransmitter at receptor sites.

reuptake transporters proteins on the presynaptic membrane that transfer neurotransmitter substances in the synaptic gap back into the terminal button.

reward pathway a pathway of dopaminergic neurons originating in the ventral tegmentum and projecting to the nucleus accumbens and prefrontal cortex. *See also* mesolimbic system and mesolimbic-cortical system.

Rimonabant (SR141716) a cannabinoid CB1 receptor antagonist. May be useful in treating substance abuse.

Ro15-4513 a competitive antagonist of alcohol at GABA delta receptors.

second messenger a substance in the cell that becomes activated during cell signaling. Second messengers initiate biochemical processes that result in opening or closing ion channels, the activation of cell enzymes or hormones, and the expression of genes.

second messenger systems chemical signaling within a cell that results in the opening of ion channels, protein synthesis, or the activation of a variety of other cellular events.

second-generation drug a class of drugs that has supplemented or replaced first-generation drugs and that differ significantly in its mechanism of action.

selective serotonin reuptake inhibitor (SSRI) a class of antidepressant drugs that selectively inhibit serotonin reuptake, leaving serotonin available at receptor sites.

self-administration an experimental procedure where animals are trained to lever-press for drug administration intravenously or directly into the brain via a cannula.

sensory thalamus regions of the thalamus that receive sensory information and project it to the cortex via the thalamocortical pathway.

septum a structure of the mesolimbic system adjacent to the nucleus accumbens.

serotonin syndrome a toxic reaction caused by excessive serotonin activity. Symptoms may include disorientation, confusion, visual disturbances, agitation, and mania.

spinothalamic pathway the pathway of ascending neurons from the dorsal horn of the spinal cord to the thalamus, somatosensory cortex, and anterior cingulate cortex.

state-dependent learning a form of operant conditioning or behavioral adaptation in which animals tend to perform better when tested under the same physiological or drug state they were in while being trained. *See* behavioral tolerance.

stereotyped behavior rigid repetitive movements observed in experimental animals after the administration of psychomotor stimulants such as cocaine and amphetamine.

substance abuse disorder a pattern of drug use that leads to significant impairment in functioning and personal relations. A disorder defined by DSM-IV-TR.

substance dependence disorder an impairment caused by drug use that is manifest by drug tolerance, physical withdrawal symptoms, and persistent unsuccessful attempts to control or discontinue its use. A disorder defined by DSM-IV-TR.

substance P an excitatory neurotransmitter released in the dorsal horn of the spinal cord by pain-transmitting neurons.

suicidality attempts, both successful and unsuccessful, at committing suicide.

suicide ideation experiencing thoughts of suicide and/or planning suicide attempts.

synesthesia a perceptual phenomenon where sensations in one modality are experienced or mixed with another.

tardive dyskinesia a severe motor disorder characterized by facial tics, lip smacking, tongue extensions, and rapid eye blinking. Can be caused by long-term use of antipsychotic medication.

thalamic reticular nucleus (TRN) the outer cortex of the thalamus that regulates the sensory thalamus and activity along the thalamocortical pathway. Functions as an "attentional gate" by allowing or inhibiting sensory input to the cortex.

theobromine an active metabolite of caffeine. May be used to treat asthma.

therapeutic index the range between a drug's therapeutically effective dose and its lethal or toxic dose. The therapeutic index can decrease as tolerance develops.

theta activity cortical electroencephalograph activity in the range of 3.5–7.5 Hz often observed during the early stages of sleep.

tolerance a decrease in the effectiveness of a drug after repeated administration. This is observed as a shift to the right in the dose response curve.

transcription a step in the process of expressing the activity of genes for the building of a specific protein.

tricyclic antidepressant an antidepressant characterized by its three-ring molecular structure.

tripartite synapses synapses between glial cells and neurons that appear to regulate neuronal activity.

tuberomammillary nucleus a nucleus of histaminergic cell bodies located in the ventral surface of the hypothalamus. Believed to be involved in cortical arousal.

upregulation a process that results in an increase in synaptic activity caused by increasing neurotransmitter synthesis, its release, and/or the availability if its receptors.

valerian an herbal remedy promoted to treat insomnia and anxiety. Derived from the root of valerian plants.

ventral tegmental area (VTA) an area of the midbrain that is the origin of dopaminergic cell bodies that comprise the mesolimbic system.

ventral tegmentum a structure containing dopamine neurons located in the midbrain. Part of the mesolimbic system.

white matter large groups of fast-conducting myelinated axons that interconnect regions of the brain. Often compared to gray matter, which consists of unmyelinated neurons. Inside the brain, the white myelinating matter consists of a kind of glial cell called an oligodendrocite. Outside the brain in the spinal cord, this myelinating glia is called a Schwann cell.

BIBLIOGRAPHY

Abi-Dargham, A., & Moore, H. (2003). Prefrontal DA transmission at D1 receptors and the pathology of schizophrenia. *The Neuroscientist, 9*(5), 404–416.

Abi-Dargham, A., Rodenhiser, J., Printz, D., Zea-Ponce, Y., Gil, R., Kegeles, L., et al. (2000). Increased baseline occupancy of D2 receptors by dopamine in schizophrenia. *Proceedings of the National Academy of Sciences of the United States of America, 97*(14), 8104–8109.

Adolphs, R., Tranel, D., Damasio, H., & Damasio, A. (1995). Fear and the human amygdala. *The Journal of Neuroscience, 15*(9), 5879–5891.

Aghajanian, G. K., & Marek, G. J. (1999). Serotonin and hallucinogens. *Neuropsychopharmacology, 21*(2), 16–23.

Agrawal, A., & Lynskey, M. T. (2008). Are there genetic influences on addiction: Evidence from family, adoption and twin studies. *Addiction, 103*(7), 1069–1081.

Altar, C. A. (1999). Neurotrophins and depression. *Trends in Pharmacological Sciences, 20*(2), 59–61.

Amato, J. L., Bankson, M. G., & Yamamoto, B. K. (2007). Prior exposure to chronic stress and MDMA potentiates mesoaccumbens dopamine release mediated by the 5-HT(1B) receptor. *Neuropsychopharmacology, 32*(4), 946–954.

American Psychiatric Association. (2000). *Diagnostic and statistical manual of mental disorders* (4th ed.). Arlington, VA: Author.

Amiri, S., Mohammadi, M. R., Mohammadi, M., Nouroozinejad, G. H., Kahbazi, M., & Akhondzadeh, S. (2008). Modafinil as a treatment for attention-deficit/hyperactivity disorder in children and adolescents: A double blind, randomized clinical trial. *Progress in Neuro-Psychopharmacology & Biological Psychiatry, 32*(1), 145–149.

Andreatini, R., Sartori, V. A., Seabra, M. L., & Leite, J. R. (2002). Effect of valepotriates (valerian extract) in generalized anxiety disorder: A randomized placebo-controlled pilot study. *Phytotherapy Research, 16*(7), 650.

Antrop, I., Roeyers, H., Van Oost, P., & Buysse, A. (2000). Stimulation seeking and hyperactivity in children with ADHD. *The Journal of Child Psychology and Psychiatry and Allied Disciplines, 41*, 225–231.

Appel, J. B., West, W. B., & Buggy, J. (2004). LSD, 5-HT (serotonin), and the evolution of a behavioral assay. *Neuroscience & Biobehavioral Reviews, 27*(8), 693–701.

Atmaca, M., Yildirim, H., Ozdemir, H., Tezcan, E., & Poyraz, A. K. (2007). Volumetric MRI study of key brain regions implicated in obsessive-compulsive disorder. *Progress in Neuro-Psychopharmacology & Biological Psychiatry, 31*(1), 46–52.

Barnea-Goraly, N., Kwon, H., Menon, V., Eliez, S., Lotspeich, L., & Reiss, A. L. (2004). White matter structure in autism: Preliminary evidence from diffusion tensor imaging. *Biological Psychiatry, 55*(3), 323–326.

Basavarajappa, B. S. (2007). The endocannabinoid signaling system: A potential target for the next-generation therapeutics for alcoholism. *Mini Reviews in Medicinal Chemistry, 7*(8), 769–779.

Battista, N., Fezza, F., Finazzi-Agro, A., & Maccarrone, M. (2006). The endocannabinoid system in neurodegeneration. *Italian Journal of Biochemistry, 55*(3–4), 283–289.

Bechara, A., & Damasio, H. (2002). Decision-making and addiction (part 1): Impaired activation of somatic states in substance dependent individuals when pondering decisions with negative consequences. *Neuropsychologia, 40*(10), 1675–1689.

Bechara, A., Damasio, H., & Damasio, A. (2003). Role of the amygdala in decision-making. *Annals of the New York Academy of Sciences, 985*, 356–369.

Belin, D., & Everitt, B. J. (2008). Cocaine seeking habits depend upon dopamine-dependent serial connectivity linking the ventral with the dorsal striatum. *Neuron, 57*(3), 432–441.

Benedetti, F., Mayberg, H. S., Wager, T. D., Stohler, C. S., & Zubieta, J. K. (2005). Neurobiological mechanisms of the placebo effect. *The Journal of Neuroscience, 25*(45), 10390–10402.

Benjamin, J., Levine, J., Fux, M., Aviv, A., Levy, D., & Belmaker, R. H. (1995). Double-blind, placebo-controlled, crossover trial of inositol treatment for panic disorder. *The American Journal of Psychiatry, 152*, 1084–1086.

Bergh, C., Eklund, T., Sodersten, P., & Nordin, C. (1997). Altered dopamine function in pathological gambling. *Psychological Medicine, 27*(2), 473–475.

Berk, M., Hallam, K., Lucas, N., Hasty, M., McNeil, C., Conus, P., et al. (2007). Early intervention in bipolar disorders: Opportunities and pitfalls. *The Medical Journal of Australia, 187*(7), S11–S14.

Biederman, J. (2005). Mixed amphetamine salts extended release for the treatment of ADHD. *CNS Spectrums, 10*(12), 5.

Biederman, J., Quinn, D., Weiss, M., Markabi, S., Weidenman, M., Edson, K., et al. (2003). Efficacy and safety of Ritalin, a new, once daily, extended-release dosage form of methylphenidate, in children with attention deficit hyperactivity disorder. *Pediatric Drugs, 5*(12), 833–841.

Bionomics. (2007, May). Bionomics validates drug candidate for anxiety. *Bionomics.*

Blom, J. M., Tascedda, F., Carra, S., Ferraguti, C., Barden, N., & Brunello, N. (2002). Altered regulation of CREB by chronic antidepressant administration in the brain of transgenic mice with impaired glucocorticoid receptor function. *Neuropsychopharmacology, 26*(5), 605–614.

Bonese, K. F., Wainer, B. H., Fitch, E. W., Rothberg, R. M., & Schuster, C. R. (1974). Changes in heroin self-administration by a rhesus monkey after morphine immunisation. *Nature, 252*(5485), 708–710.

Bossert, J. M., Poles, G. C., Wihbey, K. A., Koya, E., & Shaham, Y. (2007). Differential effects of blockade of dopamine D1-family receptors in nucleus accumbens core or shell on reinstatement of heroin seeking induced by contextual and discrete cues. *The Journal of Neuroscience, 27*(46), 12655–12663.

Bradberry, C. W. (2000). Acute and chronic dopamine dynamics in a nonhuman primate model of recreational cocaine use. *The Journal of Neuroscience, 20*(18), 7109–7115.

Braga, R. J., & Petrides, G. (2005). The combined use of electroconvulsive therapy and antipsychotics in patients with schizophrenia. *The Journal of ECT, 21*(2), 75–83.

Brederlau, A., Correia, A., Anisimov, S., Elmi, M., Paul, G., Roybon, L., et al. (2006). Transplantation of human embryonic stem cell-derived cells to a rat model of Parkinson's disease: Effect of in vitro differentiation on graft survival and testoma formation. *Stem Cells, 24*(6), 1433–1440.

Bremner, J. D. (1999). Does stress damage the brain? *Biological Psychiatry, 45*(7), 797–805.

Bridge, J. A., Iyengar, S., Salary, C. B., Barbe, R. P., Birmaher, B., Pincus, H. A., et al. (2007). Clinical response and risk for reported suicidal ideation and suicide attempts in pediatric antidepressant treatment: A meta-analysis of randomized controlled trials. *The Journal of the American Medical Association, 297*(15), 1683–1696.

Broderick, P. A. (1992). Cocaine's colocalized effects on synaptic serotonin and dopamine in ventral tegmentum in a reinforcement paradigm.

Pharmacology Biochemistry & Behavior, 42(4), 889–898.

Brunello, N. (2004). Mood stabilizers: Protecting the mood . . . protecting the brain. *Journal of Affective Disorders, 79*(1), S15–S20.

Brunello, N., & Tascedda, F. (2003). Cellular mechanisms and second messengers: Relevance to the psychopharmacology of bipolar disorders. *The International Journal of Neuropsychopharmacology, 6*(2), 181–189.

Buchanan, R. W., Javitt, D. C., Marder, S. R., Schooler, N. R., Gold, J. M., McMahon, R. P., et al. (2007). The cognitive and negative symptoms in schizophrenia trial (CONSIST): The efficacy of glutamatergic agents for negative symptoms and cognitive impairments. *The American Journal of Psychiatry, 164*(10), 1593–1602.

Bueno, C. H., Zangrossi, H., Jr., & Viana Mde, B. (2007). GABA/benzodiazepine receptors in the ventromedial hypothalamic nucleus regulate both anxiety and panic-related defensive responses in the elevated T-maze. *Brain Research Bulletin, 74*(1–3), 134–141.

Buisson, B., & Bertrand, D. (2001). Chronic exposure to nicotine upregulates the human alpha 4beta 2 nicotinic acetylcholine receptor function. *The Journal of Neuroscience, 21*(6), 1819–1829.

Burns, E. K., & Levinson, A. H. (2008). Discontinuation of nicotine replacement therapy among smoking-cessation attempters. *American Journal of Preventive Medicine, 34*(3), 212–215.

Butterweck, V. (2003). Mechanism of action of St John's wort in depression: What is known? *CNS Drugs, 17*(8), 539–562.

Byrnes-Blake, K. A., Carroll, F. I., Abraham, P., & Owens, S. M. (2001). Generation of anti-(+)methamphetamine antibodies is not impeded by (+)methamphetamine administration during active immunization of rats. *International Immunopharmacology, 1*(2), 329–338.

Cade, J. (1949). Lithium salts in the treatment of psychotic excitement. *The Medical Journal of Australia, 36,* 349.

Canli, T., Qiu, M., Omura, K., Congdon, E., Haas, B. W., Amin, Z., et al. (2006). Neural correlates of epigenesis. *Proceedings of the National Academy of Sciences of the United States of America, 103*(43), 16033–16038.

Carlson, N. R. (2007). *Physiology of behavior* (9th ed.). Boston: Allyn and Bacon.

Carlsson, A., & Lindqvist, M. (1963). Effect of chlorpromazine or haloperidol on formation of 3methoxytyramine and normetanephrine in mouse brain. *Acta Pharmacologica et Toxicologica, 20,* 140–144.

Carter, L. P., Koek, W., & France, C. P. (2009). Behavioral analysis of GHB: Receptor mechanisms. *Pharmacological Therapy, 121*(1), 100–114.

Caspi, A., Sugden, K., Moffitt, T. E., Taylor, A., Craig, I. W., Harrington, H., et al. (2003). Influence of life stress on depression: Moderation by a polymorphism in the 5-HTT gene. *Science, 301*(5631), 386–389.

Cassidy, F., Zhao, C., Badger, J., Claffey, E., Dobrin, S., Roche, S., et al. (2007). Genome-wide scan of bipolar disorder and investigation of population stratification effects on linkage: Support for susceptibility loci at 4q21, 7q36, 9p21, 12q24, 14q24, and 16p13. *American Journal of Medical Genetics Part B: Neuropsychiatric Genetics, 144*(6), 791–801.

Castren, E., Voikar, V., & Rantamaki, T. (2007). Role of neurotrophic factors in depression. *Current Opinion in Pharmacology, 7*(1), 18–21.

Centers for Disease Control and Prevention. (2005). Mental health in the United States: Prevalence of diagnosis and medication treatment for attention-deficit/hyperactivity disorder—United States. *Morbidity and Mortality Monthly Report, 54*(34), 842–847.

Chen, C. Y., O'Brian, M. S., & Anthony, J. C. (2005). Who becomes cannabis dependent soon after onset of use? Epidemiological evidence from the United States: 2000–2001. *Drug and Alcohol Dependence, 79,* 11–22.

Chen, P. S., Peng, G. S., Yang, S., Wu, X., Wang, C. C., Wilson, B., et al. (2006). Valproate protects dopaminergic neurons in midbrain neuron/glia cultures by stimulating the release of neurotrophic factors from astrocytes. *Molecular Psychiatry, 11*(12), 1116–1125.

Cheng, J. K., & Chiou, L. C. (2006). Mechanisms of the antinociceptive action of gabapentin. *Journal of Pharmacological Sciences, 100*(5), 471–486.

Cheng, J. Y., Chen, R. Y., Ko, J. S., & Ng, E. M. (2007). Efficacy and safety of atomoxetine for attention-deficit/hyperactivity disorder in children and adolescents-meta-analysis and meta-regression analysis. *Psychopharmacology, 194*(2), 197–209.

Cheng, V. Y., Bonin, R. P., Chiu, M. W., Newell, J. G., MacDonald, J. F., & Orser, B. A. (2006). Gabapentin increases a tonic inhibitory conductance in hippocampal pyramidal neurons. *Anesthesiology, 105*(2), 325–333.

Chenu, F., & Bourin, M. (2006). Potentiation of antidepressant-like activity with lithium: Mechanism involved. *Current Drug Targets, 7*(2), 159–163.

Chessick, C. A., Allen, M. H., Thase, M., Batista Miralha da Cunha, A. B., Kapczinski, F. F.,

de Lima, M. S., et al. (2006). Azapirones for generalized anxiety disorder [Electronic version]. *Cochrane Database of Systematic Reviews, 3,* CD006115.

Choi, S. (2003). Nefazodone (Serzone) withdrawn because of hepatotoxicity. *Canadian Medical Association Journal, 169*(11), 1187.

Chuang, D. M. (2005). The antiapoptotic actions of mood stabilizers: Molecular mechanisms and therapeutic potentials. *Annals of the New York Academy of Sciences, 1053,* 195–204.

Clayton, A. H., & Montejo, A. L. (2006). Major depressive disorder, antidepressants, and sexual dysfunction. *The Journal of Clinical Psychiatry, 67*(Suppl. 6), 33–37.

Clayton, A. H., Warnock, J. K., Kornstein, S. G., Pinkerton, R., Sheldon-Keller, A., & McGarvey, E. L. (2004). A placebo-controlled trial of bupropion SR as an antidote for selective serotonin reuptake inhibitor-induced sexual dysfunction. *The Journal of Clinical Psychiatry, 65*(1), 62–67.

Collins, A. C., Romm, E, & Wehner, J. M. (1990). Dissociation of the apparent relationship between nicotine tolerance and up-regulation of nicotinic receptors. *Brain Research Bulletin, 25,* 373–379.

Comer, S. D., Collins, E. D., MacArthur, R. B., & Fischman, M. W. (1999). Comparison of intravenous and intranasal heroin self-administration by morphine-maintained humans. *Psychopharmacology, 143,* 327–338.

Comings, D. E., Rosenthal, R. J., Lesieur, H. R., Rugle, L. J., Muhleman, D., Chiu, C., et al. (1996). A study of the dopamine D2 receptor gene in pathological gambling. *Pharmacogenetics, 6*(3), 223–234.

Cooper, J. B., Jane, J. A., Alves, W., & Cooper, E. (1999). Right median nerve electrical stimulation to hasten awakening from coma. *Brain Injury, 13*(4), 261–267.

Cooper, J. C., & Knutson, B. (2008). Valence and salience contribute to nucleus accumbens activation. *NeuroImage, 39*(1), 538–547.

Cornelius, J. F., Clark, D. B., Bukstein, O. G., Birmaher, B., Salloum, I. M., & Brown, S. A. (2005). Acute phase and five-year follow-up study of fluoxetine in adolescents with major depression and a comorbid substance use disorder: A review. *Addictive Behaviors, 30*(9), 1824–1833.

Cornelius, J. R., Chung, T., Martin, C., Wood, D., & Clark, D. (2008). Cannabis withdrawal is common among treatment-seeking adolescents with cannabis dependence and major depression, and is associated with rapid relapse dependence. *Addictive Behaviors, 33*(11), 1500–1505.

Cottler, L. B. (2007). Drug use disorders in the National Comorbidity Survey: Have we come a long way? *Archives of General Psychiatry, 64*(3), 1–2.

Cowen, M. S., Adams, C., Kraehenbuehl, T., Vengeliene, V., & Lawrence, A. J. (2005). The acute anti-craving effect of acamprosate in alcohol-preferring rats is associated with modulation of the mesolimbic dopamine system. *Addiction Biology, 10*(3), 233–242.

Cox, G. R., Desbrow, B., Montgomery, P. G., Anderson, M. E., Bruce, C. R., Macrides, T. A., et al. (2002). Effect of different protocols of caffeine intake on metabolism and endurance performance. *Journal of Applied Physiology, 93,* 990–999.

Coyle, J. T. (2006). Glutamate and schizophrenia: Beyond the dopamine hypothesis. *Cellular and Molecular Neurobiology, 26*(4–6), 365–384.

Cromberg, H., Badiani, A., Chan, J., Dell'Orco, J., Dineen, P., & Robinson, T. (2001). The ability of environmental context to facilitate psychomotor sensitization to amphetamine can be dissociated from its effect on acute drug responsiveness and on conditioned responding. *Neuropsychopharmacology, 24,* 680–690.

Cunningham, M. O., Woodhall, G. L., Thompson, S. E., Cooley, D. J., & Jones, R. S. (2004). Dual effects of gabapentin and pregabalin on glutamate release at rat entorhinal synapses in vitro. *European Journal of Neuroscience, 20*(6), 1566–1576.

Cuzon, V. C., Yeh, P. W., Yanagawa, Y., Obata, K., & Yeh, H. H. (2008). Ethanol consumption during early pregnancy alters the disposition of tangentially migrating GABAergic interneurons in the fetal cortex. *The Journal of Neuroscience, 28*(8), 1854–1864.

Czapinski, P., Blaszczyk, B., & Czuczwar, S. J. (2005). Mechanisms of action of antiepileptic drugs. *Current Topics in Medicinal Chemistry, 5*(1), 3–14.

Daly, J. W., & Fredholm, B. B. (1998). Caffeine—an atypical drug of dependence. *Drug and Alcohol Dependence, 51,* 199–206.

Damasio, A. (1995). On some functions of the human prefrontal cortex. *Annals of the New York Academy of Sciences, 769,* 241–251.

Daniela, E., Gittings, D., & Schenk, S. (2006). Conditioning following repeated exposures to MDMA in rats: Role in the maintenance of MDMA self-administration. *Behavioral Neuroscience, 120*(5), 1144–1150.

da Silva Lobo, D. S., Vallada, H. P., Knight, J., Martins, S. S., Tavares, H., Gentil, V., et al. (2007). Dopamine genes and pathological gambling in discordant sib-pairs. *Journal of Gambling Studies, 23*(4), 421–433.

Davidson, J. R. (2002). Hypericum trial study group: Effect of Hypericum perforatum (St. John's wort) in major depressive disorder. *Journal of the American Medical Association, 287,* 1807–1814.

DeSanty, K. P., & Dar, M. S. (2001). Cannabinoid-induced motor incoordination through the cerebellar CB(1) receptor in mice. *Pharmacology Biochemistry & Behavior, 69*(1–2), 251–259.

Devane, W. A., Dysarz, F. A., III, Johnson, M. R., Melvin, L. S., & Howlett, A. C. (1988). Determination and characterization of a cannabinoid receptor in rat brain. *Molecular Pharmacology, 34*(5), 605–613.

Devane, W. A., Hanus, L., Breuer, A., Pertwee, R. G., Stevenson, L. A., Griffin, G., et al. (1992). Isolation and structure of a brain constituent that binds to the cannabinoid receptor. *Science, 258*(5090), 1946–1949.

de Villiers, S. H., Lindblom, N., Kalayanov, G., Gordon, S., Malmerfelt, A., Johansson, A. M., et al. (2002). Active immunization against nicotine suppresses nicotine-induced dopamine release in the rat nucleus accumbens shell. *Respiration: International Review of Thoracic Diseases, 698*(3), 247–253.

Dickstein, S. G., Bannon, K., Castellanos, F. X., & Milham, M. P. (2006). The neural correlates of attention deficit hyperactivity disorder: An ALE meta-analysis. *The Journal of Child Psychology and Psychiatry, 47*(10), 1051–1062.

DiFranza, J. R. (2008). Hooked from the first cigarette. *Scientific American, 298*(5), 82–87.

DiMarzo, V. (2008). BB(1) receptor antagonism: Biological basis for metabolic effects. *Drug Discovery Today, 13*(23), 1026–1041.

Doggrell, S. A. (2005). Fluoxetine—do the benefits outweigh the risks in adolescent major depression? *Expert Opinion on Pharmacotherapy, 6*(1), 147–150.

Doyon, W. M., Ramachandra, V., Samson, H. H., Czachowski, C. L., & Gonzales, R. A. (2004). Accumbal dopamine concentration during operant self-administration of a sucrose or a novel sucrose with ethanol solution. *Alcohol, 34*(2–3), 261–271.

D'Sa, C., & Duman, R. S. (2002). Antidepressants and neuroplasticity. *Bipolar Disorders, 4*(3), 183–194.

Duman, R. S., & Monteggia, L. M. (2006). A neurotrophic model for stress-related mood disorders. *Biological Psychiatry, 59*(12), 1116–1127.

Eckstein-Ludwig, U., Fei, J., & Schwarz, W. (1999). Inhibition of uptake, steady-state currents, and transient charge movements generated by the neuronal GABA transporter by various anticonvulsant drugs. *British Journal of Pharmacology, 128*(1), 92–102.

Einat, H., Yuan, P., Gould, T. D., Li, J., Du, J., Zhang, L., et al. (2003). The role of the extracellular signal-regulated kinase signaling pathway in mood modulation. *The Journal of Neuroscience, 23*(19), 7311–7316.

Eisenberg, M. J., Filion, K. B., Yavin, D., Belisle, P., Mottillo, S., Joseph, L., et al. (2008). Pharmacotherapies for smoking cessation: A meta-analysis of randomized controlled trials. *Canadian Medical Association Journal, 179*(2), 135–144.

El-Zein, R., Abdel-Rahman, S., Hay, M., Lopez, M., Bondy, M., Morris, D., et al. (2005). Cytogenetic effects in children treated with methylphenidate. *Cancer Letters, 230*(2), 284–291.

Engblom, D., Bilbao, A., Sanchis-Segura, C., Dahan, L., Perreau-Lenz, S., Balland, B., et al. (2008). Glutamate receptors on dopamine neurons control the persistence of cocaine seeking. *Neuron, 59*(3), 497–508.

Ettinger, R. H., Ettinger, W. F., & Harless, W. E. (1997). Active immunization with cocaine-protein conjugate attenuates cocaine effects. *Pharmacology Biochemistry & Behavior, 58*(1), 215–220.

Fadda, R., Scherma, M., Spano, M. S., Salis, P., Melis, V., Fattore, L., et al. (2006). Cannabinoid self-administration increases dopamine release in the nucleus accumbens. *Neuroreport, 17*(15), 1629–1632.

Faraone, S. V., & Upadhyaya, H. P. (2007). The effect of stimulant treatment for ADHD on later substance abuse and the potential for medication misuse, abuse, and diversion. *The Journal of Clinical Psychiatry, 68*(11), e28.

Fava, M., Alpert, J., Nierenberg, A. A., Mischoulon, D., Otto, M. W., Zajecka, J., et al. (2005). A double-blind, randomized trial of St. John's wort, fluoxetine, and placebo in major depressive disorder. *Journal of Clinical Psychopharmacology, 24*(5), 441–447.

Federici, M., Sebastianelli, L., Natoli, S., Bernardi, G., & Mercuri, N. B. (2007). Electrophysiologic changes in ventral midbrain dopaminergic neurons resulting from (+/−)-3, 4-methylenedioxymethamphetamine (MDMA- "Ecstasy"). *Biological Psychiatry, 62*(6), 680–686.

Fehr, C., Yakushev, I., Hohmann, N., Buchholz, H. G., Landvogt, C., Deckers, H., et al. (2008). Association of low striatal dopamine d2 receptor availability with nicotine dependence similar to that seen with other drugs of abuse. *The American Journal of Psychiatry, 165*(4), 507–514.

Fehsel, K., Loeffler, S., Krieger, K., Henning, U., Agelink, M., Kolb-Bachofen, V., et al. (2005). Clozapine induces oxidative stress and proapoptotic gene expression in neutrophils of schizophrenic patients. *Journal of Clinical Psychopharmacology, 25*(5), 419–426.

Fernandez-Guasti, A., Ulloa, R. E., & Nicolini, H. (2003). Age differences in the sensitivity to clomipramine in an animal model of obsessive-compulsive disorder. *Psychopharmacology, 166*(3), 195–201.

Ferrario, C. R., Shou, M., Samaha, A. N., Watson, C. J., Kennedy, R. T., & Robinson, T. E. (2008). The rate of intravenous cocaine administration alters c-fos mRNA expression and the temporal dynamics of dopamine, but not glutamate, overflow in the striatum. *Brain Research, 1209*, 151–156.

Foley, K. F., DeSanty, K. P., & Kast, R. E. (2006). Bupropion: Pharmacology and therapeutic applications. *Expert Review of Neurotherapeutics, 6*(9), 1249–1265.

Food and Drug Adminstration. (2007). FDA proposes new warnings about suicidal thinking, behavior in young adults who take antidepressant medications. *FDA News* (PO7–77).

Ford, C. P., Mark, G. P., & Williams, J. T. (2006). Properties and opioid inhibition of mesolimbic dopamine neurons vary according to target location. *The Journal of Neuroscience, 26*(10), 2788–2797.

Fox, B. S. (1997). Development of a therapeutic vaccine for the treatment of cocaine addiction. *Drug and Alcohol Dependence, 48*(3), 153–158.

Fredholm, B., Battig, K., Holmen, J., Nehlig, A., & Zvartua, E. (1999). *Actions of caffeine in the brain with special reference to factors that contribute to its widespread use. Pharmacological Reviews, 51*(1), 83–133.

Frey, B. N., Andreazza, A. C., Cereser, K. M., Martins, M. R., Valvassori, S. S., Reus, G. Z., et al. (2006). Effects of mood stabilizers on hippocampus BCNF levels in an animal model of mania. *Life Sciences, 79*(3), 281–286.

Gaoni, Y. E., & Mechoulam, R. (1964). Isolation, structure and partial synthesis of an active constituent of hashish. *Journal of American Chemical Society, 86*(8), 1646–1647.

Gaudiano, B. A., & Herbert, J. D. (2003). Antidepressant-placebo debate in the media: Balanced coverage or placebo hype? *Commission for Scientific Medicine and Mental Health, 2*(1).

Gelenberg, A. J., Shelton, R. C., Crits-Christoph, P., Keller, M. B., Dunner, D. L., Hirschfeld, R. M., et al. (2004). The effectiveness of St. John's wort in major depressive disorder: A naturalistic phase 2 follow-up in which nonresponders were provided alternate medication. *The Journal of Clinical Psychiatry, 65*(8), 1114–1119.

Gerdeman, G., & Lovinger, D. M. (2001). CB1 cannabinoid receptor inhibits synaptic release of glutamate in rat dorsolateral striatum. *Journal of Neurophysiology, 85*(1), 468–471.

Geuze, E., vanBerckel, B., Lammertsma, A., Boellaard, R., de Kloet, C., Vermetten, E., et al. (2008). Reduced GABAa benzodiazepine receptor binding in veterans with post-traumatic stress disorder. *Molecular Psychiatry, 13*, 74–83.

Gibbons, R. D., Brown, C. H., Hur, K., Marcus, S. M., Bhaumik, D. K., Erkens, J. A., et al. (2007). Early evidence on the effects of regulators' suicidality warnings on SSRI prescriptions and suicide in children and adolescents. *The American Journal of Psychiatry, 164*(9), 1356–1363.

Gobbi, G., & Janiri, L. (2006). Sodium- and magnesium-valproate in vivo modulate glutamatergic and GABAergic synapses in the medial prefrontal cortex. *Psychopharmacology, 185*(2), 255–262.

Gonzales, R. A., Job, M. O., & Doyon, W. M. (2004). The role of mesolimbic dopamine in the development and maintenance of ethanol reinforcement. *Pharmacology & Therapeutics, 103*(2), 121–146.

Gonzalez-Maeso, J., Weisstaub, N. V., Zhou, M., Chan, P., Ivic, L., Ang, R., et al. (2007). Hallucinogens recruit specific cortical 5-HT2A receptor-mediated signaling pathways to affect behavior. *Neuron, 53,* 439–452.

Goodman, A. (2008). Neurobiology of addiction. An integrative review. *Biochemical Pharmacology, 75*(1), 266–322.

Goodman, W. K., Price, L. H., Rasmussen, S .A., Mazure, C., Delgado, P., Heninger, G. R., et al. (1989). The Yale-Brown obsessive compulsive scale. *Archives of General Psychiatry, 48*(10), 1012–1018.

Graeff, N. G., Netto, C. F., & Zangrossi, H., Jr. (1998). The elevated T-maze as an experimental model of anxiety. *Neuroscience & Biobehavioral Reviews, 23*(2), 237–246.

Gresch, P. J., Strickland, L. V., & Sanders-Bush, E. (2002). Lysergic acid diethylamide-induced Fos expression in rat brain: Role of serotonin-2A receptors. *Neuroscience, 114*(3), 707–713.

Griffiths, R. R., Lamb, R. J., Sannerud, C. A., Ator, N. A., & Brady, J. V. (1991). Self-injection of barbiturates, benzodiazepines and other sedative-anxiolytics in baboons. *Psychopharmacology, 103(2),* 154–161.

Griggs, E. A., & Ward, M. (1977, April). LSD Toxicity: A Suspected Cause of Death. *The Journal.*

Gronli, J., Bramham, C., Murison, R., Kanhema, T., Fiske, E., Bjorvatn, B., et al. (2006). Chronic mild stress inhibits BDNF protein expression and CREB activation in the dentate gyrus but not in the hippocampus proper. *Pharmacology Biochemistry & Behavior, 85(4),* 842–849.

Guzzetta, F., Tondo, L., Centorrino, F., & Baldessarini, R. J. (2007). Lithium treatment reduces suicide risk in recurrent major depressive disorder. *The Journal of Clinical Psychiatry, 68(3),* 380–383.

Halpern, J. H., & Pope, H. G, Jr. (2002). Hallucinogen persisting perception disorder: What do we know after 50 years? *Drug and Alcohol Dependence, 69*(2), 109–119.

Hamet, P., & Tremblay, J. (2005). Genetics and genomics of depression. *Metabolism: Clinical and Experimental, 54*(5)(Suppl. 1), 10–15.

Hamilton, M. C. (1959). The assessment of anxiety states by rating. *British Journal of Medical Psychology, 32,* 50–55.

Han, D. H., Lee, Y., Yang, K., Kim, E., Lyoo, I., & Renshaw, P. (2007). Dopamine genes and reward dependence in adolescents with excessive Internet game play. *Journal of Addiction Medicine, 1*(3), 133–139.

Hardan, A. Y., Minshew, N. J., & Keshavan, M. S. (2000). Corpus callosum size in autism. *Neurology, 55,* 1033–1036.

Harlan, R. E., & Garcia, M. M. (1998). Drugs of abuse and immediate-early genes in the forebrain. *Molecular Neurobiology, 16*(3), 221–267.

Hashimoto, K., Shimizu, E., & Iyo, M. (2004). Critical role of brain-derived neurotrophic factor in mood disorders. *Brain Research Reviews, 45*(2), 104–114.

Hatsukami, D. K., Stead, L. F., & Gupta, P. C. (2008). Nicotine addiction: Prevalence and treatment. *Lancet, 371,* 2027–2038.

Hatzidimitriou, G., McCann, U. D., & Ricaurte, G. A. (1999). Altered serotonin innervation patterns in the forebrain of monkeys treated with (+/−)3, 4-methylenedioxymethamphetamine seven years previously: Factors influencing abnormal recovery. *The Journal of Neuroscience, 19*(12), 5096–5107.

Haynes, L. E., Barber, D., & Mitchell, I. J. (2004). Chronic antidepressant medication attenuates dexamethasone-induced neuronal death and sublethal neuronal damage in the hippocampus and striatum. *Brain Research, 1026*(2), 157–167.

Hazlett, E. A., Romero, M. J., Haznedar, M. M., New, A. S., Goldstein, K. E., Newmark, R. E., et al. (2007). Deficient attentional modulation of startle eyeblink is associated with symptom severity in the schizophrenia spectrum. *Schizophrenia Research, 93*(1–3), 288–295.

Hensler, J. G. (2003). Regulation of 5-HT1A receptor function in brain following agonist or antidepressant administration. *Life Sciences, 72*(15), 1665–1682.

Hernandez, C. M., & Terry, A. (2005). Repeated nicotine exposure in rats: Effects on memory function, cholinergic markers and nerve growth factor. *Neuroscience, 130*(4), 997–1012.

Hnasko, T. S., Sotak, B. N., & Palmiter, R. D. (2007). Cocaine-conditioned place preference by dopamine-deficient mice is mediated by serotonin. *The Journal of Neuroscience, 27*(46), 12484–12488.

Ho Pian, K. L., van Megan, H. J., Ramsey, N. F., Mandi, R., can Rijk, P. P., Wynne, H. J., et al. (2005). Decreased thalamic blood flow in obsessive-compulsive disorder patients responding to fluvoxamine. *Psychiatry Research, 138*(2), 89–97.

Hoffman, A. F., Oz, M., Yang, R., Lichtman, A. H., & Lupica, C. R. (2007). Opposing actions of chronic delta9-tetrahydrocannabinol and cannabinoid antagonists on hippocampal long-term potentiation. *Learning and Memory, 14*(1–2), 63–74.

Hughes, J. R. (2007). Autism: The first firm finding = underconnectivity? *Epilepsy & Behavior, 11*(1), 20–24.

Hurley, M. J., & Jenner, P. (2006). What has been learnt from study of dopamine receptors in Parkinson's disease? *Pharmacology & Therapeutics, 111*(3), 715–728.

Hyman, S. E., Malenka, R. C., & Nestler, E. J. (2006). Neural mechanisms of addiction: The role of reward-related learning and memory. *Annual Review of Neuroscience, 29,* 565–598.

Ichikawa, J., Chung, Y. C., Dai, J., & Meltzer, H. Y. (2005). Valproic acid potentiates both typical and atypical antipsychotic-induced prefrontal cortical dopamine release. *Brain Research, 1052*(1), 56–62.

Ichikawa, J., Dai, J., & Meltzer, H. Y. (2005). Lithium differs from anticonvulsant mood stabilizers in prefrontal cortical and accumbal dopamine release: Role of 5-HT(1A) receptor agonism. *Brain Research, 1049*(2), 182–190.

Iqbal, U., Dringenberg, H. C., Brien, J. F., & Reynolds, J. N. (2004). Chronic prenatal ethanol exposure alters hippocampal GABA(A) receptors and impairs spatial learning in the guinea pig. *Behavioral Brain Research, 150*(1–2), 117–125.

Ivanov, A., & Aston-Jones, G. (2001). Local opiate withdrawal in locus coeruleus neurons In vitro. *The Journal of Neurophysiology, 85,* 2388–2397.

Iverson, L. L. (2000). *The science of marijuana.* Oxford: Oxford University Press.

Izzo, A. A. (2004). Drug interactions with St. John's wort (Hypericum perforatum): A review of the clinical evidence. *International Journal of Clinical Pharmacology and Therapeutics, 42*(3), 139–148.

Javitt, D. C. (2007). Glutamate and schizophrenia: Phencyclidine, N-methyl-d-aspartate receptors, and dopamine-glutamate interactions. *International Review of Neurobiology, 78,* 69–108.

Javitt, D. C., & Coyle, J. T. (2004, January). Decoding schizophrenia. *Scientific American,* 1–4.

Job, M. O., Tang. A., Hall, F. S., Sora, I., Uhl, G. R., Gergeson, S. E., et al. (2007). Mu (mu) opioid receptor regulation of ethanol-induced dopamine response in the ventral striatum: Evidence of genotype specific sexual dimorphic epistasis. *Biological Psychiatry, 62*(6), 627–634.

Joel, D. (2006). The signal attenuation rat model of obsessive-compulsive disorder: A review. *Psychopharmacology, 186*(4), 487–503.

Johnson, M. W., & Ettinger, R. H. (2000). Active immunization attenuates cocaine's discriminative properties. *Experimental and Clinical Psychopharmacology, 8,* 163–167.

Joyce, J. N. (1993). The dopamine hypothesis of schizophrenia: Limbic interactions with serotonin and norepinephrine. *Psychopharmacology, 112*(1)(Suppl. 1), S16–S34.

Just, M. A., Cherkassky, V. L., Keller, T. A., Kana, R. K., & Minshew, N. J. (2007). Functional and anatomical cortical underconnectivity in autism: Evidence from an fMRI study of an executive function task and corpus callosum morphometry. *Cerebral Cortex, 17*(4), 951–961.

Just, M. A., Cherkassky, V. L., Keller, T. A., & Minshew, N. J. (2004). Cortical activation and synchronization during sentence comprehension in high-functioning autism: Evidence of underconnectivity. *Brain, 127,* 1811–1821.

Justinova, Z., Tanda, G., Redhi, G. H., & Goldberg, S. R. (2003). Self-administration of delta9-tetrahydrocannabinol (THC) by drug naive squirrel monkeys. *Psychopharmacology, 169,* 135–140.

Kalechstein, A. D., De La Garza, R., II, Mahoney, J. J., III, Fantegrossi, W. E., & Newton, T. F. (2007). MDMA use and neurocognition: A meta-analytic review. *Psychopharmacology, 189*(4), 531–537.

Kalivas, P. W., McFarland, K., Bowers, S., Szumlinski, K., Xi, Z. X., & Baker, D. (2003). Glutamate transmission and addiction to cocaine. *Annals of the New York Academy of Sciences, 1003,* 169–175.

Kalivas, P. W., & Volkow, N. D. (2005). The neural basis of addiction: A pathology of motivation and choice. *The American Journal of Psychiatry, 162*(8), 1403–1413.

Kang-Park, M. H., Kieffer, B. L., Roberts, A. J., Siggins, G. R., & Moore, S. D. (2007). Presynaptic delta opioid receptors regulate ethanol actions in central amygdala. *The Journal of Pharmacology and Experimental Therapeutics, 320*(2), 917–925.

Kang-Park, M. H., Wilson, W. A., Kuhn, C. M., Moore, S. D., & Swartzwelder, H. S. (2007). Differential sensitivity of GABA A receptor-mediated IPSCs to cannabinoids in hippocampal slices from adolescent and adult rats. *Journal of Neurophysiology, 98*(3), 1223–1230.

Kapur, S., Zipursky, R., Jones, C., Remington, G., & Houle, S. (2000). Relationship between dopamine D(2) occupancy, clinical response, and side effects: A double-blind PET study of first-episode schizophrenia. *The American Journal of Psychiatry, 157*(4), 514–520.

Karl, A., Schaefer, M., Malta, L. S., Dorfel, D., Rohleder, N., & Werner, A. (2006). A meta-analysis of structural brain abnormalities in PTSD. *Neuroscience & Biobehavioral Reviews, 30*(7), 1004–1031.

Kasper, S., Anghelescu, I. G., Szegedi, A., Dienel, A., & Kieser, M. (2006). Superior efficacy of St. John's wort extract WS5570 compared to placebo in patients with major depression: A randomized, double-blind, placebo-controlled, multi-center trial (ISRCTN77277298). *BMC Medicine, 4,* 14.

Kato, T. (2007). Molecular genetics of bipolar disorder and depression. *Psychiatry and Clinical Neurosciences, 61*(1), 3–19.

Kehoe, W. A., Jr. (2008). Substance abuse: New numbers are a cause for action. *The Annals of Pharmacotherapy, 42*(2), 270–272.

Kendler, K. S. (2006, December). Major depression and generalised anxiety disorder. Same genes, (partly) different environments—revisited. *The British Journal of Psychiatry, 189*(6), 540–546.

Kendler, K. S., Gardner, C. O., Gatz, M., & Pedersen, N. L. (2007). The sources of co-morbidity between major depression and generalized anxiety disorder in a Swedish national twin sample. *Psychological Medicine, 37*(3), 453–462.

Kessler, R. C., Berglund, P., Demler, O., Jin, R., Merikangas, K. R., & Walters, E. E. (2005). Lifetime prevalence and age-of-onset distributions of DSM-IV disorders in the National Comorbidity Survey Replication. *Archives of General Psychiatry, 62*(6), 1–11.

Khom, S., Baburin, I., Timin, E., Hohaus, A., Trauner, G., Kopp, B., et al. (2007). Valerenic acid potentiates and inhibits GABAa receptors: Molecular mechanism and subunit specificity. *Neuropharmacology, 20,* 1–10.

Khundaker, A. A., & Zetterstrom, T. S. (2006). Biphasic change in BDNF gene expression following antidepressant drug treatment explained by differential transcript regulation. *Brain Research, 1106*(1), 12–20.

Kim, S. W., Shin, I. S., Kim, J. M., Lee, S. H., Lee, J. H., Yoon, B. H., et al. (2007). Amisulpride versus risperidone in the treatment of depression in patients with schizophrenia: A randomized, open-label, controlled trial. *Progress in Neuro-Psychopharmacology & Biological Psychiatry, 31*(7), 1504–1509.

Kim, Y-K., Lee, H-P., Won, S-D., Park, E-Y., Lee, H-Y., Lee, B-H., et al. (2007). Low plasma BDNF is associated with suicidal behavior in major depression. *Progress in Neuro-Psychopharmacology & Biological Psychiatry, 31*(1), 78–85.

Kim, Y. K., Yoon, I. Y., Shin, Y. K., Cho, S. S., & Kim, S. E. (2007). Modafinil-induced hippocampal activation in narcolepsy. *Neuroscience Letters, 422*(2), 91–96.

Kirsch, I., & Sapirstein, G. (1998). Listening to Prozac but hearing placebo: A meta-analysis of antidepressant medication. *Prevention and Treatment, 1*(2).

Knutson, B., Adams, C. M., Fong, G. W., & Hommer, D. (2001). Anticipation of increasing monetary reward selectively recruits nucleus accumbens. *The Journal of Neuroscience, 21*(16), RC159.

Koepp, M. J., Gunn, R. N., Lawrence, A. D., Cunningham, V. J., Dagher, A., Jones, T., et al. (1998). Evidence for striatal dopamine release during a video game. *Nature, 393*(6682), 266–268.

Kogan, M., Blumberg, S. J., Schieve, L. A., Boyle, C. A., Perrin, J. M., Ghandour, R. M., et al. (2009). Prevalence of parent-reported diagnosis of autism spectrum disorder among children in the U.S., 2007. *Pediatrics, 124*(4),1–8.

Kogan, N. M. (2005). Cannabinoids and cancer. *Mini Reviews in Medicinal Chemistry, 5*(10), 941–952.

Koponen, E., Rantamaki, T., Voikar, V., Saarelainen, T., MacDonald, E., & Castren, E. (2005). Enhanced BDNF signaling is associated with an antidepressant-like behavioral response and changes in brain monoamines. *Cellular and Molecular Neurobiology, 25*(6), 973–980.

Kozisek, M. E., Middlemas, D., & Bylund, D. B. (2008). Brain-derived neurotrophic factor and its receptor tropomyosin-related kinase B in the mechanism of action of antidepressant therapies. *Pharmacology & Therapeutics, 117*(1), 30–51.

Krall, C. M., Richards, J. B., Rabin, R. A., & Winter, J. C. (2008). Marked decrease of LSD-induced stimulus control in serotonin transporter knockout mice. *Pharmacology Biochemistry & Behavior, 88*(3), 349–357.

Kropotov, J. D., Grin-Yatsenko, V. A., Ponomarev, V. A., Chutko, L. S., Yakovenko, E. A., & Nikishena, I. S. (2005). ERPs correlates of EEG relative beta training in ADHD children. *International Journal of Psychophysiology, 55*(1), 23–34.

Kumar, S., Fleming, R. L., & Morrow, A. L. (2004). Ethanol regulation of gamma-aminobutyric acid A receptors: Genomic and nongenomic mechanisms. *Pharmacology & Therapeutics, 101*(3), 211–226.

Kumar, S., Kralic, J. E., O'Buckley, T. K., Grobin, A. C., & Morrow, A. L. (2003). Chronic ethanol consumption enhances internalization of alpha1 subunit-containing GABAA receptors in cerebral cortex. *Journal of Neurochemistry, 86*(8), 700–708.

Kumari, V., Antonova, E., Geyer, M. A., Ffytche, D., Williams, S. C., & Sharma, T. (2007). A fMRI investigation of startle gating deficits in schizophrenia patients treated with typical or atypical antipsychotics. *The International Journal of Neuropsychopharmacology, 10*(4), 463–477.

Kumari, V., Soni, W., & Sharma, T. (2002). Prepulse inhibition of the startle response in risperidone-treated patients: Comparison with typical antipsychotics. *Schizophrenia Research, 44*(1–2), 139–146.

Laeng, P., Pitts, R. L., Lemire, A. L., Drabik, C. E., Weiner, A., Tang, H., et al. (2004). The mood stabilizer valproic acid stimulates GABA neurogenesis from rat forebrain stem cells. *Journal of Neurochemistry, 91*(1), 238–251.

LaLumiere, R. T., & Kalivas, P. W. (2008). Glutamate release in the nucleus accumbens core is necessary for heroin seeking. *The Journal of Neuroscience, 23*(12), 3170–3177.

Landry, D. W., & Yang, G. (1997). Anti-cocaine catalytic antibodies—a novel approach to the problem of addiction. *Journal of Addictive Diseases, 16*(3), 1–17.

Landry, D. W., Zhao, K., Yang, G., Glickman, M., & Georgiadis, T. (1993). Antibody-catalyzed degradation of cocaine. *Science, 259*(5103), 1899–1901.

Laruelle, M. (1998). Imaging dopamine transmission in schizophrenia. A review and meta-analysis. *The Quarterly Journal of Nuclear Medicine, 42*(3), 211–221.

Lecca, D., Cacciapaglia, F., Valentini, V., & Di Chiara, G. (2006). Monitoring extracellular dopamine in the rat nucleus accumbens shell and core during acquisition and maintenance of intravenous WIN 55,212-2 self-administration. *Psychopharmacology, 188*(1), 63–74.

Lee, B-H., Kim, H., Park, S-H., Kim, Y. K. (2006). Decreased plasma BDNF level in depressive patients. *Journal of Affective Disorders, 101*(1–3), 239–244.

Le Foll, B., & Goldberg, S. R. (2005). Cannabinoid CB1 receptor antagonists as promising new medications for drug dependence. *The Journal of Pharmacology and Experimental Therapeutics, 312*(3), 875–883.

Lejoyeux M., S., J., & Ades, J. (1998). Benzodiazepine treatment for alcohol-dependent patients. *Alcohol and Alcoholism, 33*(6), 563–575.

Lemos, J. C., Pan, Y. Z., Ma, X., Lamy, C., Akanwa, A. C., & Beck, S. G. (2006). Selective 5-HT receptor inhibition of glutamatergic and GABAergic synaptic activity in the rat dorsal and median raphe. *European Journal of Neuroscience, 24*(12), 3415–3430.

Lepicier, P., Bibeau-Poirier, A., Lagneux, C., Servant, M. J., & Lamontagne, D. (2006). Signaling pathways involved in the cardioprotective effects of cannabinoids. *Journal of Pharmacological Sciences, 102*(2), 155–166.

Lepicier, P., Lagneux, C., Sirois, M. G., & Lamontagne, D. (2007). Endothelial CB1-receptors limit infarct size through NO formation in rat isolated hearts. *Life Sciences, 81*(17–18), 1373–1380.

LeSage, M. G., Keyler, D. E., Hieda, Y., Collins, G., Burroughs, D., Le, C., et al. (2006). Effects of a nicotine conjugate vaccine on the acquisition and maintenance of nicotine self-administration in rats. *Psychopharmacology, 184*(3–4), 409–416.

Levin, E. D., Conners, C., Silva, D., Ninton, S., Meck, W., March, J., et al. (1998). Transdermal nicotine effects on attention. *Psychopharmacology, 140*(2), 135–141.

Levin, G. M., Bowles, T. M., Ehret, M. J., Langaee, T., Tan, J. Y., Johnson, J. A., et al. (2007). Assessment of human serotonin 1A receptor polymorphisms and SSRI responsiveness. *Molecular Diagnosis & Therapy, 11*(3), 155–160.

Levine, J. D., Gordon, N. C., & Fields, H. L. (1978). The mechanism of placebo analgesia. *Lancet, 2*(8091), 654–657.

Li, Z., DiFranza, J. R., Wellman, R. J., Kulkarni, P., & King, J. A. (2008). Imaging brain activation in nicotine-sensitized rats. *Brain Research, 1199*, 91–99.

Liang, J., Suryanarayanan, A., Abriam, A., Snyder, B., Olsen, R. W., & Spigelman, I. (2007). Mechanisms of reversible GABAA receptor plasticity after ethanol Intoxication. *The Journal of Neuroscience, 27*(45), 12367–12377.

Lin, P. Y. (2007). Meta-analysis of the association of serotonin transporter gene polymorphism with obsessive-compulsive disorder. *Progress in Neuro-Psychopharmacology & Biological Psychiatry, 31*(3), 683–689.

Linde, K., Mulrow, C. D., Berner, M., & Egger, M. (2005). St. John's wort for depression. [Electronic version]. *Cochrane Database of Systematic Reviews*, CD000448.

Lohoff, F. W., Sander, T., Ferraro, T. N., Dahl, J. P., Gallinat, J., & Berrettini, W. H. (2005). Confirmation of association between the Val66Met polymorphism in the brain-derived neurotrophic factor (BDNF) gene and bipolar 1 disorder. *American Journal of Medical Genetics Part B: Neuropsychiatric Genetics, 139*(1), 51–53.

Lombard, C., Nagarkatti, M., & Nagarkatti, P. (2007). CB2 cannabinoid receptor agonist, JWH-015, triggers apoptosis in immune cells: Potential role for CB2 - selective ligands as immunosuppressive agents. *Clinical Immunology, 122*(3), 259–270.

Loo, S. K., Hopfer, C., Teale, P. D., & Reite, M. L. (2004). EEG correlates of methylphenidate response in ADHD: Association with cognitive and behavioral measures. *Journal of Clinical Neurophysiology, 21*(6), 457–464.

Machado-Vieira, R., Dietrich, M. O., Leke, R., Cereser, V. H., Zanatto, V., Kapczinski, F., et al. (2007). Decreased plasma brain derived neurotrophic factor levels in unmedicated bipolar patients during manic episode. *Biological Psychiatry, 61*(2), 142–144.

Mack, A. (2003). Examination of the evidence for off-label use of gabapentin. *Journal of Managed Care Pharmacy, 9*(6), 559–568.

Madras, B. K., Xie, Z., Lin, Z., Jassen, A., Panas, H., Lynch, L., et al. (2006). Modafinil occupies dopamine and norepinephrine transporters in vivo and modulates the transporters and trace amine activity in vitro. *The Journal of Pharmacology and Experimental Therapeutics, 319*(2), 561–569.

Mai, L., Jope, R. S., & Li, X. (2002). The BDNF-mediated signal transduction is modulated by GSK3beta and mood stabilizing agents. *Journal of Neurochemistry, 82*(1), 75–83.

Marek, G. J., Martin-Ruiz, R., Abo, A., & Artigas, F. (2005). The selective 5-HT2A receptor antagonist M100907 enhances antidepressant-like behavioral effects of the SSRI fluoxetine. *Neuropsychopharmacology, 30*(12), 2205–2215.

Martell, B. A., Mitchell, E., Poling, J., Gonsai, K., & Kosten, T. R. (2005). Vaccine pharmacotherapy for the treatment of cocaine dependence. *Biological Psychiatry, 58*(2), 158–164.

Mateo, Y., Budygin, E. A., John, C. E., & Jones, S. R. (2004). Role of serotonin in cocaine effects in mice with reduced dopamine transporter function. *Proceedings of the National Academy of Sciences of the United States of America, 101*(1), 372–377.

McAlonan, G. M., Cheung, V., Cheung, C., Suckling, J., Lam, G. Y., Tai, K. S., et al. (2004). Mapping the brain in autism. A voxel-based MRI study of volumetric differences and intercorrelations in autism. *Brain, 128*(2), 268–276.

McClung, C. A., & Nestler, E. J. (2003). Regulation of gene expression and cocaine reward by CREB and DeltaFosB. [Electronic version]. *Nature Neuroscience, 6*(11).

McKallip, R. J., Lombard, C., Martin, B. R., Nagarkatti, M., & Nagarkatti, P. S. (2002). Delta 9-tetrahydrocannabinol-induced apoptosis in the thymus and spleen as a mechanism of immunosuppression in vitro and in vivo. *Pharmacology & Experimental Therapeutics, 302*(2), 451–465.

McKinney, D. L., Cassidy, M. P., Collier, L. M., Martin, B. R., Wiley, J. L., Selley, D. E., et al. (2008). Dose-related differences in the regional pattern of cannabinoid receptor adaptation and in vivo tolerance development to delta9-tetrahydrocannabinol. *The Journal of Pharmacology and Experimental Therapeutics, 324*(2), 664–673.

Mechan, A., Yuan, J., Hatzidimitriou, G., Irvine, R. J., McCann, U. P., & Ricaurte, G. A. (2006). Pharmacokinetic profile of single and repeated oral doses of MDMA in squirrel monkeys: Relationship to lasting effects on brain serotonin neurons. *Neuropsychopharmacology, 31*(2), 339–350.

Mechoulam, R., & Gaoni, Y. (1965). A total synthesis of dl-delta1-tetrahydrocannabinol, the active constituent of hashish. *Journal of the American Chemical Society, 87*(14), 3273–3275.

Merikangas, K. R., Akiskal, H., Angst, J., Greenberg, P., Hirschfield, R., Petukhova, M., et al. (2007). Lifetime and 12-month prevalence of bipolar spectrum disorder in the National Comorbidity Survey replication. *Archives of General Psychiatry, 64*(5), 543–552.

Miller, M. M., & McEwen, B. S. (2006). Establishing an agenda for translational research on PTSD. *Annals of the New York Academy of Sciences, 1071*, 294–312.

Mirza, N. R., & Nielsen, E. O. (2006). Do subtype-selective gamma-aminobutyric acid A receptor modulators have a reduced propensity to induce physical dependence in mice? *The Journal of Pharmacology and Experimental Therapeutics, 316*(3), 1378–1385.

Miyasaka, L. S., Atallah, A. N., & Soares, B. G. O. (2007). Valerian for anxiety disorders. *Cochrane Database of Systematic Reviews, 4.*

Moffitt, T. E., & Melchior, M. (2007). Why does the worldwide prevalence of childhood attention deficit hyperactivity disorder matter? *The American Journal of Psychiatry, 164*, 856–858.

Moncrieff, J. (2003). A comparison off antidepressant trials using active and inert placebos. *International Journal of Methods in Psychiatric Research, 12*(3), 117–127.

Monteggia, L. M., Luikart, B., Barrot, M., Theobold, D., Malkovska, I., Nef, S., et al. (2007). Brain-derived neurotrophic factor conditional knockouts show gender differences in depression-related behaviors. *Biological Psychiatry, 61*(2), 187–197.

Moresco, R. M., Pietra, L., Henin, M., Panzacchi, A., Locatelli, M., Bonaldi, L., et al. (2007). Fluvoxamine treatment and D2 receptors: A pet study on OCD drug-naive patients. *Neuropsychopharmacology, 32*(1), 197–205.

Muller, D. J., de Luca, V., Sicard, T., King, N., Strauss, J., & Kennedy, J. L. (2006). Brain-derived neurotrophic factor (BDNF) gene and rapid-cycling bipolar disorder: Family-based association study. *The British Journal of Psychiatry, 189*, 317–323.

Muller, W. E. (2003). Current St. John's wort research from mode of action to clinical efficacy. *Pharmacological Research, 47*(2), 101–109.

Murphy, K., Kubin, Z., Shepherd, J. N., & Ettinger, R. H. (2010). Valeriana officinalis root extracts have potent anxiolytic effects in laboratory rats. *Phytomedicine.*17, 674–678.

Murray, K. N., & Abeles, N. (2002). Nicotine's effect on neural and cognitive functioning in an aging population. *Aging and Mental Health, 6*(2), 129–138.

Nair, A., Vadodaria, K. C., Banerjee, S. B., Benekareddy, M., Dias, B. G., Duman, R. S., et al. (2007). Stressor-specific regulation of distinct brain-derived neurotrophic factor transcripts and cyclic AMP response element-binding protein expression in the postnatal and adult rat hippocampus. *Neuropsychopharmacology, 32*(7), 1504–1519.

Nakata, K., Ujike, H., Sakai, A., Uchida, N., Nomura, A., Imamura, T., et al. (2003). Association study of the brain-derived neurotrophic factor (BDNF) gene with bipolar disorder. *Neuroscience Letters, 337*(1), 17–20.

National Institute of Mental Health. (2008). Autism spectrum disorders (pervasive developmental disorders), Bethesda, MD: Author.

National Institute on Drug Abuse. (2007). *High school and youth trends*. Bethesda, MD: National Institutes of Health.

Niaura, R., Hays, J. T., Jorenby, D. E., Leone, F. T., Pappas, J. E., Reeves, K. R., et al. (2008). The efficacy and safety of varenicline for smoking cessation using a flexible dosing strategy in adult smokers: A randomized controlled trial. *Current Medical Research and Opinion, 24*(7), 1931–1941.

Nibuya, M., Nestler, E. J., & Duman, R. S. (1996). Chronic antidepressant administration increases the expression of cAMP response element binding protein (CREB) in rat hippocampus. *The Journal of Neuroscience, 16*(7), 2365–2372.

Nilsson, M., Joliat, M. J., Miner, C. M., Brown, E. B., & Heiligenstein, J. H., (2004). Safety of subchronic treatment with fluoxetine for major depressive disorder in children and adolescents. *Journal of Child and Adolescent Psychopharmacology, 41*(3), 412–417.

Nowicky, A. V., Teyler, T. J., & Vardaris, R. M. (1987). The modulation of long-term potentiation by delta-9-tetrahydrocannabinol in the rat hippocampus, in vitro. *Brain Research Bulletin, 19*(6), 663–672.

Nyberg, S., Eriksson, B., Oxenstierna, G., Halldin, C., & Farde, L. (1999). Suggested minimal effective dose of risperidone based on PET-measured D2 and 5-HT2A receptor occupancy in schizophrenic patients. *The American Journal of Psychiatry, 156*(6), 869–875.

Olds, J., & Milner, P. (1954). Positive reinforcement produced by electrical stimulation of septal area and other regions of rat brain. *Journal of Comparative and Physiological Psychology, 47*(6), 419–427.

Olie, J. P., Spina, E., Murray, S., & Yang, R. (2006). Ziprasidone and amisulpride effectively treat negative symptoms of schizophrenia: Results of a 12-week, double-blind study. *International Clinical Psychopharmacology, 21*(3), 143–151.

Olney, J. W., Newcomer, J. W., & Farber, N. B. (1999). NMDA receptor hypofunction model of schizophrenia. *Journal of Psychiatric Research, 33*(6), 523–533.

Olsen, R. W., Hanchar, H. J., Meera, P., & Wallner, M. (2007). GABAA receptor subtypes: The "one glass of wine" receptors. *Alcohol, 41(3)*, 201–209.

Osaka, T., & Matsumura, H. (1994). Noradrenergic inputs to sleep-related neurons in the preoptic area of the locus coeruleus and the ventromedial medulla in the rat. *Neuroscience Research, 19*(1), 39–50.

Overstreet, D. H., Commissaris, R., De La Garza, R., File, S., Knapp, D., & Seiden, L. (2003). Involvement of 5-HT1A receptors in animal tests of anxiety and depression: Evidence from genetic models. *Stress, 6*(2), 101–110.

Palatnik, A., Frolov, K., Fux, M., & Benjamin, J. (2001). Double-blind, controlled, crossover trial of inositol versus fluvoxamine for the treatment of panic disorder. *Journal of Clinical Psychopharmacology, 21*(3), 335–339.

Papakostas, G., Perlis, R., Scalia, M., Petersen, T., & Fava, M. (2006). A meta-analysis of early sustained response rates between antidepressants and placebo for the treatment of major depressive disorder. *Journal of Clinical Psychopharmacology, 26*(1), 56–60.

Parsey, R. V., Oquendo, M. A., Ogden, R. T., Olvet, D. M., Simpson, N., Huang, Y. Y., et al. (2006). Altered serotonin 1A binding in major depression: A {carbonyl-C-11}WAY100635 positron emission tomography study. *Biological Psychiatry, 59*(2), 106–113.

Patel, S., & Hillard, C. J. (2001). Cannabinoid CB(1) receptor agonists produce cerebellar dysfunction in mice. *The Journal of Pharmacology and Experimental Therapeutics, 297*(2), 629–637.

Pattij, T., Groenink, L., Hijzen, T. H., Oosting, R. S., Maes, R. A. A., van der Gugten, J., et al. (2002). Autonomic changes associated with enhanced anxiety in 5-HT1A receptor knockout mice. *Neuropsychopharmacology, 27*, 380–390.

Pederson, D. J., Lessard, S. J., Coffey, V. G., Churchley, E. G., Wootton, A. M., Ng, T., et al. (2008). High rates of muscle glycogen resynthesis after exhaustive exercise when carbohydrate is coingested with caffeine. *Journal of Applied Physiology, 105*, 7–13.

Pentel, P. R., Malin, D. H., Ennifar, S., Hieda, Y., Keyler, D. E., Lake, J. R., et al. (2000). A nicotine conjugate vaccine reduces nicotine distribution to brain and attenuates its behavioral and cardiovascular effects in rats. *Pharmacology Biochemistry & Behavior, 65*(1), 191–198.

Phend, C. (2007, May). Bipolar disorder prevalence hidden by diagnostic thresholds. *Medpage Today.*

Philip, N. S., Carpenter, L. L., Tyrka, A. R., & Price, L. H. (2008). Augmentation of antidepressants with atypical antipsychotics: A review of the current literature. *Journal of Psychiatric Practice, 14*(1), 34–44.

Pianezza, M. L., Sellers, E., & Tyndale, R. (1998). Nicotine metabolism defect reduces smoking. *Nature, 393*(6687), 750.

Ping, A., Xi, J., Prasad, B. M., Wang, M. H., & Kruzich, P. J. (2008). Contributions of nucleus accumbens core and shell GluR1 containing AMPA receptors in AMPA- and cocaine-primed reinstatement of cocaine-seeking behavior. *Brain Research, 1215,* 173–182.

Pinna, G., Agis-Balboa, R. C., Zhubi, A., Matsumoto, K., Grayson, D. R., Costa, E., et al. (2006). Imidazenil and diazepam increase locomotor activity in mice exposed to protracted social isolation. *Proceedings of the National Academy of Sciences of the United States of America, 103*(11), 4275–4280.

Plaze, M., Bartres-Faz, D., Martinot, J. L., Januel, D., Bellivier, F., De Beaurepaire, R., et al. (2006). Left superior temporal gyrus activation during sentence perception negatively correlates with auditory hallucination severity in schizophrenia patients. *Schizophrenia Research, 87*(1–3), 109–115.

Pliszka, S. R. (2007). Pharmacologic treatment of attention-deficit/hyperactivity disorder: Efficacy, safety and mechanisms of action. *Neuropsychology Review, 17*(1), 61–72.

Pobbe, R. L., & Zangrossi, H., Jr. (2005). 5-HT(1A) and 5-HT(2A) receptors in the rat dorsal periaqueductal gray mediate the antipanic-like effect induced by the stimulation of serotonergic neurons in the dorsal raphe nucleus. *Psychopharmacology, 183*(3), 314–321.

Porrino, L. J. (1993). Functional consequences of acute cocaine treatment depend on route of administration. *Psychopharmacology, 112*(2–3), 343–351.

Porsolt, R. D., Anton, G., Blavet, N., & Jalfre, M. (1979). Behavioural despair in rats: A new model sensitive to antidepressant treatment. *European Journal of Pharmacology, 47*(4), 379–391.

Post, R. M. (2007). Role of BDNF in bipolar and unipolar disorder: clinical and theoretical implications. *Journal of Psychiatric Research, 41*(12), 979–990.

Posternak, M. A., & Zimmerman, M. (2007). Therapeutic effect of follow-up assessments on antidepressant and placebo response rates in antidepressant efficacy trials. *The British Journal of Psychiatry, 190,* 287–292.

Potter, A. S., & Newhouse, P. (2008). Acute nicotine improves cognitive deficits in young adults with attention-deficit/hyperactivity disorder. *Pharmacological Biochemical Behavior, 88*(4), 407–417.

Preet, A., Ganju, R. K., & Groopman, J. E. (2008). Delta9-tetrahydrocannabinol inhibits epithelial growth factor-induced lung cancer cell migration in vitro as well as its growth and metastasis in vivo. *Oncogene, 27*(3), 339–346.

Punch, L. J., Self, D. W., Nestler, E. J., & Taylor, J. R. (1997). Opposite modulation of opiate withdrawal behaviors on microinfusion of a protein kinase A inhibitor versus activator into the locus coeruleus or periaqueductal gray. *The Journal of Neuroscience, 17*(21), 8520–8527.

Randrup, A., & Munkvad, I. (1965). Special antagonism of amphetamine-induced abnormal behavior. Inhibition of stereotyped activity with increase of some normal activities. *Psychopharmacologia, 7,* 416–422.

Ranganathan, M., & D'Souza, D. C. (2006). The acute effects of cannabinoids on memory in humans: A review. *Psychopharmacology, 188*(4), 425–444.

Rao, Y., Liu, Z. W., Borok, E., Rabenstein, R. L., Shanabrough, M., Lu, M., et al. (2007). Prolonged wakefulness induces experience-dependent synaptic plasticity in mouse hypocretin/orexin neurons. *The Journal of Clinical Investigation, 117*(2), 4022–4033.

Rasmussen, K., Beitner-Johnson, D. B., Krystal, J. H., Aghajanian, G. K., & Nestler, E. J. (1990). Opiate withdrawal and the rat locus coeruleus: Behavioral, electrophysiological, and biochemical correlates. *The Journal of Neuroscience, 10,* 2308–2317.

Resnick, R. B., Kestenbaum, R. S., & Schwartz, L. K. (1977). Acute systemic effects of cocaine in man: A controlled study by intranasal and intravenous route. *Science, 195*(4279), 695–698.

Ricaurte, G. A., Yuan, J., Hatzidimitriou, G., Cord, B. J., & McCann, U. D. (2002). Severe dopaminergic neurotoxicity in primates after a common recreational dose regimen of MDMA ("ecstasy"). *Science, 297*(5590), 2260–2263.

Richardson, K., Baillie, A., Reid, S., Morley, K., Teesson, M., Sannibale, C., et al. (2008). Do acamprosate or naltrexone have an effect on daily drinking by reducing craving for alcohol? *Addiction, 103*(6), 953–959.

Robbins, T. W., & Murphy, E. R. (2006). Behavioral pharmacology: 40 years of progress, with a focus on glutamate receptors and cognition. *Trends in Pharmacological Sciences, 27*(3), 141–148.

Rocca, P., Beoni, A. M., Eva, C., Ferrero, P., Zanalda, E., & Ravizza, L. (1998). Peripheral benzodiazepine receptor messenger RNA is decreased in lymphocytes of generalized anxiety disorder patients. *Biological Psychiatry, 43*(10), 767–773.

Rodd, Z. A., Melendez, R. I., Bell, R. L., Kuc, K. A., Zhang, Y., Murphy, J. M., et al. (2004). Intracranial self-administration of ethanol within the ventral tegmental area of male Wistar rats: Evidence for involvement of dopamine neurons. *The Journal of Neuroscience, 24*(5), 1050–1057.

Rogawski, M. A., & Loscher, W. (2004). The neurobiology of antiepileptic drugs for the treatment of nonepileptic conditions. *Nature Medicine, 10*(7), 685–692.

Rogoz, Z., Skuza, G., & Legutko, B. (2005). Repeated treatment with mirtazepine induces brain-derived neurotrophic factor gene expression in rats. *Journal of Physiology and Pharmacology, 56*(4), 661–671.

Rojas, D. C., Peterson, E., Winterrowd, E., Reite, M. L., Rogers. S. J., & Tregellas, J. R. (2006). Regional gray matter volumetric changes in autism associated with social and repetitive behavior symptoms. *BMC Psychiatry, 6*, 56.

Rosack, J. (2002). Switching drug classes benefits treatment-resistant patients. *Psychiatric News, 37*(9), 31.

Rose, J. E., Behm, F. M., Westman, E. C., & Johnson, M. (2000). Dissociating nicotine and nonnicotine components of cigarette smoking. *Pharmacology Biochemistry & Behavior, 67*(1), 71–81.

Rowe, D. L., Robinson, P. A., & Gordon, E. (2005). Stimulant drug action in attention deficit hyper-activity disorder (ADHD): Inference of neurophysiological mechanisms via quantitative modelling. *Clinical Neurophysiology, 116*(2), 324–335.

Rowe, D. L., Robinson, P. A., Lazzaro, I. L., Powles, R. C., Gordon, E., & Williams, L. M. (2005). Biophysical modeling of tonic cortical electrical activity in attention deficit hyperactivity disorder. *International Journal of Neuroscience, 115*(9), 1273–1305.

Roz, N., Mazur, Y., Hirshfeld, A., & Rehavi, M. (2002). Inhibition of vesicular uptake of monoamines by hyperforin. *Life Sciences, 71*(19), 2227–2237.

Roz, N., & Rehavi, M. (2004). Hyperforin depletes synaptic vesicles content and induces com-partmental redistribution of nerve ending monoamines. *Life Sciences, 75*(23), 2841–2850.

Ruelaz, A. R. (2006). Treatment-resistant depression: Strategies for management. *Psychiatric Times, 23*(11).

Russo-Neustadt, A., Beard, R. C., & Cotman, C. W. (1999). Exercise, antidepressant medications, and enhanced brain derived neurotrophic factor expression. *Neuropsychopharmacology, 21*, 679–682.

Rybakowski, J. K., Suwalska, A., Skibinska, M., Dmitrzak-Weglarz, M., Leszczynska-Rodziewicz, A., & Hauser, J. (2007). Response to lithium prophylaxis: Interaction between serotonin transporter and BDNF genes. *American Journal of Medical Genetics Part B: Neuropsychiatric Genetics, 144*(6), 820–823.

Sagredo, O., Garcia-Arencibia, M., de Lago, E., Finetti, S., Decio, A., & Fernandez-Ruiz, J. (2007). Cannabinoids and neuroprotection in basal ganglia disorders. *Molecular Neurobiology, 36*(1), 82–91.

Sahay, A., & Hen, R. (2007). Adult hippocampal neurogenesis in depression. *Nature Neuroscience, 10*(9), 1110–1115.

Sallette, J., Bohler, S., Benoit, P., Soudant, M., Pons, S., Le Novere, N., et al. (2004). An extracellular protein microdomain controls up-regulation of neuronal nicotinic acetylcholine receptors by nicotine. *The Journal of Biological Chemistry, 279*(18), 18767–18775.

Samaha, A.-N., Mallet, N., Ferguson, S. M., Gonon, F., & Robinson, T. E. (2004). The rate of cocaine administration alters gene regulation and behavioral plasticity: Implications for addiction. *The Journal of Neuroscience, 24*(28), 6362–6370.

Samaha, A.-N., & Robinson, T. E. (2005). Why does the rapid delivery of drugs to the brain promote addiction? *Trends in Pharmacological Sciences, 26*(2), 82–87.

Samat, A., Tomlinson, B., Taheri, S., & Thomas, G. N. (2008). Rimonabant for the treatment of obesity. *Recent Patents on Cardiovascular Drug Discovery, 3*(3), 187–193.

Sanna, E., Busonero, F., Talani, G., Mostallino, M. C., Mura, M. L., Pisu, M. G., et al. (2005). Low tolerance and dependence liabilities of etizolam: Molecular, functional, and pharmacological correlates. *European Journal of Pharmacology, 519*(1–2), 31–42.

Santhakumar, V., Wallner, M., & Otis, T. S. (2007). Ethanol acts directly on extrasynaptic subtypes of GABAA receptors to increase tonic inhibition. *Alcohol, 41*(3), 211–221.

Saxena, S., Brody, A. L., Schwartz, J. M., & Baxter, L. R. (1998). Neuroimaging and frontal-subcortical circuitry in obsessive-compulsive disorder. *The British Journal of Psychiatry, Supplement, 35*, 26–37.

Saxena, S., Brody, A. O., Ho, M. L., Zohrabi, N., Maidment, K. M., & Baxter, L. R., Jr. (2003). Differential brain metabolic predictors of response to paroxetine in obsessive-compulsive disorder versus major depression. *The American Journal of Psychiatry, 160*(3), 522–532.

Schotanus, S. M., & Chergui, K. (2008). Dopamine D1 receptors and group 1 metabotropic glutamate receptors contribute to the induction of long-term potentiation in the nucleus accumbens. *Neuropharmacology, 54*(5), 837–844.

Schule, C., Zill, P., Baghai, T. C., Eser, D., Zwanzger, P., Wenig, N., et al. (2006). Brain-derived neurotrophic factor Val66Met polymorphism and dexamethasone/CRH test results in depressed patients. *Psychoneuroendocrinology, 31*(8), 1019–1025.

Sciotto, M. J. (2007). Evaluating the evidence for and against the overdiagnosis of ADHD. *Journal of Attention Disorders, 11*(2), 106–113.

Scragg, R., Wellman, R. J., Laugesen, M., & DiFranza, J. R. (2008). Diminished autonomy over tobacco can appear with the first cigarettes. *Addictive Behaviors, 33*(5), 389–398.

Seeman, P. (2002). Atypical antipsychotics: Mechanism of action. *Canadian Journal of Psychiatry, 47*(1), 27–38.

Seeman, P., Schwarz, J., Chen, J. F., Szechtman, H., Perreault, M., McKnight, G. S., et al. (2006). Psychosis pathways converge via D2high dopamine receptors. *Synapse, 60*(4), 319–346.

Seeman, P., & Tallerico, T. (1998). Antipsychotic drugs which elicit little or no Parkinsonism bind more loosely than dopamine to brain D2 receptors, yet occupy high levels of these receptors. *Molecular Psychiatry, 3*(2), 123–134.

Sena, L. M., Bueno, C., Pobbe, R. L., Andrade, T. G., Zangrossi, H., Jr., & Viana, M. B. (2003). The dorsal raphe nucleus exerts opposed control on generalized anxiety and panic-related defensive responses in rats. *Behavioral Brain Research, 142*(1–2), 125–133.

Sharkey, K. A., Cristino, L., Oland, L. D., Van Sickle, M. D., Starowicz, K., Pittman, Q. J., et al. (2007). Arvanil, anandamide and N-arachidonoyl-dopamine (NADA) inhibit emesis through cannabinoid CB1 and vanilloid TRPV1 receptors in the ferret. *European Journal of Neuroscience, 25*(9), 2773–2782.

Shaw, P., Eckstrand, K., Sharp, W., Blumenthal, J., Lerch, J. P., Greenstein, D., et al. (2007). Attention-deficit/hyperactivity disorder is characterized by a delay in cortical maturation. *Proceedings of the National Academy of Sciences of the United States of America, 104*(49), 19694–19654.

Shelton, R. C. (2007). The molecular neurobiology of depression. *Psychiatric Clinics of North America, 30*(1), 1–11.

Shelton, R. C., Keller, M. B., Gelenberg, A., Dunner, D., Hirschfield, R., Thase, M., et al. (2001). Effectiveness of St. John's wort in major depression: A randomized controlled trial. *The Journal of the American Medical Association, 285*(15), 1978–1986.

Shin, L. M., Rauch, S. L., & Pitman, R. K. (2006). Amygdala, medial prefrontal cortex, and hippocampal function in PTSD. *Annals of the New York Academy of Sciences, 1071*, 67–79.

Siegel, S. (1975). Evidence from rats that morphine tolerance is a learned response. *Journal of Comparative and Physiological Psychology, 89*, 498–506.

Siegel, S. (1987). Pavlovian conditioning of ethanol tolerance. *Alcohol and Alcoholism, 1*, 25–36.

Silk, T. J., Rinehart, N., Bradshaw, J. L., Tonge, B., Egan, G., O'Boyle, M. W., et al. (2006). Visuospatial processing and the function of prefrontal-parietal networks in autism spectrum disorders: A functional MRI study. *The American Journal of Psychiatry, 163*(8), 1440–1443.

Siu, E. C. K., & Tyndale, R. F. (2008). Selegiline is a mechanism-based inactivator of CYP2A6 inhibiting nicotine metabolism in humans and mice. *The Journal of Pharmacology and Experimental Therapeutics, 324*(3), 992–999.

Siu, E. C. K., Wildenauer, D. B., & Tyndale, R. F. (2006). Nicotine self-administration in mice is associated with rates of nicotine inactivation by CYP2A5. *Psychopharmacology, 184*(3), 401–408.

Slatkin, N. E. (2007). Cannabinoids in the treatment of chemotherapy-induced nausea and vomiting: Beyond prevention of acute emesis. *The Journal of Supportive Oncology, 5*(Suppl. 3), 1–9.

Snead, O. C. (2000). Evidence for a G protein-coupled gamma-hydroxybutyric acid receptor. *Journal of Neurochemistry, 75*(5), 1986–1996.

Snyder, J. L., & Bowers, T. G. (2008). The efficacy of acamprosate and naltrexone in the treatment of alcohol dependence: A relative benefits analysis of randomized controlled trials. *The American Journal of Drug and Alcohol Abuse, 34*(4), 449–461.

Snyder, S. M., & Hall, J. R. (2006). A meta-analysis of quantitative EEG power associated with attention-deficit hyperactivity disorder. *Journal of Clinical Neurophysiology, 23*(5), 440–455.

Solinas, M., Goldberg, S. R., & Piomellli, D. (2008). The endocannabinoid system in brain reward processes. *British Journal of Pharmacology, 154*(2), 369–383.

Song, D. H., Shin, D. W., Jon, D. I., & Ha, E. H. (2005). Effects of methylphenidate on quantitative EEG of boys with attention-deficit hyperactivity disorder in continuous performance test. *Yonsei Medical Journal, 46*(1), 34–41.

Sora, I., Hall, F. S., Andrews, A. M., Itokawa, M., Li, X-F., Wei, H-B., et al. (2001). Molecular mechanisms of cocaine reward: Combined dopamine and serotonin transporter knockouts eliminate cocaine place preference. *Proceedings of the National Academy of Sciences of the United States of America, 98*(9), 5300–5305.

Soyka, M., Koller, G., Schmidt, P., Lesch, O. M., Leweke, M., Fehr, C., et al. (2008). Cannabinoid receptor 1 blocker rimonabant (SR 141716) for treatment of alcohol dependence: Results from a placebo-controlled, double-blind trial. *Journal of Clinical Psychopharmacology, 28*(3), 317–324.

Spencer, T., Heiligenstein, J. H., Biederman, J., Faries, D. E., Kratochvil, C. J., Conners, C. K., et al. (2002). Results from 2 proof-of-concept, placebo-controlled studies of atomoxetine in children with attention-deficit/hyperactivity disorder. *The Journal of Clinical Psychiatry, 63*, 1140–1147.

Spencer, T. J., Biederman, J., Madras, B. K., Dougherty, D. D., Bonab, A. A., Livini, E., et al. (2007). Further evidence of dopamine transporter dysregulation in ADHD: A controlled PET imaging study using Altropane. *Biological Psychiatry, 62*(9), 1059–1061.

Stahl, S. M., Pradko, J. F., Haight, B. R., Modell, J. G., Rockett, C. B., & Learned-Coughlin, S. (2004). A review of the neuropharmacology of bupropion, a dual norepinephrine and dopamine reuptake inhibitor. *The Primary Care Companion Journal of Clinical Psychiatry, 6*(4), 159–166.

Stein, M. B., Seedat, S., & Gelernter, J. (2006). Serotonin transporter gene promoter polymorphism predicts SSRI response in generalized social anxiety disorder. *Psychopharmacology, 187*(1), 68–72.

Stolerman, I. P., Fink, R., & Jarvik, M. (1973). Acute and chronic tolerance to nicotine measured by activity in rats. *Psychopharmacologia, 30*(4), 329–342.

Stone, J. M., Morrison, P. D., & Pilowsky, L. S. (2007). Glutamate and dopamine dysregulation in schizophrenia—a synthesis and selective review. *Journal of Psychopharmacology, 21*(4), 440–452.

Strakowski, S. M., DelBello, M. P., & Adler, C. M. (2005). The functional neuroanatomy of bipolar disorder: A review of neuroimaging findings. *Molecular Psychiatry, 10*(1), 105–116.

Strakowski, S. M., DelBello, M. P., Zimmerman, M. E., Getz, G. E., Mills, N. P., Ret, J., et al. (2002). Ventricular and periventricular structural volumes in first- versus multiple-episode bipolar disorder. *The American Journal of Psychiatry, 159*(11), 1841–1847.

Suh, J. J., Pettinati, H. M., Kampman, K. M., & O'Brien, C. P. (2006). The status of disulfiram: A half of a century later. *Journal of Clinical Psychopharmacology, 26*(3), 290–302.

Suzdak, P. D., Glowa, J. R., Crawley, J. N., Schwartz, R. D., Skolnick, P., & Paul, S. M. (1986). A selective imidazobenzodiazepine antagonist of ethanol in the rat. *Science, 234*(4781), 1243–1247.

Swanson, J. M., Kinsbourne, M., Nigg, J., Lanphear, B., Stefanatos, G. A., Volkow, N., et al. (2007). Etiologic subtypes of attention-deficit/ hyperactivity disorder: Brain imaging, molecular genetic and environmental factors and the dopamine hypothesis. *Neuropsychology Review, 17*(1), 39–59.

Swerdlow, N. R., Light, G. A., Cadenhead, K. S., Sprock, J., Hsieh, M. H., & Braff, D. L. (2006). Startle gating deficits in a large cohort of patients with schizophrenia: Relationship to medications, symptoms, neurocognition, and level of function. *Archives of General Psychiatry, 63*(12), 1325–1335.

Szabo, B., Siemes, S., & Wallmichrath, I. (2002). Inhibition of GABAergic neurotransmission in the ventral tegmental area by cannabinoids. *European Journal of Neuroscience, 15*(12), 2057–2061.

Szechtman, H., Sulis, W., & Eilam, D. (1998). Quinpirole induces compulsive checking behavior in rats: A potential animal model of obsessive-compulsive disorder (OCD). *Behavioral Neuroscience, 112*(6), 1475–1485.

Tabet, N. (2006). Acetylcholine inhibitors for Alzheimer's disease: Anti-inflammatories in acetylcholine clothing! *Age and Aging, 34*(4), 336–338.

Tadic, A., Rujescu, D., Szegedi, A., Giegling, I., Singer, P., Moller, H. J., et al. (2003). Association of a MAOA gene variant with generalized anxiety disorder, but not with panic disorder or major depression. *American Journal of Medical Genetics Part B: Neuropsychiatric Genetics, 117*(1), 1–6.

Tao, X., Finkbeiner, S., Arnold, D. B., Shaywitz, A. J., & Greenberg, M. E. (1998). Ca2+ influx regulates BDNF transcription by a CREB family transcription factor-dependent mechanism. *Neuron, 20*(4), 709–726.

Tapper, A. R., McKinney, S. L., Nashmi, R., Schwarz, J., Deshpande, P., Labarca, C., et al. (2004). Nicotine activation of a4* receptors: Sufficient for reward, tolerance, and sensitization. *Science, 306*(5698), 1029–1032.

Taylor, W. D., & Doraiswamy, P. M. (2003). A systematic review of antidepressant placebo-controlled trials for geriatric depression: Limitations of current data and directions for the future. *Neuropsychopharmacology, 29*, 2285–2299.

Thalemann, R., Wolfling, K., & Grusser, S. M. (2007). Specific cue reactivity on computer game-related cues in excessive gamers. *Behavioral Neuroscience, 121*(3), 614–618.

Thanos, P. K., Michaelides, M., Benvenista, H., Wang, G. J., & Volkow, N. D. (2008). The effects of cocaine on regional brain glucose metabolism is attenuated in dopamine transporter knockout mice. *Synapse, 62*(5), 319–324.

Thase, M. E., Jonas, A., Khan, A., Bowden, C. L., Wu, X., McQuade, R. D., et al. (2008). Aripiprazole monotherapy in nonpsychotic bipolar I depression: Results of 2 randomized, placebo-controlled studies. *Journal of Clinical Psychopharmacology, 28*(1), 13–20.

Theile, J. W., Morikawa, H., Gonzales, R. A., & Morrisett, R. A. (2008). Ethanol enhances GABAergic transmission onto dopamine neurons in the ventral tegmental area of the rat. *Alcoholism: Clinical & Experimental Research, 32*(6), 1040–1048.

Thomas, M. J., Kalivas, P. W., & Shaham, Y. (2008). Neuroplasticity in the mesolimbic dopamine system and cocaine addiction. *British Journal of Pharmacology, 154*(2), 327–342.

Thomas, R. M., & Peterson, D. A. (2003). A neurogenic theory of depression gains momentum. *Molecular Interventions, 3,* 441–444.

Thome, J., Sakai, N., Shin, K-H., Steffen, C., Zhang, Y-J., Impey, S., et al. (2000). cAMP response element-mediated gene transcription is upregulated by chronic antidepressant treatment. *The Journal of Neuroscience, 20*(11), 4030–4036.

Ticku, M. K., & Mehta, A. K. (2009). Characterization and pharmacology of the GHB receptor. *Annals of the New York Academy of Sciences, 1139,* 374–385.

Tiihonen, J., Lonnqvist, J., Wahlbeck, K., Klaukka, T., Tanskanen, A., & Haukka, J. (2006). Antidepressants and the risk of suicide, attempted suicide, and overall mortality in a nationwide cohort. *Archives of General Psychiatry, 63*(12), 1358–1367.

Tiraboschi, E., Tardito, D., Kasahara, J., Moraschi, S., Pruneri, P., Gennarelli, M., et al. (2004). Selective phosphorylation of nuclear CREB by fluoxetine is linked to activation of CaM kinase IV and MAP kinase cascades. *Neuropsychopharmacology, 29,* 1831–1840.

Torrens, M., Fonseca, F., Mateu, G., & Farre, M. (2005). Efficacy of antidepressants in substance use disorders with and without comorbid depression. A Systematic review and meta-analysis. *Drug and Alcohol Dependence, 78*(1), 1–22.

Tsai, L. (2005). *Diagnostic confusion in Asperger disorder.* Paper presented at the ASC-US Annual Conference, Orlando, FL.

Tuominen, H. J., Tiihonen, J., & Wahlbeck, K. (2006). Glutamatergic drugs for schizophrenia. *Cochrane Database of Systematic Reviews, 2,* CD003730.

Turner, T. (2007). Chlorpromazine: Unlocking psychosis. *British Medical Journal , 334*(Suppl. 1), s7.

Vallance, A. K. (2006). Something out of nothing: The placebo effect. *Advances in Psychiatric Treatment, 12,* 287–296.

Vallejo, Y. F., Buisson, B., Bertrand, D., & Green, W. N. (2005). Chronic nicotine exposure upregulates nicotinic receptors by a novel mechanism. *The Journal of Neuroscience, 25*(23), 5563–5572.

Vanelle, J. M., & Douki, S. (2006). A double-blind randomised comparative trial of amisulpride versus olanzapine for 2 months in the treatment of subjects with schizophrenia and comorbid depression. *European Psychiatry, 21*(8), 523–530.

Vann, R. E., James, J. R., Rosecrans, J. A., & Robinson, S. E. (2006). Nicotinic receptor inactivation after acute and repeated in vivo nicotine exposures in rats. *Brain Research, 1086,* 98–103.

van Rossum, J. M. (1966). The significance of dopamine-receptor blockade for the mechanism of action of neuroleptic drugs. *Archives Internationales de Pharmacodynamie et de Therapie, 160*(2), 492–494.

Van Sickle, M. D., Oland, L. D., Ho, W., Hillard, C. J., Mackie, K., Davison, J. S., et al. (2001). Cannabinoids inhibit emesis through CB1 receptors in the brainstem of the ferret. *Gastroenterology, 121*(4), 767–774.

Varvel, S. A., Martin, B. R., & Lichtman, A. H. (2007). Lack of behavioral sensitization after repeated exposure to THC in mice and comparison to methamphetamine. *Psychopharmacology, 193,* 511–519.

Vasconcelos, M. M., Werner, J., Jr., Malheiros, A. F., Lima, D. F., Santos, I. S., & Barbosa, J. B. (2003). Attention deficit/hyperactivity disorder prevalence in an inner city elementary school. *Arq Neuropsiquiatr, 61*(1), 67–73.

Volkow, N. D., & Swanson, J. (2003). Variables that affect the clinical use and abuse of methylphenidate in the treatment of ADHD. *The American Journal of Psychiatry, 160*(11), 1909–1918.

Volkow, N. D., Wang, G-J., Fischman, M. W., Foltin, R. W., Fowler, J. S., Abumrad, N. N., et al. (1997). Relationship between subjective effects of cocaine and dopamine transporter occupancy. *Nature, 396,* 827–830.

Volkow, N. D., Wang, G-J., Newcorn, J., Telang, F., Solanto, M. V., Fowler, J. S., et al. (2007). Depressed dopamine activity in caudate and preliminary evidence of limbic involvement in adults with attention-deficit/hyperactivity disorder. *Archives of General Psychiatry, 64*(8), 932–940.

Volkow, N. D., Wang, G-J., Telang, F., Fowler, J. S., Logan, J., Childress, A. R., et al. (2006). Cocaine cues and dopamine in dorsal striatum: Mechanism of craving in cocaine addiction. *The Journal of Neuroscience, 26*(24), 6583–6588.

Volkow, N. D., Wang, G-J., Telang, F., Fowler, J. S., Logan, J., Childress, A. R., et al. (2008). Dopamine increases in striatum do not elicit craving in cocaine abusers unless they are coupled with cocaine cues. *NeuroImage, 39*(3), 1266–1273.

Vyas, A., Mitra, R., Shankaranarayana Rao, B. S., & Chattarji, S. (2002). Chronic stress induces contrasting patterns of dendritic remodeling in hippocampal and amygdaloid neurons. *The Journal of Neuroscience, 22*(15), 6810–6818.

Walitza, S., Werner, B., Romanos, M., Warnke, A., Gerlach, M., & Stopper, H. (2007). Does methylphenidate cause a cytogenetic effect in children with attention deficit hyperactivity disorder? *Environmental Health Perspectives, 115*(6), 936–940.

Walsh, B. T., Seidman, S. N., Ryski, R., Sysko, R., & Gould, M. (2002). Placebo response in studies of major depression. *The Journal of the American Medical Association, 287,* 1840–1847.

Walsh, H., Govind, A. P., Mastro, R., Hoda, J. C., Bertrand, D., Vallejo, Y., et al. (2008). Up-regulation of nicotinic receptors by nicotine varies with receptor subtype. *The Journal of Biological Chemistry, 283*(10), 6022–6032.

Walsh, S. (2007). FDA proposes new warnings about suicidal thinking, behavior in young adults who take antidepressant medications. *FDA News.*

Wang, J., Michelhaugh, S. K., & Bannon, M. (2007). Valproate robustly increases Sp transcription factor-mediated expression of the dopamine transporter gene within dopamine cells. *European Journal of Neuroscience, 25*(7), 1982–1986.

Wang, Z., Faith, M., Patterson, F., Tang, K., Kerrin, K., Wileyto, E. P., et al. (2007). Neural substrates of abstinence-induced cigarette cravings in chronic smokers. *The Journal of Neuroscience, 27*(51), 14036–14040.

Wenger, J. R., Tiffany, T. M., Bombardier, C., Nicholis, K., & Woods, S. C. (1981). Ethanol tolerance in the rat is learned. *Science, 213*(4507), 575–577.

Westenberg, H. G., Fineberg, N. A., & Denys, D. (2007). Neurobiology of obsessive-compulsive disorder: Serotonin and beyond. *CNS Spectrums, 12*(2)(Suppl. 3), 14–27.

White, J. D. (1999). Review personality, temperament and ADHD: A review of the literature. *Personality and Individual Differences, 27*(4), 589–598.

Wikgren, J., Lavond, D. G., Ruusuvita, T., & Korhonen, T. (2006). Cooling of the cerebellar interpositus nucleus abolishes somatosensory cortical learning-related activity in eyeblink conditioned rabbits. *Behavioural Brain Research, 170*(1), 94–98.

Wilens, T., McBurnett, K., Stein, M., Lerner, M., Spencer, T., & Wolraich, M. (2005). ADHD treatment with once-daily OROS methylphenidate: Final results from a long-term open-label study. *Journal of the American*

Academy of Child Adolescent Psychiatry, 44(10), 1015–1023.

Wilson, L. D., & French, S. (2002). Cocaethylene's effects on coronary artery blood flow and cardiac function in a canine model. *Journal of Toxicology-Clinical Toxicology, 40*(5), 535–546.

Wisor, J. P., & Eriksson, S. (2005). Dopaminergic-adrenergic interactions in the wake promoting mechanism of modafinil. *Neuroscience, 132*(4), 1027–1034.

Wolf, M. E., Sun, X., Mangiavacchi, S., & Chao, S. Z. (2004). Psychomotor stimulants and neuronal plasticity. *Neuropharmacology, 47*(1), 61–79.

Wu, D. F., Yang, L. Q., Goschke, A., Stumm, R., Brandenburg, L. O., Liang, Y. J., et al. (2008). Role of receptor internalization in the agonist-induced desensitization of cannabinoid type 1 receptors. *Journal of Neurochemistry, 104*(4), 1132–1143.

Wynn, J. K., Green, M. F., Sprock, J., Light, G. A., Widmark, C., Reist, C., et al. (2007). Effects of olanzapine, risperidone and haloperidol on prepulse inhibition in schizophrenia patients: A double-blind, randomized controlled trial. *Schizophrenia Research, 95*(1–3), 134–142.

Xiao, C., Zhang, J., Krnjevic, K., & Ye, J. H. (2007). Effects of ethanol on midbrain neurons: Role of opioid receptors. *Alcoholism: Clinical & Experimental Research, 31*(7), 1106–1113.

Yerevanian, B. I., Koek, R. J., & Mintz, J. (2007). Bipolar pharmacotherapy and suicidal behavior. Part I: Lithium, divalproex and carbamazepine. *Journal of Affective Disorders, 103*(1–3), 5–11.

Yolkow, N. D., Wang, G. J., Newcorn, J., Telang, F., Solanto, M. V., Fowler, J. S., et al. (2007). Depressed dopamine activity in caudate and preliminary evidence of limbic involvement in adults with attention-deficit/hyperactivity disorder. *Archives of General Psychiatry, 64*(8), 932–940.

Yoshida, K., Higuchi, H., Kamata, M., Takashashi, H., Inoue, K., Susuki, T., et al. (2007). The G196A polymorphism of the brain-derived neurotrophic factor gene and the antidepressant effect of milnacipran and fluvoxamine. *Journal of Psychopharmacology, 21*(6), 650–656.

Yoshimura, R., Mitoma, M., Sugita, A., Hori, H., Okamoto, T., Umene, W., et al. (2007). Effects of paroxetine or milnacipran on serum brain-derived neurotrophic factor in depressed patients. *Progress in Neuro-Psychopharmacology & Biological Psychiatry, 31*(5), 1034–1037.

Yuan, C.-S., Mehendale, S., Xiao, Y., Aung, H. H., Xie, J-T., & Ang-Lee, M. K. (2004). The gamma-aminobutyric acidergic effects of valerian and valerenic acid on rat brainstem neuronal activity. *Anesthesia & Analgesia, 98*, 353–358.

Zakzanis, K. K., Campbell, Z., & Jovanovski, D. (2007). The neuropsychology of ecstasy (MDMA) use: A quantitative review. *Human Psychopharmacology, 22*(7), 427–435.

Zang, Y. F., He, Y., Zhu, C. Z., Cao, Q. J., Sui, M. Q., Liang, M., et al. (2007). Altered baseline brain activity in children with ADHD revealed by resting-state functional MRI. *Brain & Development, 29*(2), 83–91.

Zangrossi, H., Jr., & Graeff, F. G. (1997). Behavioral validation of the elevated T-maze, a new animal model of anxiety. *Brain Research Bulletin, 44*(1), 1–5.

Zanoli, P. (2004). Role of hyperforin in the pharmacological activities of St. John's wort. *CNS Drug Reviews, 10*(3), 203–218.

Zanoli, P., Rivasi, M., Baraldi, C., & Baraldi, M. (2002). Pharmacological activity of hyperforin acetate in rats. *Behavioral Pharmacology, 13*(8), 645–651.

Zhang, J., Zhang, L., Jiao, H., Zhang, Q., Zhang, D., Lou, D., et al. (2006). c-Fos facilitates the acquisition and extinction of cocaine-induced persistent changes. *The Journal of Neuroscience, 26*(51), 13287–13296.

Zikopoulos, B., & Barbas, H. (2006). Prefrontal projections to the thalamic reticular nucleus form a unique circuit for attentional mechanisms. *The Journal of Neuroscience, 26*(28), 7348–7361.

Zimmerman, M., & Thongy, T. (2007). How often do SSRIs and other new-generation antidepressants lose their effect during continuation treatment? Evidence suggesting the rate of true tachyphylaxis during continuation treatment is low. *The Journal of Clinical Psychiatry, 68*(8), 1271–1276.

Zubieta, J. K., Bueller, J. A., Jackson, L. R., Scott, D. J., Xu, Y., Koeppe, R. A., et al. (2005). Placebo effects mediated by endogenous opioid activity on mu-opioid receptors. *The Journal of Neuroscience, 24*(34), 7754–7762.

INDEX